Current Debates in the Lone Star State

Brandon Rottinghaus

New York   Oxford

OXFORD UNIVERSITY PRESS

Oxford University Press is a department of the University of Oxford.
It furthers the University's objective of excellence in research, scholarship,
and education by publishing worldwide.

Oxford New York
Auckland   Cape Town   Dar es Salaam   Hong Kong   Karachi
Kuala Lumpur   Madrid   Melbourne   Mexico City   Nairobi
New Delhi   Shanghai   Taipei   Toronto

With offices in
Argentina   Austria   Brazil   Chile   Czech Republic   France   Greece
Guatemala   Hungary   Italy   Japan   Poland   Portugal   Singapore
South Korea   Switzerland   Thailand   Turkey   Ukraine   Vietnam

For titles covered by Section 112 of the US Higher Education
Opportunity Act, please visit www.oup.com/us/he for the latest
information about pricing and alternate formats.

Published in the United States of America by
Oxford University Press
198 Madison Avenue, New York, NY 10016
http://www.oup.com

Library of Congress Cataloging-in-Publication Data

Names: Rottinghaus, Brandon, 1977- author.
Title: Current debates in the Lone Star State / Brandon Rottinghaus.
Description: New York : Oxford University Press, [2019]
Identifiers: LCCN 2018023059 | ISBN 9780190855086 (paperback)
Subjects: LCSH: Texas—Politics and government.
Classification: LCC JK4816 .R66 2019 | DDC 320.4764—dc23 LC record
available at https://lccn.loc.gov/2018023059

Printing number: 9 8 7 6 5 4 3 2 1
Printed by Sheridan Books, Inc., United States of America
on acid-free paper

Brief Contents

Table of Contents

"I done drew a line. Just like the Alamo. You're either on one side of the line or the other. I don't want to ever leave Texas again."

—Bum Phillips

Acknowledgements

Texas writer Gary Cartwright once pontificated that "success is something you measure in scar tissue: fame and fortune are products of luck, but success is an element torn from its socket." I often feel this way after writing a book, but any success to be had is not mine alone.

Working with Oxford University Press has been one of the most rewarding and exciting experiences of my professional career (or, as the old-timers say, "like whiskey over ice"). Jennifer Carpenter set this book in motion and drove a straight trail, even over bumps in the landscape. Editorial assistants Andrew Blitzer and Alison Ball were patient and consistently spot-on with helpful replies to my constant questions.

Special thanks also to my fall 2017 Advanced Texas Politics course students, who helped test out the tone and content of this book in a real-life classroom setting. Their feedback was influential in shaping the final version of the work. Five anonymous reviewers helped early on to hone the scope of the content and provide guidance on the type of details they wanted to see in the book.

My most humble thanks to my little rodeo crew in Houston. To BJ and Ben, growing quick as rain, consider this a promise for more frequent wild road trips across the state. To Tracy, my most heartfelt thanks for sharing your life with me. None of this would be without you.

About the Author

Brandon Rottinghaus, a proud graduate of Plano East High School in Plano, Texas, holds a Ph.D. in political science from Northwestern University. His teaching and research interests center on Texas politics, public opinion, and executive and legislative relations. His research has been funded by the National Science Foundation, the Dirksen Center for Congressional Research, the Scowcroft Institute for International Affairs, and the White House Historical Association. His work on these subjects has appeared in several academic journals, including *Journal of Politics, Political Research Quarterly, Public Opinion Quarterly, Political Science Quarterly, Political Communication, Social Science Quarterly, PS: Political Science and Politics, American Politics Research, Presidential Studies Quarterly,* and *Congress and the Presidency.* He is the author of *The Provisional Pulpit: Modern Conditional Presidential Leadership of Public Opinion* (Texas A&M University Press, 2010), *The Institutional Effect of Executive Scandals* (Cambridge University Press, 2014), and *The Dual Executive: Unilateral Orders in a Separated and Shared Power System* (Stanford University Press, 2017). Most recently his book *Inside Texas Politics* (Oxford University Press) was published in its second edition.

He has provided commentary on national and Texas politics in hundreds of media outlets, including the *New York Times,* the *Texas Tribune, U.S. News and World Report,* the *Atlantic, USA Today,* the *Dallas Morning News,* the *Fort Worth Star Telegram,* the *San Antonio Express-News,* the *Washington Post,* the *Houston Chronicle,* BBC Radio, and local NBC, CBS, and Fox television stations—but never his home newspaper, the *Plano Star-Courier.* He is the co-host of *Party Politics,* a Texas and national podcast on Houston Public Media; co-host of *59 Seconds,* a digital series on Houston Public Media; and the creator of and a weekly contributor to *Monday Morning Politics* on Houston's Fox 26. He lives on the west side of Houston with his family and his "labish" rescue dog Annie, named after a former Texas governor.

Introduction

During a midsession debate in the Texas House, former Speaker and frequent mangler of the English language "Gib" Lewis was confused about a particular issue facing the chamber . "There's a lot of uncertainty that's not clear in my mind," he said, to the great confusion of the assembled body. With this classic "Gibbism" in mind, I decided that the primary intents of this book would be to clarify some of the confusion that exists about policy and politics in Texas, to inform the reader about impending questions that face the Lone Star State, and to generate debate about the major controversies presently troubling it.

The twists and turns and wheres and wherefores of Texas government and policy can perplex even the most clued-in observer. The interplay of a short legislative session, a modestly powerful governor but robust lieutenant governor, an expansive bureaucracy, and an elected judiciary encourage frequent power struggles in the state. The politics of policy issues like public education, immigration and border security, abortion and reproductive health, and taxation are consistently contentious. The thrusts and parries of the political parties during elections create unbroken tension that colors and shapes the political process. *Current Debates in the Lone Star State* tackles these issues and more in an effort to give readers an insider's view of the form and function of Texas's government and politics. Simply put, this book examines the perplexing debates that have shaped and are shaping policy and government in the Lone Star State.

These queries span geography and political culture as well. For instance, let us start with a simple question: What region of the country is Texas in? When Texas senator William Blakely was asked if Texas is southern or western, he simply replied, "Texas is Texas." The vastness of the Lone Star State contributes to its uniqueness and its sense of independence and individuality. Noted folklorist and English professor J. Frank Dobie at the University of Texas wrote, "Like longhorns, seedless grapefruit and hot-oil companies, ruggedness has thriven in Texas." The distinctiveness of the state's topography and geography is but one layer of its diversity. In her famous book about Texas, Mary Lasswell commented, "I am forced to conclude that God made Texas on his day off, for pure entertainment, just to prove what diversity could be crammed into one section of earth by a really top hand." Texas celebrates its diversity of languages, cultures, politics, races, ethnicities, and industries, but this variety can also create conflict.

It is the diversity of its economy that has kept Texas on more stable financial footing in recent years. The state, however, has historically experienced economic ups and downs, often connected to natural resources like oil, which have made and lost the fortunes of many Texans. In boom times, Texans celebrate. One story from a moment of peak oil prices tells of an oil baron who had four Cadillacs—one for each geographic direction. In bust times, Texans can be frugal—as one old saying goes, a sign of hard times in Texas is that those in the oil and gas industry wear ten-quart hats instead of the iconic ten-gallon hats. *Current Debates in the Lone Star State* offers a contemporary perspective on the state's massive economy that is both optimistic and pessimistic.

The politics of Texas is as unique as the state's wild history. For most of Texas's modern political history, it has been dominated by one political party or another. From the New Deal to the 1990s, the Democrats tightly held the reins of power. Native son, U.S. House member, U.S. Senate majority leader, and (eventually) president Lyndon Johnson once joked that a Republican would need a passport to enter Texas. However, demographic changes and a resurgence of the Republican Party cracked the Democrats' hold on Texas in the 1990s and early 2000s, and years of Republican dominance of state politics followed. *Current Debates in the Lone Star State* recaps these changes and discusses the political future of Texas in terms of both its political parties and its elections. As political power changes hands and modern political warfare unfolds into what former governor Ann Richards called "a contact sport," questions about voting rights and election practices emerge. This book offers perspectives on the present and future of these important issues.

We wouldn't have half the fun in Texas if we didn't talk about corruption and scandal, but we would miss the point if we ignored the profound effect of these moments on how the state is governed. The state's history of corruption and lawbreaking involving officials across the political spectrum would make other states blush. Judge Roy Bean, one of the few appointed lawmen west of the Pecos River before the Civil War, was infamous for "fining" men shot and killed in gunfights for carrying weapons. A common joke in Austin claims that the state park service installed lights to illuminate the capitol dome so that the politicians wouldn't steal it. Famed journalist (and humorist) Molly Ivins counseled readers concerned about ethics in government in the following way: "For virtue, try Minnesota." These anecdotes are as revealing of the current state of Texas government as they are humorous, illustrating the ways in which major scandals shape the accountability of state government. *Current Debates in the Lone Star State* highlights these profound moments in Texas history and relates contemporary ethical struggles through a discussion of interest groups and ethics reform.

Texas is, according to various observers, the finest portion of the globe, where everything is bigger (even the toast), and where the stars at night are big and bright. The wealth of opinions on and analysis of Texas that have been put forth shows that the Lone Star State is vast. The selections in this volume help to facilitate further debate and discussion to explore and explain just how vast it is indeed.

HOW TO USE THIS BOOK

The goal of this book is to examine past and current key debates in the Lone Star State by stimulating discussion about these important perspectives and controversies. Each section of *Current Debates in the Lone Star State* broadly introduces the scope of a particular part of elected government, public policy, or parties and elections. The book concludes with a section on the future of Texas—where the state is headed and what challenges remain. Each chapter wraps up with several questions that either check your understanding of the content or ask you to convey your own impression of the issues or arguments. Each reading includes a short but informative summary of the article, book chapter, or primary source to prep the reader for the content.

The selections draw from sources ranging from contemporary political documents to journalistic articles to academic book chapters. It was admittedly difficult to pare down the massive body of work that has been produced on these important events and political happenings into this handful of readings. Ultimately, these selections represent both core work in the field and contemporary views of important issues being debated in the Lone Star State.

Like the companion textbook, *Inside Texas Politics*, this book is designed to give readers an insider's view of government, politics, and policy in the Lone Star State. Interbranch and intrabranch skirmishes, battles over the budget, fights about voter registration and turnout, and lingering constitutional questions all demonstrate the role that those inside and outside of government play in defining modern Texas. This book offers an updated and enticing entry into contemporary issues, problems, and solutions confronting the nation's second-largest state. Looking past the changing daily headlines to core issues of importance to Texas will make readers savvier and help prepare the state's next generation of leaders.

The perspectives included in *Current Debates in the Lone Star State* necessarily span the ideological spectrum—left, right, and center. The resulting range of views should give readers a sense of the ideological divisions that confront the state today. Yet, despite intense intraparty divisions and record-high interparty divisions, moments of bipartisan agreement abound, and *Current Debates in the Lone Star State* highlights these moments of shared policy concurrence. More perspectives mean more engaged debate!

Chapter 1

Cultural and Political Trends

Province. Nation. State. Texas is a land much revered by its inhabitants, a place where everything is bigger, and where the people have a distinct state of mind. As the saying goes, Texas is not to be "messed with." The size of the state has made it a major player in the economy of the nation and the extraction of natural resources. Its location on the U.S. border with Mexico links the two nations socially and economically, providing both tension and opportunity. Furthermore, the tendency of the state to be dominated by a single political party for long stretches of time, first the Democrats and then the Republicans, has made it central to presidential aspirants striving to raise money and find political backing.

Texas has always been exceptional because of its size, geographic role, resources, and larger–than–life politics. The myths about Texas could fill libraries and occupy students of history and politics for generations. Rooted in the state's rich history is a sense of Texas exceptionalism, a sentiment that the state is great and without peer. Historian T. R. Fehrenbach makes a strong case for the "independent Texan," the characteristic figure who harnessed an entrepreneurial spirit and strength to settle the hostile land that Texas was in its infancy. Still, it may be that Texas exceptionalism has its limits. Fehrenbach suggests that the Texan myth has been used to justify some historic wrongs like slavery and the exploitation of the poor by the rich.

Several common themes of political culture characterize the citizens of Texas, which tells us something important about where political power resides in the state. Political culture is the product of shared broad political goals, shaped by a common set of values and preferences and reinforced by social and political organizations. The pioneers who originally shaped the early Texas colony and the Texas Republic infused Texas with a spirit of rugged individualism and a strong sense of fair play, both of which continue to permeate the political environment today. Texans have always had an expansive and grandiose vision of their state.

Texans' opinions on a variety of issues and policies, their relationship with the government, and their desire to protect individual rights are all important factors in explaining how Texas is governed. Texas's political culture both enhances and restrains the types of actions its government can take, from what policies the legislature enacts to the types of executive actions governors take, how agencies in Austin enforce laws, how judges rule on cases, and how much power local governments have. The excerpt from Erica Greider's book *Big, Hot, Cheap, and Right* outlines the evolution of the state's desire for small government but also makes the case that a limited-government philosophy isn't always practical in a modern state like Texas, with its vast and thriving industry and pressing problems to solve.

Political scientist Daniel Elazar developed a classification of states' political cultures, arguing that the states vary in terms of citizens' beliefs and values regarding the appropriate goals of the political system, citizens' activities, and the relationship of government to the people. Elazar places Texas at the intersection of individualistic and traditionalistic political cultures. Those who settled Texas infused the state with the political cultures they brought with them. Texas shows elements of individualistic political culture through its support for free enterprise, fierce opposition to big government (especially at the federal level), and emphasis on entrepreneurship. Its traditionalistic political culture is seen in characteristics like low voter participation, one-party dominance, and conservative social values informed by strict religious beliefs. In 2016, the debate about the proper role of religion in public schools became a statewide issue when a public school nurse's aide posted a Charlie Brown Christmas cartoon containing a Bible verse on her school door, as *Breitbart* reporter Lana Shadwick describes. The resulting actions of a school administrator in Killeen, Texas, demonstrate how pro-religious forces in the state often conflict with rules about public schools being neutral on religion and how the state's culture has formed around these two positions.

CHAPTER QUESTIONS

1) Is Texas really that different from other places, or is it just the *myth* of Texas that's larger?
2) Are these myths used to justify actions that inhibit minority participation or to promote policies that benefit groups who fit that (possibly incorrect) historical motif?
3) What are your impressions of the Texas mystique? Put another way, how do you describe Texas to people not from Texas?
4) Values often conflict (like freedom of religion versus freedom *from* religion)—how do these conflicts play out in Texas's politics and law?

1.1) The Ungoverned (Chapter 7)

Big, Hot, Cheap, and Right: What America Can Learn from the Strange Genius of Texas, 2013

ERICA GREIDER

Grieder starts her chapter with a simple and direct summary: "Texas today is a state that prefers limited government." From the days when Texas sat on the United States' western frontier to the present struggles over funding for social programs, Republicans and Democrats alike have embraced a "do it yourself" mentality. Grieder calls the distinct brand of Texan who embraces this personal and professional ethos that government should be limited, stay *out* of peoples' lives, and have a small imprint on the economy "the ungoverned." This notion of desired distance is spun from a political tale as wild as the Texas frontier: in post–Civil War Texas, resurgent Democrats challenged incumbent Republicans, who during Reconstruction had centralized authority and disenfranchised whites who they considered disloyal to the Union.

The "ungoverned" limited-government philosophy is a mindset, but it is also welded into the state's political, economic, and constitutional structure. The revamped Texas Constitution of 1876 (which is still in use today) cements limited state government and enhanced individual liberty. Texas has no income tax. The state legislature meets for only 140 grueling days . . . every two years. The executive branch is weak because it is divided among several statewide elected offices. Efforts to make changes to this government architecture have failed. Much of the rejection of these changes has come from the voters themselves; the fact that amending the constitution requires the approval of a majority of voters is itself a testament to the "rule by the people" mentality.

Changes may be necessary, though, according to Grieder. Many of the constitution's provisions are outdated or unnecessary, and the amendment process itself is sluggish and difficult to control. She describes these circumstances as "bugs"—glitches that could (and should) be fixed. How can you govern a modern state like Texas with an outdated constitution? Beyond that, how can a state that views the role of government as unimportant expect citizens to come out to participate in the process through voting?

Texas today is a state that prefers limited government. Even its Democrats are more conservative in that sense than their national counterparts. As with so many aspects of the state's culture, the small-government stance took root long ago. The reason for that wasn't just that Texans had a history of conflict with the various governments they happened to be held under at the time. They also never developed the habit of expecting much from their government.

After annexation, for example, Texas had serious public health problems. Its citizens were riddled with such diseases as malaria, cholera, yellow fever, dysentery, and gonorrhea. The public sector had few resources for sanitation or other public health interventions. It was hard to recruit doctors to the frontier, anyway, because so many settlers had no way to pay them other than in cows, pigs, and chickens. The government, fragile as it was, could do little other than pressure the newspapers not to write stories about the various outbreaks of disease: if word got out, then it would be even harder to get doctors to come to Texas. People got used to making do on their own.

They might have developed a different view, but they never really had a chance. In 1876, in the wake of Reconstruction, Texas wrote a new constitution that has effectively guaranteed a limited government ever since. Barring some kind of overhaul—which has been attempted several times, never successfully—the state's role is bound to be a small one.

Texas is one of only four states, for example, that doesn't have a personal income tax. Creating one would require an amendment to the state constitution, which would have to be passed by a two-thirds majority in both houses of the legislature and then approved by a majority of voters. Another unusual thing about Texas is that its legislature meets for only 140 days, every *other* year. This creates problems because the legislature does have some responsibilities, such as writing the budget for the following two-year span. In January 2011, the state comptroller told legislators they would have $72.2 billion to spend in the 2012–2013 biennium. The projection resulted in harsh budget cuts, and turned out to be too low, by nearly $20 billion.

One way to interpret the Texas constitution is that the delegates who wrote it had nothing but contempt for the government. That's why they took care to limit it in perpetuity. That is, in fact, pretty much what happened. The state's current constitution was written in 1876, less than a decade after the state had been taken over by Radical Republicans, who had saddled the state, during the Reconstruction, with a government that was much bigger than Texans were used to or wanted. The 1876 delegates were determined to keep politicians from having so much power ever again. They largely succeeded, because even though the anger of that era has abated, the document it gave rise to continues to hold sway. In a superficial respect, of course, the delegates' plan failed, because the Texas Capitol has once again been infiltrated by Radical Republicans, but we'll come back to that later.

When the Civil War came to an ignominious end, all of the Confederate states understood their defeat as a military failure rather than a moral one. Texans, in addition, liked to tell themselves that their state was unique. This was a preoccupation that had obviously preceded that war. Among the grievances listed in Texas's secession ordinance, for example, was that the federal government had failed to protect Texan settlers from Indian attacks on the frontier.

This attitude was clearly self-serving. Slavery had been the cause of secession in Texas as in every other Confederate state. Although there were relatively few slaves in the poor and sparsely populated Republic of Texas—that is, between 1836 and 1845—the state's population had grown steadily since annexation, and slavery had taken root firmly by the time of the Civil War. The 1850 US Census counted 58,161 slaves in Texas and an overall population of 212,592. By 1860, the state's population had nearly tripled and included 182,566 slaves.

Still, Texas had lost less than many states during the war, largely because it had had less to lose. Being at the western edge of the Confederacy, the state had seen minimal fighting. Also, the abolition of slavery didn't threaten Texas's future the way that it did the other formerly slaveholding states. Despite the growth of slavery in the antebellum era, Texas was the whitest state in the Confederacy, and after the Civil War about 30 percent of its people were freedmen. In Mississippi, by contrast, the 1860 Census had counted about 354,000 white people and about 437,000 slaves. African Americans were also the majority in South Carolina, which went into the war with 291,000 whites and some 402,000 slaves. Emancipation in those states posed a potentially existential threat to white supremacy. White Texans didn't like the end of slavery, but they had less reason to fear it.

In the aftermath of the Civil War, then, Texas was resigned to being readmitted to the Union under the lenient terms that Abraham Lincoln had set out. Andrew Johnson, the Southern Democrat who ascended to the presidency after Lincoln was assassinated in 1865, planned to follow his predecessor's plan, after declaring the insurrection over in August 1866.

What followed would be a crucial chapter in the development of Texas's political identity. By 1867, Republicans in Congress had realized they didn't like President Johnson and they didn't need him either. Annoyed by his magnanimity to the beaten Southerners, the Republicans preferred to reconstruct the South according to their own specifications. They swiftly passed a series of acts, overriding Johnson's veto, that took a harder line. The advent of Radical Reconstruction put most of the former Confederacy under military control. Texas was lumped into a district with Louisiana. Anyone who had done anything in public life on behalf of the Confederacy was barred from future public service, from serving on a jury to holding office. Whites could be disenfranchised for disloyalty, and many were. Meanwhile, the freedmen would have full civil rights, including the right to vote.

Besides being a tremendous blow to the ego of Texans, Reconstruction also threatened to upend the political order. By 1868, Texas had about 100,000 registered voters, lower than might be expected given that the 1870 Census would find that Texas had about 800,000 people. Anglos maintained a whopping majority in terms of population, but they had been whittled to a narrow majority of the electorate, because the Republicans had been busily registering the freed slaves and summarily dismissing thousands of white voters. Partisan affiliation fell mostly along racial lines, but given how small the white majority was, and the ban against former Confederates holding office, Texas Democrats were thoroughly driven from power. In 1869, they were so discouraged they didn't even have a candidate for governor; a Republican, E. J. Davis, won the office.

Having asserted unprecedented power in the state, Republicans sought to put their stamp on Texas. As the majority party at the state constitutional convention called in 1869, they drew up a constitution that reflected a governing vision unlike anything Texas had seen before. The document favored centralized authority for the first time in Texas's history. It brought public schools under state, rather than local, purview; introduced several new tax streams; and expanded the governor's role.

The message was clear enough: national Republicans weren't even going to bother reconstructing Texas as it had been before the war. They wanted to raze the state's political infrastructure, such as it was, and build it from scratch—effectively by force but with the humiliation of democratic pretense.

Resentment was mounting. White Texans felt they were being subdued for political reasons, which of course they were; the carpetbaggers were attempting to remediate the condition of the freedmen, no small task given that white Texans would have been happy for African Americans to be second-class citizens indefinitely. During the previous constitutional convention, in 1866—after the passage of the Thirteenth Amendment but before the insurrection in Texas had officially ended—delegates had abolished slavery, and authorized some economic rights for the freedmen, but they had also barred African Americans from voting or holding office.

When Texas was readmitted to the Union in 1870, it was still in effect an occupied state under Republican rule. Even Texans who had opposed secession to begin with were becoming far less sympathetic to the national government. The policies and tactics of the Reconstruction government were unpopular with everyone except the Republicans who had written and enforced them. Texas being Texas, the very idea of having a superempowered governor, an elaborate school bureaucracy, and occasional and arbitrary imposition of martial law was a bridge too far.

In 1872, Democrats finally mustered enough seats in the legislature to force a gubernatorial election. The following year Democrat Richard Coke, a former Confederate officer, won the governorship.

The Republicans did not take the results gracefully. Governor Davis outright declined to accept that he had lost. Republicans locked the Democratic legislators out of the capitol and stationed guards around the first floor so that they couldn't sneak back in to vote. But the Democrats outtricked them by sneaking into the second floor of the legislature, where they were able to quickly count the votes and announce that Richard Coke was indeed the new governor.

The new administration set to work summarily undoing the previous one. In 1875, a new constitutional convention met. The document its delegates produced limited the state government severely. It also bolstered individual rights. The writ of habeas corpus was reaffirmed, as were due process, the right to bear arms, the right to free speech, the right to free religious expression, and the separation of church and state. All in all, more than two dozen rights were detailed in the first article of the constitution, including a metaright: "To guard against transgressions of the high powers herein delegated, we declare that everything in this 'Bill of Rights' is excepted out of the general powers of government, and shall forever remain inviolate, and all laws contrary thereto, or to the following provisions, shall be void."

The convention delegates whittled away the governor's job description until his office was one of the weakest in the country. The legislature, they decided, needed to meet only once every two years (under Reconstruction, it had been convened annually). Most of the public sector took a salary cut, including the delegates themselves, who slashed their per diem at the start of the discussions. Joe B. Frantz, a former head of the Texas State Historical Association, notes that the delegates were so hostile to government and public administration that they didn't even hire a stenographer—a real disservice to the future heads of the state's historical associations, because it meant there were no official records of the deliberations.

Perhaps most significantly, the delegates severely limited the state's authority to borrow, tax, and spend. Though this might sound appealing to today's Republican Party, many scholars, not to mention Texans themselves, would come to regret that the delegates went to such lengths to tie their own hands. They had come up with dozens of tax rules, most of them concentrated in one article, others jammed haphazardly throughout the document. Some of these were in direct contradiction with each other, and none of them showed much thought, foresight, or even awareness of what other parts of the constitution were saying about the state's responsibility to its citizens.

In Article 7, for example, the constitution tasks the legislature with finding out a way to create and support an efficient system of free public schools ("a general diffusion of knowledge," it explains, is "essential to the preservation of the liberties and rights of the people"). This is a worthy standard, which Texas can hardly meet. Schools cost money, and the constitution didn't provide for a state-level income tax or sales tax or property tax, which are the usual ways that states raise money.

"In a state constitution there is no need to mention any power to tax," sighed George Braden,

a constitutional law expert, in a 1976 analysis. "The legislature has all the taxing power anybody can dream up." Similarly, he observed, there was no need for a state constitution to explicitly limit both taxing and spending; a limit on the former was bound to achieve the latter. His advice came one hundred years too late. The whole thing was a "mess," concluded Braden, having attempted to explain the matter in nearly one hundred pages of Talmudic detail.

Texans were so upset by the federal government, in other words, that they took out their frustration on the state. Counterintuitive, perhaps; maybe they would have done better to create a stronger state, so as to guard against encroachment by the feds. But the feeling seemed to be that government was government. If the federal government could commandeer the state government, as it had during Reconstruction, the difference was immaterial. "In almost every way possible they indicated that public administrators were a nuisance who needed to be turned out almost as quickly as they assumed office," concluded state historian Joe Frantz. "The system provided for little continuity or time for planning, and Texas has suffered from it for a century." The new constitution became the law of the land on February 15, 1876. And with that, Texas's hostility to government—its own and everyone else's—became a self-fulfilling prophecy.

There were several movements in subsequent years to replace the 1876 constitution, none of them successful. The most sustained effort came in 1974 when the legislature set out to replace the old constitution with one that would be less erratic and less restrictive. "Its members repeated all the old mistakes and added a few new ones," according to Frantz.

The US Constitution works, in part, because of its elasticity. The Texas legislature, and the lobbyists, took the opposite tack; they tried to preempt future interpretations the state might come up with by detailing their specific preferences on the issues of the day. By the time they were through, the legislature itself didn't even approve its own document. The next year, the state went to the voters directly and offered them eight propositions that had been suggested during the drafting attempt; the voters rejected all of them. The result, Frantz concluded, was that "Texas lumbers along with a constitution that was written for a horse-and-buggy age."

Individualist, small-government ideology can't explain this much commitment to the old constitution, especially considering how ideologically impure Texans are in practice when government is able to provide something they want. Throughout the twentieth century, for example, Texans were receptive to government spending and occasionally pursued it with ardor. Nor does an explanation lie in a solemn respect for tradition. Texans are fond of tradition, but they fiddle with the constitution all the time. As of 2012, voters had considered 653 amendments to it and approved more than two-thirds of them.

Here's another way of looking at the matter: it might be that Texans believe in small government because their government is small. In 2010, computer scientist Jaron Lanier published *You Are Not a Gadget*, a jeremiad against the unanticipated consequences of technological design. The details of any new device or system, he explained, reflect any number of factors—the designer's conscious decisions, of course, but also the designer's unexplored assumptions and habits, the technological constraints of the time, the materials available, and so on. Regardless of whether these constraints are deliberate, users often receive them as such. The tools teach the user how they should be used. "We tinker with your philosophy by direct manipulation of your cognitive experience, not indirectly, through argument," Lanier asserted.

This might apply to the political habits in Texas. The delegates who wrote the 1876 constitution clearly intended to limit the government forever. Certainly, they hamstrung the state with arbitrary restraints that made governing difficult. But, as Lanier argued, the effects of a design may start to seem normal, even right. The governor can hardly do anything, so no one expects much from him. The legislature isn't even there most of the time. The state agencies don't have much room for encroachment. There aren't that many regulations, which is lucky, because there aren't that many regulators. The State Board of Education can't even force its local counterparts to teach kids that premarital sex is a sin. Some aspects of the Texas constitution were clearly intentional and would be included if the document were rewritten today. Other aspects, though, are bugs. One of Texas's problems is that it's not entirely clear which is which.

The best example of this dilemma is probably the state's skimpy legislative schedule. The framers of the Texas constitution clearly didn't want state legislators to do much; the only task they are required to tackle is drawing up a state budget. Given that they have only four months every other year to manage that, the budget does end up subsuming much of the legislature's time. In theory, a small-government conservative might think that's a fine idea. In practice, however, even Texas's small-government conservatives sometimes complain. It's hard to write a good budget that spans two years, takes effect more than a year later, and is largely based on projections about how much money the somewhat unpredictable sales tax is going to bring in.

There have, of course, always been Texans who wanted a more active government. That's one of the major points made by Jim Hightower, a Democrat who served as agriculture commissioner of Texas from 1982 to 1990 before losing that office to Rick Perry, then a little-known state representative who snuck up with a propesticide platform.

Today, Hightower is one of America's most high-profile populist[s]—on the left, at least. One of his themes is that the parties have been co-opted and the people misled (unlike Thomas Frank, he thinks this is true of Democrats as well as Republicans). In his view, Texas is a Republican state because the people have gotten so discouraged that they don't bother to vote. If they did vote, the Democrats—the progressive Democrats—would surely take control. After all, he observes, there was a time when Texas was [one of] America's [most] populist states.

That's true, but there are complications in the picture. One is that Texas's populists were actually relatively conservative. They even had a big hand in writing the supe rstrict 1876 constitution. About half of the delegates were affiliated with the

Grange, one of the farmers' coalitions. (The state has big tax exemptions for agricultural interests even today, when it isn't just lowly farmers who get to take advantage of them. Michael Dell, the founder and CEO of Dell, is one of the beneficiaries; Rick Perry is another. Put up a few birdfeeders, house a roadside zoo, and, presto, your land is farmland.)

The version of populism that flourished in Texas wasn't strictly a philosophical indictment of big business or a vote in favor of a robust public sector. It was a reaction to the big business interests that already existed and were making it harder for Texas businesses to get big.

Texas's populist politicians, in fact, talked up the virtues of free enterprise. In 1895, when James Hogg (who was then attorney general) went to the legislature to promote the antitrust law, he made the case that it would be good for business: "The contention that this anti-trust law is a menace to prosperity and will deter capital from investing in this State, is, logically, to insist that the way to induce the investment of capital, and to promote prosperity, is to welcome monopoly and legalize trusts—to substitute combination to fetter trade for competition to give it freedom."

By the late 1800s, the aspirational ideal of success through entrepreneurship had already taken hold. Even before the oil strike at Spindletop, Texans had gotten the idea that any of them could become entrepreneurs. They saw themselves as workers allied against bosses, but also, importantly, as potential bosses allied against the established, moneyed bosses of the North. Regardless of whether it was true, that belief would prove salient.

You can see the tension if you compare the 1892 Omaha Platform of the national populist movement with the Texas party's version. Both documents argued that the working people of the United States, particularly farmers, were being systemically disadvantaged by federal policies that favored established moneyed interests—bankers, corporations, etc. They called for many of the same things—a graduated income tax, free silver, labor protections, electoral reforms—and the Texas platform specifically endorsed the populist platforms presented elsewhere, including Omaha.

The Omaha Platform, however, called for a more robust government to step in. "We believe that the power of government—in other words, of the people—should be expanded (as in the case of the postal service) as rapidly and as far as the good sense of an intelligent people and the teachings of experience shall justify, to the end that oppression, injustice, and poverty shall eventually cease in the land." With regard to the railroads, a major issue at the time, the national populists wanted a government takeover: "Transportation being a means of exchange and a public necessity, the government should own and operate the railroads in the interest of the people. The telegraph, telephone, like the post-office system, being a necessity for the transmission of news, should be owned and operated by the government in the interest of the people."

The Texas platform preferred a smaller role for government: "We demand that all revenues—national, state, or county—shall be limited to the necessary expenses of the government, economically and honestly administered." It advocated more government oversight of certain industries, but government takeover only as a last resort: "We demand the most rigid, honest, and just national control and supervision of the means of public communication and transportation, and if this control and supervision does not remove the abuses now existing, we demand the government ownership of such means of communication and transportation."

It's as if the national populists saw the political system as a potential bulwark against private greed, whereas Texas populists still thought the political system was part of the problem. "The fruits of the toil of millions are boldly stolen to build up colossal fortunes for a few, unprecedented in the history of mankind," said the national platform, "and the possessors of those, in turn, despise the republic and endanger liberty." The Texas take was this: "[Politicians] have snatched our government from the hands of the economy and now a billion dollars is spent by a single Congress, both parties vying with each other in making big appropriations for rivers, harbors, public buildings, extravagances of officials, congressmen, the pensioning of rich widows, burying dead congressmen, etc."

Accordingly, the national platform called for government to have a broader mandate so that it could help more people. The Texas platform called for government to do more in some respects—one of its complaints was that the state had failed to provide effective schools, as the state constitution required—but it also suggested that government be reined in, or at least subject to more oversight by the people.

The Texan skepticism about government would be reinforced, at times, by bad government. James "Pa" Ferguson, who served as governor from 1915 to 1917, had some progressive inclinations. "Let us have more business and less talk," he announced in his first gubernatorial platform, in 1914. "Instead of wrangling over the question of whether man shall drink, let us consider for a time how he and his loved ones may get something to eat and to wear." He was also a crook; the legislature impeached him in 1917 after a Travis County jury indicted him on nine charges, including embezzlement.

In 1924, his wife, Miriam (or "Ma") Ferguson, ran for office as a proxy for her husband. She was the first woman to be elected governor of Texas (and one of the first in the United States; on November 4, 1924, Wyoming also elected a woman, Nellie Tayloe Ross, who was inaugurated two weeks before Ferguson, in January 1925). In Ma Ferguson's case, though, a heavy asterisk must be applied, since there was never any question who was calling the shots. "Two governors for the price of one" was her campaign promise, which exaggerated how much governing she was fixing to do.

After such experiences with government, the Texas framing might start to seem logical. If government is inept, making it bigger and more powerful might not be the best idea.

How do today's Texans feel about their feeble government?

The fact that the state has long posted some of the lowest voter turnout rates in the country has sometimes been considered a sign of voter disgust, if not suppression. Utah, however, also has low voter turnout, and rarely is it dinged for bad government; that state is run with Mormon discipline.

Another possibility, then, is that Texans have been happy enough with the status quo. The government might not do much, but at the same time it doesn't meddle with people that much, nor does it ask for much in terms of taxes. That has apparently been an acceptable deal for most Texans, particularly because the people have been able to look elsewhere for the services the government can't provide or won't provide or both.

Lobbyists, for example, are happy to take on some of the legislative opportunities and responsibilities that in a normal state would be handled by legislators. The media, state and national, occasionally provide oversight. Churches and charities supplement the threadbare safety net, and the private sector provides a considerable number of public goods. Not the most elegant system, perhaps—but it hasn't failed hard enough to compel real change.

ARTICLE QUESTIONS

1) Can a liberal or progressive ideology that seeks to distribute wealth and protect those with little means ever work in a moderate to conservative state like Texas?

2) How do issues such as attempts to limit abortion rights run up against the state's philosophy of limited government?

3) What do you feel should be the proper role of government in the lives of Texans? Is there too much or not enough government at present?

4) Why are Texans so reluctant to change the structure of government according to the author?

1.2) The Society (Chapter 5)

The Seven Keys to Texas, 1996

T. R. FEHRENBACH

> The mythology of Texas is rooted in the people who settled the lands, and it abounds with individual independence, pragmatism, and, very often, pure exaggeration. Famed Texas historian T. R. Fehrenbach in his book *The Seven Keys to Texas* wrestles with the theme of the state's struggle for identity. This struggle demonstrates Texas's tension between culture and practicality, dreams and reality, and myth and truth. It also helps us explain the cultural and political values Texans hold.
>
> Independence is the cornerstone of the typical Texas hero, who is a mix of reality and fiction. Fehrenbach argues that the iconic independent Texan assumes personal responsibility; is futuristic, reactionary, and entrepreneurial; and "takes orders with poor grace." This ethos has certainly served Texas well: its heroes have fought for Texas's independence, developed the state's natural resources, and settled a wild land. However, it has a negative side as well, according to Fehrenbach. Violence against Native Americans was justified as a muscular expansion of civilization, and slavery and sharecropping were justified in the name of economic expansion. What other groups have been excluded or ostracized by this type of viewpoint?
>
> Religion also frames the state's attachment to independence and self-identification. Some of this framework is formal: church services and invocations at Friday night football games. Religious sentiment also permeates Texan society more broadly, however, emerging in a distaste for pretension and luxury, the assertion of the importance of community, and a puritanical work ethic.
>
> These ingredients have been blended to create Texans who are a mix of contradictions: the newly rich seeking to hold onto an essential belief of what it means to be Texan by dressing in western wear or clinging to ideals of egalitarianism in what is clearly not an egalitarian economic system. These ingredients have also created and sustained class conflict between the rich and the not-so rich and have placed power in the hands of relatively few leaders.

The economy of Texas has moved closer to the national norm; 80 percent of Texans have left the land since 1940 and live in cities; a quarter of the Texan work force is engaged in some sort of manufacturing. On the surface, the Texas social scene seems to be a principal tributary of the American mainstream.

But there are subtle and not-so-subtle differences beneath the common plasticized surfaces, especially between Texas and the industrialized states.

For example, it is not uncommon for Texas corporate executives of national standing and top-rung remuneration to introduce or identify themselves as hired hands. The statement is neither coy, satirical, nor self-demeaning. It clarifies something that is still important in Texas, where even a corporate superstar, if he does not own his company, may stand in the position similar to that of a prime athlete vis-à-vis the owner of the New York Yankees.

While the tendency of Texans living outside the state to form "Texans in Exile" or other such nostalgic groups is well known, outlanders who have moved to Dallas and other Texas communities in recent years have formed "Damn Yankee" and similar organizations. This is only partly satirical; it is also a psychic and cultural protective measure frequently taken by many immigrants who feel they need reassurance in an alien society.

Meanwhile, in a pattern at least as old as King David's soldier Uriah the Hittite, who became more Hebrew than the Hebrews, many newcomers to Texas turn into the most ardent converts of all, even surpassing natives in their devotion to "Texanism."

Such things point up a fact that many Americans fail to recognize—and some will deny or resent—that the boundaries of Texas are not mere administrative lines of jurisdictional convenience drawn on the map of the United States. Texas society still shows profound differences from those of New York or California. And these are not confined to the quaint small towns or the backwoods; they flourish in Dallas, Houston, and San Antonio.

Many of the differences are not unique to Texas; in some way or other most of them are found across the region now called the Sunbelt. But just as Texas is bigger, nearly everything in Texas becomes exaggerated and commands attention.

Texas society springs in part from its economy—but only in part. Birth, place, and race, and perhaps religion, come before occupation in its processes of self-identification. When a person in Texas asks immediately, "What do you do?" instead of "Where are you from?" the odds are high that he or she is an outlander who lacks a deep-seated personal sense of place and belonging.

Texas society also springs from its people, their ethic and culture, their ideals and mythology, and their history, which includes the way urbanization and industrialization have come about. If all industrial societies inevitably followed the same course in societal and cultural terms, then the whole world would be like nineteenth-century England, and modern Frenchmen would resemble modern Russians. It is a truism in Texas that, except in and around the industrialized enclaves of Houston and Dallas, the state has never joined the "industrial society" as that concept is recognized nationally. But the actual truth is that the United States has been busy creating several "industrial" societies. There is the industrial society of the Northern manufacturing states, the industrializing society of the South, and the modern society of Texas, all of which have similarities but are not the same.

Texans *have* created a modern society during the long struggle upward from the frontier. But they have not surrendered everything in the process, especially the ancient, independent, inherently asocial consciousness of their ancestors who first rejected European society and then forged their own culture on the Southern frontiers. Texas

intellectuals, noticeably, are almost never marxist, determinist, or collectivist in their world views. The very notions are repugnant, not intellectually, but culturally. Thinking Texans with average incomes may hate rich men and worry about the "interests" that politicians love to lambaste—but they also tend to hate "socialism" more.

This culture has always made the individual the base of society—and of religion as well—and put individual responsibility above all forms of corporate responsibility or other social claims.

Its dictum is that people—individuals—should and do get pretty much what they deserve in all things, whether success on earth or later entry into heaven.

This is a view that much of the modern world regards as reactionary, while Texans themselves like to see it as futuristic, the hoped-for shape of things to come.

Meanwhile, it is a source of tension, not only between Texans and Northern "liberals" (many Texans are liberal, so long as liberalism does not touch religion, private property, the family, or openly enhance the powers of the state), but within the Anglo-Texan soul itself. For in the modern world of Texas as in all worlds there is a struggle between culture and practicality, dreams and reality, symbolism and structure, myth and truth, in short, a conflict with many names but which might be called, man wrestling with himself.

The old society is gone, but its imagery, mentality, and mythology live on. These are as alive in boardrooms across Texas as among the oil derricks and on the cattle ranges. The residue still shows in a hard pragmatism and absence of ideology, a worship of action and accomplishment, a disdain for weakness or incompetence, and a thread of belligerence—and finally, a cultural mythology stemming from the Alamo that even a Texan in the White House could not shake off.

Cultural survival is perhaps strongest in the ideal of the independent Texan. Now, this is not a purely Texan trait; it is American, found as much in the stony soil of New Hampshire as on the flinty plateaus of the Texas Hill Country. But the myth and cultural reality of personal independence is peculiarly and historically prevalent west of the Sabine and south of the Red River. The term "independent Ohioan" or "independent New Yorker" is essentially meaningless; if anything it conjures up images of political ticket-splitters. "Independent Texan," however, immediately strikes a chord of response among Texans, and even among other Americans who could not hope to define it.

The reality exists, from an H. L. Hunt to a Don Meredith to Howard Hughes to a Bill Clements. Whether Texans damn such persons or praise them, they all evoke a haunting uneasiness and sense of loss that we associate with endangered species. For the person who demands independence and assumes personal responsibility—but not responsibility for others—has taken on the aspect of a vanishing tribe in modern America.

There were never so many "independent" Texans as folklore insists, just enough to fashion that folklore and impress it upon the Texan consciousness. There were the tall men who died at the Alamo and won at San Jacinto, all the while taking orders with poor grace. There were Rangers who rode alone like paladins; cattlemen who held their ranges against writs and wire as stubbornly as any feudal baron confronted with the king's cannon. There were the farmers who took their families into the Post Oak belt when it was still Comanche country and lived, by choice, miles from every neighbor. There were statesmen like Sam Houston who saved the nation one day and dared and damned the popular fury the next—heroes in heroic times, who stood for many different things, but created a rich Texas symbolism.

Like the society itself, the Texan hero was both futuristic and reactionary, in the vanguard but also representing something very old, seizing upon the latest techniques in the pursuit of primordial drives and goals.

Both old-coot cattlemen and early wildcatters fit the image, together with modern entrepreneurs. And this image has another dimension in Texas—that of men and women who jeer at the pretensions and hypocrisies of overly organized societies, whether they be European or Yankee or even those closer to home. It is the image of a Texan who speaks his mind in pungent, barnyard terms, and who can outwit, ignore, or overcome the absurdities and humiliations forced on most people by civilization.

This hero can just as easily be a cowboy as a range king, a jackleg as well as a millionaire tycoon. Texas is the last home of the jackleg (the person who would never join a labor union, a trade association, or a cooperative) as much as it is the refuge of the entrepreneur. The hero can be right-wing or radical, football player or country sheriff, or horse doctor—the view and style are not so important as is the ability to be one's own man and make it stick.

It helps, but is not necessary, for the hero to be a "good ole boy" in the Southern tradition.

To those with a sense of social organism this Texan is distasteful and even dangerous. But the ethos is not truly anti-social. The Texas hero is not set against society as such so long as society lets him be. Nor is this Texan a revolutionary in the modern sense. He is a rebel but has no interest in building a brave new world or reforming society; he rebels, like the rebels of 1836, to secure his own freedoms *within* society.

The independent Texan rarely is interested in pushing his own ideas or biases on others, so long as others do not try to make him abide by theirs. Then, there is a thin line between belligerence and aggressive self-defense, and because of this, an aura of violence always surrounds the Texan folk ideal.

If Texans often seem to be "agin" something or somebody, it is because independence is not a normal civilized human condition. Man is a social animal, seemingly as hierarchical as baboons (but not so successful at making hierarchies). Independence, the assertion of the individual under self-control, is only achieved with strain, preserved only by isolation or combat. The Texan ideal is the antithesis of the dropout—but also the antithesis of the organization man. It suggests constant, dubious battle.

Over most of the United States "independence" has a fine sound; it cannot be given a pejorative meaning in the American tongue, but it is something celebrated on July Fourth and forgotten the rest of the year. It is a wishful ideal, perhaps the last heritage of the old frontier.

Most Americans do not think independently or act independently, whether voting, buying, dressing, investing, or holding forth in intellectual circles. The independent person is praised but not often tolerated, a wonderful American kind of hypocrisy.

Financial independence rather than riches is probably the most prized American goal, which Merrill Lynch, land developers, and the Social Security planners all exploit expertly. Millions of Americans profess political independence, forcing countless politicians to portray themselves as "independent" Democrats or Republicans. The word still has magic in a vast, impersonal socio-economic-political system which in fact has made most forms of independence increasingly unobtainable.

But it is still this unsurrendered ideal that keeps some people slaving eighteen hours a day at personal enterprises when they could make more money on someone's payroll. It drives women professionals as well as would-be entrepreneurs. It drives a few from the rat race, but it hounds far more to the smogs of Denver or Houston, because Texas, like most of America, has developed irreconcilable imperatives.

The Frenchman Raymond Aron, perhaps the best observer of the American scene since Tocqueville, wrote that since the democratic revolutions of the eighteenth century, Western civilization has fostered strong, splendid ideals of personal freedom but at the same time created industrial, economic, and social forms which limit genuine liberty for the individual and family.

But capitalism is hardly the villain; the fault lies in any society driven to mass production, mass employment, mass consumption, and mass social organization. Under either a modern "capitalist" or "socialist" system, the roles, education, status, and psychological problems of clerks, sanitation workers, factory hands, educators, and engineers are much the same.

The clash between imperatives is also not new. The Texas-Mexican, Texas-Indian wars were cultural confrontations with racial overtones—but the struggle for the land was and is a war of cultural imperatives. The Indian ranges were appropriated by conquerors who were themselves conquered by an all-engulfing civilization.

All these successive battles for cultural survival left their mark on the land, and on both the Texan and American soul. They form, at bottom, the stuff of Western literature, that most American of art forms, in which some lonely soul, perhaps aided by family and a friend or two, is always arrayed against vast odds at High Noon.

Those who find the Texan character uncomfortable or distasteful—including some Texans—disparage this image of the Texan hero, mock the myth of the man who stands alone, criticize the constant chimera of the Alamo. No matter—every successive generation of Texans seeks its Alamos, and sometimes finds them.

The society of the Republic of Texas was remarkably simple, a rawer Old South writ large. It continued the traditions and tensions of Cohee and Tuckahoe between the upland corn farmers and the cotton-growing coastal plains. It was comprised of a horde of subsistence farmers and a smaller number of planter capitalists whose major investment was in Negro slaves. But rich man and poor man were racially, culturally, and religiously homogeneous—for all that the planters tended to be Anglican or Presbyterian and the others, (formally unchurched) puritan fundamentalist—in a characteristically American fashion. The rich man's life style was light years removed from the poor man's in many ways, but it was only what the poor man would have chosen, if he had had the means. There were few intimations of aristocracy, for aristocracy on the European pattern was despised. The planters were capitalistic rather than paternalistic in their world view, and the nearest insinuation of aristocratic notions was a reference to origins in Virginia or South Carolina. Such ancestry was considered—and to some, still is—more prestigious than that from other states.

Out of this odd mix was forged a genuine white democracy in which social and political equality, but never economic equality, prevailed. The cement was not so much class as the racism a black-owning society must have. The slaves provided a social floor.

The "respectable" occupations had already been established: landowner, farmer, doctor, lawyer. Texas was overrun with members of this last category from the earliest days. Anglo-Texans almost never engaged in merchandising or banking. The first practitioners of these trades came from the North—Presbyterian merchants who came down the Ohio and Mississippi Valleys—or directly out of Europe. Northern businessmen, like Richard King and Mifflin Kenedy and others less well-known from New England or New York, tended to become landowners and even slaveholders quite rapidly. This left commerce almost entirely to German or German-Jewish immigrants, and it was they who established almost all the stores and businesses across Texas from the Red River to the Rio Grande.

The Civil War desolated and demoralized this society but did not essentially change it across the eastern half of the state. Its basic human and cultural patterns were in fact reinforced by wholesale immigration of whites from the more devastated regions of the South, most of whom headed toward the frontiers.

By 1865, however, there was a very high proportion of blacks in Texas, partially because slavery was profitable here before the war, and partially because during the federal invasions of nearby states such as Louisiana and Arkansas, thousands of blacks had been sent by their owners to the relative safety west of the Sabine. What to do with this people—more than twenty percent of the population—and with the increasing numbers of poor whites ruined by the economic conditions that punished small farmers during the rest of the century after emancipation, could have become an insoluble problem without the institution of share-cropping.

This was a form of tenantry that did not involve cash payments, in which land was parceled out in small acreages to both white and ex-slave families. The landowner financed seed and other expenses, sometimes groceries, and after "deducts" took at least 20 percent of the value of the harvest. Reduced to his labor, the sharecropper found it almost impossible to rise from poverty. The system was not so pernicious as slavery or the debt-peonage that prevailed in Mexico, where debts legally bound the workers to the soil.

It was even necessary in its time and place, if the population was to work and the land be used at all. But the effects on large parts of Texas society were profound.

It maintained the two-tier system of owners and workers—and as thousands of white families were driven into tenantry by the economic crises of the last part of the century, it created a newer class of "white trash." These were people of little ambition and slovenly habit, whose children, fed on a staple of syrup and cornbread, developed pellagra and worse, what in Texas came to be called the sharecropper mentality. The deprivations, real and cultural, of tenantry were harder to erase than the physical effects when country people moved to town in this century. Lyndon Johnson's grandfather was a community-founding pioneer, but his father was reduced to tenantry, and the President never quite escaped from or shook off the incubus.

Meanwhile, the ethnic Mexican population in Texas remained very small. It was no more than 12,000 (out of more than 600,000) before the Civil War, and was confined to the border regions south of San Antonio. In the towns and counties along the Rio Grande, political control passed entirely to Anglos, while the tenor of Mexican life remained unchanged. Texas Mexicans were rarely sharecroppers in this era. They were landowners themselves—as oppressed as the Anglo small farmers and gradually losing their lands—or laborers; they also made up a great proportion of the cowboys on Texas ranches in the Southwest.

Before 1900 there was almost no Mexican immigration, simply because there was nothing to attract it to the state. In 1900, ethnic Mexicans, who lived mostly in the borderlands, made up only five percent of all Texans, and they were almost ignored in the consciousness of the rest of the population—which was also to have its effects.

The rural character of Texas persisted very late. In 1860 the largest town, San Antonio, held only 8,000 citizens, and there were only twenty communities in all that boasted 1,000 inhabitants. In 1875, Washington County on the Brazos River was the most populous in Texas, and it did not contain a single town.

However, the movement from the land had already begun. This was to come in a steady tide, with repeated waves in the bad times of recurrent drouth and economic depression. But as late as 1910 there was no city with 100,000, and San Antonio, then as now without significant industry, was the largest in the state—a rank it was to hold until the 1930s when Houston, with its new man-made port, expanded under the impetus of the East Texas oil fields.

The trend toward urbanization accelerated throughout the twentieth century, with two-thirds of all Texas counties steadily losing population, while the Texas population itself grew prodigiously. However, as late as 1940 Texas was still predominantly rural, a fact that is not always understood outside the state.

The Texas cities, with a few exceptions such as Galveston and San Antonio, are all essentially twentieth-century creations. They all grew basically as mercantile, distribution, or financial centers for the countryside, or as ports of entry. And until well past the middle of this century, they were peopled primarily from the surrounding rural areas, from Old American agrarian stock. In most cases, they became metropolitan areas, some fifty in all, without the development of manufacturing industry.

Here there was a great difference from the patterns of the North and Midwest, where cities swelled from direct immigration from Europe, by populations that bypassed the trans-Appalachian experience, and most quickly developed industries.

Texas cities also grew up in the automobile age and were founded in almost every case in prairie or open country, unhindered by older surrounding settlements. Thus they expanded laterally rather than upward, without internal compression or close patterns forced by transportation needs. Few if any row houses were ever built in Texas; few if any neighborhoods—except for black and later Mexican enclaves—were ever formed.

Houston drew from the piney woods and surrounding rice plains; Dallas from the cotton belt; San Antonio from the limestone hills and dusty *brasada* country; four-score lesser cities did the same. Most Texans, moving from country to town, moved less than 200 miles—and this was not so much like Scotsmen going to London or Poles to Chicago but more like Frenchmen moving from their villages to neighboring Lyons.

City dwellers took up new occupations, but culture and world views did not immediately change. Farmers who saw themselves as middle class became white-collar employees—however, they did not, and still have not, become urbanites in cities with old, established urbane traditions.

During most of this century there was no fundamental change. Despite the profound depopulation of the rural counties, strong ties with them remained. Texans living in the burgeoning cities retained much of their rural outlook and ethos, along with their fried foods and small-town gaucheries.

Significantly, while each Texas city took on a certain ambience and character of its own—Dallas, earnest, eager, on the make; Houston, with its eye on the big buck; San Antonio and El Paso, less ambitious, more laid back and with virtually closed social circles at the top—none of them developed a true civic culture or civic type, like Parisians or Londoners or the natives of Hamburg. Texas culture, not civic culture, dominates. When a Texan is asked his place of origin, the native will almost always say "Texas," never "Houston" or "Amarillo." Sub-identifications come later, like the exchange of religious denomination or occupation.

The Texans also kept their Christian culture virtually unchanged. Texas is not a more merciful or more deeply religious society than others, but it is a *Christian* society. Religious forms permeate society and culture, from grace-saying to the public invocations by preachers—which some outlanders find uncomfortable or even distasteful—at football games. The churches are large, filled, and whatever effect they have upon faith and morals, they are an important means of Texan self-identification. Denomination is often as important as ancestry or occupation in defining identity, and each plays its role in society in a way that is unfathomable to many Americans to whom religion is no longer of significance.

If Texas had an established church—though the very notion goes against the grain of frontier American tradition—it would undoubtedly have emerged as Southern Baptist. For many years Baptists formed an absolute majority in the state, and their influence is still pervasive. Baptists evolved more powerfully in Texas than perhaps in any other region, and they have exported themselves more successfully than any other denomination into other American regions. Baptist polity fits Texas, both molding and reinforcing its world views: the essential priesthood of all believers, the lack of tension between God and Mammon and the acceptance of worldly success from effort, the separation of different ethnic groups as natural (which Catholics and mainstream Protestants handle uncomfortably), the puritan ethic with its distaste for pretension and luxury, belief in personal sin and personal salvation with the individual at the center of the religious universe, and suspicion of alcohol, disinterest in formal credos, and the utter independence of each congregation with disdain of elaborate hierarchies and rituals.

Besides the Baptists, many other pentecostal churches abound, both in the big cities and the rural areas.

Their influence in and on the culture has often been obscured, because other presences have been more visible. The early church buildings in Texas towns were all built by Episcopalians, Presbyterians, and Roman Catholics—who perhaps had greater need for edifices. In fact, until well into this century, Baptists and Methodists in Texas rarely erected buildings, and the first ones look more like courthouses than churches. As in most other parts of America, the socially elite—but not necessarily all rich people—gravitate toward more genteel denominations, and they draw more attention and make more news than the thousands of individual fundamentalist congregations who more often than not live in a state of truce with each other.

However, all the Texas churches—like all trans-Appalachian Protestants and even Roman Catholics assimilated into Anglo culture—are suffused with certain Calvinistic or puritan cultural values having nothing to do with their formal theology. On most issues, Anglicans and Baptists in Texas

in the same community think, act, and vote much the same, leaving their disdains and quarrels, except for a few things like drinking, to distant theologians.

Texans also carried their basic social and economic forms from the countryside into the cities. While it is too simplistic to say the underclass is still black or brown and the rest of society is divided between owners and hired hands, something of this pattern clearly remains.

But since urbanization took place without the large-scale industrialization that was normal in the North, and was carried out by a different type of population, the forms and attitudes of American Northern industrial society have been slow to appear in Texas. In fact, they probably never will appear in exactly the same form. Here there is a very real difference between the society of Texas and the other "imperial" states. Texas did not create a new American urban culture out of many diverse parts; it adapted the rural frontier culture to an urban environment—but again, a different type of urban setting.

While urban Texas grew rich from the effects of extracting, processing, financing, and selling the state's products—and servicing all the processes—it was difficult for a real management structure to arise. Owners continued to profit most, but without the employment of large, blue-collared work forces, there was also nothing like the Eastern millowner-millhand relationship. Because most enterprise stayed small, there was no formation of private business into private bureaucracies in the classic American pattern.

The property owner has remained boss. All managers, from ranch foremen to employed corporate executives to symphony conductors, hold at least something of the status of hired hands. And few things cause more misunderstandings, confusion, and sometimes fury, among the newcomers who have entered Texas.

This pattern permitted Texas business to remain small and entrepreneurial, and it kept its ethic pure—but the side effects puzzle and even infuriate skilled people from other regions, whether music directors in Dallas who believe themselves above patrons' beck and call, or executives—but not owners—who see themselves as movers and shakers in some cities but are not invited into the most prestigious local businessmens' clubs.

In most Texas communities, certainly in the medium-sized cities and until very recently in such larger cities as Houston and San Antonio, economic, social, and political power have not fragmented as they have in the complex, ethnically mixed North. These have stayed in the same hands, a manifestation that Texas society remains more like American society of the last century than the present one. The society of Texas towns, like the basic Texas property laws, resembles that of America everywhere in the eighteenth century more than that of modern Boston.

This society has enormous disparities of wealth and divisions between the social classes—but these gulfs still tend to be obscured, or even unadmitted, because of the white population's essential homogeneity.

And this has the effect of enforcing a certain egalitarianism in what is not an egalitarian society, even within a rural Baptist congregation. Texans are awkward about expressing notions of birth or breeding, except as applied to those outside the Anglo race and culture. Ancestry is often traced to the older Southern states, with the inference that it was there high-up on the social scale—unprovable and immaterial in any case. Rich Texans, especially those descended from the old breed, manifest their wealth in certain visible symbols, but the automobile, great house, and private airplane are much more "right" in feel and practice than assertions of superior culture, whether of education, musical awareness, or the collection of antiques. Above all, wealth and power are most properly displayed in one's business, by buying a company, a vast ranch, prime breeding stock, or a bank.

Some of this, like the wearing of diamond jewelry by men, is mere gaucherie by the standards of old money, but some of it still comes from deep cultural springs. Many prominent Texans have their clothing custom-made, but still styled to make them look like cowboys.

As a major figure in the petroleum industry once said—both belligerently and defensively—compared to Eastern investment types most Texas oil men live like slobs, and would be made nervous by having a butler around the house.

Texas money is mostly new, though there is more "old money" around than even many Texans realize, but it has not taken all the courses followed by the mainstream. Just as some Scottish lairds still survive in stone castles on a damp rock surrounded by their gillies and pipers, some Texans who prepared with Greek for Harvard wear khakis and drive pickup trucks and surround themselves, not with baronial splendor, but with "Mexican" hired hands.

But beneath the ranks of owners and the handfuls of high executives, what was once an American middle class—bankers, merchants, professional people—tends more and more to become a New Class of salaried hands, privileged compared to those who perform manual labor, but hired hands all the same. They find the same fragmentation, in Texas, between emotion and intellect in their work, which often is not directly productive and in which they are judged less by results than by the approval of superiors and peers.

No part of life, from the university to the highway department, has escaped the pressures of modern organization and bureaucratization. The old discipline of self-reliance, still held, struggles with the newer social discipline of conformity. National norms and fashions batter continually at the Texas frontiers, and the barriers do not always hold.

But there is still an instinctive clinging to a sense of time and place and uniqueness, however damaged by the national insistence upon total pluralism. As Joe Frantz, the Texas historian has observed, Texans find themselves somewhat in the position of eighteenth-century Scots confronting union with England. They treasure their differences, their social ethic and independence and society suffused with the forms, practices, and imagery of puritan Christianity, but at the same time are aware that others despise these and deprecate those who cling to them. The Texan who hopes to succeed in all senses of the word is torn between imperatives.

There is still a deep attachment to the land and its history, and pride in the way it all turned out, a pride lost in the ephemeral present of most American cities. This is what Texans mean when they say they are proud to be Texans, to newcomers who have shown their own pride and attachment to the place of their birth by their alacrity to leave them forever for a few more dollars.

Many Americans see these Texan traits as provincialism. And so they are, for Texans are provincial in most meanings of the word. But provincialism has always placed more strain on native intellectuals—born to a country where intelligence, but not intellectuality, is prized—than upon citizens who do what comes naturally, whether they be workers or businessmen. Texas intellectuals face the provincial's eternal dilemma: to go or not to go to Rome, and when in Rome, to try to become a Roman or make his living explaining his barbarian ways to Romans—who may find them greatly entertaining. It is a problem every Texas writer and artist faces in his own way. Some, like Scots or Gascons, make their way to London or Paris—but few ever really feel comfortable with the choice unless they can easily repudiate their heritage.

Modern American liberalism, for example, has its ironies: it asserts the right of Nigerians and Vietnamese to be Nigerians and Vietnamese—even when removed to America—but casts deep suspicions on the Texan who insists upon being a Texan.

This accounts for an agonizing confusion, both in and outside of Texas, about what Texas is and stands for and means to the greater nation.

It accounts for the self-exiled Texan, making a big to-do about it all in alien places, and for the agony of the Texas politician with ambitions beyond the state—who knows that he cannot placate both Dallas and New York, and that what may be conventional wisdom in one is likely to be anathema in the other.

And it also accounts for that ever-recurring phenomenon, the returning prodigal, come home at last.

ARTICLE QUESTIONS

1) As the politics of the state become more ideological, both liberal and conservative, are these values fracturing the pragmatism that has made Texans so independent?
2) How does the image of Texans in the popular mind contradict reality?
3) In what ways does religion shape the political and cultural opinions of Texans?
4) Think about your own expressions of Texas—are you perpetuating this mythology, and to what effect?

1.3) Charlie Brown Christmas Decoration Banned from Texas School

Breitbart, December 9, 2016

LANA SHADWICK

The traditionalistic character of Texas's political culture emphasizes rules and values that support existing institutions, such as the church and traditional family structure. Three-quarters of all Texans indicate that religion is "extremely important" in their lives. The state gave rise to the phenomenon of the "megachurch"—a church that has an average weekly attendance of more than 2,000. Houston alone has thirty-seven such churches, with the ten largest having a combined weekly attendance of around 200,000. Texas even passed the "Merry Christmas" law, which permits school holiday displays as long as more than one faith is represented.

Although religion is important to Texans, there are limits about where it can be practiced. Public schools have rules forbidding materials or events that can be said to promote religion.

Breitbart (an online conservative news outlet) reporter Lana Shadwick, an attorney, former prosecutor, and former judge, in the following story relays the tale of a nurse's aide named Dedra Shannon in Killeen, Texas, who taped to her school door a handmade six-foot poster featuring Linus from *A Charlie Brown Christmas* reciting a Bible verse about the birth of Christ. The holiday spirit quickly turned litigious as the Killeen school district asked her to take it down, Republican Attorney General Ken Paxton came to her defense, and a district judge ruled the decoration could stay if she wrote "Ms. Shannon's Christmas message" on the poster.

In this debate, two powerful forces clashed. On one side, freedom of speech advocates claimed that school employees have as much right to express themselves through their religion as anyone else, and that such expressions are not coercive to students. Backing this claim up is the "Merry Christmas" law, which allows students and teachers to express their religious preferences without fear of retribution. Opponents argue that as a government employee, Shannon could not express a religious preference in her work setting if government was to be kept neutral with respect to religion. The Killen school district stated that employees were free to celebrate the holiday season as they wished but were not permitted to "impose their beliefs on students." The courts have weighed in on these matters over the years, but do their rulings contradict the strongly religious Texas identity?

A Texas school principal forced a staffer to take Charlie Brown Christmas decorations off a school door because it included a quote from Linus which had the word "Christ" in it.

The principal reportedly said it was "an issue of separation of church and state." The Texas Attorney General called the action "an attack on religious liberty and a violation of the First Amendment and state law."

The door, covered in brown paper with a picture of Charlie Brown, bore the following quote from "A Charlie Brown Christmas":

> For unto you is born this day in the city of David a Savior which is Christ the Lord. That's what Christmas is all about, Charlie Brown.

Dedra Shannon who is a staffer at Charles E. Patterson Middle School in Killeen, Texas, was told to take the decorations down two days after she decorated the door of the nurse's office with it, reported Todd Starnes.

Ms. Shannon was reported to say, "She [the Principal] said, 'please don't hate me, but unfortunately you're going to have to take your poster down.'" Shannon added, "I'm disappointed. It is a slap in the face of Christianity."

"Throughout the school there are talks about diversity. Well, you aren't being very diverse if you are not allowing the Christians to put something up that refers to a Christian holiday," Starnes reported. Her father, Danny Breyeris, who is the pastor for the Soldiers of the Cross Cowboy Fellowship near Fort Hood contacted Starnes.

The war on the meaning of Christmas met with this response from the president of Texas Values, "a non-profit organization dedicated to standing for faith, family, and freedom in Texas." Jonathan Saenz noted: "This kind of outrageous attack on Christmas is exactly why the Texas 'Merry Christmas Law' was passed in 2013—to protect the Constitutional rights of students, parents and staff."

As reported by *Breitbart* Texas, Texas State Representative Dwayne Bohac was the author of the "Merry Christmas Bill." HB 308 amended Texas Education Code section 29.920 to protect the right of students and teachers to celebrate Christmas and Hanukkah without fear of retribution. Bohac said the bill protects school teachers and others from litigation and harassment.

The "Merry Christmas" bill was signed into law in 2013 by then Governor Rick Perry. Bohac said he got the idea for the bill when he picked up his 6-year-old son Reagan from school and he was talking about the "holiday tree" they had decorated.

Rep. Bohac and his former staffer, Kay Glenn Clinton, are the authors of *Merry Christmas, Y'all, Texas Style!* The Christmas book takes you through Santa's journey through the Lone Star State.

Texas Attorney General Ken Paxton responded to the episode by saying:

> I am proud to have voted for the Merry Christmas law in 2013, when I was a member of the Legislature. We passed that law precisely because of this type of discrimination against people of faith. No school official in Texas can silence a Biblical reference to Christmas. This is an attack on religious liberty and a violation of the First Amendment and state law. I am calling on the school board of the Killeen ISD to immediately reverse their unlawful decision.

Texas Values has a project on a website called "Merry Christmas Texas." It contains a summary of the "Merry Christmas" legislation which can be shared with the schools and school districts. It also provides a method of reporting on a school or district, or simply sharing how your school district is acknowledging Christmas.

Saenz, the president of Texas Values, chastised the principal saying:

> The public school principal in this case has directly attacked, banned and censored a reference to the religious history of Christmas while allowing a secular symbol to remain. This outrageous religious discrimination is a violation of the First Amendment and a direct violation of state law and must be stopped. The school should apologize immediately and allow the full display to go back up.

The Killeen ISD released a statement Friday afternoon:

> The Killeen ISD administration has reviewed the decision made in regards to the Christmas door decoration, and supports the actions taken by the Principal in requesting that the reference to the Bible verse be removed. Our employees are free to celebrate the Christmas and Holiday season in the manner of their choosing. However, employees are not permitted to impose their personal beliefs on students. The display in question was a six-foot-plus tall door decoration in the main hallway of the school building, and included a reference to a Bible verse covering much of the door. Upon review, it is clear that this display was not in keeping with the Merry Christmas Bill (House Bill 308), which requires that a display not encourage adherence to a particular religion.

ARTICLE QUESTIONS

1) Do you believe the school district was right to ask Ms. Shannon to take down the display, or do you side with the attorney general and Ms. Shannon's attorneys, who argue she has the right to express her religion in school?
2) Why are the courts stricter on questions about religion in public schools than in other settings?
3) Can Texas's religious identity justify greater flexibility for school districts in allowing religious displays, or should the rule be the same nationally?

Chapter 2

Economics

Everything is bigger in Texas, as the saying goes—even the economy. If Texas were an independent nation, its economy would have been ranked tenth in the world in 2017. Texas is home to six of the top fifty companies on the Fortune 500 list and a diverse set of industries, including real estate, manufacturing, and technology, each of which has contributed to the state's economic success.

This wealth, however, has not been spread evenly throughout the pocketbooks of Texans. Fluctuations in the state's economy and concentrations of low-wage employment make some Texans vulnerable to tough economic times. Brandon Formby, Chris Essig, and Annie Daniel, investigative reporters for the *Texas Tribune*, examine one key area in which Texas's economic might does not help all Texans: affordable housing. They find that home and apartment prices are outpacing the salaries of many Texans, the income gap between renters and owners is continuing to widen, and the number of high-poverty neighborhoods is increasing.

Boomtowns are not new to Texas—spikes in oil extraction, production, and refining have produced multiple shabbily thrown-together towns across east and south Texas from 1901 to the present. But even as some industries falter, others are thriving. The diversity of the Texas economy creates a stable floor for Texas's economy, even in uncertain economic times. Also helpful for economic growth, according to *Washington Monthly*'s Philip Longman, are the state's high rates of immigration and birth. Both factors have accelerated the state's population growth, leading to more demand for jobs but scarcity of state resources and lower wages.

The ever-changing economic fortunes of the state have tended to follow boom and bust cycles, benefiting some greatly and others very little. The "Texas Miracle" increased the state's economic horsepower but didn't tame its economic inequality. In short, this "miracle" did not bless all groups equally. Since 2009, the state's number of minimum-wage and low-pay, low-skilled positions has exploded, prompting some to claim that Texas's job growth has all been in low-paying jobs, with median family income remaining flat (Texas is ranked twenty-fifth out of the fifty states on this measure). Economic sluggishness following a dramatic drop in the price of oil, from $108 per barrel in June 2015 to $48 per barrel in January 2016, hurt the state, affecting everything from hiring in the oil patch to decisions in corporate boardrooms, but did not cripple it. Because Texas's fiscal well-being is tied closely to energy, the watchful eye of the state followed these developments closely.

Texas has long used economic incentives to encourage businesses to locate in or relocate to the Lone Star State. Some Republicans argue that stimulating business through efforts such as incentives for groups to film movies in Austin or locate a corporate hub in Dallas is a legitimate use of taxpayer money. Other more conservative Republicans, often from the party's more orthodox Tea Party wing, decry such efforts as "corporate welfare" and ask the state to not "pick winners and losers" by violating free-market principles. Philip Longman points out in his *Washington Monthly* article that the state has consistently sided with business interests over lower- and middle-income taxpayers—examples include a regressive tax structure that taxes what residents buy (taking more of a bite out of the income of lower- and middle-class earners) and slush funds that the state uses to attract "favored businesses with special subsidies and incentives."

Brian Wellborn of the Texas Comptroller's Office, the executive office responsible for tracking the Texas economy, cautions that as of 2017, the Lone Star State's finances are "looking tight." Why, in a state with such a diverse and strong economy, is the state budget so precarious? Wellborn argues that state revenue has been compressed by the dedication of funds to specific priorities (like transportation), lower revenues from taxes (like sales tax), and "ongoing weakness" in the oil and gas industry. Economic diversity, a term that describes the operation of many different economic sectors within the state, has allowed state revenues to stay ahead of the sluggish economy in some areas.

The picture painted by the articles in this section show a strong and stable state economy, but one that is not as rosy as the boosters of the Texas Miracle may imply. Economic downturns in specific sectors, low pay, income inequality, and regressive taxation policies have produced mixed economic effects—good for some and less good for others.

CHAPTER QUESTIONS

1) Why has the Texas economy benefited some but not others?
2) How does Texas's small government and individualistic mentality square with government spending to encourage business development?
3) Does the state have an obligation to improve every Texan's economic position?
4) Does the state's budget reflect the priorities of Texas? Why or why not?

2.1) Despite "Texas Miracle," Affordable Housing Difficult for Many Urban Dwellers

Texas Tribune, July 16, 2017

BRANDON FORMBY, CHRIS ESSIG, AND ANNIE DANIEL

Texas has made and lost several fortunes through boom and bust cycles involving natural resources and agriculture. The modern Texas economy is humming, but the economic boom isn't just about oil, gas, or any other single entity—today, Texas is the hub for twenty-one major corporations, including American Airlines, Exxon Mobil, and J. C. Penney, and boasts high-tech industry, a host of startups, and aerospace employment. Although we learned in the first chapter that Texans favor smaller government, business interests embrace more government spending on infrastructure (like roads and airports) as a way to generate new business. Government also plays a role in attracting new businesses to the state. The governor serves as an "economic cheerleader" to woo businesses to locate in the Lone Star State, and state and local government cooperate to provide incentives to businesses to collaborate and expand.

This sunny economic picture, however, is challenged by *Texas Tribune* writers Brandon Formby, Chris Essig, and Annie Daniel. In urban Texas, affordable housing is difficult to find despite strong economic growth. Why? The price of homes and apartments is outpacing salaries, land prices are rising in some high-demand areas, the income gap between renters and owners is continuing to widen, and the number of high-poverty neighborhoods is increasing. Their analysis finds that "not all households and not all markets are thriving," although unemployment rates and drops in housing value haven't been as bad in Texas as in other areas of the country. Even so, conditions are tighter at the lower end of the market because of higher demand for quality properties and population growth.

The impact of these trends on Texans can be significant. One affordable housing advocate notes that a family's housing budget puts pressure on its ability to succeed. Outcomes are related to where a family resides and how much salary it earns, with the state's poorest residents more likely to face financial burdens in paying housing costs and Austin residents more likely to have trouble finding affordable housing.

It's becoming harder for urban-dwelling Texans to find an affordable home to buy or decent place to rent as house prices outpace salaries, the income gap between renters and owners continues to widen and the number of high-poverty neighborhoods increases.

Those are among several findings from a *Texas Tribune* analysis of data that underpins a study that Harvard University's Joint Center for Housing Studies released Friday. The data were part of a report called "The State of the Nation's Housing" which found that while the U.S. housing market is returning to normal after the Great Recession, "not all households and not all markets are thriving."

Unemployment rates and downward spirals in home values weren't nearly as bad in Texas during the national economic downturn as they were in other parts of the country. But the state's large urban areas are still experiencing similar mismatches between housing stock and income as other American metropolitan areas.

Harvard researchers, elected Texas officials and development industry experts point to a number of reasons for the lack of affordable housing. They say that everything from stricter financing requirements to government regulations and labor shortages can drive project costs up to the point where smaller homes and rental properties for low-income people aren't cost effective to build.

"Conditions are particularly tight at the lower end of the market, likely reflecting both the slower price recovery in this segment and the fact that fewer entry-level homes are being built," the Harvard report said.

High demand for properties in Texas—a side effect of the state's relative economic success and continued population growth—is also a contributing factor to increased project costs that typically get passed on to home buyers or renters.

"Land costs in rapidly growing or hot markets is always a big driver," said Scott Norman, executive director of the Texas Association of Builders.

Meanwhile, more than 2 million urban Texan households, most of them renters, are considered financially burdened by housing costs because they spend 30 percent or more of their income on housing—and more than 950,000 of them spend more than half of their income on housing costs.

Experts and a litany of academic studies say that Americans who spend that much of their income to keep a roof over their heads have a harder time climbing out of poverty or moving up the socioeconomic ladder.

"There are so many other budgetary pressures, and the more you spend on housing, the less you can spend in other areas that impact your family's ability to succeed," said Mandy DeMayo, executive director of the housing advocacy group Housing-Works Austin.

The report and data were released on the heels of a legislative session that some city officials and lawmakers said further hamstrung attempts to create more affordable housing—especially for the state's poorest residents. And they were released one day after Gov. Greg Abbott vetoed a bill from State Rep. Eddie Rodriguez that was designed to keep in place districts that protect the affordability of houses in parts of gentrifying Austin.

"Directing large amounts of property tax revenue to select city projects has the effect of increasing the tax burden on other property owners," Abbott wrote in a proclamation explaining the veto of House Bill 3281. "We should not empower cities to spend taxpayer money in a futile effort to hold back the free market."

Rodriguez lambasted the veto and accused Abbott, a Republican, of hurting residents as part of state leaders' ongoing attempts to pre-empt local officials' governance of their cities.

"There is a real affordability crisis in my district, and the governor's cruel veto will hurt hardworking Texans who rely on their government to work for them," Rodriguez said in a statement Thursday.

Income and House Prices

According to the *Tribune*'s review of data Harvard collected, median Texas house prices outpaced median incomes in all five of the state's major metro areas from 1990 to 2016.

In Austin, that gap is most pronounced. That means it's harder for a resident there to find a house to buy than it is in the state's other large urban areas.

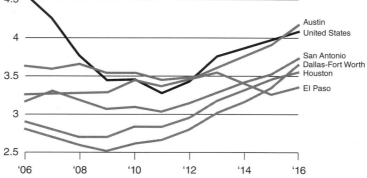

Ratio of median income to median house price

Figure 2.1 **Austin Metro Area Outpaces U.S. in Median Income to Median House Price Ratio** The ratios of median incomes-to-median house prices in Texas metro regions show how salaries have not kept pace with the cost of an existing single-family house since 1990.
Source: Harvard University

DeMayo said demand is keeping land prices high. Compound that with increased labor and construction costs and the price to build ends up getting rolled into monthly mortgages that remain out of reach for many.

"Some of that is land economics, which I wish I had the answer to," she said.

Austin Mayor Steve Adler said prices will continue to rise until the city and real estate industry figure out ways to provide more housing. He said the city wanted to talk to developers about creating a program where development fees would be set aside and used to build affordable housing units. But the Legislature passed a bill forbidding such programs during their recent regular session.

"The state cut off the conversation even before it could begin," he said.

What Can Texans Afford?
The Harvard study found that low-income Americans are having particular trouble finding affordable apartments to rent or houses for which they can secure a mortgage.

The Austin area had the smallest percentage of homeowners and renters—59 percent and 40 percent, respectively—able to afford the monthly payments of a median priced home. El Paso was the only major Texas urban area where more than half of renters were able to afford such monthly payments.

Meanwhile, the income gap between renters and homeowners was most pronounced in Houston, where a typical renter's income of $39,500 was 64 percent of a typical homeowner's income of $61,470.

Veon McReynolds is a Houston housing advocate and president of the board of the Texas Low Income Housing Information Service. He said it is frequently difficult for renters to become owners—a key way Americans build personal wealth—because minimum wage is no longer enough to cover the costs of buying a home.

"I have to be making three times minimum wage to maybe be able to save just a little bit of money," McReynolds said.

Share of income for homeowners (mortgage) and renters

Metro area		Median Income	Percent who can afford median priced home
Austin-Round Rock	Homeowners:	$67,200	59%
	Renters:	$45,230	40%
Dallas-Fort Worth-Arlington	Homeowners:	$61,640	65%
	Renters:	$41,110	48%
El Paso	Homeowners:	$43,630	68%
	Renters:	$30,780	54%
Houston-The Woodlands-Sugar Land	Homeowners:	$61,470	64%
	Renters:	$39,500	45%
San Antonio-New Braunfels	Homeowners:	$55,080	64%
	Renters:	$38,110	48%

Figure 2.2 Austin Ranks Low in Housing Affordability Not all urban areas are equal when it comes to the shares of residents who can afford the median cost of a house without spending more than 30 percent of household income.
Source: Harvard University

He said if minimum wage isn't increased, there will continue to be high demand for subsidized housing.

"The opportunity is not there," he said.

Higher Salary Helps, but Not Always

The state's poorest residents—those making under $30,000 a year—are far more likely to be considered financially burdened by housing costs. But even those making $50,000 and $60,000 can have a hard time finding an affordable place to live.

Residents who make less than $30,000 a year in the Austin, Dallas–Fort Worth, Houston and San Antonio areas are more likely to spend more than 30 percent on housing costs than typical Americans earning the same salaries. In Austin, Dallas–Fort Worth and Houston, that's also true for people who make between $30,000 and $44,999.

Austin is the only Texas urban area where people who earn between $45,000 and $74,999 per year are more likely to be burdened by housing costs than a typical American in the same income bracket.

Harvard researchers point to a growing number of high-end housing units and decreasing number of low-cost units as a major culprit. And state Rep.

Eric Johnson, D-Dallas, said gentrification is only making that situation worse.

His district covers part of West Dallas, which has become the epicenter of that city's mounting affordable housing crisis in the past year. A new signature downtown Dallas bridge has attracted new businesses to the aging and low-income neighborhood, which in turn has lured new residents to high-end apartment complexes and townhouses that are replacing some low-cost properties and driving up the rents and property taxes on homes that remain.

"So much that's occurring in those areas is leading to the destruction or the elimination of affordable housing where it already exists," he said.

Concentrations of Poverty Grow

Data reviewed by the *Tribune* found that Dallas–Fort Worth between 2000 and 2015 saw the biggest increase—more than 1 million people—in the number of residents living in high concentrations of poverty. Those are neighborhoods where at least 20 percent of residents live below the federal poverty threshold. At least one-fifth of residents there and in the Austin, Houston and San Antonio areas now live in concentrated poverty.

	Earning under $15,000	$15,000–$29,999	$30,000–44,999	$45,000–74,999	$74,999 and over
United States	84%	65%	43%	22%	7%
Austin	92%	84%	62%	25%	5%
Dallas–Fort Worth	89%	77%	50%	21%	5%
El Paso	77%	56%	28%	10%	2%
Houston	88%	74%	46%	21%	4%
San Antonio	85%	67%	40%	17%	4%

Figure 2.3 Austin Residents More Likely to be Burdened by Housing Costs Texans earning the lowest incomes are the most likely to be burdened by housing costs—meaning they spend at least 30 percent of their income on housing. The chart below shows the percentage of households considered burdened by housing costs in the state's urban areas.
Source: Harvard University, Credit: Chris Essig

Percent of residents in poor areas

Metro area	2000	2015	Percent change
Austin	16%	20%	+28% ↑
Dallas - Fort Worth	16%	26%	+67% ↑
El Paso	58%	51%	−13% ↓
Houston	25%	28%	+15% ↑
San Antonio	33%	29%	−11% ↓

Figure 2.4   Dallas Sees Sharp Rise in Residents in Poor Areas   As housing costs increased, so did the number of urban Texas neighborhoods where at least 20 percent of residents live at or below the federal poverty line.
Source: Harvard University and the U.S. Census Bureau, Credit: Chris Essig

More than half of El Paso area residents do, though the share of residents in such high levels of poverty there and in the San Antonio region declined during the 15-year period.

Experts say that it is more difficult for people to move up the socio-economic ladder when they live in concentrated poverty. DeMayo, the Austin housing advocate, said that studies show that living in more affluent neighborhoods or areas with more socioeconomic diversity helps improves people's job prospects, quality of life, health care access and educational opportunities.

She said people in Austin often assume their city is the only one experiencing rapid growth and dramatically increased housing prices. But, DeMayo said, a lack of affordable housing is becoming common across America, something the Harvard report echoed.

"It's all at a different scale, but these are growing cities and these are challenges we're all facing together and nobody has the answer yet," she said.

ARTICLE QUESTIONS

1) What are three reasons mentioned why affordable housing is difficult for many Texans to find?
2) What challenges facing Texans in the housing market are described?
3) Much of the reluctance to embrace affordable housing is a "not in my backyard" mindset. Can anything be done to change individuals' perception of people who live in low-income housing?
4) What are some policies the Texas legislature might pass to address the problem of affordable housing?

2.2) Oops: The Texas Miracle That Isn't

Washington Monthly, March–May 2014

PHILIP LONGMAN

Texas is famous for the formula for Dr. Pepper, a distinctive type of barbecue, and, if Texas Republicans are right, the strong economic growth that led the nation from 2000 to 2015. Rick Perry, the state's governor for most of that time, argued that the growth formula was simple: low taxes (including no income tax), little regulation, tort reform, and a "don't spend all the money" position. Arguing that other states make it difficult to do business, Governor Perry hit the road to persuade businesses in other states to migrate to Texas for a more favorable economic climate. Some of the results during this period are hard to argue with: job creation that outpaced the national rate, more middle- and high-wage jobs, a booming energy sector, and lower costs of living.

However, according to *Washington Monthly*'s Philip Longman, the "Texas Miracle" was less scriptural and more like good luck. In his article, he challenges the idea that Texas created its own good fortune, arguing that national and global changes in energy prices favored Texas at just the right time. Job growth may have simply reflected population growth: with more population (either by birth or migration) come expanded needs for jobs in the building, medical, and service industries. The assertion that Texas attracts people fleeing high-tax, aggressively regulated states is not accurate either—Texas's net migration from other states is lower than the figures referenced by Miracle defenders.

The Miracle has also been a nightmare for some Texans. Texas's tax structure, Longman argues, disproportionately hurts lower- and middle-income taxpayers. Upward mobility, the capacity for a child in a family to move up the economic ladder and earn more than his or her parents, is lower in Texas than in other states. Texas is also falling behind other states in individual income, even those states on the east coast that Texas representatives often demonize as ignoring free-market principles. The state's record in the early 2000s is in fact considerably more mixed than many of the its boosters would have us believe. Does the state have an obligation to make the economy better for everyone, or is it enough to make it better for most?

Is Texas our future? The question got kicked around during the last presidential campaign when Texas Governor Rick Perry was briefly riding high. Everywhere Perry went he appealed to Republican primary voters by describing what he called the "Texas Miracle." As Perry told conservative talk show host Glenn Beck, "Since June 2009, about 48 percent of all the jobs created in America were in Texas. Come add to it." In his stump speech Perry would click off what he said were the four major reasons his state had come to lead the nation in job creation—without ever forgetting a one of them. They were, he said, low taxes, low regulation, tort reform, and "don't spend all the money."

Perry's prospects in that political season quickly faded, of course, after that moment—instantly viral—when he froze during a debate while trying to remember which three federal cabinet agencies he had vowed to eliminate. Neither his cringe-inducing exclamation of "oops" nor his subsequent explanations that he had experienced a "brain fart" while distracted by Mitt Romney's smile were enough to save his candidacy.

But the debate over whether Texas has anything important to teach the rest of America has continued to build. One reason is that even though Perry didn't get to replace Barack Obama in the White House, he has continued to boast about his Texas Miracle, including in radio ads that have caused an uproar everywhere they've aired across the country. "Building a business is tough, but I hear building a business in California is next to impossible," Perry intones in one, before pitching California businesses to move to Texas. In another, he announces, "I have a word of advice for employers frustrated by Illinois's shortsighted approach to business. You need to get out while there is still time. The escape route leads straight to Texas."

When Perry launched a similar radio campaign attacking New York for excessive regulation and inviting its businesses to "Go Big in Texas," he inspired the comedian Lewis Black to strike back with a "Don't F*** with NY" video that aired on *The Daily Show* with Jon Stewart. "You say we got too much regulation," Black countercharged. "We've got Wall Street. They break the law for a living and never get punished."

Yet that observation wasn't enough to prevent more and more rank-and-file conservatives, along with a growing number of nonpartisan observers, both in and out of Texas, from also taking up talk of the Texas Miracle. Among conservatives, a typical formulation contrasts Texas with the supposedly failed state of California. For example, Chuck DeVore, a Republican member of the California State Assembly before decamping in disgust for the Lone Star State, has a new book out entitled *The Texas Model: Prosperity in the Lone Star State and Lessons for America*. In it, DeVore explains that

> Texas spends less, taxes less, sues less, and secures for their people the liberty to earn a living, keep more of what they earn, and live where they want. Is it any wonder that for more than ten years, Americans have been moving to Texas while Californians have been fleeing as fast as they can sell their home and pack? Texas and California represent two opposing versions of the American Dream, one based on liberty, the other, government.

The idea that vast numbers of Americans are "voting with their feet" for liberty and prosperity by abandoning blue states and moving to Texas has become conservative gospel.

Another typical formulation appeared recently in the *American Spectator*. After celebrating Texas's lack of an income tax, John R. Coyne Jr. went on to exclaim that "with its coolness toward regulation, its suspicion of government stretching back to Reconstruction, and its respect for private enterprise, Texas provides a model for any part of the country willing to set aside the conventional collectivist economic pieties." Few conservatives, especially Tea Party types, want to defend the economic record of the last Republican president. But that still leaves them with the Texas Miracle as putative proof of concept for the benefits that would accrue if, say, the country would just accept the economic prescriptions of Texas Senator Ted Cruz.

Some liberal voices have, of course, risen up to offer rebuttal. In 2012, *New York Times* columnist Gail Collins published a book entitled *As Texas Goes . . . How the Lone Star State Hijacked the American Agenda*. Within Texas, liberal legislators (and there are a few) have updated a publication every year since 2003 entitled "Texas on the Brink," which provides rankings meant to point out the state's worst deficiencies, such as being last in the percentage of the adult population who graduated from high school while being first among the states in carbon dioxide emissions and in the share of the population lacking health insurance.

Yet within the last year or so, the Texas Miracle meme has nonetheless gained more promoters and attention in the wider culture. *Time* magazine, for example, recently ran the headline "Why Texas Is Our Future," arguing in a cover story "that Americans are seeking a cheaper cost of living and a less regulated climate in which to do business; Texas has those in spades." A new book written by a former correspondent for the *Economist* and respectfully reviewed by the *New York Times* is entitled *Big, Hot, Cheap, and Right: What America Can Learn from the Strange Genius of Texas*. Another new book, *Texas Got It Right*, contains a foreword by veteran mainstream media executive Walter Isaacson, currently CEO of the Aspen Institute, in which he proclaims that Texas's "can-do spirit and love of independent thinkers, innovators, and entrepreneurs is something that could help kick up our whole economy."

So rest assured that Texas boosterism will loom large again in the next presidential election, and not just because Rick Perry is showing clear signs of another run at the White House. Texas has indeed outperformed the nation as a whole in job creation during the Obama years. And it has done so with a state government under the total control of ever-more-conservative Republicans, who now hold up that fact as validation of their whole economic agenda. Progressives, and everyone earnestly interested in improving the nation's economic performance, need to confront all this Texas bragging and find out what, if anything, it proves.

In recent remarks before the Dallas Breakfast Group, Richard W. Fisher, president and CEO of the Federal Reserve Bank of Dallas, exclaimed, "I am never shy on Texas brag." This is saying the least. In countless speeches, Fisher has laid out what is probably the most substantive case for a Texas Miracle, using mostly Dallas Fed data.

Fisher first emphasizes Texas's comparatively rapid rate of job creation. Over the last twenty-three years, the number of jobs has increased twice as fast in Texas as it has in the rest of the country. Many people might imagine that most of those new jobs pay low wages, but that turns out not to be true. To be sure, Texas has more minimum-wage jobs than any other state, and only Mississippi exceeds it with the most minimum-wage workers per capita.

But Fisher is talking here about new jobs, and according to the Dallas Fed, only 28 percent of the jobs created in or relocated to Texas since 2001 pay in the lowest quarter of the nation's wage distribution. By comparison, jobs paying in the top half account for about 45 percent of the new jobs in Texas.

This means that Texas has been creating or attracting middle- and high-wage jobs at a far faster pace than the rest of the country taken as whole. For example, between 2001 and 2012, the number of Texas jobs in the upper-middle quarter of the nation's wage distribution increased by 25.6 percent. This compares with a 4.1 percent decline in the number of such jobs outside of Texas. Though coming off a comparatively small base, Texas has also outperformed the rest of the country in its growth of high-paying jobs.

That's potentially a very big deal. During the eight years of George W. Bush's presidency, the country as a whole experienced zero net job creation, and the continuing decline in middle-class jobs is arguably the largest single threat to the economy's viability. If Texas has figured out a replicable and enduring fix for America's broken jobs machine, then the rest of the country does indeed have something important to learn. But as we'll see, there's much less to

the Texas Miracle than meets the eye, and its lessons hardly confirm conservative ideology.

The first and most obvious question to ask about the Texas boom in jobs is how much it simply reflects the boom in Texas oil and gas production. Texas boosters say the answer is very little, and play up how much the Texas economy has diversified since the 1970s. And indeed, Texas has more high-tech, knowledge-economy jobs than it did forty years ago. But so does the rest of America, and the stubborn truth is that, despite there being more computer programmers and medical specialists in Texas than a generation ago, oil and gas account for a rapidly rising, not declining, share of the Texas economy.

Unless you've been to Texas lately, you might have missed just how gigantic its latest oil and gas boom has become. Thanks to fracking and other new drilling techniques, plus historically high world oil prices, Texas oil production increased by 126 percent just between 2010 and 2013. Only a few years ago, Texas's oil production had dwindled to just 15 percent of U.S. output; by May of last year it had jumped to 34.5 percent, as new drilling methods opened up vast new plays in once-forgotten corners of south and west Texas with names like Eagle Ford, Spraberry Trend, and Wolfcamp. Thanks to the bonanza of drilling, Texas already produces more oil than Venezuela, and is headed to become the ninth-largest producer of oil in the world, ahead of Kuwait, Mexico, and Iraq.

Meanwhile, Texas accounts for 27 percent of U.S. natural gas production, which is more than the production of any nation except Russia. NASA satellites now record an arc of white light at night stretching from San Antonio to the Mexican border produced by gas flares. As a recent issue of *Texas Monthly* notes, in once-sleeping towns like Cotulla, where a young Lyndon Johnson taught migrant Mexican children in the 1920s, the population has more than tripled in the past two years, and no fewer than thirteen new hotels have opened, along with numerous "man camps," to accommodate the influx of oil rig workers.

Though Texas boosters point to the growth of the high-tech industry in Austin, the so-called "telecom corridor" in Dallas, and the growth of health care jobs in Houston, this can't hide the fact that oil and gas are by far the fastest-growing sources of the state's economic growth. Between 1998 and 2011, for example, the percent of Texas GDP produced directly by oil and gas extraction more than doubled, according to the U.S. Commerce Department's Bureau of Economic Analysis. This doesn't even count the growth of related industries, like oil refining and a petrochemical sector now thriving on the state's abundant supplies of natural gas. Meanwhile, the share of the Texas economy produced by the information, communications, and technology sectors is 27 percent *smaller* than it was in 1998.

To be sure, only about 8 percent of the new jobs in Texas are directly involved in oil and gas extraction, but the multiplier effects of the energy boom create a compounding supply of jobs for accountants, lawyers, doctors, home builders, gardeners, nannies, you name it. Saying that Texas doesn't depend very much on oil and gas just because most Texans are not formally employed in drilling wells is like saying that the New York area doesn't depend very much on Wall Street because only a handful of New Yorkers work on the floor of the stock exchange.

The next big question is how much Texas's growth in jobs just reflects its growth in population. For many decades, Texas has grown much faster in population than the U.S. as a whole, indeed about twice as fast since the 1990s. On its face, there is nothing particularly impressive about a rate of job formation that is just keeping pace with increases in population.

But in the conservative narrative, this population growth is largely driven by individual Americans and businesses fleeing the high taxes and excessive regulation of less-free states. In other words, Texas's rate of job creation is supposedly more a cause than a consequence of its population growth. If that were true, the Texas boosters would be right to brag. But among the many problems with this story is the reality that, even with an oil boom on, nearly as many native-born Americans are moving *out* of Texas as are moving *in*.

For example, according to Census Bureau data, 441,682 native-born Americans moved to Texas from other states between 2010 and 2011. Sounds like a lot. But moving (fleeing?) in the opposite direction were 358,048 other native-born Americans

leaving Texas behind. That means that the net domestic migration of native-born Americans to Texas came to just 83,634, which in a nation of 315 million isn't even background noise. It's the demographic equivalent of, say, the town of Lawrence, Kansas, or Germantown, Maryland, "voting with its feet" and moving to Texas while the rest of America stays put.

And despite all the gloating by Texas boosters about how the state attracts huge numbers of Americans fleeing California socialism, the numbers don't bear out this narrative either. In 2012, 62,702 people moved from California to Texas, but 43,005 moved from Texas to California, for a net migration of just 19,697. That's a population flow amounting to the movement of one village in a continental nation. Far from proving the merits of the so-called Texas model, it shows just how few Californians have seen fit to set out for the Lone Star State, despite California's high cost of housing and other very real problems. The same is true for all but a handful of Americans living in other states. Net domestic migration to Texas peaked after Hurricane Katrina devastated Louisiana and Mississippi, and has been falling off ever since.

This comparatively low level of net domestic migration to Texas is consistent with another little-appreciated fact that runs counter to the conservative narrative about the Texas Miracle. It is that, for most Americans, as well as for most businesses, moving to Texas would not mean paying less in taxes, and for many it would mean paying more.

Oh yes, I know what you've heard. And it's true, as the state's boosters like to brag, that Texas does not have an income tax. But Texas has sales and property taxes that make its overall burden of taxation on low-wage families much heavier than the national average, while the state also taxes the middle class at rates as high or higher than in California. For instance, non-elderly Californians with family income in the middle 20 percent of the income distribution pay combined state and local taxes amounting to 8.2 percent of their income, according to the Institute on Taxation and Economic Policy; by contrast, their counterparts in Texas pay 8.6 percent.

And unlike in California, middle-class families in Texas don't get the advantage of having rich people share equally in the cost of providing government services. The top 1 percent in Texas have an effective tax rate of just 3.2 percent. That's roughly two-fifths the rate that's borne by the middle class, and just a quarter the rate paid by all those low-wage "takers" at the bottom 20 percent of the family income distribution. This Robin-Hood-in-reverse system gives Texas the fifth-most-regressive tax structure in the nation.

Middle- and lower-income Texans in effect make up for the taxes the rich don't pay in Texas by making do with fewer government services, such as by accepting a K–12 public school system that ranks behind forty-one other states, including Alabama, in spending per student.

Moving a business to Texas also turns out to have tax consequences that are inconsistent with the conservative narrative of the Texas Miracle. Yes, some businesses manage to strike lucrative tax breaks in Texas. As part of an industrial policy that dares not speak its name, the state government, for example, maintains the Texas Enterprise Fund (known to some as a slush fund and to others as a "deal-closing" fund), which the governor uses to lure favored businesses with special subsidies and incentives.

But most Texas businesses, especially small ones, don't get such treatment. Instead, they face total effective tax rates that are, by bottom-line measures, greater than those in even the People's Republic of California. For example, according to a joint study by the accounting firm Ernst & Young and the Council on State Taxation, in fiscal year 2012 state and local business taxes in California came to 4.5 percent of private-sector gross state product. This compares with a 4.8 percent average for all fifty states—and a rate of 5.2 percent in Texas. With the exception of New York, every major state in the country, including New Jersey, Massachusetts, Pennsylvania, Ohio, Michigan, Indiana, Illinois, Wisconsin, and Minnesota, *has a lower total effective business tax rate than Texas*. If you think that means Texas might not offer as much "liberty" as advertised, well, you're right.

The same study compares how much businesses in different states pay in taxes for every dollar they get back in government-provided benefits. Using methodology developed by the Federal Reserve Bank of Chicago, the study first allocates public spending between households and businesses.

Certain expenditures, such as for health care and welfare, are treated as benefiting only households; others, such as for police, fire, and highway transportation, are treated as benefiting businesses as well. The big question mark here is how to treat education spending, since businesses differ in how much education they require from their workers. But regardless of how that allocation is made, California businesses as a whole still get a far better deal on their taxes than those in Texas.

For example, under the assumption that spending on education benefits only households and not businesses, California businesses pay $2.30 in taxes for every dollar they get in benefits, while Texas businesses pay $5. By this measure, Texas is the ninth-worst state in the country in the cost/benefit ratio it offers businesses on their taxes. Assuming that 50 percent of education spending benefits business, California businesses pay $1 in taxes for every dollar they get in benefits, while Texas business pay $1.50. Either way, it's no wonder that Texas's economic development efforts rely so heavily on (largely false) advertising.

The business case for Texas does not speak for itself. It may be a great place to be a big oil or petrochemical company, or a politically favored large corporation able to wring out tax concessions. Its state laws are also hostile to unions, and its wage levels are generally lower than in much of the rest of the country. But for the vast majority of businesses, which are small and not politically connected, Texas doesn't offer any tax advantages and is in many ways a harder place to do business. This is consistent with Census Bureau data showing that a smaller share of people in Texas own their own business than in all but four other states.

Before the 1980s, Texas followed a long, populist tradition that tried to protect family farmers and other small-scale businesses and consumers. Under its 1876 constitution, for example, Texas enacted consumer protections against predatory mortgage lending, with provisions that ironically helped to hold down foreclosures in Texas during the Great Recession. In 1889, Texas became the second state in the country to enact an antitrust law. Two years later, it further pioneered government regulation of big business by establishing the Texas Railroad Commission, which went on to protect wildcatters and other small-scale oil producers by regulating the oil industry in ways that kept outside Goliaths like Standard Oil at bay. But since the 1980s, "pro business" in Texas has more and more come to mean just pro Big Business.

The comparatively low levels of entrepreneurship in Texas in turn help to explain its comparatively low rates of upward mobility over the last generation. Here the evidence comes from a recent study, led by Raj Chetty and colleagues at Harvard University and the University of California, Berkeley, which tracked children born into families of modest means in different parts of the country and determined how many of them managed to move up the economic ladder when they became adults. The findings are illuminating.

In the San Francisco Bay Area, for example, children who grew up in families in the bottom fifth of the income distribution had only a 12.2 percent chance of rising to the top fifth as adults. Those who grew up in or near San Diego or Los Angeles had even lesser odds—only 10.4 and 9.6 percent, respectively. It's depressing that for so many Californian children, the chances of realizing the American Dream are so slim. But California looks like the land of opportunity compared to Texas.

In the greater Austin area, children who grew up in families of modest means had only a 6.9 percent chance of joining the top fifth of earners when they became adults; in Dallas, only 7.1 percent; in San Antonio, just 6.4 percent. Yes, Texas offers more chances for upward mobility than places like Detroit and some Deep South cities like Atlanta. Yet the claim that Texas triumphs over the rest of America as the land of opportunity is all hat and no cattle. Children raised in the postindustrial wasteland of Newark, New Jersey, during the 1980s, it turns out, had a better chance of going from rags to riches than did children born in Houston, which was the best city in Texas for upward mobility during that time.

No wonder then, that the flow of Americans moving to Texas is so modest. The state may offer low housing prices compared to California and an unemployment rate below the national average, but it also has low rates of economic mobility, minimal public services, and, unless you are rich, taxes that are as high or higher than most anywhere else

in America. And worse, despite all the oil money sloshing around, Texas is no longer gaining on the richest states in its per capita income, but rather getting comparatively poorer and poorer.

It's hard to think of any two states more different than Texas and Vermont. For one, Texas has gushers of oil and gas, while Vermont has, well, maple syrup. As early as the 1940s, Texas surpassed Vermont in per capita income. Vermont had virtually nothing going for it—no energy resources except firewood, no industry except some struggling paper mills and failing dairies. By 1981, per capita income in Vermont had fallen to 17 percent below that of Texas. That year, the state's largest city elected a self-described "democratic socialist," Bernie Sanders, to be its mayor. Vermont, it might seem, was on the road to serfdom and inevitable failure.

But then a great reversal in the relative prosperity of the two states happened, as little Vermont started getting richer faster than big Texas. By 2001, Texas lost its lead over Vermont in per capita income. By 2012, despite its oil and gas boom and impressive job creation numbers, Texas was 4.3 percent poorer than Vermont in per capita income.

This is not an isolated example. Since the early 1980s, Texas has also been falling behind many other states in its income per person. In 1981, per capita income in Texas came to within 92 percent of that of Maryland; now Texans earn only 79 percent as much as Marylanders. In 1981, per capita income in Texas almost equaled that of Massachusetts; now Texans on average earn only about three-quarters of what residents of Massachusetts do. Relative to Connecticut, Texans have seen their per capita income slip from 82 percent to 71 percent.

Now let's compare Texas with a big, demographically and economically diverse state like New York. Same pattern. As with Vermont, Texas started out poorer than New York. Into the 1930s, per capita personal income in Texas was less than half that of the Empire State. But gradually, Texans began to catch up. By the mid-1950s, Texans on average earned a full three-quarters as much as New Yorkers, thanks to a combination of New Deal–era investments in rural electrification, paved roads and other infrastructure, huge increases in federal military spending during and after World War II, and, of course, the oil boom.

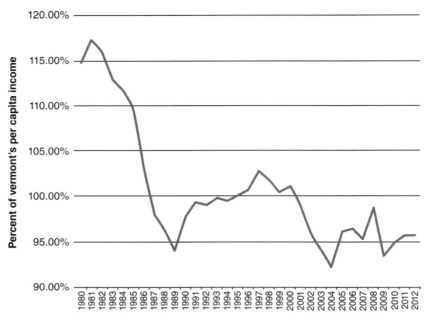

Figure 2.5   Texans Falling Behind Vermonters in Per Capita Income
Per Capita Personal Income of Texas as a share of Per Capita Personal Income
of Vermont: 1980–2012
Source Data: U.S. Department of Commerce, Bureau of Economic Analysis

In this era the state was under the firm control of Democrats like Sam Rayburn and Lyndon Johnson, who passionately believed in big federal spending projects, especially if, as with the early space program, a significant share of the spending flowed to Texas. By the beginning of the 1980s, per capita personal income for Texas reached 92 percent of that of New York.

Yet since then, per capita income in Texas has fallen to as low as 72 percent that of New York, and still remains at just 80 percent. This is true even though most of New York's major cities, including Buffalo, Rochester, Syracuse, and pretty much the whole northern tier, have been in deep recession since the 1980s, and even though it's only within the last few years that upstate New York has derived any income from shale oil. Meanwhile, per capita income in metro Houston has fallen from 4 percent above that of metro New York City in 1981 to 13 percent below in 2012.

A big part of the reason that Texas has not been able to keep up with New York in per capita income is, of course, the fantastical, world-historical fortunes that have been racked up on Wall Street since the 1980s, which inflate the per capita income numbers for not just New York City but the state as a whole. And Texans would be right in saying that their tax dollars, along with everyone else's, went to bail out those big New York investment banks back in 2009. But that does not explain why Texas, even as it has led the nation in job formation, has fallen further behind states like Vermont, Maryland, and Massachusetts in per capita income.

So what is the explanation for that riddle? Here's a stab. As we've seen, the flow of native-born Americans moving to Texas has been quite modest over the last generation, and for good reason. Few native-born Americans could lower their taxes, or raise their standard of living, by moving there. But Texas population has nonetheless boomed due to two main factors: immigration from abroad, mostly Mexico, and a birthrate that is the second highest in the nation after Utah.

Both come with challenges. Texas leads the nation, for example, in the percentage of teenagers with multiple children. And one factor driving down Texas's per capita income is simply a compositional effect of having a high and rising percent of its population comprised of young, low-skilled, recent immigrants.

But regardless of its sources, population growth fuels economic growth. It swells the supply and lowers the cost of labor, while at the same time adding to the demand for new products and services. As the population of Texas swelled by more than 24 percent from 2000 to 2013, so did the demand for just about everything, from houses to highways to strip malls. And this, combined with huge new flows of oil and gas dollars, plus increased trade with Mexico, favored Texas with strong job creation numbers.

But this model of economic development, which also combines a highly regressive tax system with minimal levels of public investment, has not allowed Texas to keep up with America's best-performing states in per capita income or rates of upward mobility. And that's what most people, including in Texas, most want the economy to deliver. The real Texas miracle is that its current leaders get away with bragging about it.

ARTICLE QUESTIONS

1) What are the reasons conservatives argue that the Texas Miracle blessed Texas (and would do so again)?
2) How should the state balance its need for business development with its protection of those residents most vulnerable to economic downturns?
3) When evaluating the factors that contributed to the Texas "Miracle," how much importance does Longman ascribe to the oil and gas boom during this time period?
4) Is a tax system that taxes consumption (sales taxes) more fair than one that taxes income? How would you design a more fair system?

2.3) Fiscal Notes: 2017 Legislative Wrap-Up

Office of the State Comptroller, 2017

BRIAN WELLBORN

Texas's economy in recent years has outperformed that of many other states, but crafting a biennial budget is always a challenge. In the following report, Office of the State Comptroller financial analyst Brian Wellborn highlights the challenges confronting Texas lawmakers in crafting the 2018–2019 budget. Wellborn warns that the Lone Star State's finances are "looking tight," with revenues estimated to be low because of the dedication of funds to specific priorities (like transportation), lower revenues from taxes (like sales tax), and "ongoing weakness" in the oil and gas industry.

Ultimately, the legislature passed a $216.8 billion budget, which included state revenue and federal aid for specific programs. Texas must pass a budget every legislative session, but the sources of revenue to fund that budget rarely change. The Office of the State Comptroller's report notes that no legislation was passed that significantly altered such sources of revenue, although legislators toyed with the idea of altering or eliminating the franchise tax. . . . Because no changes were made, lawmakers still had to find revenue to balance the budget as required by state law. To accomplish this, they delayed a $1.8 billion payment to the State Highway Fund, a controversial move that drew the ire of some fiscal hawks in the Republican Party.

In the following report, Wellborn highlights the continuities and changes of the fiscal year 2018–2019 budget compared to the prior biennial budget. Many long-term obligations like pension systems, methods of school finance, and the reauthorization of five state agencies did not change, while other items such as additional funding for public schools and requirements that the state assist victims of crimes in receiving restitution payments did.

Financial Highlights of New Laws

The regular session of the Texas Legislature concluded on May 29, 2017. State policymakers filed and deliberated on thousands of bills. More than 1,200 of them became law (Figure 2.6), including Senate Bill (SB) 1, the General Appropriations Act, which will fund state government operations for the next two years.

The 2018–19 biennial budget was widely regarded as a significant challenge for legislators. In January, Texas Comptroller of Public Accounts Glenn Hegar provided the Legislature with a $104.9 billion Biennial Revenue Estimate (BRE) for general revenue that reflected a low starting balance, increased dedication of sales tax revenues and lower revenue collections from 2016 due to ongoing weakness in the oil and gas industries.

The BRE shows the state's financial condition and estimates the revenue it can expect to receive during the next two-year budget period. Legislators are constitutionally required to keep spending below that threshold if no additional revenue is generated or freed up.

The state's finances were looking tight in January.

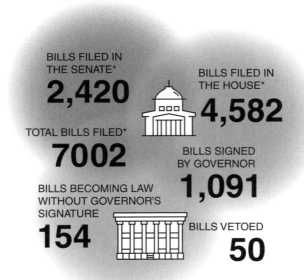

BILLS FILED IN THE SENATE*

2,420

BILLS FILED IN THE HOUSE*

4,582

TOTAL BILLS FILED*

7002

BILLS SIGNED BY GOVERNOR

1,091

BILLS BECOMING LAW WITHOUT GOVERNOR'S SIGNATURE

154

BILLS VETOED

50

Figure 2.6 Regular Session of the 85th Legislature: By the Numbers   *Does not include House and Senate resolutions, which generally honor various individuals, communities, and initiatives.
Source: Texas Legislature Online

"Passing the budget was a key challenge in the 85th Legislature's regular session," says Tom Currah, chief revenue estimator at the Comptroller's office. "I think a lot of people worried legislators wouldn't get it passed before the end of the session, but ultimately they did."

The Legislature's final budget for 2018 and 2019 appropriates $107.7 billion in general revenue and $216.8 billion from all funds, including federal aid and revenues dedicated to specific purposes such as the State Highway Fund. The Legislature also appropriated about $1 billion in general revenue and almost $1.6 billion in federal funds as supplemental appropriations for 2017 to cover outstanding obligations from the previous biennium, such as Medicaid obligations, not fully covered by the previous budget.

When lawmakers submitted their budget to the Comptroller for certification, Hegar praised their efforts.

"Even before I released the Biennial Revenue Estimate back in January, lawmakers understood this session would be difficult, and coming to a budget consensus would require sacrifice and compromise," Hegar said. "I commend legislators for crafting a conservative budget that remains within my revenue forecast."

Finding the Money

The 2017 regular session of the Legislature didn't pass legislation that would significantly affect revenue collections, according to Currah.

"Proposals were made regarding the franchise tax," Currah said. "But nothing was decided and that issue died along with others that might have significantly affected revenue available to spend."

Still, the Legislature needed to free up additional revenue to make the budget work. To appropriate $107.7 billion for the biennium, plus another $1 billion of general revenue in supplemental appropriations for 2017, legislators needed about $4 billion in additional funds.

The Legislature was able to identify nearly half of that, $1.8 billion, by delaying a payment to the State Highway Fund. This was accomplished through a rider in the General Appropriations Act.

Another $668 million came from deeming a number of dedicated accounts within general revenue

as available for Comptroller certification, through a funds consolidation bill, House Bill (HB) 3849.

The Comptroller's office also was able to certify an additional $500 million for spending by expediting the sales of certain securities held by the state.

Looking to Long-Term Obligations

One area the Legislature always considers in creating the budget is state employee and teacher pay and benefits, as well as pensions, health care and other post-employment benefits administered by the Employees Retirement System of Texas (ERS) and the Teacher Retirement System of Texas (TRS).

The 2017 regular session changed little for state employee retirement. For fiscal 2018 and 2019, retirement contribution rates will remain the same for Texas state government (9.5 percent), individual agencies (0.5 percent) and employees (9.5 percent). The Legislature made no changes to retirement eligibility or benefits.

One retirement benefit change, however, will prevent certain state and local elected officials from receiving pension benefits if convicted of a felony related to the performance of their official duties. SB 500 enacted this restriction immediately.

ERS plan beneficiaries also saw few major changes to their insurance. The state will continue to fund insurance at 100 percent for full-time employees and 50 percent for dependents. New changes to ERS insurance include laws meant to expand the use of mediation for out-of-network bills and improve benefits for breast cancer testing, hearing aids and cochlear implants.

With the passage of HB 3976, however, the Legislature took significant action to maintain the solvency of TRS-Care, the health care plan used by about 265,000 retired public school employees. In a November 2016 report, the Joint Interim Committee to Study TRS Health Benefit Plans projected a TRS-Care shortfall of $1.3 billion to $1.5 billion for the 2018–19 biennium.

To protect the system, HB 3976 eliminates three coverage tiers for retirees receiving TRS-Care benefits as of Jan. 1, 2018. Those under age 65 will be moved to a high-deductible health care plan with a $3,000 deductible and maximum out-of-pocket costs of $7,150. Older retirees will

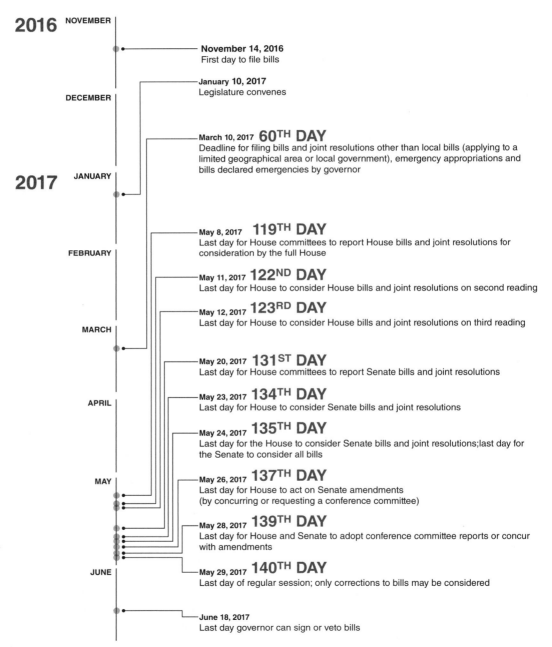

2016 NOVEMBER

November 14, 2016
First day to file bills

January 10, 2017
Legislature convenes

DECEMBER

March 10, 2017 60TH **DAY**
Deadline for filing bills and joint resolutions other than local bills (applying to a limited geographical area or local government), emergency appropriations and bills declared emergencies by governor

2017 JANUARY

May 8, 2017 119TH **DAY**
Last day for House committees to report House bills and joint resolutions for consideration by the full House

FEBRUARY

May 11, 2017 122ND **DAY**
Last day for House to consider House bills and joint resolutions on second reading

May 12, 2017 123RD **DAY**
Last day for House to consider House bills and joint resolutions on third reading

MARCH

May 20, 2017 131ST **DAY**
Last day for House committees to report Senate bills and joint resolutions

May 23, 2017 134TH **DAY**
Last day for House to consider Senate bills and joint resolutions

APRIL

May 24, 2017 135TH **DAY**
Last day for the House to consider Senate bills and joint resolutions;last day for the Senate to consider all bills

May 26, 2017 137TH **DAY**
Last day for House to act on Senate amendments
(by concurring or requesting a conference committee)

MAY

May 28, 2017 139TH **DAY**
Last day for House and Senate to adopt conference committee reports or concur with amendments

May 29, 2017 140TH **DAY**
Last day of regular session; only corrections to bills may be considered

JUNE

June 18, 2017
Last day governor can sign or veto bills

Figure 2.7 Legislative Calendar The Texas Constitution and legislative rules establish key dates and deadlines for each 140-day regular legislative session. For 2017, the above included.

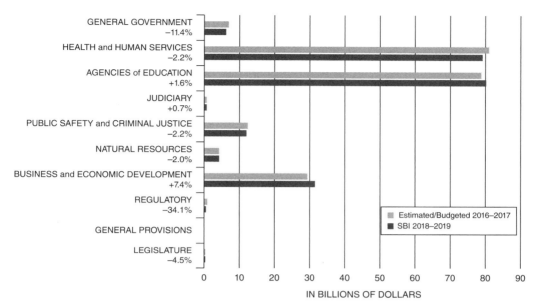

Figure 2.8 Legislative Budget Comparison 2016–2017 vs. 2018–2019 In drafting the budget for the 2018–19 biennium, the Texas Legislature faced significant challenges due to a low starting balance, increased dedication of sales tax revenues and lower revenue collections from 2016 due to ongoing weakness in the oil and gas industries. Because of these constraints, the Legislature's 2018–19 budget added only $18 million in general revenue spending above the budget for the preceding biennium.

Notes: Includes supplemental spending adjustments pursuant to House Bill 2, 85th Legislature, 2017. Excludes interagency contracts. Figures for the 2018–19 biennium have been adjusted to reflect vetoes from the governor.
Source: Legislative Budget Board

participate in a Medicare Advantage plan with a $500 annual deductible and a $3,500 maximum out-of-pocket cost.

While such decisions are always tough, Hegar commended legislators for addressing an issue that could have become a crisis.

"Delaying action on some of our long-term obligations will only cost us more over time, much like compounding interest on a loan," Hegar said. "If the state had turned a blind eye to TRS-Care, the program could have failed in the upcoming biennium."

Laws of Note to the Comptroller's Office
As bill filing and deliberation progressed, the Comptroller's office monitored the proceedings, assisted with fiscal notes and kept an especially close

watch on a number of bills affecting the agency and state taxation. Some that became law include:

HB 1866—Under Texas law, criminal defendants may be ordered to make restitution payments to their victims, but probation departments sometimes find it difficult to locate crime victims, and their funds then become "unclaimed property" as administered by the Comptroller's office. HB 1866 requires probation departments to provide detailed information on crime victims, including last known addresses and other identifying information, to our office when restitution payments become classified as unclaimed. It also permits the agency to publicize restitution payments along with other Texas unclaimed property on our website, making it easier for victims to find and claim their property themselves.

"With the enrollment of HB 1866, we can ensure our office receives more of the information necessary to find crime victims who are owed money," Hegar says. "Getting them their money as quickly as possible is the right thing to do and will have a beneficial impact on their lives."

SB 255—State law requires the Comptroller's office to train and certify all state agency purchasing personnel. The agency, however, believes some of the requirements involved were overly prescriptive and inflexible.

SB 255 streamlines the training process by eliminating inefficient policies for training purchasing personnel, while maintaining previous content requirements. It also eliminates a years-of-experience requirement for certification, which proved to be a significant barrier to entry in the field of public procurement. The bill also increases training requirements for all agency contract managers.

SB 745—This bill tightens the language of the Texas Tax Code relating to when certain employers can claim an exemption on sales taxes due for services provided by temporary employees.

Same Song, Second Verse

The 85th Texas Legislature met in special session from July 18 to Aug. 15, 2017. Among other issues, the session addressed one holdover from the regular session, "Sunset" reauthorization of five Texas state agencies.

The Legislature also appropriated an additional $351 million for public schools, including $150 million in "hardship grants" for districts expecting significant revenue losses in the 2017–18 or 2018–19 school years. Lawmakers also appropriated $212 million in general revenue to reduce health insurance premiums for retired public school teachers who participate in the state's TRS-Care insurance plan.

Bills related to other, thornier issues, such as school finance, didn't pass.

The Comptroller's office—and *Fiscal Notes*—will continue to monitor legislation that could affect the state's finances and economy.

A Bit of Background

We'll report more on the special session in our online feature *Line Items*, coming soon.

For more information about the state's long-term financial challenges, be sure to read our March 2017 special edition, *Texas State Government and Long-Term Obligations*, which examines state employee pension funding, the TRS-Care program, the Texas Guaranteed Tuition Plan, a state-sponsored prepaid tuition plan, and the ever-growing backlog of deferred maintenance projects for state buildings.

To better understand the role fiscal notes play in the legislative process—and fully explore the meaning of this publication's name—read "The Fiscal Noting Process: Doing the Math on New Legislation."

And if you're interested in Texas' "rainy day fund," a sometimes-contentious source of funding for legislative projects, dig into our archives to read "The Texas Economic Stabilization Fund: Saving for Rainy Days."

ARTICLE QUESTIONS

1) What are three reasons for the modest biennial revenue estimate?
2) How large is Texas's 2018–2019 budget? How much of this funding comes from general revenue and how much from the federal government?
3) Legislators debated the hot-button topic of delaying a previously agreed-upon payment to the State Highway Fund, with some comparing the delay to budget fraud. Do you agree or disagree with the state's decision to delay this payment to balance the budget?
4) Several key bills were passed that affect state taxation policy. Which do you believe to be the most consequential to the state?

Chapter 3

Demographics

In the story of the politics and culture of Texas, the first passage must be about the state's immense population size coupled with its growing diversity. Political power in Texas is significantly shaped by the people who inhabit the state and the shifting interactions between racial and ethnic groups that occur there. In Texas, the trajectory of political change hugs the arc of demographic changes that have rapidly redefined the Lone Star State's economy, culture, and politics.

The state has always been big, but population booms have regularly swelled its ever-expanding population base. Texas's population was a mere 212,592 in 1850 but ballooned to almost 28 million by 2017. In every census taken since 1850, Texas has grown faster than the United States as a whole. These waves of migration and immigration (six of them, according to Richard Parker in his book *Lone Star Nation: How Texas Will Transform America*) have radically changed Texas's economy and political structures. This transformation continues. By 2050, the state's population is expected to double to 54.4 million people. Much of this growth will be due to people moving to the state rather than current inhabitants having more children, a trend in the sixth great wave. Iconic images of the vast Texas frontier dotted with cattle and cowboys notwithstanding, the state has over the years become less rural and more urban (and increasingly suburban), making its citizens less reliant on government.

As important as *where* people live is *who* lives there. The state has also become more racially and ethnically diverse, creating pockets of political power in major cities and in specific regions. Data from Steven Murdoch, the former state demographer, reveal that immigration and natural birth among young Latino families is one of the "three pillars" of Texas's population growth. Although Anglos (whites) constituted a clear supermajority of Texans in the 1980s, the rapid growth of the Hispanic population since then has altered the social and political shape of the state. In 1980, Anglos accounted for more than 9 million of the state's 14 million population (66 percent of the polity), while Hispanics accounted for almost 3 million (21 percent). By 2010, the Anglo population had increased by only a modest 23 percent, while the Hispanic population had grown an incredible 216 percent. Furthermore, the state's Hispanic residents overall are younger than its non-Hispanic residents and tend to have more children. Taking all of these trends together, Texas has more robust population growth than other states, with a slowdown in one not likely to reverse its explosive population growth.

Driving some of the growth of the state's Hispanic population are foreign-born Hispanics. More than 15 percent of Texas's population was born in another country—another of the "three pillars" driving population growth in the Lone Star State. Immigration has shaped the state's politics as well—as foreign-born populations grow (and the children of these immigrants grow up), the state has confronted new demands for social services, concerns over discrimination, and questions about access to schools.

The political implications of this change are potentially profound, especially as Latinos begin to vote in larger numbers. Rogelio Sáenz of the *San Antonio News-Express* focuses on the idea of "demographics as destiny" and the potential for a "blue" (Democratic) Texas, an outcome he disputes as unlikely. Anglos are generally more likely to vote for Republicans and Hispanics for Democrats, but Anglos are more likely to vote in general than Hispanics, despite the latter's rising population numbers. A report from the Texas Demographic Center also foretells a more heterogeneous Texas, especially as significant numbers of immigrants settle there. Will the political parties adapt to these changes by courting more diverse voters, incorporating more diverse messages, or recruiting more diverse candidates? Texas will also face other problems related to these shifts: as smaller counties lose population to larger counties, the state may have difficulty delivering resources (medical care, schools, and transportation) to the former.

The state is also aging, prompting new debates about health care, pensions, and school finance. Texas currently has 3 million residents aged sixty-five and older. The baby boomers, defined as those born after the Second World War (1946–1964), are now rapidly aging. By 2050, the number of citizens aged sixty-five years and older is expected to reach about 6.5 million. However, the growth of younger cohorts of Texans is not significant enough to replace those aging cohorts, with projections of the total number of individuals under the age of eighteen remaining constant over the period. The Texas Demographic Center report indicates that as the state "ages in place," this phenomenon may inhibit economic development, restrain community vitality, and reduce population growth through natural increase.

The Lone Star State's demographics help tell its story. What challenges do you see the state facing as its demographics change? What opportunities do you see as demographics reshape Texas?

CHAPTER QUESTIONS

1) Why has the state's population grown in waves? What characterizes a "wave"?
2) How does each reading characterize the state's ever-changing demographics: as an opportunity or as a crisis? What policies need to be examined or reexamined to address these changes?
3) Which demographic trend do you believe will have the most significant impact on Texas's future?

3.1) Great Migrations (Chapter 2)

Lone Star Nation: How Texas Will Transform America, 2014

RICHARD PARKER

> The vastness of Texas has always held promise to migrants. Richard Parker, author of *Lone Star Nation: How Texas Will Transform America*, argues that successive waves of migration have altered the course of history by changing economic structures, creating new social pressures, and shifting the balance of political power. In his accounting, the recent population wave is the sixth that has occurred in the state's history. This most recent migration, he claims, has the most potential to change Texas's political character forever.
>
> Each wave of migration in Texas has engineered new conflicts, some violent, but all revolutionary. Native tribes encroached on each other's territory and displaced one another. Anglo settlement pushed Native Americans out of their territory. Anglo settlers pressed for their own rights from Spain and Mexico. Polish and German immigrants clashed with other settlers over slavery. After the conflict of the Civil War, economic expansion framed subsequent migrations to Texas. The last three waves of migration have had more dramatic impacts on the economic order than the political order, but political change remains potent. What challenges face Texas after the sixth wave of migration?

On an isolated stretch of desert an imaginary line slices the land, separating New Mexico from Texas.

This is a land of boundaries. A few miles to the west, the muddy Rio Grande cuts its way south, separating Mexico from the United States. To the east, the Organ Mountains mark the southern end of the Rocky Mountains and the purple Franklin Mountains to the southeast note the beginning of the harsh Chihuahuan Desert, which unfolds for hundreds of miles. Interstate 10 stretches out across the mesas, a pair of double-wide, blacktop ribbons between the mountains and the river, connecting the Atlantic and Pacific coasts. Eighteen wheelers push on in both directions. But most of the cars are going east. One after another bears the same license plate: California.

Quickly, a bright yellow sign framed by rustic wooden posts bids them a farewell to New Mexico: "Now Leaving the Land of Enchantment!" A few seconds later, a modest, green highway sign with a red, white, and blue flag comes into view: "Welcome to Texas." A giant stone lone star monument slides into view. For many travelers from California a brief elation will set in. They have crossed 761 miles of desert from, say, Southern California, after all. But that feeling is dashed by the very next mileage sign:

> EL PASO 18
> BEAUMONT 852

And it is still some 600 miles to the big cities in between East Texas and West Texas. Dallas, San Antonio, Austin, and Houston are all still a full day's drive away. Between 2005 and 2010, some 3.4 million Californians left the Golden State. For many in the middle class the reasons were simple: High housing prices, scarce jobs, and mounting taxes. Housing was expensive and then, when the real estate bubble popped, it took the economy and jobs with it. But taxes remained high. And so, those that could—and those who had to—got out, reversing decades in which California gained more people than they lost.

California once embodied the American dream of orange groves, opportunities, and sunny beaches. Now, the California diaspora dispatched people to neighboring states like Oregon and Arizona. Yet the single largest number, about 1 million in the initial years, went to Texas, with many making that long trek through the desert, past the state line, and onward to reach the big cities of Texas: Houston, Dallas, San Antonio, and Austin.

Yet California was not the only home Americans left behind for a new life in the Lone Star State. Over the same five-year period, nearly 3.5 million Americans arrived in Texas from all points in the United States: California, yes, but also New York, Washington, D.C., Chicago, Miami, Portland, Seattle—and hundreds of other towns and cities. America was in the throes of one of its periodic and epic mass migrations. Among them were the westward expansion and European migration of the 19th century, the Great Migration of African Americans from the agrarian South to the industrializing Midwest in the early 20th century, and the Great Depression migrations from the Dust Bowl to the fields and groves of California.

When these occur, they alter the course of history. Entire economies arise. New social pressures are created. Power changes hands. Texas has seen five such great migrations. This is the sixth. In each case, the migrations to Texas created economic, social, and political change that reverberated across America and, in some cases, around the world. Indeed, Texas may be one of the great magnets of mass migration in human history, given the number of times that millions have picked up and moved here.

Like the current of a strong, new river suddenly carved into the earth, the Sixth Migration has delivered 3.6 million people to the state and deposits over 1,000 fresh arrivals every single day. In the 1970s and 1980s, the collapse of the Industrial Rustbelt drove the first large wave of non-southerners to Texas, the Fifth Migration. These migrants decisively moved the state's conservative politics from the Democratic column into the Republican one, where Texas remains today. No Republican has won the White House in the last quarter century without Texas, nor could they. Early in the 20th century, oil brought Southerners in the Fourth Migration to create an industry that, to this day and for better or for worse, fuels modern economies around the globe.

The Third Migration, the mass arrival of Southerners in the early 19th century led to war, independence, the expansion of slavery and the Indian wars; then it triggered still more war with Mexico and ultimately, after Texas was granted statehood, tipped America into its bloodiest conflict, the Civil War. The Second Migration from Asia spawned the Native American cultures that, in turn, brought with them agriculture, trade and war. The arrival of the first humans, also from Asia, 16,000 years ago constituted the First Migration; for the first time, the pristine natural order of North America met with hunting, harvesting, and the hand of a creature it had never known: Man.

In the morning, 150 miles east of El Paso, the sun comes up and the interstate roars across the creosote-studded flats into little Van Horn, population 2,000. The town has a truck stop, a couple thousand residents, and a jam-packed breakfast rush at McDonald's. Everybody here is headed somewhere else, true to form for a town that has been a way station since it was founded as a stagecoach stop in the 1850s in the midst of Apache country. Off in the distance, the Davis Mountains rise.

Back on the road and coming fast, big green highway signs warn drivers that a fork in the road approaches and the time zone is about to change from mountain to central time. A lengthy drive beckons. Soon enough, a fork in the road arises: Bear left and head for the big cities of Dallas–Fort Worth, though many hours away. Bear right and hours from now, Austin, San Antonio and, later, Houston will eventually come into view. I bear right across the creosote-studded Trans Pecos and the hours slip by as slowly as the highway signs: Exits for Balmorea, Pecos, Fort Davis, Marfa, Big Bend. Each remains hours away, hidden from view of the interstate which crossed the middle of nowhere on its way to Fort Stockton. A little south, at Iraan, an exit reveals a back road into the Hill Country, leaving the big interstate behind for the Llano Uplift. Narrowing to just two lanes, U.S. 377 jogs across the Edwards Plateau. It is afternoon now and the spring light is bright and clear. The limestone remains of a Spanish presidio, established on the San Saba River in 1757, come into view. This is as far west as the Spanish ventured in Texas.

All these towns out here, from Junction to Mason to Llano, wait patiently for fall, when city hunters fill up the hotels, little restaurants, and the bars for deer season. But now, the next deer season is nearly as far ahead in the calendar as the last and the towns seemed empty. The light reflected off the broad, rushing waters of the Llano River bounces off the struts and girders of the big metal bridge, as the road leads toward the town square. It is getting close to fishing time, in fact. The giant schools of white bass are forming up, even now, in the deep water of the Highland Lakes to run the shallow rivers to spawn.

By early afternoon on a Tuesday, the square is empty, the parking lot around the town hall largely devoid of cars. A faded Confederate flag hangs limp over the memorial to the Civil War dead. The plaque reveals the short list of the small town deceased who set off for a very faraway conflict. I turn right on State Highway 16 and, in a little while the road begins to climb, the town slipping out of sight. The cell phone signal falters as the road climbs through a narrow saddle, heads due south and backwards—to the beginning of time itself.

Rocks, big and nearly square, rise up in a ruddy color, as if a giant playing with red blocks had forgetfully dropped them here and there, forming whole escarpments. Off to the right, Enchanted Rock rises, a pink granite dome reaching some 425 feet above the rest of the countryside, the result of magma from the earth's crust bubbling upward as long as a billion years ago. The giant rocks and hills of the Llano country are literally the blocks from the bottom of the world. No younger than 600 million years old, these Precambrian rocks come from the foundations of the very continents themselves, the basement of the earth and the beginning of geologic time.

The ones lying here, scattered, big as whole buildings, are the only ones still visible in Texas, and one of only seven sites where they are visible in North America. All come from a silent vault in time that still encompasses nearly 90 percent of the earth's history. From here, though, history pressed relentlessly forward. A quarter of a billion years ago, this area was bordered by salt water to the east and south. Then the Ouchita Mountains arose, stretching from present day Arkansas across northern Texas. Rivers drained westward into

the shallow seas that covered West Texas. By the Permian Period, the sea began to withdraw, leaving only flats and basins. Some 140 million years ago, dinosaurs and flying reptiles roamed Texas.

From here, Highway 16 presses determinedly south, toward the Pedernales River. The land flattens. Thick Spanish oaks and formidable thickets arise. A quick left turn onto Farm Road 1323 deepens the isolation. A solitary sign warns: "Watch for cattle crossing road." Not even a house in sight, cows and calves impassively chew their cud while watching the car go by, just yards away. At the one-house junction at Sandy, the land changes yet again. The exposed limestone, lifted out of those ancient seas, turns the ground white and rocky. Here the road enters the Cretaceous Period: 65 million years ago when the extinction of the giant reptiles brought forth the mammoths, sloths, and the large cats.

The last great Ice Age came and brought with it, as far back as 15,500 years ago, the first humans: The First Migration to Texas as people from Asia crossed the Bering Strait from Russia to Alaska and then headed south, away from the ice, to hunt the giant Columbian mammoth. Predating even Clovis man, once thought to be the earliest Americans, these ancient people settled in places like Buttermilk Creek, in Bell County near present day Waco, for its water and game, certainly, but mostly for its rich supply of chert rock, used to shape trademark spearheads and blades, cut with funnels along the side. The blades not only cut into the animal's flesh but their clever design deftly allowed their quarry to bleed out even as it fled. Once pierced with an arrow or spear point, the more the prey moved, the more it bled. But these people vanished, too, as suddenly and inexplicably extinct as the giant mammals they had hunted.

Yet before the land bridge sank from view, more people came from Asia, arriving in waves 7,000 years ago and making their way southward, too, away from the ice to hunt the ancient bison, twice as big as the modern buffalo. The last great Ice Age concluded, the land bridge sank into the rising waters of the Bering Sea and the glaciers retreated northward. The once lush Great Plains dried out and the sea in Texas conducted its final retreat, sulking into the shallow Gulf of Mexico some 3,000 years ago.

The people of the Second Migration, who would become known first as Indians, and later as Native Americans, were like any migrants. They sought opportunity and moved to find it. Racially similar, they quickly became linguistically and culturally diverse, spreading across vast distances. The Caddoan people of East Texas were close in culture, for example, to the Mound Builders of the Mississippi and showed strong Mexican influences. Smaller tribes, reputed to be cannibals, spread along the coast of the Gulf of Mexico and fiercely repelled any intrusions. Coahuiltecans inhabited the harshest scrub desert and adapted by digging, grubbing, and eating anything from pecans to spiders to undigested seeds harvested from deer dung, not to mention agave bulbs, flies, and even maggots. Before they came to know the horse, the Tonkawa lived on the fringes of bison country on the Edwards Plateau in the forested Hill Country.

A still newer culture arrived from the Rocky Mountains, speaking Athabaskan, the language of the Pacific Northwest. Known simply as Apaches by other Native Americans, they spread out onto the plains and down into Texas, taking on different permutations themselves, Jicarillas, Lipans, and others. After washing ashore in 1529 near present-day Galveston, the Spanish explorer Álvar Núñez Cabeza de Vaca recorded Native American tribes that herded hundreds of deer into enclosures for food, dug up roots, and plucked the fruit of prickly pears as he and a dwindling group of shipwreck survivors battled starvation, the landscape, the weather, and disease, while trying to get back to Mexico City: "One third of our people were dangerously ill, getting worse hourly and we felt sure of meeting the same fate, with death as our only prospect, which in such a country was much worse yet."

Cabeza de Vaca, one other Spanish adventurer, and the slave Estevanico de Dorantes were the only men to finally reach the capital of New Spain. The two adventurers married well. For his trouble, Estevanico was sold back into slavery and killed by Indians, eventually, in what became New Mexico while scouting routes for the return of the Spanish, this time en masse. When the Spanish arrived in numbers in 1540 during the disastrous expedition of Coronado, the oldest living cypress trees in the Texas Hill Country today were young saplings. In 1680, the Spanish horse dispersed throughout the American Southwest and yet another mountain tribe came out on the plains: The Comanche—a Ute word for "enemy"—who mastered the feral mustang. By 1750, the Native American horse culture spread from Texas to Canada. Soon enough, the Comanche and the Apache would struggle over their rights to the Southern Plains, one displacing the other in wars for food and territory. Other tribes migrated to Texas, too, or were pushed across it by aggressive neighboring tribes. In the 19th century, the Kickapoo, an Algonquian tribe of the Great Lakes region, dispersed to regions as far as Texas after pressure from white settlers and other Native Americans.

While the French presence in Texas was inconsequential, the Spanish occupation of Texas and the Southwest was a long but half-hearted affair; a global kingdom had far more pressing concerns than the rough and untamed wilderness of Texas, after all. Paramount among these concerns was Mexico, the Viceroyalty of New Spain. On behalf of Madrid, Mexico City governed a swath of earth that stretched from Cuba, Puerto Rico, and the Cayman Islands in the Caribbean, encompassed all of Mexico and Central America, all of Texas and most of what is now the American West, including California—and then stretched westward across the Pacific Ocean, to include the Philippines and the Marianna Islands. Each year, a Spanish fleet would drop anchor in Acapulco Bay to fill cargo holds with Mexican gold. Then the heavily-laden vessels sailed west, stopping in Manila and Guam, following the setting sun home to the mother country, half a world away.

So Spain invited American southerners from the Missouri territory led by Moses Austin to settle in Texas in 1820, as new citizens of a rough, backwater outpost of their global empire. After independence from Spain the very next year, Mexico, too, failed at sparking a migrant culture of its own to move into Texas. So, by 1830 some 30,000 Anglo settlers—largely of Scotch and Irish descent—filled the void, traveling from the ports of the Carolinas to Tennessee and Kentucky and into Texas, eclipsing in a few short years the Mexican and Native American populations combined that had arisen or arrived over centuries and millennia.

This was the Third Migration to Texas. This period became most infamous for the Battle of the Alamo as well as victory on the field at San Jacinto and the region's subsequent independence. Like all the great migrations to Texas, this one had an impact felt well beyond those early years in the 19th century and one felt well beyond the borders of Texas itself.

But why? Why would these people travel to a foreign land which held meager promise but was fraught with risk from Indian attacks, disease, thirst, and outright starvation?

The answer was simple: These people not only had the desire to come but the need to come. Their drive was a perfect balance of ambition and desperation—as it is, frankly, with many people who decide to move, whether across the country or across the world. T. R. Fehrenbach accurately noted that the southerners sweeping into Texas numbered among them a few rich men, certainly, but most were Scotch-Irish from the Appalachian South. Many landed at the port of Charleston, South Carolina. There they had generally found limited opportunity in the settled Carolinas. So they pushed into the wilderness of Tennessee, Kentucky, and northern Alabama only to scratch out small farms on land that quickly played out, fighting recurring Indian wars and carrying the burden of staggering debt.

Like a lot of members of the Third Migration, one Tennessean named David Crockett found Texas a vast and beautiful place, when compared to the broken down plots people like himself had left behind in the East. It was true. Texas was a wide open space that just a little rain, now and again, could turn thick with vegetation, rich with water in some places and promising. "I must say as to what I have seen of Texas it is the garden spot of the world," Crockett wrote in 1836. It held "the best land and the best prospects for health I ever saw, and I do believe it is a fortune to any man to come here. There is a world of country to settle."

The records of the original Austin colony showed 776 colonial families, most coming from Louisiana, Alabama, Arkansas, Tennessee, and Missouri. "The vast majority emigrated to Texas for no other reason than economic opportunity: the chance to get cheap land," Fehrenbach wrote. "Some left debts behind in the States, but most brought some form of capital: Seeds, equipment, stock, or slaves. . . . For the price of 80 acres of plantation ground in the South, a Texas settler could acquire a square league or 4,428 acres." Even leaders, like Sam Houston, who would be president of the Republic of Texas, senator, and governor, fled the failure of his marriage, the stall of his political career, and a mountain of debt in Tennessee for a potent mix of opportunity and uncertainty in Texas.

The Austin family, of course, was quite happy to extend credit, even to fleeing debtors. Stephen F. Austin, heir to the colony after Moses died, had vacillated over the increasing arrival of slaves with the new migrants; it was one important source of friction with the Mexicans who had abolished slavery in 1829. Ultimately, though, he came down on the side of slavery, declaring, "Texas must be a slave country!" Austin himself purchased a slave for $1,200—for no apparent purpose. The Mexican government then cracked down, banning immigration from those in the United States who might bring their slaves into the region.

The Mexicans, in turn, called on European Catholics, namely Germans, to settle and balance out the new and largely Protestant migrants from the American South in the hopes that fellow Catholics and Europeans might not be eager to join the United States. A few initially answered the call and settled an arc that stretched from Galveston on the coast to Kerrville out in the western edge of the Hill Country. After war and independence from Mexico in 1836, more European Catholics followed: Germans, Czechs, and Poles, though they were still a decided minority among the settlers and they were culturally, linguistically and religiously different from the Scotch-Irish from the American South. There were political differences, too, namely over that original American sin: Slavery.

Texas joined the Union on December 29, 1845 and the Third Migration now birthed global consequences. War against Mexico in 1848 had a devastating effect on the Mexicans who ceded what became the American West, including the gold fields and Pacific ports of California. Mexico would descend into political tyranny, economic privation, and eventually the chaos of revolution. America would become a rich power, its ambitions spanning two oceans. The gold of California would fuel the industrial revolution, the Indian wars, the settlement of the American west and reach across the world to remove the remnants of the Spanish empire in the Caribbean and the Pacific at the close of the 19th century, replacing it with an American one.

A vague concept in the early 1800s, Manifest Destiny was the belief that the American people alone possessed both the virtue and God's will to remake the continent in their own image; its ideological heirs would include present-day American Exceptionalism. President James Polk and his supporters created the concept of Manifest Destiny to justify war with Mexico and realized its birth with expansion to the sparkling waters of the Pacific Ocean. But Manifest Destiny was midwifed in Texas first.

In 1850, new Polish settlers joined their European counterparts on that arc that stretched from Galveston to the Hill Country. A small settlement, christened Panna Maria, grew up in the mesquite country at the confluence of the San Antonio and Cibolo creeks, east of San Antonio. The dusty cattle track that led through it would soon enough become the Chisholm Trail. And the town would become the oldest Polish settlement in the United States.

In Texas, slavery divided European Catholics and Mexicans from the American Southerners. For Mexicans, the issue had been settled in 1829 when Mexico forbade slavery and gave Texas a one-year extension to abolish the practice. For the Germans, the trade in human flesh was an abhorrent throwback to the Middle Ages. The *Sachsenspiegel*, the most important German legal code of that era, shunned slavery beginning in the early 13th century.

But the practice of slavery in Texas reached far beyond the Sabine River into Washington, D.C.

The issue delayed the accession of Texas into the Union because of the well-placed fear that it would expand slavery; so the impoverished Texas Republic floated in the limbo of independence at the fringes of the Union. John C. Calhoun devised a scheme in which Texas would be divided into six states to give it more power on behalf of slavery in Congress. Debates over slavery in the Midwest dragged—often because of Texas. And as war approached, Texas inadvertently also strengthened the inaccurate perception of Southerners that Texas would strengthen the Confederacy to the point of invulnerability, opening a new Manifest Destiny to the south this time, expanding an empire of plantation servitude into a conquered Mexico and Central America.

These calculations and miscalculations about Texas helped to trigger and then prolong the deadliest conflict in American history, the American Civil War. Already much has been said about the Civil War and nearly as much has been said about the Civil War and Texas. But this tragic conflict was proof positive of how the great migrations to Texas had consequences of national and international scale. While the Third Migration of American Southerners became legendary for its battle against the Mexicans, less understood was how the Third Migration played a crucial role in the American crucible over human chattel. The men who followed the heroes of the Alamo and San Jacinto helped tip America into a war that left as many as 750,000 Americans dead, according to a recent estimate—more than in any other war.

Because of weather and topography, plantation farming could only thrive in the southeastern quadrant of Texas, where the land was rich with alluvial soil and rivers and bayous allowed for the easy shipment of crops to market. And these were no subsistence crops. Plantation crops like sugar and cotton were just about the only cash crops in nearly 700,000 square miles. There had been just 20 Africans in Texas out of a population of 3,000 in the late 18th century, according to the 1777 Spanish census. By the end of the 1830s, around 5,000 slaves toiled in Texas, despite Mexico's ban on the practice.

The plantation economy, originally centered near present-day Houston on the Colorado and

Brazos Rivers, greedily demanded more and more free labor. "We want more slaves," wrote Charles DeMorse in the Clarksville *Northern Standard*. "We need them." Independence from Mexico and statehood in the United States actually accelerated the spread of slavery, north and west on to the blackland prairies, a grassland east of San Antonio and Austin stretching north toward the Red River. On the eve of war in 1860, the slave population had increased 40-fold since independence from Mexico to 182,000 men, women, and children.

Texas had far fewer slaves than many southern states and large slaveholders were a decided minority—though with their wealth a disproportionately powerful one. Out of a population of 600,000 people in 1860, only 20,000 white males owned slaves. Of these, half owned fewer than three. Only three men owned more than 200 but they also owned nine out of ten cotton bales bound for export and the cash that came in return. The Knights of the Golden Circle, a secret society established by Kentucky plantation owners to spread slavery westward, now engulfed Texas, encouraging secession as the fear of a Republican presidency in 1860 was realized with the election of Abraham Lincoln.

By early 1861, southern states were leaving the Union and on February 1, 1861 an unruly mob disproportionately dominated by slaveholders was convened on the question of secession at the capitol in Austin, despite the determined opposition of Governor Sam Houston, who fumed, as he said, at "the mob upstairs." Houston disliked abolitionists but foresaw that leaving the Union would prove disastrous. As former president and part of the original American wave of migrants, he held no special love for the men who followed him. "All new states are invested, more or less, by a class of noisy, second-rate men who are always in favor of rash and extreme measures," he wrote as newcomers followed the original colonists. "But Texas was absolutely overrun by such men." All of the delegates had migrated relatively recently to Texas from the American South, and fully 70 percent were slaveholders—wildly unrepresentative of the white population at large. Many were Knights of the Golden Circle, with fantasies of slave empires stretching toward South America. There were just

eight unionists in the crowd, led by the respected James W. Throckmorton. But their voices were all drowned out.

Calling "the African race . . . an inferior and dependent race" for which slavery was beneficial, the convention voted at 11:00 a.m. the next day 166 to eight "to dissolve the union between the State of Texas and the other States, united under the compact styled, 'The Constitution of the United States of America.'" Houston himself was in grudging attendance. Texans ratified secession later that month by a margin of four to one even as North Texas threatened to secede and San Antonio seethed with pro-Union sentiment—as did the Germans, Poles, and Czechs.

In Austin, Houston was presented with a loyalty oath to the new Confederacy, which he steadfastly refused to sign. "In the name of the constitution of Texas, which has been trampled upon, I refuse to take this oath," he said. "I love Texas too well to bring civil strife and bloodshed upon her." For his refusal, the old general was summarily fired by the state legislature and he left Austin. Now, events in Texas helped to prolong the war that it helped to start with a struggle over the real strategic importance of the state, schemes of hubris, obsessive compulsion, and that which seems, now, to have verged on madness. In exchange for safe passage to the sea and the evacuation of his 3,000 troops, U.S. Army General David Twiggs surrendered the federal arsenal in San Antonio to 700 Texans. Every single U.S. Army post in Texas was abandoned. Nearly all of Texas, save the coast, would be uncontested by the Union Army for the duration of the war as Twiggs practically ceded Texas single-handedly.

Cowboys began herding thousands of rangy longhorns eastward across Louisiana and the Mississippi River; the Confederate Army became dangerously dependent upon the beef supplied by Texas for its hungry, then starving, troops. A year before the Battle of Gettysburg, Confederate President Jefferson Davis foolishly launched a bloody and ill-fated attempt to invade the California gold fields and Pacific ports from West Texas. No army since Hannibal had survived so far from home and its supply lines and this one was no exception, never getting farther than neighboring New Mexico. Instead of encountering flag-waving Confederate sympathizers, the troops in gray met only local resistance, snow, and better-supplied Union troops. Their wagon train captured, the survivors tried to avoid dying of thirst or starvation or being unmercifully killed by Apaches as they stumbled southward, in rags, back into Texas.

At home, some Texans turned on one another especially after forced conscription into the Confederate Army. Death threats arrived in the mailboxes of suspected Unionists; 25 of them were hanged outright in Cooke County, north of Dallas, followed by 40 more. In 1862, Confederate cavalry and a home guard of Partisan Rangers tracked 100 Germans on the move to Mexico, where they planned to enlist in the Union Army, and killed 32 men as they slept by the banks of the Nueces River. While it was called the Battle of the Nueces afterward, it was really a massacre. In fact, it was a war crime as the commanding officer exceeded his orders and his subordinate officer simply began murdering prisoners. Nine more Germans were summarily executed. Fifty other German Texans were caught in Gillespie and hanged.

With fevered dreams of a Confederate West now turned to desert dust, President Lincoln in Washington had his own obsession with Texas: Capturing it and severing it from the union. Urged on by New York merchants eager for Union Texas cotton, in short supply because of the blockade of Confederate ports, Lincoln commanded his admirals as part of Operation Anaconda to blockade, bombard, and land troops on the Texas coast repeatedly. Only once, at Galveston, did they briefly succeed before being driven back into the sea. Lincoln's Texas obsession was nearly as fantastical as Davis's. Nearly 400 miles of sparsely populated coastline would have left invading troops—unless they could successfully occupy Galveston—far from population centers, depending on supply lines that stretched unimaginably. By 1863, Houston, the hero of the revolution, president, senator, and governor, lay dying near Huntsville as his prophecy came true. Passing in and out of consciousness on July 26, 1863 his final words to his wife were: "Texas, Texas, Margaret."

In the very heart of the fighting in the eastern theatre, the Texas Brigade commanded by John Bell Hood was considered the finest in the Army of Northern Virginia and a favorite of none other than General Robert E. Lee. He called them "my Texans," for their valor in battle. They fought heroically and sometimes recklessly across Virginia to Sharpsburg, Gettysburg and back to Virginia in the desperate Battle of the Wilderness. Lee loved the Texans so much that he offered to lead them into the battle there; the Texans said they would charge but only if Lee, astride his horse, Traveler, remained at a safe distance.

When Lee surrendered amidst the burning bridges of Appomattox on April 9, 1865, his Texans were still there, though just 600 of the 3,500 original men still stood. Back in Texas, Lincoln's Emancipation Proclamation, issued over two full years earlier, had been kept a secret from slaves in Texas. They finally knew that they were free with the arrival of Union occupation forces under Major General Gordon Granger at Galveston over two months later, on June 19, 1865, known ever after as Juneteenth.

The true legacy of the Third Migration had been felt, now, not just in Texas but across America itself. The great American sin of slavery had been expanded by Texas, but only briefly, and as a result it had been violently expunged, if never completely erased. A Confederacy with a weak hand from the start had overplayed it, in part because of Texas and, as defender of the institution of slavery, the South now lay in righteously smoldering ruins. Following the public triumphs and disasters, the tragic consequences now came home to roost. But the matter was settled. Slowly, the country would pull itself back together. The industrializing North, not the agrarian South, would become the power center and economic engine of the country, propelling Americans into the West that Texas had been crucial in opening. Manifest Destiny could now gaze across the ocean at a new empire for America, a Pacific one. Because of Texas, the entire 19th century was recast amidst equal parts of hubris and madness, triumph and tragedy, sorrow and hope.

ARTICLE QUESTIONS

1) What has been the common theme of migration to Texas, from the first migration to the sixth one?
2) What brought you or your family to Texas? In what "wave" did you and your family arrive?
3) Think to the future: What will the next major migration to Texas look like?

3.2) Texas Migration

Texas Demographic Center, January 2017

STEVE WHITE, LLOYD B. POTTER, HELEN YOU, LILA VALENCIA, JEFFREY A. JORDAN, AND BEVERLY PECOTTE

Anyone who has been on a highway in Texas or has seen the cranes spanning the skies above its cities lately can tell you the state is swelling with residents. The Texas Demographic Center notes that the state's 254 counties cover more than 261,000 square miles and are home to more than 27 million residents. Texas's population gains since 2015 have topped the list of population growth in all U.S. states, exploding by 7 million people in just seventeenth years. From 2009 to 2013, Texas had a net growth of 4 percent, and up to 6 percent in large counties. How did Texas get this large in terms of population?

There were two key factors in this wave of migration. The first was immigration from other nations, which produced growth at a rate of 12 percent overall and above 13 percent in the state's largest counties. Those counties—Harris, Dallas, Tarrant, and Bexar—were the most common settling point for immigrants. On the other hand, Texas's ten least populated counties received the fewest immigrants—collectively, only two. Counties along the Texas border with Mexico would have had negative population growth if it were not for soaring immigration rates.

Migration from other states was also a big factor in this population wave, as we read about in the previous excerpt by Richard Parker. Net migration (those arriving in Texas minus those leaving) was again most robust in the state's largest counties, cementing Texas's identity as an urban state. In reality, however, Texas is more of a suburban state, with most major internal migration occurring from cities to surrounding suburban counties. Summing these two trends together, smaller-population counties were more affected by internal migration, while larger-population counties were more affected by external migration (immigration).

The boom has had impacts on the state's economy and residents, in ways both big and small. Where do you see this growth having the most consequential impacts in your life?

Included in this Brief:

- Migration patterns vary across Texas counties.
- Smaller population counties are more affected by internal migration.
- Larger population counties are more affected by external migration.
- Border counties would have negative migration if not for strong immigration rates.

With millions of Texans moving each year, a basic question is: *Which parts of Texas are most impacted by this migration?*

The first brief in this series on Texas migration, *Texas Mobility*, described the volumes and types of mobility for the state as a whole. It noted more than four million Texans change residence each year. Of these four million plus movers, 16 percent originated outside of the state—coming from other U.S. states or from abroad—and the remaining 84 percent originated within the state.

Together, these streams of external and internal migrants represent an important source of demographic change in Texas.

The present brief expands on the first by examining how these internal and external migration streams are affecting different areas within the state. Toward this end, we use the state's 254 counties as units of analysis.

In terms of political geography, Texas represents a single state that has 27,862,596 residents living within an area of 261,232 square miles. As a whole, the state gains around a quarter million additional residents a year through domestic migration and immigration. However, not all parts of the state are affected equally by this migration and variations in migration can lead to profound differences in local population growth patterns.

Migration Terms
Based on migrant origins and destinations:

- **Internal Migration**—migration between two Texas counties.
- **Domestic Migration**—migration between a Texas county and another U.S. state
- **International Migration or Immigration**—migration from another nation to a Texas county

Based on migration volume:

- **Net Migration**—the number of in-migrants minus the number of out-migrants.
- **Gross Migration**—the number of in-migrants plus the number of out-migrants

Note: *Net migration tells us how much population growth or decline occurs through migration. Gross migration counts all of the people who move into and out of a place during a period of time and, as such, provides a gauge of overall population mobility.*

Unlike other population events such as births and deaths, when a person moves, it affects both an origin and a destination. That is, one place's in-migrant is another place's out-migrant. When migration is viewed this way, certain areas in Texas have become favorite destinations for other areas' out-migrants.

Here are some highlights:

- Migration patterns vary across Texas counties.
- Smaller population counties are more affected by internal migration.
- Larger population counties are more affected by external migration.
- Border counties would have negative migration if not for strong immigration rates.

County Volumes and Linkages
Volumes
In general, gross migration volume is proportional to a county's population size. For example, in Table 3.1, the five most populous Texas counties, Bexar, Dallas, Harris, Tarrant, and Travis, also have the state's five largest total gross migration flows. Similarly, the state's least populated counties rank at the bottom for gross migration. Reflecting the counties' population extremes, Table 3.1 shows that total gross migration ranges from over 300,000 in Harris County, the state's most populous county, down to less than 20 persons in Kenedy County which ranks 252nd in population size.[1]

The other source of migration is international migration or immigration.[2] Table 3.1 again shows a close correspondence between county population size and immigration volume. For example, among the top 10 population size counties, nine of these also are in the top 10 immigration counties. As a group, the top 10 received 125,962 immigrants. As with gross migration, the 10 least populated counties are at the bottom for immigration, collectively receiving a total of 2 immigrants.

When net internal migration is examined, the relationship between migration flows and population size is not as straightforward. For example, Dallas County has the state's second largest population but ranks last, at 254th, for net internal migration. This occurs because Dallas County lost more than 25,000 persons through net internal migration. Thus, a large gross migration stream does not necessarily lead to large population gains because the outcome depends on the balance between in-migrants and out-migrants.

Table 3.1 Selected Migration Characteristics for the 10 Most and 10 Least Populous Counties in Texas, 2009–2013

County Name	Population		Total Gross Migration*		Net Internal Migration		Net Domestic Migration		Total Net Migration*		International Migration (Immigration)		Total Net Migration* & Immigration	
	Size	Rank	Size	Rank	Size	Rank	Size	Rank	Size	Rank	Size	Rank	Size	Rank
Harris	4,119,266	1	318,064	1	-18,297	253	21,693	1	3,396	14	38,780	1	42,176	1
Dallas	2,377,637	2	241,434	2	-27,155	254	2,811	11	-24,344	254	17,992	2	-6,352	254
Tarrant	1,823,073	3	186,758	3	-363	204	8,965	4	8,602	6	10,782	5	19,384	6
Bexar	1,728,176	4	161,793	4	2,746	8	9,477	2	12,223	3	12,960	3	25,183	2
Travis	1,047,764	5	152,850	5	2,019	13	9,031	3	11,050	4	10,146	6	21,196	4
El Paso	801,745	6	66,453	10	-3,493	251	550	26	-2,943	252	12,507	4	9,564	9
Collin	799,867	7	109,013	6	-1,428	246	4,587	8	3,159	15	5,646	9	8,805	10
Hidalgo	775,494	8	38,569	17	-1,667	248	1,964	12	297	75	7,094	7	7,391	15
Denton	679,254	9	106,999	7	13,267	1	5,000	7	18,267	1	4,659	12	22,926	3
Fort Bend	600,966	10	66,721	9	1,304	18	913	19	2,217	17	5,396	10	7,613	14
......	......		......		......		......							
Motley	1,170	245	315	237	-2	120	-91	222	-93	155	0	211	-93	174
Foard	1,122	246	118	246	2	117	30	141	32	127	0	211	32	144
Roberts	1,022	247	198	243	-25	130	17	154	-8	142	0	211	-8	157
Kent	887	248	149	244	103	90	42	133	145	93	0	211	145	109
Terrell	825	249	106	248	96	94	0	170	96	106	0	211	96	129
Borden	625	250	113	247	49	106	0	170	49	121	2	200	51	140
McMullen	605	251	101	249	22	112	-29	203	-7	141	0	211	-7	156
Kenedy	507	252	19	254	-17	126	0	170	-17	143	0	211	-17	160
King	319	253	58	251	1	119	1	168	2	137	0	211	2	153
Loving	87	254	32	253	-26	132	6	163	-20	146	0	211	-20	161

Note: *Internal and Domestic migration combined.
Source: U.S. Census Bureau, 2014. ACS 5-Year Summary Data, 2009–2013

At the same time, a small net migration flow does not necessarily mean that migration has no impact on local populations. A good example is Harris County. In the process of gaining 3,396 persons through total net migration, 160,730 new residents moved to Harris County while 157,334 established residents moved out of Harris County. Together, this in-migration and out-migration represented a gross migration flow of 318,064 persons or 7.7 percent of the total Harris County population. With this, gross migration produced a 7.7 percent "turnover" in population even though the 3,396 net migrants represented less than 0.1 percent of the total county population.

Linkages

In addition to migration volume, another way to characterize migration is by linkages. Migration involves a move between an origin and a destination. As such, a migration flow forms a linkage between two places. A primary distinction for migration linkages is whether they are internal (connected within Texas) or external (connected to another state through domestic migration or another country through international migration).

Referring again to Table 3.1, six of the 10 most populous counties lost population through net internal migration. As a group, the top 10 lost 33,067 persons from migration within Texas. However, all of the top 10 gained population through domestic migration, collectively gaining 64,991 persons from other U.S. states. In addition, the top 10 gained 125,962 new residents through immigration.

The opposite patterns emerge for the 10 least populated counties. Collectively, the bottom 10 gained 203 persons through internal migration but lost 24 persons through net domestic migration. As a group, the bottom 10 gained 2 residents from immigration.

Table 3.1 suggests that external migration, from both other states and other nations, is the prime source of migration-based population growth for large population counties. With almost no immigration and negative domestic migration, the group of least populated counties appears to be most affected by internal migration—moves that begin and end in Texas.

Border Counties

Two of the 10 most populated counties, El Paso and Hidalgo, share a border with Mexico. While these counties share some migration similarities with large population counties, they also have some noticeable differences. Both have total gross migration flows that are proportionately small compared to their population sizes. For example, Hidalgo County ranks 8th in population size but 17th in gross domestic migration. These two border counties have relatively small flows of internal and domestic migrants. For example, El Paso County ranks 26th in net domestic migration while Hidalgo County ranks 12th. Finally, both border counties have proportionately large population gains from immigration. As an example, El Paso County is 6th in population size but ranks 4th in immigration.

Table 3.1 has revealed some distinctions among and between the state's 10 most populated and 10 least populated counties. For example: gross migration and immigration flows tend to be proportional to population size; the largest population counties tend to lose population to internal migration and gain population through external migration; and the smallest population counties have an opposite pattern where population is gained through internal migration and lost through external migration. However, these 20 counties are but a small sample of the state's 254 total counties.

County Groupings

While it would be informative to examine migration patterns for each of the state's 254 counties, it is difficult to generalize from this amount of detail. One way to examine similarities and differences is to group the counties by size. To further explore the trends noted above, the Texas counties were grouped by population size as follows.

The 254 counties were ranked by population size and divided into quintiles: five groups where each group represents 20 percent of the state's total counties. An additional Border County group was extracted from the five size categories. This resulted in the following six county classifications:

Tier 1 (Smallest): 87–5,044 (N = 47)
Tier 2: 5,045–12,676 (N = 49)
Tier 3: 12,677–24,461 (N = 49)

Tier 4: 24,462–64,725 (N = 48)
Tier 5 (Largest): 64,726–4,119,266 (N = 47)
Border Counties: 825–801,745 (N = 14)

These six groups represent all 254 Texas counties. The Border Counties are the 14 Texas counties that share a border with Mexico. In terms of population size, the Border Counties are represented in all five tiers.[3] Please refer to Appendix A for a more detailed description of the county groupings.

Mobility Versus Migration

Local moves are a change of residence within the same county. These moves within a county represent mobility but not migration. This is because local moves inside a county have no impact on the size or composition of that county's total population.

Figure 3.1 presents local moves, in-migration, and total mobility rates per 1,000 residents using the six county classifications described above. The in-migration rate includes all inflows by combining internal migration, domestic migration, and immigration. The total mobility rate combines local moves and in-migration to derive an overall gauge of mobility. By using rates instead of absolute values, migration patterns can be compared directly across the different county groupings.

Figure 3.1 also shows some general relationships between mobility patterns and county classification. Large population counties have higher total mobility than smaller population counties. Tier 5 has the highest rate of total mobility at 181.3 movers per 1,000 residents while Tier 1 has the least at 133.9.

In general, the rate of local moves increases as county population size increases. Tier 5 has the highest rate of local moves at 112.1 movers per 1,000 residents while Tier 1 has the lowest rate at 51.6. In Tiers 1–4, the lower local moves rates could be due to differences in housing availability, employment opportunities, and age structures that exist between the low- and high-population counties.

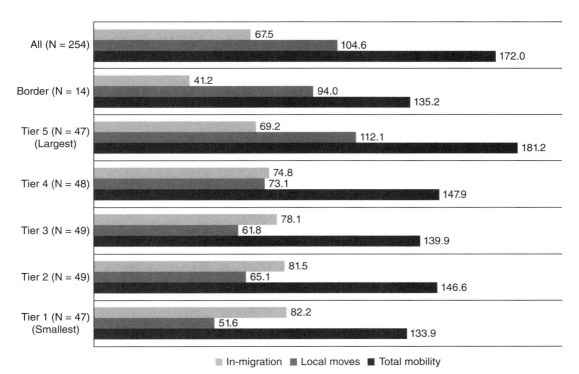

Figure 3.1 Local Moves, In-Migration, and Total Mobility Rates per 1,000 Residents in Texas Counties, 2009–2013
Source: U.S. Census Bureau, 2014. ACS 5-Year Summary Data, 2009–2013

Tiers 1–4 have in-migration rates that exceed their local moves rates. The smallest population counties in Tier 1 have the highest in-migration rate of 82.3 in-migrants per 1,000 residents. The largest population counties in Tier 5 have an in-migration rate of 69.2.

For Tiers 1–5, higher rates of local moves are associated with higher total mobility rates. The Border Counties do not follow this pattern. These counties have the second highest rate of local moves (94.0) but the second lowest rate of total mobility (135.2). Total mobility is low because the Border Counties have the lowest in-migration rate, 41.2 in-migrants per 1,000 residents.

Migration Flows

Figure 3.2 has the percentage shares by in-migration type for the six county categories. The types are: internal in-migrants (originating in another Texas county); domestic in-migrants (originating in another U.S. state); and immigrant in-migrants (originating in another country). These are the three migration flows that can alter the size and composition of a county's population.

For the less populated counties in Tiers 1–4, around 74 to 79 percent of all in-migrants are internal in-migrants, originating from other counties within Texas. This compares to 57.5 percent for

the most populated counties in Tier 5. Internal in-migration is least important in the Border Counties where it comprises 32.3 percent of all in-migration.

Domestic in-migration is most substantial in the Border Counties where 40.4 percent of all in-migrants originated from other U.S. states. For the top population counties of Tier 5, domestic migration is 31.7 percent of all in-migration. Domestic migration is least important in Tiers 1–4 where it ranges from 16.3 to 21.7 percent.

As for immigrant in-migrants, the Border Counties are most impacted with 27.3 percent of all in-migrants originating in another country. Tier 5 has the next highest share at 10.8 percent while Tiers 1–4 have immigrant in-migration shares of less than 5.0 percent.

Based on the patterns in Figures 3.1 and 3.2, several generalizations can be made:

- Tiers 1–4, the smaller population counties, are more connected with migrants originating within Texas.
- Tier 5, the largest population counties, is more affected by in-migration from outside of Texas.
- The 14 Border Counties are characterized by relatively high immigration from other countries.

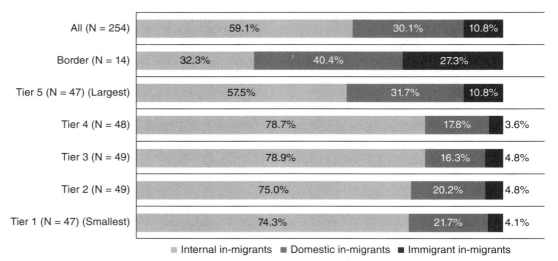

Figure 3.2   Percentage Shares of Internal, Domestic and International In-Migration in Texas Counties, 2009–2013
Source: U.S. Census Bureau, 2014. ACS 5-Year Summary Data, 2009–2013

Net Migration

The in-migration data in Figure 3.2 identified the origins of people moving into Texas counties. However, in-migration data alone do not capture the full effects of migration. Another gauge of migration is net migration which describes the total or net effect of in-migration and out-migration flows.

Figure 3.3 presents net migration rates for internal, domestic, and total net migration (Note: total net migration is internal and domestic net migration combined). Here, we see that the rate of population gain from total net migration is closely related to population size:

- Tier 5, with the largest population counties, had the highest total net rate at 5.8 net migrants per 1,000 residents.
- Conversely, in Tier 1, the smallest population group, had the lowest total net rate of –6.9.

Figure 3.3 also suggests the sources of net migration vary by county category:

- All county categories gained population from domestic migration.

- Four county categories, Tiers 1–3 and the Border Counties, had negative or flat net internal migration rates.
- In Tier 4, internal migration represented 63.1 percent of the total net migration rate.
- In Tier 5 domestic migration made up close to 90.0 percent of the total net migration rate.

Table 3.2 has the percentage of counties with positive net migration. It shows the share of counties in each group that gained population from internal and domestic migration as well as internal and domestic migration combined.

For the state as a whole, 140 of the 254 counties or 55.1 percent gained population from both internal and domestic migration. Tiers 1–4 had similar proportions gaining population, ranging from 49.0 to 56.3 percent. The largest population counties in Tier 5 had close to 75 percent gaining population from both internal and domestic migration while the proportion for Border Counties was only 28.6 percent.

Each of the county categories had more counties gaining population from domestic migration than from internal migration. The difference

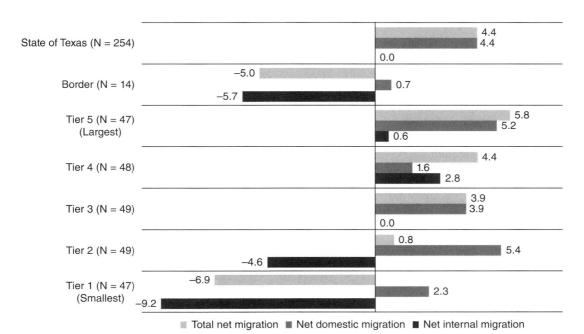

Figure 3.3   Net Migration Rates per 1,000 Residents for Counties in Texas, 2009–2013
Source: U.S. Census Bureau, 2014. ACS 5-Year Summary Data, 2009–2013

Table 3.2   Percentage of Counties with Positive Net Migration in Texas, 2009–2013

	Positive Internal	Positive Domestic	Positive Combined
(Smallest) Tier 1: (N = 47)	46.80%	59.60%	53.20%
Tier 2: (N = 49)	40.80%	63.30%	51.00%
Tier 3: (N = 49)	44.90%	65.30%	49.00%
Tier 4: (N = 48)	52.10%	60.40%	56.30%
(Largest) Tier 5: (N = 47)	59.60%	91.50%	74.50%
Border: (N = 14)	21.40%	64.30%	28.60%
All: (N = 254)	47.20%	67.70%	55.10%

Source: U.S. Census Bureau, 2014. ACS 5-Year Summary Data, 2009–2013

between internal and domestic sources is most apparent in the top population tier. For Tier 5, 91.5 percent of the counties gained from domestic migration while 59.6 gained from internal migration.

Among the smaller population counties, Tiers 1–3 had less than 50 percent gaining population

from internal migration. This means that more than half of the counties in Tiers 1–3 lost population due to migration within Texas. For the Border Counties, 21.4 percent gained population from internal migration and, as such, almost 80 percent lost population from migration within Texas.

Immigration's Contribution

Figure 3.4 shows how immigration interacts with internal and domestic net migration. In Figure 3.4, Total Net Migration is net internal and net domestic migration combined.

Here are some highlights:

- Immigration rates are highest in the largest counties (Tier 5) and the Border Counties at 7.5 and 11.2 immigrants per 1,000 residents respectively. For Tier 5, the 7.5 immigration rate helps this group have the highest combined migration rate (13.3).

- The Border Counties would have lost population from migration were it not for strong immigration. Without immigration, the total net migration rate was negative at −5.0 migrants

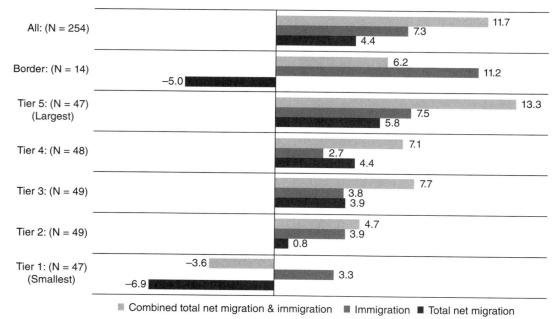

■ Combined total net migration & immigration   ■ Immigration   ■ Total net migration

Figure 3.4   Total Net Migration, Immigration, and Combined Migration Rates, 2009–2013
Source: U.S. Census Bureau, 2014. ACS 5-Year Summary Data, 2009–2013

per 1,000 residents. The 11.2 immigration rate was enough to make the combined migration rate positive at 6.2 migrants per 1,000.

- In contrast, the 3.3 immigration rate in the least populated group (Tier 1) is not enough to make its combined migration rate positive.

Migration Connectivity

One last way to examine migration is to look at the linkages between county pairs. Figure 3.5 shows the net migrants per county-to-county link. Here, a link represents one or more persons moving between a pair of counties. For example, each of Texas' 254 counties could have up to 253 internal migration links. This would occur if a county shared at least one in-migrant or out-migrant with each of the other 253 Texas counties. Similarly, for domestic migration, each Texas county could have up to 2,889 links to all counties and county equivalents in the other 49 states. In this way, migrants per link data provide information on the counties' degree of connectivity as well as the efficiency of migration links.

Figure 3.5 indicates that the number of links ranges from 955 in Tier 1 up to 18,053 in Tier 5. This large difference occurs because the number of links is closely related to the volume of gross migration and Tier 5 counties have much higher gross migration than Tier 1 counties. When viewed as a per capita rate, the relationship between migration links and population size reverses. For example,

the number of links per 1,000 residents is 7.8 in the Tier 1 counties and 0.9 in the Tier 5 county group.

In Figure 3.5, the number of net migrants per link is a gauge for link efficiency. Using this concept, Tier 5 has the most efficient internal migration connectivity with 2.0 net internal migrants per county-to-county link. For domestic migration, Tier 5 also leads the way with 8.2 net migrants per link.

The Border Counties have the least efficient internal migration, losing 18.9 net migrants for each internal link. The Border Counties and Tier 1 counties have the least efficient domestic migration connectivity, with each group gaining 1.2 net domestic migrants per domestic link.

Figure 3.5 again illustrates how migration from outside of Texas predominates in the largest population counties. Tier 5 gains 8.2 domestic migrants per each external link compared to 2.0 migrants per each internal link. As with other measures, the connectivity data suggest that the smallest population counties are characterized by population loss through internal migration. Tier 1 loses 1.6 migrants for each county-to-county link within Texas while it gains 1.2 migrants per domestic link.

Tables 3.3 and 3.4 examine linkages at the individual county level. Table 3.3 shows net internal migration while Table 3.4 presents net domestic migration. Each table shows the three counties with the largest losses or largest gains from net migration as well as each county's five largest migration links.

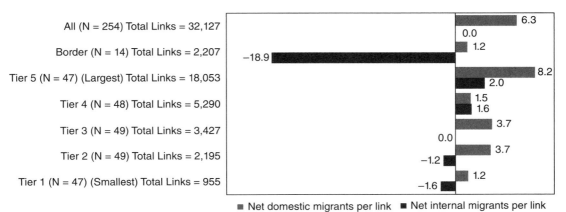

Figure 3.5 Net Internal and Net Domestic Migrants per County-to-County Link, 2009–2013
Source: U.S. Census Bureau, 2014. ACS 5-Year Summary Data, 2009–2013

Table 3.3   Select County-to-County Links for Texas Internal Migration, 2009–2013

Table 3.3A   Top Three Population Losses from Net Internal Migration with Five Largest Negative Links

	Cameron County, TX Internal Links = 102 Net Internal Migration = -3,979		Dallas County, TX Internal Links = 203 Net Internal Migration = -27,155		Harris County, TX Internal Links = 199 Net Internal Migration = -18,297	
Top 5	Name	Net	Name	Net	Name	Net
1	Hidalgo County, TX	-957	Denton County, TX	-7,669	Montgomery County, TX	-3,398
2	Bexar County, TX	-660	Tarrant County, TX	-7,588	Travis County, TX	-2,552
3	Nueces County, TX	-592	Collin County, TX	-1,088	Liberty County, TX	-1,775
4	Hays County, TX	-309	Smith County, TX	-1,021	Fort Bend County, TX	-1,706
5	Williamson County, TX	-294	Travis County, TX	-799	Hays County, TX	-1,149

Source: U.S. Census Bureau, 2015a. County-to-County Migration Flows: 2009–2013 ACS.

Table 3.3B   Top Three Population Gains from Net Internal Migration with Five Largest Positive Links

	Brazos County, TX Internal Links = 158 Net Internal Migration = 8,132		Denton County, TX Internal Links = 143 Net Internal Migration = 13,267		Williamson County, TX Internal Links = 140 Net Internal Migration = 8,658	
Top 5	Name	Net	Name	Net	Name	Net
1	Bexar County, TX	767	Dallas County, TX	7,669	Travis County, TX	4,250
2	Tarrant County, TX	637	Tarrant County, TX	1,575	Bell County, TX	955
3	Grimes County, TX	544	Collin County, TX	1,342	McLennan County, TX	482
4	Burleson County, TX	374	Rockwall County, TX	641	Dallas County, TX	380
5	Brazoria County, TX	362	Harris County, TX	625	Hidalgo County, TX	340

Source: U.S. Census Bureau, 2015a. County-to-County Migration Flows: 2009–2013 ACS.

In Table 3.3, all of the top three loss and top three gain counties are Tier 5 in population size. In Table 3.3A, the two largest losses from internal migration occur in the state's two most populous counties: Dallas and Harris. The third largest loss is in Cameron County, a border county that ranks 13th in population size. For each of these three counties, the largest county-to-county population losses are to adjacent counties: Dallas to Denton; Harris to Montgomery; and, Cameron to Hidalgo.

Table 3.3B has the three counties with the largest net internal migration gains. The counties gaining from internal migration also have large populations but of the three, only Denton County is among the state's ten most populous counties. For Denton and Williamson Counties, the largest county-to-county population gains are from adjacent counties: Denton from Dallas; and, Williamson from Travis.

Table 3.4 shows the largest negative and positive net domestic migration links for individual Texas counties. Table 3.4A has the top three domestic migration loss counties. None is among the top ten most populous. Two of these, Cameron and Val Verde, are Border Counties. In terms of population size, the top domestic migration losses are small when compared to the top internal migration losses. County-to-county links for the top three domestic

Table 3.4   Select County-to-County Links for Texas Domestic Migration, 2009–2013

Table 3.4A   Top 3 Population Losses from Net Domestic Migration with Five Largest Negative Links

Top 5	Cameron County, TX *Domestic Links = 231* *Net Domestic Migration = –884*		Johnson County, TX *Domestic Links = 125* *Net Domestic Migration = –673*		Val Verde County, TX *Domestic Links = 76* *Net Domestic Migration = –702*	
	Name	**Net**	**Name**	**Net**	**Name**	**Net**
1	Lee County, FL	–374	Lancaster County, NE	–198	San Bernardino County, CA	–435
2	Maricopa County, AZ	–278	Grady County, OK	–129	Hamilton County, IN	–128
3	Kandiyohi County, MN	–204	Berkeley County, SC	–116	Broward County, FL	–117
4	Alexandria city, VA	–203	Ward County, ND	–66	Olmsted County, MN	–102
5	Terrebonne Parish, LA	–137	Lincoln County, OK	–54	Chaves County, NM	–80

Source: U.S. Census Bureau, 2015a. County-to-County Migration Flows: 2009–2013 ACS.

Table 3.4B   Top 3 Population Gains from Net Domestic Migration with Five Largest Positive Links

Top 5	Bexar County, TX *Domestic Links = 944* *Net Domestic Migration = 9,477*		Harris County, TX *Domestic Links = 1,032* *Net Domestic Migration = 21,693*		Travis County, TX *Domestic Links = 628* *Net Domestic Migration = 9,031*	
	Name	**Net**	**Name**	**Net**	**Name**	**Net**
1	Los Angeles County, CA	813	Los Angeles County, CA	3,073	Los Angeles County, CA	733
2	Cook County, IL	586	Cook County, IL	1,200	Fulton County, GA	645
3	Orange County, CA	576	Miami-Dade County, FL	1,001	Cook County, IL	573
4	Cochise County, AZ	522	Fairbanks North Star, AK	967	Orange County, CA	493
5	Hillsborough County, FL	515	Queens County, NY	657	Miami-Dade County, FL	386

Source: U.S. Census Bureau, 2015a. County-to-County Migration Flows: 2009–2013 ACS.

loss counties are dispersed. The 15 negative links involve 12 different states and 15 different counties.

In Table 3.4B, the top domestic migration gains occur in three of the state's top five most populous counties. In terms of absolute size, the top domestic gains are much larger than the top domestic losses. Compared to the domestic loss counties, the county-to-county links for the top gainers are more concentrated. The 15 positive links involve seven states and nine counties. Many of these links are with other major U.S. metropolitan areas. Los Angeles County (Los Angeles) is the largest domestic link for all three top gaining Texas counties. Cook County (Chicago), Orange County (Anaheim), and Miami-Dade (Miami) are other major sources of domestic migration gain.

Overall, the county-to-county links suggest that the state's most populated counties are impacted by migration in two ways. In the first instance, internal migration redistributes people from the state's most populated counties to less-populated, adjacent counties. In the second instance, domestic migration from major U.S. metropolitan areas adds people to the state's most populated counties. With this, the state's most populous counties are losing existing residents from internal migration while simultaneously gaining new residents from domestic migration. Moreover, these same counties are primary destinations for new immigrants. A continuation of these trends promises to reshape both the population distributions and population compositions of the state's most populated areas. . . .

Summary and Conclusions

Summary

In recent years, Texas has become a favorite destination for domestic and international migrants, adding close to 250,000 people a year through migration. In addition to this external migration, over a million Texans move from one county to another within the state. Together, these migration streams produce a substantial population redistribution within Texas every year.

Though contemporary Texas consistently adds population through migration, the same is not true for all of the state's 254 counties. Population change from migration has been uneven and the sources of migration have varied across the state.

This brief has examined migration in Texas counties by total mobility, migration flows, net migration, immigration, and connectivity. With each of these migration measures, there is a strong contrast between the largest population counties and the smallest population counties in Texas. In addition, the group of 14 Border Counties has its own distinctive migration characteristics.

Population change from migration in Texas can be generalized as follows:

- Smaller population counties are more affected by internal migration—movements beginning and ending in Texas. The three least populated tiers had population loss or zero growth from internal migration. They also tend to have flat or low rates of domestic and international migration. As for migration linkages, these counties are less connected to other counties than the largest population counties and tend to gain fewer migrants per county-to-county link.

- The largest population counties tend to have the highest mobility rates, greatest migration volumes, highest overall migration rates, and highest overall connectivity with other counties. Larger population counties are most affected by domestic and international migration flows. More than 90 percent of the total net migration in these counties comes from external sources that originate outside of Texas. At the same time, some of the state's most populated counties are losing population through internal migration to nearby counties.

- Border counties have low volumes and low rates of internal and domestic migration and, as a group, experience negative total net migration. Were it not for high immigration rates, these counties would have negative overall migration rates.

Conclusions

It has long been believed that migration is associated with basic social change and cultural diffusion (Bogue 1959; Bogue et al. 1982). Given this dynamic, the state's major metropolitan areas have become the focal points of substantial change. While all of Texas is affected by migration, the counties encompassed by major metropolitan areas are experiencing large population increases through the in-migration of people from other states and nations. This growth from external migration sources suggests a future with increasingly heterogeneous populations, both demographically and culturally, residing in the state's major metropolitan areas.

At the same time, some of the state's least populated counties are losing population through both internal and domestic migration. Because migrants tend to be young adults, this pattern of youth outmigration can lead to increasingly older populations remaining in these counties. In turn, this "aging in place" can inhibit economic development, restrain community vitality, and reduce population growth through natural increase. To the extent this pattern of out-migration continues, some of the state's least populated counties will face continuing population loss.

In many respects, the Texas counties that share a border with Mexico are an enigma. Domestic migration is minimal and negative in 10 of the

14 counties. As a group, their total net migration rate is –5.0 per 1,000 residents. At the same time, this group gains 11.2 persons per 1,000 residents through immigration. Thus, the border counties are experiencing population gain through immigration and losing population from internal and domestic migration. Yet, even with this, some of these counties are among the fastest growing in the state. This is because high fertility rates are producing large population gains through natural increase. Thus, while the loss of population from migration is similar to that of the state's least populated counties, the border counties are growing rapidly from immigration and natural increase. If these trends persist, these counties will continue to have populations that are younger and more international than the state as a whole.

Given the differences in these three types of counties, it might be said that Texas is one state with three demographic destinies. As a whole, Texans are very mobile and Texas is growing from migration. But, within the state, the sifting and sorting of these population movements is uneven. These trends underlie a reshaping of the state's population geography with some counties losing population while others gain population, some counties growing older while others are attracting young people, and some counties becoming more heterogeneous while others fail to thrive. Should these trends persist, Texas could see a future where migration sharpens the state's geographical differences in opportunities and challenges.

NOTES

1. Data used in this report are derived from the 2014 5-Year American Community Survey (ACS). The 2014 5-Year ACS Summary File covers the 2009–2013 time period. With this, five years of data are accumulated on a continuous basis. This is done to increase the sample size, which improves the survey's accuracy and permits the inclusion of geographic areas with populations of less than 20,000 persons. Conceptually, these period surveys measure the average characteristics of a geographic area over five years (U.S. Census Bureau 2008).

   As with all survey data, the ACS is subject to sampling error which occurs when a random sample does not fully represent the whole population that is being evaluated. Sampling error becomes less problematic with larger sample sizes. For a more detailed description of the ACS data accuracy, please see the U.S. Census Bureau (2015b) reference.

2. Here we use the terms international migration and immigration interchangeably. The American Community Survey does not have data on net international migration. The U.S. Census Bureau produces several annual reports that include the mobility patterns of Americans. Two of the primary sources are surveys: The American Community Survey and the annual supplement to the Current Population Survey. The other primary source, Population Estimates, is not a survey. The Population Estimates Program uses various data sources to produce annual estimates of the population and components of population change. Using various estimation techniques, the Population Estimates are able to calculate Net International Migration as well as Net Domestic Migration. By contrast, the surveys are based on respondents' answers. Because these surveys are administered only in the United States and its territories, they do not get information on persons who emigrate from the U.S. to other countries.

3. The 14 border counties and their respective population tiers (quintiles) are as follows: Hudspeth (Tier 1); Jeff Davis (Tier 1); Kinney (Tier 1); Terrell (Tier 1); Brewster (Tier 2); Presidio (Tier 2); Zapata (Tier 3); Maverick (Tier 4); Starr (Tier 4); Val Verde (Tier 4); Cameron (Tier 5); El Paso (Tier 5); Hidalgo (Tier 5); and, Webb (Tier 5). For more information, please refer to Appendix A.

REFERENCES

Bogue, D. J. 1959. "Internal Migration." In *The Study of Population*. Edited by P. M. Hauser and O. D. Duncan. Chicago: University of Chicago Press.

Bogue, D. J., Kenneth Hinze, and Michael White. 1982. *Techniques of Estimating Net Migration*. Chicago: Community and Family Study Center, University of Chicago Press.

U.S. Census Bureau. 2008. "A Compass for Understanding and Using American Community Survey Data: What General Data Users Need to Know." (Available: https://www.census.gov/content/dam/Census/library/publications/2008/acs/ACSGeneralHandbook.pdf 03/03/2016)

U.S. Census Bureau. 2014. American Community Survey (ACS): Five-Year Summary Data, 2009–2013. (Available: http://factfinder.census.gov/faces/nav/jsf/pages/index.xhtml 09/03/2015).

U.S. Census Bureau. 2015a. County-to-County Migration Flows: 2009–2013 ACS. (Available: http://www2.census.gov/programs-surveys/demo/tables/geographic-mobility/2013/county-to-county-migration-2009-2013/county-to-county-2009-2013-ins-outs-nets-gross.xlsx 11/20/2015)

U.S. Census Bureau. 2015b. "American Community Survey: Accuracy of the Data (2014). (Available: https://www2.census.gov/programs-surveys/acs/tech_docs/accuracy/ACS_Accuracy_of_Data_2014.pdf 09/12/2016)

Appendix A: County Classifications

Table 3.5A

Tier 1			Tier 2			Tier 3		
FIPS	Name	Population*	FIPS	Name	Population*	FIPS	Name	Population*
48011	Armstrong	1,768	48009	Archer	8,786	48003	Andrews	15,300
48023	Baylor	3,641	48017	Bailey	7,053	48007	Aransas	23,388
48033	Borden	625	48031	Blanco	10,500	48019	Bandera	20,344
48045	Briscoe	1,598	48047	Brooks	7,110	48035	Bosque	18,005
48079	Cochran	3,028	48063	Camp	12,166	48051	Burleson	16,966
48081	Coke	3,233	48065	Carson	6,078	48057	Calhoun	21,111
48087	Collingsworth	3,033	48069	Castro	7,864	48059	Callahan	13,427
48095	Concho	4,048	48075	Childress	6,978	48089	Colorado	20,591
48101	Cottle	1,530	48077	Clay	10,539	48093	Comanche	13,603
48103	Crane	4,375	48083	Coleman	8,558	48115	Dawson	13,695
48105	Crockett	3,811	48107	Crosby	5,985	48117	Deaf Smith	18,721
48109	Culberson	2,345	48111	Dallam	6,709	48123	DeWitt	20,121
48125	Dickens	2,358	48119	Delta	5,143	48133	Eastland	18,241
48129	Donley	3,598	48127	Dimmit	10,001	48145	Falls	17,529
48137	Edwards	2,070	48131	Duval	11,604	48161	Freestone	19,494
48151	Fisher	3,898	48153	Floyd	6,315	48163	Frio	17,329
48155	Foard	1,122	48159	Franklin	10,496	48165	Gaines	17,573
48173	Glasscock	1,176	48169	Garza	6,324	48177	Gonzales	19,631

Tier 1			Tier 2			Tier 3		
FIPS	Name	Population*	FIPS	Name	Population*	FIPS	Name	Population*
48191	Hall	3,286	48175	Goliad	7,204	48179	Gray	22,519
48197	Hardeman	4,035	48193	Hamilton	8,348	48219	Hockley	22,775
48211	Hemphill	3,884	48195	Hansford	5,503	48225	Houston	23,176
48235	Irion	1,595	48205	Hartley	6,029	48233	Hutchinson	21,770
48261	Kenedy	507	48207	Haskell	5,791	48239	Jackson	13,970
48263	Kent	887	48237	Jack	8,921	48253	Jones	19,943
48267	Kimble	4,543	48247	Jim Hogg	5,179	48255	Karnes	14,742
48269	King	319	48283	La Salle	6,830	48279	Lamb	13,717
48275	Knox	3,711	48297	Live Oak	11,468	48281	Lampasas	19,692
48295	Lipscomb	3,283	48305	Lynn	5,811	48285	Lavaca	19,126
48301	Loving	87	48307	McCulloch	8,187	48287	Lee	16,406
48311	McMullen	605	48315	Marion	10,383	48289	Leon	16,513
48317	Martin	4,898	48335	Mitchell	9,263	48293	Limestone	23,219
48319	Mason	3,991	48357	Ochiltree	10,301	48299	Llano	19,052
48327	Menard	2,187	48369	Parmer	9,988	48313	Madison	13,511
48333	Mills	4,851	48379	Rains	10,851	48331	Milam	24,135
48345	Motley	1,170	48387	Red River	12,661	48337	Montague	19,358
48359	Oldham	2,042	48391	Refugio	7,192	48341	Moore	21,637
48383	Reagan	3,422	48399	Runnels	10,250	48343	Morris	12,743
48385	Real	3,322	48403	Sabine	10,557	48351	Newton	14,172
48393	Roberts	1,022	48405	San Augustine	8,788	48353	Nolan	14,856
48413	Schleicher	3,316	48411	San Saba	5,953	48365	Panola	23,609
48417	Shackelford	3,333	48425	Somervell	8,429	48371	Pecos	15,482
48421	Sherman	3,020	48429	Stephens	9,373	48389	Reeves	13,571
48431	Sterling	1,338	48437	Swisher	7,712	48395	Robertson	16,351
48433	Stonewall	1,347	48445	Terry	12,625	48415	Scurry	16,737
48435	Sutton	4,026	48475	Ward	10,678	48455	Trinity	14,314
48447	Throckmorton	1,603	48483	Wheeler	5,469	48457	Tyler	21,314
48461	Upton	3,272	48495	Winkler	7,120			
			48501	Yoakum	7,865			
			48507	Zavala	11,690			

Note: *Population is from the 2009–2013 5-Year ACS Summary Data for the population 1 year of age and older.

Tier Population Key

	Tier 1	Tier 2	Tier 3	Tier 4	Tier 5	Border Counties
Population	87–5,044	5,045–12,676	12,677–24,461	24,462–64,725	64,726–4,119,266	825–801,745

Table 3.5B

Tier 4			Tier 5			Border Counties			
FIPS	Name	Population*	FIPS	Name	Population*	FIPS	Name	Population*	Tier
48001	Anderson	57,722	48005	Angelina	85,910	48043	Brewster	9,136	2
48013	Atascosa	45,173	48021	Bastrop	73,842	48061	Cameron	404,024	5
48015	Austin	28,339	48027	Bell	311,127	48141	El Paso	801,745	5
48025	Bee	31,836	48029	Bexar	1,728,176	48215	Hidalgo	775,494	5
48049	Brown	37,287	48037	Bowie	91,402	48229	Hudspeth	3,327	1
48053	Burnet	42,759	48039	Brazoria	315,036	48243	Jeff Davis	2,290	1
48055	Caldwell	38,128	48041	Brazos	194,767	48271	Kinney	3,563	1
48067	Cass	30,064	48085	Collin	799,867	48323	Maverick	53,743	4
48071	Chambers	35,086	48091	Comal	110,923	48377	Presidio	7,495	2
48073	Cherokee	50,311	48099	Coryell	74,832	48427	Starr	60,423	4
48097	Cooke	38,096	48113	Dallas	2,377,637				
48143	Erath	38,400	48121	Denton	679,254				
48147	Fannin	33,452	48135	Ector	139,042				
48149	Fayette	24,544	48139	Ellis	150,264				
48171	Gillespie	24,707	48157	Fort Bend	600,966				
48185	Grimes	26,487	48167	Galveston	292,928				
48189	Hale	35,686	48181	Grayson	119,887				
48199	Hardin	54,341	48183	Gregg	120,494				
48217	Hill	34,591	48187	Guadalupe	134,362				
48221	Hood	51,196	48201	Harris	4,119,266				
48223	Hopkins	34,836	48203	Harrison	65,625				
48227	Howard	34,838	48209	Hays	162,331				
48241	Jasper	35,378	48213	Henderson	77,782				
48249	Jim Wells	40,436	48231	Hunt	85,581				
48259	Kendall	34,595	48245	Jefferson	249,062				
48265	Kerr	49,211	48251	Johnson	150,760				
48273	Kleberg	31,529	48257	Kaufman	103,926				
48277	Lamar	49,176	48291	Liberty	74,829				
48321	Matagorda	36,083	48303	Lubbock	279,272				
48325	Medina	45,983	48309	McLennan	234,221				
48347	Nacogdoches	64,116	48329	Midland	140,206				
48349	Navarro	47,173	48339	Montgomery	466,046				
48363	Palo Pinto	27,789	48355	Nueces	339,763				
48373	Polk	45,230	48361	Orange	81,452				
48401	Rusk	52,835	48367	Parker	117,373				
48407	San Jacinto	26,348	48375	Potter	119,764				

Tier 4			Tier 5			Border Counties			
FIPS	Name	Population*	FIPS	Name	Population*	FIPS	Name	Population*	Tier
48409	San Patricio	64,127	48381	Randall	121,418				
48419	Shelby	25,332	48397	Rockwall	80,095				
48449	Titus	31,858	48423	Smith	209,441				
48459	Upshur	39,131	48439	Tarrant	1,823,073				
48463	Uvalde	26,177	48441	Taylor	130,486				
48467	Van Zandt	51,986	48451	Tom Green	110,585				
48473	Waller	43,338	48453	Travis	1,047,764				
48477	Washington	33,341	48469	Victoria	86,982				
48481	Wharton	40,802	48471	Walker	67,506				
48493	Wilson	43,359	48485	Wichita	129,773				
48497	Wise	59,290	48491	Williamson	435,257				
48499	Wood	41,755							

Note: *Population is from the 2009–2013 5-Year ACS Summary Data for the population 1 year of age and older.

Tier Population Key

	Tier 1	Tier 2	Tier 3	Tier 4	Tier 5	Border Counties
Population	87–5,044	5,045–12,676	12,677–24,461	24,462–64,725	64,726–4,119,266	825–801,745

ARTICLE QUESTIONS

1) What are the pillars of Texas's population expansion? Can you think of any others?
2) How would you describe these trends in Texas migration patterns to someone not from Texas?
3) What are some of the implications of Texas's population growth identified by the authors?

3.3) White Births, Migration Explain Why Texas Remains a Red State

San Antonio News-Express, December 31, 2016

ROGELIO SÁENZ

In a deceptively simple question, University of Texas at San Antonio scholar and demographer Rogelio Sáenz marries demographic changes to political changes to ask: "When will Texas become a blue [Democratic] state?" The question is complex, but racial changes in the state's population are at the heart of the answer. In particular, Sáenz points to the balance of Anglo and Hispanic voters as central to voting power, as Anglos are generally more likely to vote for Republicans and Hispanics for Democrats.

California and Texas, two states that both have large Hispanic populations, are used as comparison points. Birth rates and the "natural increase" and "natural declines" of Anglos and

Hispanics are different in the two states, leading to California having a more Hispanic population and Texas having a more Anglo population. However, demographics alone won't "turn Texas blue," according to Sáenz—the stability of the Anglo birth rate will delay any major electoral impact. The mechanics of voting will slow the transition toward Democratic power as well, with voter identification laws (which require government-issued identification to vote) and district lines drawn to limit the impact of the Hispanic population acting as major barriers to an increase in Hispanic voting power. Sáenz suggests that the Democratic Party has some say in the matter if it commits resources to getting Hispanics to vote, but the reality of Texas turning blue is in the distant future.

When will Texas become a blue state?

This is a question that as a demographer I am often asked.

It is commonly thought that it is just a matter of time until the state's political hue will turn.

It is expected that the youthful Latino population will grow rapidly in the coming years, while the aging white population will eventually start to decline.

After all, didn't this occur in California? In 1992, California became a blue state and has become more so since then, with Hillary Clinton garnering nearly 62 percent of the state's presidential election popular vote in November.

A comparison of white voting-age citizens (WVACs, persons 18 and older who are U.S. citizens) in California and Texas allows us to assess the task at hand for Democrats in Texas. Note that voting-age citizens may not be eligible to actually vote because they may not be registered to do so or they may have committed a crime that bars them from voting.

Whites accounted for approximately 60 percent of the total population of voting-age citizens (TVACs) in California and Texas in 2000.

The similarities end there, as California has sustained some of the greatest declines in its white population in the country, while that of Texas continues to be fairly vibrant.

The white voting-age citizen population in California declined by about 120,000 (a 1 percent decline) between 2000 and 2015, while that in Texas grew by approximately one million (a rise of 12 percent), the largest growth in the nation. This demographic dynamic suggests that Democrats still have a way to go in their quest for Texas to turn blue.

The share of whites among the total population of voting-age citizens is now 48 percent in California and 53 percent in Texas.

Demographic indicators signal that the white vote will continue to erode much faster in California than in Texas in the future.

White women in California have an average of 1.5 births over their childbearing years (15–44) in 2015 compared with their counterparts in Texas having 1.8. The relative presence of white children in California continues to wane much more rapidly with white children in California declining by 26 percent between 2000 and 2015 compared to a smaller drop of 7 percent in Texas.

How do those numbers jibe with Texas Latinas? Their average number of births was 2.3 in 2015, down from 2.9 in 2001.

Over the last 15 years large numbers of whites have left California, while many from throughout the country have moved to Texas. In California, in each of the 15 years between 2001 and 2015 more white voting-age citizens moved out of California to other U.S. states in the respective previous year than moved to the Golden State. Over this time, California sustained a net loss of close to 745,000 white voting-age citizens, the greatest net loss except for New York. In contrast, Texas attracted more of these individuals from other states than it lost to them in 12 of the 15 years, representing a net gain of approximately 418,000 white voting-age citizens, with only Florida and Arizona posting greater net gains from migration.

Due, in part, to its aging population and net out-migration, there are more deaths than births among whites in California, but not in Texas.

A recent study that I conducted with my colleague, Kenneth M. Johnson at the University of New Hampshire, shows that California is a state where white deaths firmly outnumber white births, what demographers refer to as "natural decline." California experienced natural decrease among whites in 13 of 14 years between 2001 and 2014. In 2014, there were 144,318 white births in California alongside 157,486 white deaths, translating to a natural decline of 13,168. In contrast, Texas whites have always had more births than deaths, what is referred to as "natural increase." In 2014, there were 140,992 white births and 120,192 white deaths in Texas, netting a natural increase of 20,800. Only Utah, which has a youthful white population and high levels of fertility, had a higher level of natural increase (24,198) than Texas.

For Texas Latinos in 2015, there were 189,462 births and 37,795 deaths, resulting in a natural increase of 151,667.

These demographic trends suggest that the likelihood Texas will turn blue in the very near future—through demographics alone—is relatively low. The stability of white growth will delay the electoral impact.

The road toward a Democratic tilt in Texas is even rougher considering the political barriers that Republicans have erected to minimize the political power of Latinos and African Americans. These include direct measures to limit the political representation of these groups, such as voter ID laws (though the courts have made some concessions here) and the disingenuous drawing of redistricting maps (a lawsuit is still in the court system). Indirect means to diminish the political clout of Latinos and African Americans include the slashing of public education funding in public schools

that are majority non-white and mass incarceration, which has taken away the vote of many persons of color.

There are also challenges within the Latino population that contribute to delaying the time when Texas will turn blue. In particular, even though preliminary data suggest increases in the Latino voter turnout in the last presidential election, Latinos commonly register and turn out to vote at lower levels than whites and African Americans. The Latino vote is also far from homogeneous with considerable portions of Latino voters supporting Republicans including Donald Trump in the last presidential election.

The Democratic Party has major challenges in turning Texas into a blue state. The Democratic establishment has relied primarily on demographic change with the hope that one day there will be enough Latino and African American voters to outnumber white voters. Population projections indicate that in the very near future Latinos will outnumber whites in Texas. However, couched in those raw numbers are the challenges related to a large portion of Latinos not being able to vote because they are too young, they are not U.S. citizens, they are not registered to vote or they have a criminal record that does not allow them to vote. Despite projected declining numbers in the future, the Texas white population continues to be formidable, especially when a much smaller segment has barriers blocking its vote.

The Democratic establishment needs to increase its commitment and resources to and engagement of Latinos in Texas, beyond the reliance on demography to turn Texas blue. Without greater investment, the answer to that oft-asked question—"When will Texas become blue?"—becomes further in the distant future.

ARTICLE QUESTIONS

1) What are the similarities and differences between the Anglo populations in Texas and California?
2) What can the Democratic Party do to encourage Hispanics to turn out to vote for Democratic Party candidates? What can the Republican Party do?
3) What are the implications of demographic changes for Texas's political future?

Chapter 4

The Texas Constitution

Constitutional government in Texas is older than the republic itself. The story of how Texas's constitutional principles were established starts when Texas was part of Mexico; since then, these principles have been adapted as the state has expanded and the political environment has changed. Over the years, Texas's system of constitutional government has been forged in reaction to government policies or practices that have frustrated voters: Mexico's unpopular edicts limiting Texas's expansion, the Texas Republic's struggles for economic solvency, the practice of slavery, and finally resentment of a domineering governor during Reconstruction.

The Texas Constitution structures the rules of the game, shaping the moves, strategies, and struggles of Texas's government and politics. In general, a constitution lays out the principles and responsibilities of government and specifies the powers of each branch and elected officials, as well as limitations on public policy. The constitution also specifies *who* can serve—an unusual provision in the Texas Constitution requires any holder of public office to have a belief in a "supreme being." This provision is blatantly unconstitutional (on the federal level) but may affect who runs for office. It definitely affected one City Council race in Austin, when one candidate accused another of being a "self-admitted atheist" and therefore prohibited from holding public office in Texas. The issue has never been challenged directly in court, but a past interpretation by the state attorney general voided the provision without removing it from the constitution itself.

Texans have always valued an ethos of rugged individualism and are not inclined to give up their freedoms lightly. The challenge in crafting a constitution for the Lone Star State has thus been to balance freedoms and government power. This challenge continues. In recent years, the state has struggled to meet its constitutional mandate to fund its public school system. As *Texas Tribune* education reporter Kiah Collier observes, the state's ability to meet its constitutional requirements cuts across political and legal lines, with its 5 million schoolchildren left in the middle. The Texas Supreme Court ruled in 2016 that the system was "broken" but satisfied the state's "minimum constitutional requirements," a decision that put the onus of reform on the legislature.

State constitutional guidelines extend to the ability of lawmakers to make laws on certain issues, to tax and spend the public's money, and to check the power of each other. How and where money is spent is always hotly debated, particularly when the government considers spending funds on religious events or on behalf of religious institutions. John Colyandro and Russell Withers of the right-leaning Texas Conservative Coalition Research Institute scrutinize the ability of the state to set aside public money for parents to use in enrolling their children in private religious schools. They conclude that such a use of public funds is constitutionally legitimate so long as the state does not preference one religion over another or a religious school over a secular public school.

The right of self-expression, protected by both the U.S. and Texas Constitutions, can take many forms. The Texas Constitution protects the "liberty to speak, write or publish [one's] opinions on any subject" and prohibits any law from "curtailing the liberty of speech or of the press." But these rights may conflict with other rights, like the right of bystanders to document events (usually by smartphone). The rise of protests across the country, and especially on college campuses, prompted law student Dean Galaro to write a short primer on how the Texas Constitution governs protests and photography and how Texas courts have interpreted these provisions. Journalists and observers of events have broad rights to free speech, Galaro argues, limited in only a few types of incidents. Overall, he concludes, there aren't many ways that individuals can limit how they are photographed in public under Texas law, so he advises, "Be careful what you do in public."

CHAPTER QUESTIONS

1) Identify one way that the Texas Constitution's provisions affect your daily life.
2) What sorts of changes to the constitution (if any) do you see as important?
3) How flexible should the Texas Constitution be? Should it adapt to modern times, or should policymakers and judges strictly interpret what they read in the text?

4.1) Texas Supreme Court Rules School Funding System Is Constitutional

Texas Tribune, May 13, 2016

KIAH COLLIER

Perhaps the only thing more hotly contested than the state's top barbecue joints is the structure and funding of its public school system. Although this system is primarily funded by local taxes and administered by regional school boards, the state has a constitutional responsibility to design a fair and equal public education system, with the Texas Constitution declaring that "it shall be the duty of the Legislature of the State to establish and make suitable provision for the support and maintenance of an efficient system of public free schools." The state's current funding system is often referred to as a "Robin Hood" system, in which wealthy districts share property tax revenue with poorer school districts to distribute education funds more evenly.

In 2011, for the seventh time since the 1980s, two thirds of the state's school districts sued the state government on the grounds that this system of funding shortchanged some districts at the expense of others. It took five years for the case to work its way up to the Texas Supreme Court, which rendered a verdict in 2016. As Austin reporter Kiah Collier writes, the state dodged a bullet when the high court held that the current system "satisfies minimum constitutional requirements." The decision had legal, policy, and political implications. Legally, Chief Justice Don Willett argued that the courts should not supplant the will of the legislature by telling that body how to design an education system. On a policy level, without the legal grounds to force the legislature to reform the system, the present arrangement is not likely to change. Politically, education is always a heavily debated issue, with Democrats arguing that the system needs a makeover and the current system is just a "Band-Aid" and Republicans praising the ruling as a victory for taxpayers.

The Texas Supreme Court on Friday issued a ruling upholding the state's public school funding system as constitutional, while also urging state lawmakers to implement "transformational, top-to-bottom reforms that amount to more than Band-Aid on top of Band-Aid."

But without a court order directing the Legislature to fix specific provisions in the system, school groups worry that lawmakers will either do nothing or something outside the box.

"Our Byzantine school funding 'system' is undeniably imperfect, with immense room for improvement. But it satisfies minimum constitutional requirements," Justice Don Willett wrote in the court's 100-page opinion, which asserts that the court's "lenient standard of review in this policy-laden area counsels modesty."

There were no dissenting opinions; Justices Eva Guzman and Jeff Boyd delivered concurring ones.

"Good enough now . . . does not mean that the system is *good* or that it will continue to be *enough*," Guzman wrote. "Shortfalls in both resources and performance persist in innumerable respects, and a perilously large number of students is in danger of falling further behind."

Friday's ruling is the second time the state's highest civil court has upheld the state's school finance system. Since the 1980s, school districts have repeatedly sued the state in an attempt to increase public education funding, and have often prevailed. The latest case, brought by more than two-thirds of Texas school districts, is the seventh time such a case has reached the state Supreme Court.

"This is an historic ruling by the Texas Supreme Court, and a major victory for the people of Texas, who have faced an endless parade of lawsuits following any attempt to finance schools in the state,"

Attorney General Ken Paxton said in a statement Friday. "We have said all along that school financing must be debated and shaped by the Texas Legislature, not through decades' worth of ongoing litigation in the court system, and I'm pleased the court unanimously agrees."

Houston lawyer Mark Trachtenberg, who represented 88 property-wealthy school districts in the case, said the ruling "represents a dark day for Texas school children, especially given the Legislature's repeated failure to adequately fund our schools."

A recent study by the National Education Association found that Texas ranks 38th in the country in per-pupil public-education spending.

Wayne Pierce, executive director of the Equity Center, which represented more than 440 low- and medium-wealth school districts in the case, said the high court has "pretty well given a blank check to the Legislature and the only question now is if the Legislature steps up and does the right thing or if they take this as an opportunity to further hurt the system."

"I think they're going to have to do something, but will it be enough? I doubt it," said Pierce, asked about whether he thinks lawmakers will increase funding.

"Will this [court decision] be used to not fix public education but go out on some tangential rabbit trail? I think that's probably more likely," he said. "If this decision has a silver lining, it's around a huge, black cloud."

But some Democratic and Republican state lawmakers on Friday called for action on the issue.

"While I applaud and agree with the Texas Supreme Court's ruling, make no mistake: This is not the end of this journey, but the beginning," said state Rep. Jeff Leach, R-Plano. "The duly elected Texas Legislature—not the courts—has the immense responsibility to work to reform, improve and strengthen education in Texas."

"For far too long, the state has been neglecting its responsibilities, failing to pick up its fair share of the school finance tab, and pushing the costs down to overburdened local taxpayers," said state Rep. Donna Howard, D-Austin.

More than 600 Texas school districts sued the state after the Legislature cut $5.4 billion from the public education budget in 2011.

Their lawyers argued the state's method of funding public schools was unconstitutional on a variety of grounds—that the Legislature had failed to provide districts with sufficient funding to ensure students meet the state's increasingly difficult academic standards; that big disparities had emerged between property-wealthy and property-poor school districts; and that many school districts were having to tax at the maximum rate just to provide a basic education, meaning they lacked "meaningful discretion" to set rates. That amounts to a violation of a constitutional ban on a statewide property tax.

In a 2014 ruling, Travis County District Court Judge John Dietz—a Democrat—upheld all of those claims, siding with the plaintiff school districts.

He also ruled against two other parties in the lawsuit that did not represent traditional school districts, directing them to seek relief from the state Legislature.

In early 2012, a group representing parents, school choice advocates and the business community—Texans for Real Efficiency and Equity in Education—filed a suit alleging that the current school finance system is inefficient and over-regulated. The Texas Charter Schools Association also sued the state, arguing that a cap on charter school contracts and charters' lack of access to facilities funding was unconstitutional.

In Friday's ruling, the state Supreme Court upheld Dietz's ruling relating to the fairness coalition and charter schools association but struck down the rest, meaning that all plaintiffs essentially lost out on any injunctive relief.

But Robert Henneke, general counsel for the Texas Public Policy Foundation, a conservative think tank that backed the so-called efficiency intervenors, painted an optimistic picture of the ruling.

"The court thoroughly rejected the notion that the amount of funding into the system is what is constitutionally required," he said. "While the court defers to the Legislature to make policy, I think the court's opinion made clear that there is need for reform and, globally, much broader than mere funding and finance."

During oral arguments Sept. 1, state lawyers asked the court to dismiss or remand the case to a lower court so it may consider changes lawmakers recently have enacted to the state's school finance system. Last year, the Legislature increased public education funding by $1.5 billion—snubbing a $3 billion House proposal—and authorized another $118 million for a high-quality pre-kindergarten grant program that Gov. Greg Abbott championed.

Before issuing his ruling, Dietz reopened evidence for a four-week period so that he could consider changes made by the 2013 Legislature, which restored about $3.4 billion of the $5.4 billion in public education cuts made in 2011 and changed graduation and testing requirements.

Abbott, who was serving as attorney general at the time, appealed Dietz's ruling directly to the all-Republican state Supreme Court.

On Friday, Abbott called the ruling "a victory for Texas taxpayers and the Texas Constitution." He added that the decision "ends years of wasteful litigation by correctly recognizing that courts do not have the authority to micromanage the State's school finance system."

Meanwhile, the Center for Public Policy Priorities, a left-leaning think tank, called on the Legislature to "make meaningful investments in our schools so that all Texans have the chance to live up to their full potential."

And teacher groups bemoaned the decision.

"It is a sad day when the state's highest court decides that doing the least the state can do to educate our children is enough," said Texas State Teachers Association President Noel Candelaria.

Sheryl Pace, a school finance expert at the business-backed Texas Taxpayers and Research Association, said the court decision surprised her given the sheer number of school districts suing. She stressed that the decision does not preclude state lawmakers from making changes to the school finance system, which the court described as deeply flawed.

"I do think this frees up the Legislature so that they can address school finance if they want to," she said. "There won't be an injunctive deadline being held over their heads."

Whether state lawmakers will actually do so is another question, though, she said. Last year, an effort to overhaul the school finance system failed, with opponents arguing the Legislature should wait for the state Supreme Court ruling.

ARTICLE QUESTIONS

1) How should a state as large and diverse as Texas design an efficient system for equally funding public schools?
2) Think about your own high school. Would more equal funding among schools help or hurt your school?
3) If Texas's legislators are not willing to overhaul the state's system of public education funding, should its courts force them to do so by declaring the current policy unconstitutional?

4.2) Education Savings Accounts Are Constitutional

TribTalk, January 24, 2017

JOHN COLYANDRO AND RUSSELL WITHERS

Although the Texas Supreme Court called the Lone Star State's public school finance system "imperfect" and "Byzantine," it ultimately held that the system met minimum constitutional standards. Frustration with public schools has led many parents to opt to send their children to private schools, but many lack the means to pay for such schooling. John Colyandro and Russell

Withers of the Texas Conservative Coalition Research Institute argue that one solution to this problem is education savings accounts (ESAs), which allow the state to set aside funds for an individual student that would be spent in the public school system and permit parents to use that money like a bank account to spend on the school of their choice. Organizations like the Texas Association of School Boards and the Texas Parent-Teacher Association, however, reject the idea that ESAs are constitutionally allowable, calling them a violation of the separation of church and state.

Can the state legally use public money for private (often religious) schools? Isn't this un-constitutional, since it obviates the state's responsibility to provide suitable public schools? Colyandro and Withers argue that ESAs are a matter of parental choice to exercise discretion over the use of their taxpayer money, not of government advocating religion to students. In fact, the duo suggest, to limit the state's funding of private religious schools may discrimi-nate against religiously minded parents who want to educate their children in a nonsecular alternative. They claim that Texas could constitutionally establish ESAs so long as the state does not preference one religion over another or a religious school over a secular public school. Texas courts have hinted but not ruled that this might be acceptable. Ultimately, the channeling of public money to private religious institutions is likely to bring challenges. Should the state stay out of this debate or give Texans more choices when it comes to public schools?

Education savings accounts (ESAs) are a form of school choice that allows parents to remove their children from traditional public schools and re-ceive a portion of the funds that would otherwise be spent on them in a bank account. The parents may use those funds to pay for tuition at a private school, materials for homeschooling, or special-ized forms of education for students with special needs. The Texas Association of School Boards (TASB) and the Texas Parent-Teacher Associa-tion (PTA), argue that the Texas Constitution prohibits school choice programs, including ESAs.

TASB misleadingly claims in their 2016–18 Advocacy Agenda Priorities that the Texas Consti-tution's mandate for a system of public free schools, "precludes the funneling of public tax dollars to private institutions or individuals." That language is neither included in the state Constitution nor does it have such a prohibition. The PTA argues that school choice, including ESAs (which the PTA calls "a form of voucher") "violate separation of church and state" because tax dollars may not be "directed toward schools of religious origin[.]" Both of these objections are based on flawed asser-tions about the nature of ESAs and the U.S. and Texas Constitutions. The money is not "funneled" to private institutions or "directed towards schools

of religious origin." It is provided to parents who have broad discretion on how to use it.

The Texas Constitution requires the Legisla-ture "to establish and make suitable provision for the support and maintenance of an efficient system of public free schools." There is no quali-fication of that provision (Article VII, Sec. 1), and the Texas Supreme Court recently ruled 9–0 in *Morath vs. The Texas Taxpayer and Student Fair-ness Coalition* that the Legislature is meeting its constitutional obligation. The state has the author-ity to create additional education programs that complement its constitutional mandates, includ-ing school choice.

In his majority opinion, Justice Don Willett pointed out that "[i]n the Texas higher education setting, school choice has proven to be smart policy." He called arguments that efficiency in public edu-cation could be increased by more student-centered funding (i.e. school choice) "intriguing." And de-spite no constitutional mandate for school choice, he wrote, "We hope the Legislature will consider these and similar suggestions." The court would not have opined in this way if the justices believe school choice to be unconstitutional.

Indeed, courts have consistently held that choice programs are permissible where funding of religious institutions is indirect and incidental to the program's larger purpose. In *Zelman v. Simmons-Harris*, for example, the U.S. Supreme Court held that "where a government aid program is neutral with respect to religion, and provides assistance directly to a broad class of citizens who, in turn, direct government aid to religious schools wholly as a result of their own genuine and independent private choice, the program is not readily subject to challenge under the Establishment Clause." Going back to 1899 in *Bradfield v. Roberts*, the critical question in Establishment Clause cases is whether the government's principal or primary effect advances religion. Indirect benefits to religious institutions, like those derived from ESAs and similar school choice proposals, are permissible.

At the state level, the Texas Constitution has two provisions, informally called "Blaine amendments," prohibiting direct state support of religious institutions. Article I, Section 6 prohibits anyone from being compelled to "support any place of worship." More directly, Article I, Section 7 states that "[n]o money shall be appropriated, or drawn from the Treasury for the benefit of any sect, or religious society, theological or religious seminary; nor shall property belonging to the State be appropriated for any such purposes."

Similar "Blaine amendments" are found in more than half of U.S. state constitutions and have a sordid history of being adopted on a 19th century wave of anti-Catholic bigotry and discrimination. As Erica Smith explains in a recent article for *Federalist Society Review*, "[Blaine] Amendments continue to be used to discriminate against Catholic schools and religious schools of all denominations, as well as the families who wish to send their children to them."

Ironically, these state-level amendments purposefully discriminate against religion, making their constitutionality under the federal document an open question. Smith's article explains that while the U.S. Supreme Court has not ruled directly on the application of Blaine amendments to school choice programs, the lower courts are split on the issue.

"[T]he Sixth, Eighth, and Tenth Circuits have all struck down restrictions in public programs that discriminated against students attending religious schools. On the other side of the split, the First Circuit and the Vermont and Maine Supreme Courts have upheld such restrictions."

Despite their prohibitions on direct state support to religious institutions, Blaine amendments have been read by state courts in the same way that the U.S. Supreme Court has ruled on the Establishment Clause. The Arizona Supreme Court, for example, upheld that state's program because "[t]he ESA does not result in an appropriation of public money to encourage the preference of one religion over another, or religion per se over no religion. Any aid to religious schools would be a result of the genuine and independent private choices of the parents." The defining characteristic of ESAs—that parents can use the accounts for many different educational expenses—led that court to uphold ESAs although it had previously found vouchers unconstitutional under the same provision. An ESA, the court explained, "does not require any student to be enrolled in a private school, much less a 'sectarian' private school."

The Nevada Supreme Court was crystal clear on the question of constitutionality in a recent ruling on that state's plan, explaining that funds deposited into an ESA "are no longer 'public funds' but are instead the private funds of the individual parent who established the account." Using those funds to pay tuition at a religious school, the court said, does not violate Nevada's Blaine amendment.

The two Blaine amendments in the Texas Constitution do not raise constitutional concerns beyond those addressed in Arizona and Nevada, or by the U.S. Supreme Court. As long as a plan is neutral with respect to religion, the fact that a parent may choose to use public funds for tuition at a religious school would not violate the Texas Constitution.

Some opponents of school choice oppose these programs on ideological grounds. Constitutional claims are merely the vehicle through which choice programs are challenged in court when a legislative debate has been lost. If the Texas Legislature passes an ESA bill, proponents should not be surprised if a constitutional challenge is close behind.

Nor should opponents be surprised if the plan is upheld.

ARTICLE QUESTIONS

1) How do you feel about ESAs? Would you have taken advantage of this program when you were in high school?
2) If public money designated for public schools is spent on a student's enrollment in a religious school, does that violate the separation of church and state?

4.3) Protests, Photography, and the First Amendment

TribTalk, November 12, 2015

DEAN GALARO

The U.S. and Texas Constitutions protect free speech, but these protections are limited in some ways. The frequency of protests on college campuses and the rise of phone-based video technology has complicated free speech rights in Texas. In the following article, Dean Galaro, a law student at Southern Methodist University in Dallas, lays out individuals' rights under the Texas Constitution with respect to privacy and free speech.

Galaro argues that Texas courts have accepted a right of privacy but have argued that individuals have this right only in specific instances and may give it up in others (such as when an individual is in an area where privacy is not assumed). When it comes to the taking of pictures at public events, an individual's right to privacy is not guaranteed, even if the photographer (often a member of the media) "coerces" or "embarrasses" an individual. Galaro concludes that there aren't many ways that an individual can limit how he or she is photographed in public under Texas law, so he advises, "Be careful what you do in public."

A much-shared video from the recent student protests at the University of Missouri shows a professor attempting to bar a freelance photographer from taking pictures. Near a temporary tent city on campus bordered by signs warning that the media was not allowed, Melissa Click can be seen in a video shooing away the videographer and calling for "muscle" to remove the media from the students' "safe space." Click has since apologized and resigned her courtesy appointment with Missouri's School of Journalism, though she remains employed with the School of Communications.

This is not the first time protesters have clashed with journalists. Protests can be fraught with tension, and in the heat of the moment amid a swarm of local and national media (to say nothing of citizens with smartphone cameras), the zeal for getting one's message out can get in the way of clear thinking. But the First Amendment that allows protesters to shout their demands also allows cameras to capture the moment.

So what does the law say? In Texas, at least, it is pretty clear: If you're outside doing something in public, other people can take your picture. The U.S. Constitution protects the freedom of expression through the First Amendment. Additionally, the Texas Constitution protects the "liberty to speak, write or publish [one's] opinions on any subject . . . and no law shall ever be passed curtailing the liberty of speech or of the press."

These are powerful protections. Photojournalists and the media at large use these rights to document and disseminate news.

Texas has recognized a common-law right of privacy since 1973, meaning that among courts, it is accepted law even though it is not written into a statute. In Texas, an invasion of privacy must be an intentional intrusion into one's "solitude, seclusion, or private affairs" and "highly offensive to a reasonable person." This means that, unsurprisingly, when one is in a public space, one has left solitude and seclusion behind.

Vaughn v. Drennon, a 2006 appeals case out of Tyler, is illustrative of how this applies. The plaintiff brought a claim against a man who watched her with binoculars in several instances, sometimes while she was inside her home. However, the court pointed out that "[o]ne cannot expect to be entitled to seclusion when standing directly in front of a large window with the blinds open or while outside."

As the U.S. Supreme Court stated in *NAACP v. Claiborne Hardware Co.*, "Speech does not lose its protected character, however, simply because it may embarrass others or coerce them into action." A 1991 appeals case in Corpus Christi upheld a newspaper's use of a photograph from a high school soccer game where one of the player's genitalia was exposed midstride. Such publication was protected by the Texas Constitution because it accurately depicted a public, newsworthy event (even though the newspaper could have used other photographs from the game).

Another Texas court in 2014 specified photography as protected expression. Taking a picture is analogous to "applying pen to paper to create a writing or applying brush to canvas to create a painting." This helps equate journalism with protester expression. Everyone on both sides of the picket line has the freedom to express themselves with mouths and cameras alike.

Apart from the common law, there are statutes that protect against photographing certain subjects. For example, Section 21.15 of the Texas Penal Code prohibits photographing someone in a bathroom or changing room or photographing their "intimate area[s]." The subject must not consent, and the photographer must intend to invade the subject's privacy. However, the caveat is that "intimate area" photography is allowed when such sensitive places are "subject to public view." Let your imagination run wild.

The moral of the story is this: Be careful what you do in public. Student protests have shown themselves to be powerful forces for change, but if we want to live in a place where we can build a tent city to force out unwanted school administrators, we must also accept that our picture might end up on the front page of a newspaper.

ARTICLE QUESTIONS

1) What are some limitations to freedom of speech through public photography in Texas?
2) The author argues, "Be careful what you do in public." What does he mean by this?
3) After reading this passage and the author's advice, will you change your public behavior?

Federalism

Both the American and Texas Revolutions were fought over the principles of liberty, freedom, and self-governance. Texas joined the Union in part for economic stability, but also to obtain better security and resources to develop into a modern state. Having been part of a republic and having fought for that status with the blood of their sons and daughters, Texans were reluctant to give up states' rights. The balance of autonomy and authority was critical, both then and now.

The U.S. government is organized as a federal system, in which all powers are delegated to one national government. This type of centralized organization is referred to as a unitary system, in which governmental authority flows from the top down. Simply put, the central government's authority is supreme. However, state and local governments are granted powers by the federal government and exercise authority unique to them. Federalism is thus a power-sharing arrangement between a central governing authority and its political subunits. In this case, the U.S. federal government is the central authority and the states are the satellite units that orbit around it.

Texas's distrust of the federal government, individualistic culture, and robust sense of sovereignty, stemming from the days of the Republic, have prompted several intergovernmental squabbles over the years. These have included fights over health care funding, environmental regulations, voting, and whether Texas or Washington, D.C., should pay for border security. Politicians aggressively guard the state's rights against encroachment by the federal government. This defense even extends to how Texans celebrate Thanksgiving—for a time, Texas celebrated a different Thanksgiving holiday than the rest of the country, partly out of an ornery sense of pride.

The trouble for Texas (and every other state) is that the design of the American political system allows the federal government to set rules that must be followed by each state. The tension between state politics, national rules, and strings tied to federal funds used by the states complicates the power-sharing arrangement. The issues that give rise to such tensions are often grave. As *Texas Tribune* political reporter Edgar Walter writes, the state's foster care system, which saw the deaths of 144 children in its care, was such a disaster that a federal judge in 2016 ruled that it was "broken" and required Texas to follow federal guidance to fix it. A lawsuit ensued, with the Texas Attorney General's Office claiming that the state should be allowed to fix its own problems. Should the federal government worry about states' rights when children's lives are in jeopardy, or are the principles of federalism so central to the U.S. Constitution that they outweigh any policy issue?

Principles and politics clash frequently in the practice of federalism. The Texas Constitution emphasizes the importance of preserving "local self-government," and long after the Civil War, many Texans are still suspicious of the federal government. Today, the state continues to engage in conflict with the federal government over who is responsible for the lands that border it. As Jim Malewitz of the *Texas Tribune* reports, Texas and the federal government have clashed for more than a century over a parcel of land along Texas's border with Oklahoma in a dispute that could have a powerful effect on Texas's pocketbook.

The refugee crisis that emerged as a result of a civil war in faraway Syria has also become tied up in the debate about federal powers and state authority. The United States accepts a modest number of refugees annually, and a small portion of those people settle in Texas. After a terrorist attack at a mall in California, Texas governor Greg Abbott stated that Texas would no longer accept refugees out of fear of terrorism. Although the terrible attack in California was not committed by refugees and there is low probability that a person will be killed by a terrorist, the governor was firm that Texas would not accept refugees who had been given federal asylum. The debate that resulted forced Texans to ask whether or not they had a moral obligation to help and whether or not the federal government could force such resettlements. Aaron Rippenkroeger, president and CEO of Refugees Services of Texas, an organization that resettles refugees in the Lone Star State, argues for compassion and the extension of a helping hand to these newcomers. If the state turns away such immigrants, Rippenkroeger asks, what does this say about Texas's values?

CHAPTER QUESTIONS

1) What are some of the objections that Texas as a state has to federal intervention or power?
2) In the conflict between state and federal government, when and on what issues should one or the other have a greater say?
3) Do you distinguish between what the state and federal government are supposed to do when you blame or praise a policy outcome?

5.1) Texas Argues It Can Fix Foster Care Without Judge's Oversight

Texas Tribune, November 22, 2016

EDGAR WALTERS

Courts are often asked to determine the proper balance of state and federal government rights and obligations. On one grave issue, the courts stepped in to aid the state's foster care system, which was plagued by mismanagement—with deadly consequences. As reported by the *Texas Tribune*'s Edgar Walters, from 2010 to 2014, 144 children in the state's custody died, with chronic understaffing leading many cases of abuse to go uninvestigated. These deaths prompted a federal judge to rule that the system was "broken" and violated the Fourteenth Amendment, which gives people the right to be free from harm while in the custody of the state. The judge appointed a "special master" to submit recommendations for how to improve the state's foster care system.

Asserting that Texas can better fix its struggling foster care system than the federal government, Attorney General Ken Paxton asked a higher court to block the appointment of the special master and the freeze the court had put on further placements of children in certain foster homes. The attorney general acknowledged that the foster care system needed improvement but claimed that the judge's ruling was too broad and that Texas should have a chance to fix its system before federal intervention. This debate encapsulates the tension between state and federal autonomy. In what situation should the federal government let the states create and change public policy?

Texas' Republican attorney general, faced with a mounting crisis in the state's child welfare system, on Tuesday published a scathing critique of costly, court-ordered reforms meant to improve the conditions of children in the state's long-term foster care system.

Lawyers for the state argued that the court's proposed reforms—first ordered by a federal district judge, then laid out by a pair of "special masters" hired, against the state's wishes, on Texas' dime—are an example of egregious federal overreach.

The move puts the state's Republican leaders in a delicate position: While they concede that the foster care system's underlying problems are a pressing matter, they argue it's one they can address on their own. That's despite the fact that the system has been broken—and worsening—for years under their tenure.

In a new legal filing on Tuesday, part of the long-running class-action lawsuit against Gov. Greg Abbott and the child welfare system writ large, Texas Attorney General Ken Paxton's office objected to the special masters' recommendations, calling them "over-broad" and saying there is no proof they will work. The special masters have recommended lowering caseloads for child welfare workers and hiring more of them to pick up the slack.

Those recommendations were among those broadly outlined by U.S. District Judge Janis Jack of Corpus Christi, who wrote in a December 2015 opinion that the state's long-term foster care system had violated children's constitutional right to be free from an unreasonable risk of harm. Children in the state's current system, she wrote, "often age out of care more damaged than when they entered."

Lawyers for the state, though acknowledging that the foster care system has room for improvement, disputed Jack's ruling, writing in Tuesday's filing that the alleged constitutional violations "are unsupported by reliable expert testimony or other competent, admissible evidence." They argue Jack's findings were "too vague" to support the remedies recommended by special masters.

The children's rights advocates suing the state expressed dismay with the latest filing.

"Sadly, the state wants to keep fighting, rather than start fixing its system for these children," Paul Yetter, a lead attorney on the case, wrote in an email.

Texas leaders have said they are fully capable of reforming the state's child welfare system on their own, without any meddling from the federal judicial system.

Abbott, Lt. Gov. Dan Patrick and House Speaker Joe Straus have all vowed to take up a reform-minded agenda when state lawmakers convene in Austin in 2017. Hank Whitman, the newly appointed head of the Department of Family and Protective Services, which oversees child welfare, has asked lawmakers for funding to hire 550 additional investigators and offer significant pay raises to front-line caseworkers.

"It's unfortunate and disappointing that millions of dollars that could have gone to serving youth in the Texas foster care system and hiring more caseworkers will now be spent towards the legally baseless special master process," an Abbott spokesman told *The Texas Tribune* in May. The two special masters were expected to be paid $345 an hour over a six-month period.

In previous filings, state officials conceded there was room for improvement in Texas foster care. Still, they said the system's failings did not rise to the level of civil rights violations, arguing the shortcomings were not enough to "shock the conscience."

"It is true that Texas' foster care system needs improvement in certain areas," lawyers for the state wrote in their previous appeal. "But the same could be said of most states' foster care systems."

ARTICLE QUESTIONS

1) What was the cause of the federal court's judgment that the state's foster care system was broken?
2) In your opinion, should Texas have had a chance to fix its system, or should it have relied on federal assistance?
3) When principles of states' rights conflict with life and death issues, which principle do you think should predominate?

5.2) George P. Bush Wades into Red River Fight with Feds

Texas Tribune, December 1, 2016

JIM MALEWITZ

Famed Texas historian T. R. Ferhenbach has argued that Texas has been at war over her borders since birth. *Texas Tribune* reporter Jim Malewitz updates this story with a contemporary twist: in 2015, the state, spearheaded by Land Commissioner George P. Bush (the son of Jeb Bush and grandson of George H. W. Bush), joined a lawsuit initiated by families living along the Red River against the federal Bureau of Land Management (BLM), which had taken control of a 116-mile strip of land along the Texas–Oklahoma border. The BLM, the federal office charged with overseeing public lands and mineral rights owned by the U.S. government, relied on an act of Congress and a settled court case to take control of the 116-mile strip. In the lawsuit, Bush argued that the federal government was threatening mineral rights managed by the office. No one had yet drilled for oil or gas along this strip of land, but should Texas do so, the proceeds of such exploration could swell the state's coffers—a particularly pressing concern, given that revenues from Texas's General Land Office are funneled into the state's Permanent School Fund to help finance public schools. Texas's governor chimed in on the lawsuit as well, supporting the state's cause with fiery comments. The state has expressed the hope for a proactive and speedy end to the dispute.

George P. Bush is wading into a battle with the federal government over land along the Texas side of the Red River.

The land commissioner on Tuesday asked to join seven North Texas families in a federal lawsuit that accuses the U.S. Bureau of Land Management of perpetuating an "arbitrary seizure" of land along a 116-mile strip of the river, whose changing course has fueled a century's worth of property disputes along the state's border with Oklahoma.

Bush is the latest big-name Republican seeking standing in the case, filed last month in the U.S. District Court for the Northern District of Texas. Attorney General Ken Paxton has also asked to join, and lawyers from the Texas Public Policy Foundation, the state's most influential conservative think tank, are representing the families at no cost.

Wichita, Clay and Wilbarger counties have also signed onto the suit, along with Clay County Sheriff Kenneth Lemons Jr.

Bush argues the federal bureau is threatening mineral rights managed by his General Land Office. The Texas agency initially owned the rights to about 78 acres along the river in Wilbarger County, which expanded to about 113 acres due to the river's gradual move northward, according to court filings. The federal government is claiming ownership of about 35 of those acres, Bush argues.

Royalties from any future development of those minerals would flow to the state's Permanent School Fund, which provides money for state schools.

No one has drilled for oil or gas on the disputed stretch of land, which represents just a sliver of the 13 million acres of mineral rights the land office manages statewide. But Bush argues that the Obama administration's plans—despite their unique circumstances—threaten Texas' entire oil and gas portfolio.

"We had no other option," he said in an interview. "From our standpoint, it's a dangerous slippery slope."

The Bureau of Land Management, which oversees millions of acres of public land and minerals, has said it "remains committed to working with" the Red River community through its planning process.

"We share the interest of all parties in clarifying ownership and identifying appropriate management alternatives," spokesman Paul McGuire said last month.

The lawsuit came about 19 months after the dispute first grabbed national headlines and sparked fiery comments from Texas leaders, including Gov. Greg Abbott, who says he supports landowners in their fight.

Questions have swirled near the stretch of the river since December 2013, when bureau representatives arrived in North Texas to discuss updates to its resource management plans in Kansas, Oklahoma and Texas—specifically how the land would be used for the next 15 to 20 years.

The area includes about 90,000 acres along the Red River that the agency considers public land, with perhaps a third of it on the Texas side.

The agency has said its claim comes from a 1923 U.S. Supreme Court decision that delineated the boundaries between Texas and Oklahoma and assigned the feds the patches in between.

But Texans have long managed swaths of that area. They hold deeds to the land and have diligently paid their local taxes. The bureau has not fully surveyed the area, so it is not clear precisely where the public boundary lines intersect with private lands.

Bush and other Texas officials accuse the feds of poorly articulating their claim to the river stretch. The land office used a bureau map published in June 2014 to estimate that 35 of its mineral acres were threatened.

The federal bureau plans to finalize the management scheme by 2018 at the earliest, frustrating residents who want a resolution now.

It has not decided whether it will close off parts of the land or make it open to the public. But since few stretches are accessible without crossing onto indisputable private property, the most likely option would involve selling off the land.

Federal officials have said they understand why Red River dwellers are concerned, but they have a strict responsibility to manage taxpayer resources—in this case, the land.

Meanwhile, Texans in Congress are trying to hammer out a solution, led by U.S. Rep. Mac Thornberry, R-Clarendon, and Sen. John Cornyn.

Their proposal, which cleared a House committee in September, would require surveys of the entire disputed stretch and prevent any contested lands from being included in the federal resource management plan, among other provisions.

Bush called a fix in Washington a "more proactive" way to lift the cloud over the disputed land but said Texas wasn't willing to wait any longer.

"We're not leaving it to chance, and we're making clear our intent to resolve it once and for all," he said.

ARTICLE QUESTIONS

1) Should the federal government be able to appropriate Texas lands? Under what conditions?

2) The article describes one solution to the issue—excluding Texas land from federal management—do you believe this will work?

3) Is the federal government overstepping its role in this land dispute issue? What is the proper balance of authority in cases like this?

5.3) Texans Will Not Abandon Refugees in Their Hour of Need

TribTalk, October 5, 2016

AARON RIPPENKROEGER

The bloody civil war that broke out in Syria in 2011 has to date seen nearly half a million people killed and precipitated a refugee crisis involving millions of people. This crisis not only destabilized the Middle East but also had effects on the Lone Star State. The United States accepts a modest number of refugees (about 10,000 annually), and Texas only a fraction of that, but the inflow of Syrian refugees in 2016 became part of the tug of war between the federal government and Texas. In that year, Governor Greg Abbott claimed that the state would not accept refugees from Syria because of fears of terrorism within Texas's borders. He stated that the refugee system was "broken and flawed" in a letter to the federal Office of Refugee Resettlement.

Aaron Rippenkroeger, president and CEO of Refugees Services of Texas, in the following article challenges the governor's view and advocates for compassion for refugees and an embrace of the value of inclusion. Rippenkroeger pushes back against the argument that refugees are dangerous, calling such assertions "inaccurate and irresponsible political rhetoric." Almost none of the refugees have ever been charged with terrorism, the vetting process is secure and stringent, and the state government has virtually no say in who resettles where, since such decisions are handled by private organizations, he observes. Furthermore, stoking fear and resentment is not the Texas spirit, according to Rippenkroeger—just another political ploy to play to the governor's political base.

At a time when the nation and the world need the state of Texas to help welcome some of the most vulnerable populations on Earth, the state has chosen to shut its administration's door on refugees, survivors of human trafficking, military veterans with special immigrant visas, Cuban entrants and approved asylees, among others.

The decision on Sept. 30 by Gov. Greg Abbott to withdraw Texas from its role in the nation's refugee resettlement program after nearly 40 years of participation is dangerous, divisive and dehumanizing, and it panders to the most xenophobic tendencies of a small sliver of Americans.

But Texans know this truth as well as anyone on Earth: Nothing great is ever achieved by fear and by thinking small.

And, rest assured, the thousands of compassionate Texans who have helped resettle refugees for over four decades in the Lone Star State—citizen volunteers, people of faith, community groups and social service professionals—will not abandon them in their hour of need.

For the past month, state officials have regretfully ignored the voices of thousands of Texans from all walks of life who have pleaded that they not turn their backs on refugees, survivors of human trafficking, and other vulnerable people—the voices of Texas clergy from every faith background, volunteers from all political parties and residents of small towns and big cities across the state who have opened their hearts to welcome refugees fleeing violence and oppression and been forever changed through this act of compassion.

As we witness the blood of hundreds of innocent women and children spilled in the streets of Aleppo, Syria, and in villages across the Middle East—forcing the world's largest migration on record and the worst humanitarian crisis since the Second World War—Texas' refugee resettlement program is needed now more than ever.

Texas has built one of the most successful refugee integration programs in all the world—the result of a public-private partnership that has included a dedicated, devoted and hard-working group of colleagues employed by the state of Texas; professional liaisons at school districts and county health departments across Texas; partners employed by locally based nonprofit agencies with assistance from national nonprofit agencies; and partners at the federal level, including employees of the U.S. Department of State and the U.S. Department of Health and Human Services.

This relatively small but effective group of humanitarian professionals rely on a much larger group of citizen volunteers—many of whom are called by their faith to assist the needy and vulnerable—to help welcome families at airports and assist them with modest accommodations while professional case workers help the children enroll in school, get the parents enrolled in English classes, address any medical issues and join the U.S. workforce in a remarkably short period of time.

This partnership has consistently resulted in the fastest and highest levels of self-sufficiency for refugee families in the nation and serves as an international model of success. Within five years, the vast majority of these populations arriving in Texas become thriving, proud, tax-paying Texans and U.S. citizens.

Our work will continue despite the state's wrong-hearted decision. But it will not be easy to reconstruct a service infrastructure for these vulnerable groups that took nearly 40 years to build.

Recent announcements would have Texans believe that refugees are dangerous. This is inaccurate and irresponsible political rhetoric. It is tragic that refugees who have come to America seeking safety and freedom are being targeted by politicians based on the countries from which they have fled. Such sentiments are un-American and un-Texan.

We know who refugees are. The U.S. handpicks the most vulnerable families and individuals, who then undergo 18 to 24 months of rigorous security vetting before they are admitted. Most are coming to be reunited with family members who already live here. All refugees resettled in Texas and the United States undergo rigorous screenings by the Department of Homeland Security, the FBI, the Department of Defense and multiple intelligence agencies—screenings that include biometric checks, forensic tests, medical screenings and in-person interviews.

Texas' decision chooses to ignore the already stringent vetting requirement for refugees—far and away more rigorous than for anyone else coming to the United States. Texas officials would never hold themselves to the standard that they appear to require of national security officials when it comes to screening refugees—and they would never be able to personally guarantee that no American-born resident of Texas poses a security threat to other Texans.

Texas' public-private refugee partnership, recently falsely described by Abbott as "broken and flawed," must now be converted to an initiative operated not by our devoted public colleagues at the Texas Health and Human Services Department but by a private civil society model that humanitarian professionals will work with local communities to establish. Words cannot express our appreciation to the government employees across Texas who have devoted their careers to serving those so vulnerable—many of whom may now be reassigned or forced to seek new employment.

Values define us as Texans. They have shaped us from birth. And, most importantly, they are the threads that connect us, no matter our differences in appearance, religion or country of origin. Refugees and others who have been welcomed in Texas first want to be safe and secure. Then, like all Americans, they want acceptance and opportunity—the chance to thrive in freedom.

The large and compassionate refugee service community in Texas will not forsake them—even if our state does.

ARTICLE QUESTIONS

1) Was the governor posturing politically in his decision to block refugees from entering Texas, or is there a genuine concern that terrorism will be introduced to Texas via refugee resettlement?
2) What are the reasons outlined by the author that Texans should not be concerned about terrorism by refugees?
3) Is the current screening process sufficiently rigorous to limit any potential threat of terrorism?
4) If Texas refuses to resettle refugees, should the federal government relent, or should federal edicts be paramount?

Chapter 6

Local Government

The battle over what local government can and cannot control is central to the concerns embedded in the Texas Constitution. Much of the conflict between state and local authorities has played out as the Texas legislature has sought to limit local government's ability to establish policy on a range of issues, including social policy and financial autonomy. Municipal governments in Texas are granted broad authority but also fenced in by state authority, a limitation sanctified by the Texas Supreme Court in the early twentieth century. Cities are given some autonomy to act but are still tethered to the laws of the state.

Local government is often viewed as the lowest tier of government, yet the actions they take have some of the most profound effects on the daily lives of Texans. The years following World War II saw a boom in Texas's residential population that has continued through the present day. While Texas is often thought of as a rural state, an expansive land crossing forests, prairies, deserts, and mountains, in truth it is largely urban. More than 80 percent of the Lone Star State's population growth over the past fifty years has been in urban areas, with Texas now boasting two of the nation's five largest metropolitan regions. As demand for services has increased rapidly, local governments have expanded their efforts in the areas of public safety (fire and police), sanitation, maintenance of roads, and access to recreational facilities.

As local governments grow, they demand more authority to maintain and nurture that growth, especially by seeking new revenue sources. Issues such as city "sprawl," annexation, and the growth of smaller subgovernments produce friction as cities balance rising demand for services and cries from taxpayers about the strain on their wallets. State and local governments share the costs of many local amenities, but the balance of their responsibility is often in dispute. Local financing of state government operations is a major driver of these disagreements, according to Joel Nihlean of the Texas Association of Counties. State services are often technically provided by counties—for instance, up to 50 percent of a county's budget may go toward carrying out state policies, and counties cover more than 75 percent of the cost of the judicial system. The state has a major say in how these services are provided (by setting rules), but counties are on the hook for the bill.

Governor Greg Abbott has warned of the risk of Texas becoming "California-ized," with a patchwork of local rules and regulations that threaten to undermine state authority and hinder consistent economic progress. In response, Republicans in recent legislative sessions have prohibited local governments from enacting a host of policies, including bans on the use of plastic bags, the establishment of tree-trimming guidelines and transgender bathrooms, and purchases of red-light cameras. *City Journal* writer Mark Pulliam amplifies the governor's claim in his argument that the "Texas model" of low spending and low taxes has been undone by "blue" (Democratic) cities with more liberal voters and the economic problems associated with the policies they choose. Is this partisan divide between city and state responsible for economic sluggishness?

Representative Matt Rinaldi from Irving argues that the relationship between state and local government in which local governments are "creatures" of state government and can be controlled by state policy is important to the preservation of individual rights under the U.S. and Texas constitutions. Rinaldi, a Republican member of the Texas House and member of the conservative Freedom Caucus, champions local government control, but only to a point. He quotes President Reagan's edict that "government is best which remains closest to the people" but stresses the limitations of such government. When issues of local control and liberty conflict, Rinaldi claims, liberty should trump local control.

The Texas Municipal League, which represents local governments, has argued that no other state has proposed such sweeping restrictions on local governments seeking to shape policy in their communities. From bans on local tree ordinances to a statewide ban on texting while driving, the legislature has severely limited the ability of local government to legislate on some policies. Texans, it seems, don't mind this arrangement, even if it takes away from their ability to influence policy at the local level. When asked in surveys about their preferences regarding state policies overriding local control, Texans strongly supported state oversight.

Beyond their clash with the state government, local governments also confront other local problems at several critical points, with cities being handicapped by decisions made by past administrations or forces beyond their control. Some Texas cities are facing municipal bankruptcy as they confront spiraling pension debts. The four largest Texas cities alone owe more than $22 billion in fire, police, and municipal employee pensions. Because the state has oversight over local pension deals, city officials need to get permission from the legislature to make changes to such plans, as well as local buy in. Failing to address this problem will hurt Texas cities' financial ratings and damage city retirees' retirement funds.

CHAPTER QUESTIONS

1) Should local governments have no, some, or a complete say over what policies they enact?
2) On what issues is there friction between local and state control, and why?
3) Why are Texans who generally favor local control willing to let the state legislature write laws that supersede local governments' authority?
4) Texans have traditionally embraced local government. Where does the Texas public stand on state versus local control?

6.1) Red State, Blue Cities

City Journal, 2016

MARK PULLIAM

Legendary American writer John Steinbeck claimed that Texas had a tightly knit and cohesive identity. But decades later, a political divide has emerged among Lone Star State residents and politicians, creating ideological and policy friction. Conservative author Mark Pulliam of *City Journal* poses an important question: As Texas grows and becomes more urban, can it preserve the small-government identity that has been a symbol and signature of the state's success? Pulliam charts a useful history of the state's transition to solidly Republican rule, cataloguing the frequent floggings Democrats have taken at the ballot box. He also examines recent trends that may unravel Republican electoral dominance, including migration to urban areas by younger residents, who are more likely to be politically liberal.

Pulliam pins the responsibility for several economic crises facing local governments—out-of-control spending, expanding pension liabilities, and booming property tax burdens—on this liberal shift. Texas cities' move toward a "blue" orientation has also led to bans on plastic bags, measures mandating transgender restrooms, higher minimum wages, and "green energy" mandates. Pulliam is unconvinced that these liberal policies will be able to sustain Texas's strong economy in the future. His analysis cuts to the core of the debate about state–city relations: the state has an interest in the economic well-being and rights of all Texans, while cities focus on a smaller group of residents. The "Texas model" is one of low taxes and low spending, and Pulliam concludes that the cities must adhere to this model or else the state's economic engine will slow.

John Steinbeck once called Texas "a mystique closely approximating a religion"—and today, the Lone Star State remains full of myth, mystery, and paradox. Yet, as Steinbeck also noted, "Texas has a tight cohesiveness perhaps stronger than any other section of America." This strong sense of place and identity owes to Texas's distinctive origins and the hardy character of the migrants it attracts.

Texas's booming economy has produced rapid population growth, much of it in the form of migration from other states. Most new arrivals have settled in Texas's large and burgeoning cities, which, despite Texas's reputation as a red state, lean increasingly blue. As a result, Republican governor Greg Abbott warns that Texas runs the risk of being "California-ized." As Texas becomes ever more populous and urban, preserving the small-government identity that has proved vital to its prosperity and growth will pose a challenge. Will the "Texas model" become a victim of its own success?

Taking pride in a unique history, Texans value independence, freedom, and self-reliance, perhaps more than residents of any other state. Texas schoolchildren still learn about the Alamo and memorize Colonel William Barret Travis's "Victory or Death" letter. To this day, proud Texans celebrate General Sam Houston's triumph at the Battle of San Jacinto in 1836 and revel in the state's frontier heritage, with sports teams named Cowboys, Spurs, Rangers, Mavericks, and Longhorns. The state's official structures reflect this prideful attitude. Texas's magnificent red granite capitol building in Austin is taller than the U.S. Capitol in Washington; the San Jacinto Monument, near Houston, reaches higher than the Washington Monument. No other state fought for and won its independence as a sovereign republic or commands such loyalty among its residents. From El Paso to Beaumont, Amarillo to Brownsville, throughout the 268,000 square miles of this vast state, Texans—now numbering 27 million—devotedly display, and pledge allegiance to, their state flag.

New arrivals eagerly embrace Texas's customs and traditions. At the Broken Spoke, Austin's famed honkytonk, newcomers (including hipsters) crowd the dance floor, learning the two-step. Patrons line up for hours to enjoy authentic brisket, a Texas culinary staple, at Austin's Franklin Barbecue. The attitude of many recent transplants is reflected in the popular expression, "I wasn't born in Texas, but I got here as soon as I could!" Texans can display an almost cult-like camaraderie.

Texas has reinvented itself many times. In the nineteenth century, waves of migrants—Germans, Swedes, Czechs, and distressed immigrants from other states—settled the land, often leaving behind signs reading, "Gone to Texas." Like their Texan antecedents, twentieth-century opportunity-seekers—often midwesterners fleeing the Rust Belt—brought hardy values with them. Texas has always offered a fresh start to stubborn souls unwilling to accept defeat.

The state's economy has changed dramatically through the years. An early focus on cattle and agriculture gave way to the cyclical booms and busts of oil and gas production following the Spindletop gusher in 1901. (See "Texas Flood.") By the late twentieth century, Texas had also developed a richly diversified manufacturing and technology economy. Texas has a GDP of $1.6 trillion (bigger than Mexico's and just behind Canada's) and more exports than any other state (and more *technology* exports than California). Texas has survived severe droughts, the deadliest natural disaster in U.S. history (the 1900 Galveston hurricane), wildly fluctuating oil prices, the late 1980s savings and loan collapse, the bursting of the high-tech bubble in 2000, and the Enron scandal in 2001, the largest-ever corporate bankruptcy up to that time.

The nation regards Texas, and Texans regard themselves, as distinctly conservative—and justly so. Riding the Tea Party wave in 2009, then-governor Rick Perry casually mentioned the possibility of secession. National commentators were appalled, and some even accused the governor of treason—but Perry's popularity soared in Texas, where residents regarded the secession comment not as a gaffe but as an admirable statement of principle. In 2010, fresh on the heels of his anti-Washington manifesto, *Fed Up!*, Perry won reelection in a landslide, trouncing his Republican primary opponent, moderate U.S. senator Kay Bailey Hutchison, by more than 20 points.

Second only to California in population, Texas boasts two Republicans in the U.S. Senate, a delegation to the House of Representatives tilted in favor of the GOP by a lopsided 25 to 11 margin, Republican supermajorities in both houses of the state legislature, and a Republican governor. For the past two decades, every statewide elected official in Texas—including all nine justices on the Texas Supreme Court—has been a Republican. In 2012, Texans supported Mitt Romney over Barack Obama by nearly 16 points, a difference of more than 1.2 million votes. Texas hasn't voted for a Democratic presidential candidate since narrowly going for Jimmy Carter in 1976.

Texas wasn't always so Republican. For nearly a century following the Civil War—as elsewhere in the formerly Confederate South—it was solidly Democratic. The twentieth-century political realignment in Texas generally tracked the experience of other Southern states (though Barry Goldwater did not carry Texas in 1964) and had much to do with the liberal drift of the national Democratic Party during the 1960s. But Texas's rightward shift really got going in the 1970s, amid a tsunami of migration that more than doubled the state's population from 1970 to 2010. During his 14-year tenure as governor—a Texas record— Perry became a national figure and solidified GOP control over the state. His conservative swagger came to epitomize Texas politics.

With Perry gone, and a continuing influx of residents fleeing blue states such as California, Texas Democrats had high hopes for reversing their electoral misfortunes in 2014—but they failed miserably. The George Soros–funded Battleground Texas campaign spent $3.4 million, to little electoral effect. Republican Greg Abbott crushed Democrat Wendy Davis by more than 20 points in the governor's race. In the lieutenant governor's race, conservative state senator and former talk-radio host Dan Patrick defeated state senator Leticia Van de Putte by a similar margin. Critics of the outspoken Patrick had predicted his defeat in the general election, following an unusually acrimonious GOP primary and runoff. His lopsided victory over a Hispanic woman was particularly noteworthy because, in addition to being a white male, he emphasized border control, pledged to abolish sanctuary cities, and opposed in-state tuition for illegal immigrants. Exit polls showed Patrick getting 46 percent of the Hispanic vote overall and actually beating Van de Putte 53 percent to 46 percent among Hispanic men. He even outperformed Abbott among Hispanics, though Abbott ran Spanish-language campaign ads emphasizing his marriage to a Latina. The results demonstrate the deeply ingrained conservative culture in Texas, even among ethnic minorities. Hispanics were evidently swayed by Patrick's pro-life message, advocacy of school choice, and opposition to taxes—all GOP mainstays.

Winning elections doesn't necessarily pay off in policy victories—just ask the Republican-controlled Congress in Washington—but it has in Texas, where a Reconstruction-era constitution minimizes government power. The state's conservative politics consistently translate into conservative policies: no state income tax or state-imposed property tax, below-average taxes overall, minimal regulation, right-to-work laws, limited collective bargaining rights for public employees, comprehensive tort-reform legislation, relatively low state government spending per capita, a part-time legislature that meets every other year, and—at least in recent decades—business-friendly court rulings. Texas even has a constitutional cap on statewide government spending increases, limiting them to the estimated rate of economic growth.

Statewide policies—combined with abundant oil and gas reserves—have created a booming Texas economy in recent decades, with lots of jobs, affordable homes, and inexpensive electricity. Perry called it the "Texas Miracle." Paul Krugman and other liberal pundits demurred, but in 2013, Austin-based journalist Erica Grieder wrote a book-length defense of Texas's economic performance: *Big, Hot, Cheap, and Right: What America Can Learn from the Strange Genius of Texas*. Often a harsh critic of conservative policies, Grieder nonetheless concluded that the Texas model—low taxes, low spending, and low regulation—works. "[T]he bluster about how the nation has nothing to learn from Texas is just willfully obtuse," she wrote, "almost prima facie absurd. . . . The Texas model has clearly and incontrovertibly worked."

As the post-tech-crash recession wracked most of the U.S. during the opening years of the twenty-first century, Texas offered opportunity, employment, and a stable housing market, and Americans flocked to the state. The roaring economy and attractive business climate also lured employers from other states (especially Democrat-dominated California) to relocate their operations here. Texas weathered the financial crisis and subsequent downturn better than any other state, creating 40 percent of all U.S. civilian jobs during the past eight years. Combined with expansion of local businesses and the arrival of job-seeking refugees from economically distressed blue states, Texas's population grew by more than 4 million between 2000 and 2010, the most of any state. Its remarkable growth enabled it to gain four additional House seats in the last redistricting. Not all the population expansion was due to newcomers: Texas has the second-highest birthrate in the country, after Utah.

California and Texas, the nation's two largest states, stand at opposite poles of the political spectrum—and their recent population fortunes have diverged as well. During the same period, California's population grew at less than half the Texas rate, and—in a stunning reversal of long-standing trends—actually experienced a net loss in domestic migration numbers, with more people leaving than arriving from other states. California's meager population growth was fueled entirely by domestic births and foreign immigration.

Most of Texas's new residents (only a portion of whom come from California) have settled in its growing, vibrant metro areas. Urbanization is a relatively new phenomenon here. As recently as the mid-1940s, the state was sparsely populated and predominantly rural. Since the end of World War II, however, Texas's population has nearly quadrupled—the introduction of affordable air conditioning helped—and shifted overwhelmingly to metropolitan areas. Indeed, Texas is now one of the most heavily urbanized states, with 85 percent of its residents living in or near cities. As *Texas Monthly* ("the national magazine of Texas") recently reflected, while Texas's "rural population of 3.8 million is still the country's largest, we are, for the most part, a bunch of city folk." Texas is now home to three of the nation's ten largest cities—Houston (fourth), San Antonio (seventh), and Dallas (ninth). Those metropolitan areas, along with tech hub Austin (11th), are among the most dynamic and rapidly expanding cities in America. All four enjoyed double-digit job growth from 2010 through 2014, well above the national average. *Forbes* recently named all four among its top ten "Cities of the Future," and urban demographer Joel Kotkin included them in his ten cities "most likely to boom over the next 10 years." The cities are large and, for the most part, increasingly diverse. With Texas's ample open space, the surrounding suburbs extend like the outsize cattle ranches of yore.

People still move to the Lone Star State primarily for opportunity (jobs) and land (affordable homes). Many young families settle in suburbs surrounding the major cities, which—as in the case of Williamson County outside Austin, Montgomery County outside Houston, and Collin County outside Dallas—are solidly red. The most significant demographic factor among the recent arrivals, though, is arguably not their state of origin (which varies over time), or race, or ethnicity, but their age. Census data indicate that young people aged 25 to 34 make most moves. And these millennials, coming to Texas in droves, exhibit political attitudes and voting patterns strikingly different—i.e., more liberal—from those of most Texans. Recent trends in municipal governance reflect this shift.

Spending is getting out of whack, for starters. Among the nation's largest states, Texas trails only New York in local government debt per capita. Houston, Texas's largest city, dramatically illustrates how a thriving city has let its cost structure grow out of control. No longer just an oil town, Houston has become a sprawling behemoth, with more than 2.2 million residents, a bustling deepwater port, NASA's Johnson Space Center,

and more Fortune 500 corporate headquarters than any city except New York. The city's industrial base is broad and varied. Between 2000 and 2010, the Houston metropolitan area added more people than any other U.S. metropolitan area. The 1.2 million new arrivals included some 250,000 evacuees from New Orleans fleeing Hurricane Katrina in 2005 (about 100,000 of whom remained in Houston) and 400,000 foreign-born immigrants, an influx exceeded only in New York. According to a Rice University study, Houston—not New York, Los Angeles, or Miami—is the most racially and ethnically diverse city in America. Though not as heavily Latino as San Antonio or El Paso, Houston is home to more Hispanics than any American city other than Los Angeles and New York.

Yet for all its success, Houston faces crippling unfunded pension liabilities, a result of its mayors' obeisance to unionized public employees. On December 31, 2015, the latest date allowed by law, Houston restated its unfunded pension liability for city employees from $1.2 billion to $5.6 billion—a nearly fivefold increase. Houston's actual liability is even higher—it's closer to $7.7 billion—if retiree health care and outstanding pension bonds are included. To make matters worse, Rice University's John Diamond has stated that the city's 8 percent assumed rate of return is too high; using a more realistic rate, the city's unfunded liability could be $10 billion, almost twice the city's annual budget and dangerously close to the city's net worth. That, on top of $3.3 billion in general-obligation debt coming due, sharply falling oil prices, and a ratings downgrade by Moody's, has cast a shadow on Houston's future.

Worse still, reform doesn't look likely in the near future, since Houston voters, in last yea.'s mayoral election, elected the candidate pledged to preserve the status quo: Sylvester Turner, a progressive Democrat who ran with strong government-union backing. Turner narrowly prevailed over Bill King, who had run on a plan to institute a defined-contribution pension plan for new government employees. Turner will have a hard time providing basic city services—from fixing potholes to maintaining public safety—in the face of an impending budgetary calamity.

The story of Houston's pension shortfall, a nearly inevitable feature of the unaffordable defined-benefit plans no longer used in the private sector, is depressingly familiar: politically powerful public employees manage to elect friendly politicians, who then stealthily grant them inadequately funded, overly generous guaranteed pensions that impose staggering liabilities on taxpayers. Local elected officials (with the complicity of hired-gun actuaries) try to minimize and obfuscate the magnitude of these liabilities through accounting gimmicks and rosy projections regarding future investment returns. Ultimately, the extent of the underfunding gets exposed, but usually long after the responsible officials have left office. Taxpayers are left facing sharp tax hikes or cuts in municipal services, or both. In extreme cases, as in Detroit, San Bernardino, and Stockton, cities are forced to file for bankruptcy under Chapter 9.

In Texas, urban fiscal problems aren't confined to Houston. Dallas faces crippling unfunded pension liabilities, estimated at $5 billion for its public-safety retirement system. The problem arose thanks in part to gold-plated benefits enacted more than two decades ago that allow the city's police and fire personnel to start collecting pensions after 20 years on the job, even while they continue working and earning a guaranteed return of 8 percent or more on their pension money. The city faces other fiscal woes related to employee pay. Three years ago, Dallas officials restored so-called step-pay increases—automatic annual pay hikes based on years of service—to police and fire workers during negotiations with the union. (Though Texas doesn't officially have collective bargaining for public employees, city officials can allow unions to bargain with them through a process known as "meet and confer.") The weight of those extra pay increases is helping to crimp the city's budget as the Texas economy slows. The city also faces additional costs because last year, it passed a $10.37 minimum wage that it requires city contractors to pay their workers. Prompted mainly by the growing crisis in the city's pension fund and other fiscal concerns, both S&P and Moody's downgraded the city's credit rating last fall.

Further, in the guise of "local control," municipal elected officials in Texas have increasingly been adopting progressive ordinances on issues that would normally be subject to state regulation (if at all). For example, Austin and about a dozen other cities passed a ban on plastic bags at grocery stores; the city of Denton banned fracking within city limits; Houston and Dallas adopted (and voters in Houston then repealed) measures mandating transgender restrooms; other Texas cities have mandated a higher minimum wage for their employees and contractors than state law requires; Austin's city-owned electric utility has implemented "green energy" mandates—and so on. Austin—seemingly eager to become the San Francisco of the Southwest—recently enacted a "fair chance" ordinance that would forbid employers to ask applicants about prior criminal convictions. Governor Abbott has condemned these measures as "a patchwork quilt of bans and rules and regulations that are eroding the Texas model." Last year, the Texas legislature overrode the local ban on fracking; Abbott favors a categorical prohibition of such measures.

Proponents of ad hoc local regulations contend that conservative principles support experimentation and innovation by Texas's cities, using the analogy of "states' rights" in our federal system—but cities, it's important to remember, are creatures of state law. Abbott's goal to rein in Texas's unruly local governments faces massive resistance from the Texas Municipal League, a powerful lobbying organization representing the interests of 1,100 Texas towns and cities that employs more lobbyists in Austin than any other trade association. The irony is that local Texas governments use copious amounts of taxpayer money—which finances TML—to lobby the state legislature to permit them to impose more taxes and regulations. State senator Konni Burton, a Tea Party favorite from Fort Worth, has proposed legislation to bar the use of taxpayer funds for lobbying purposes.

While the state legislature lacks the constitutional authority to levy income or property taxes, local governments in Texas also impose one of the nation's heaviest property-tax burdens. The Texas comptroller recently reported that state property taxes are rising 2.5 times faster than median family income. Cities are extending boundaries to expand their property-tax base, plundering the more affluent surrounding suburbs. A recent study by WalletHub estimated that Texas homeowners pay, on average, a real-estate-tax rate equal to 1.93 percent of a value of a home, the fifth-highest rate among states. Perhaps most startlingly, Texas is way out of step with most Republican-leaning states. Thanks to high property-tax rates in cities and suburbs, Texas taxes property like a Democratic state, the study found.

Abbott is right, then, to worry that Texas's cities are drifting from the state model of low taxes, low spending, and low regulation—especially since liberal advocates at the local level seem more motivated than conservatives. Liberal activists in Texas gravitate to local government because they're effectively shut out of state government and national politics. Local elected officials have some advantages: they usually serve on a full-time basis, year-round, unlike state legislators, who meet just 140 days every other year. Even the position of lieutenant governor—thought to be more powerful than the governor—is a part-time job, paying just $7,200 annually. Moreover, compared with the state legislature, where voting districts are huge and campaign costs imposing, it's easier to win election to a city council, county board, or school district. And, as James Madison noted in *Federalist* 10, the influence of "factions" (his term for what we would now call special-interest groups) is greater in smaller governmental units than in larger ones. Public employees are an especially potent political force.

Simultaneously, many Republicans in Texas have become complacent. Content with their domination of state government, they pay too little attention to the mischief occurring in Texas's cities,

counties, and school districts. The debacle unfolding in Houston, easily preventable, illustrates the consequences of statewide conservatives' inattention to localities. During recent legislative sessions, the pressing issues of local debt, rising property taxes, and unfunded pension liabilities have taken a backseat to "red meat" issues, such as "open carry" and "campus carry" of guns, defunding Planned Parenthood, and banning gambling on certain types of horse racing.

They'll need to wake up soon, if Texas wishes to preserve its thriving economy and unique cultural identity. The secret to Texas's past success is that, even as the state became more urbanized, its citizens—drawn by opportunity—continued to view themselves as proud, self-reliant Texans. Low taxes and spending reinforce this identity. One of the primary reasons Texans support limited government, journalist Grieder suggests, is that they "never developed the habit of expecting much from their government." High taxes and excessive government spending by Texas's cities could change that. An entitlement mentality, once established, is hard to change.

In its 40th anniversary issue, devoted to "The Cities," left-leaning *Texas Monthly* mournfully noted: "Texas has great cities, but in the hearts of its citizens it is not an urban state." This is the essence of what makes Texas special and distinguishes it from its once-great counterpart, California. Texas's productive, prosperous cities, unless brought back to the Texas model, may be the long-term undoing of the Lone Star State. Statewide elected officials and the Texas legislature must recognize that the state cannot succeed—and prosper—if its cities become dysfunctional urban fiefdoms resembling Chicago or Baltimore.

ARTICLE QUESTIONS

1) What are some of the ways in which "blue" cities have created rules or policies that are contrary to state law?
2) Identify the primary causes of why cities trend more Democratic than other areas in Texas.
3) What are three impacts of changes in the state's urban environment on the economy or local government policies?
4) Do you agree with the author's assessment of the dangers of "blue" cities?

6.2) Liberty Trumps Local Control

TribTalk, March 12, 2015

MATT RINALDI

Matt Rinaldi, a member of the Texas House's Freedom Caucus, a group composed of conservative Republicans, takes a slightly different approach to explaining why the state must limit the policy reach of local governments. He argues that local control is important, but extending liberty for all Texans is more important. Consequently, he argues that when liberty and local control are in conflict, "liberty trumps local control."

While state "micromanaging" of local governments risks the implementation of policies that are out of step with local needs, Rinaldi argues that the bigger risk is the potential of local law to "infringe on individual rights." He draws out the implications of this scenario in an alternative case: if municipalities restricted other rights like free speech, he declares, no one would defend their actions. Rinaldi specifically points to bans on plastic bags and red-light cameras as policies that complicate private property rights that the state has a duty to protect.

Finally, Rinaldi emphasizes that it is the state's prerogative to craft legislation in the best interest of the state. Any bill passed could technically infringe on local control, but the organizational structure of federal and state government allows such an outcome. Some policy issues, he argues, are important enough to trump local control.

Just before his inauguration, Gov. Greg Abbott warned: "Texas is being Californianized, and you may not even be noticing it. It's being done at the city level with bag bans, fracking bans, tree-cutting bans. We're forming a patchwork quilt of bans and rules and regulations that is eroding the Texas model."

Responding to Abbott's call, I filed House Bill 1939 to repeal bag bans and surcharges like those enacted by Dallas and Austin, which erode consumer choice and the rights of business owners. Other bills filed in the Legislature this session seek to undo city ordinances that allow red-light cameras, restrict landlords' ability to choose tenants or infringe on religious freedom.

Some have pushed back, questioning whether the governor and some legislators have improvidently abandoned the principle of local control—the idea that the government closest to the people governs best. That criticism misses the point. Local control is an important governing principle, but liberty is a more important governing principle. When the two are in conflict, liberty trumps local control.

The importance of local control is obvious. As President Ronald Reagan said, the "government is best which remains closest to the people." Local governments are far superior to state governments in their ability to communicate with, aggregate feedback from and respond to issues raised by local constituents in areas like public education, zoning, fire codes and traffic regulations. State micromanagement of these areas is unnecessary and more likely to be out of line with local needs.

However, while local government is often best at implementing policy, it poses a bigger risk of enacting laws that infringe on individual rights. James Madison first warned us of this threat in the *Federalist* No. 10, penned in 1787. Smaller voter bases and donor pools mean local elections are more susceptible than statewide elections to be affected by a single special interest group. Less voter engagement in local races means local government infringements on liberty are less likely to be identified and held in check. It is the responsibility of the Legislature to correct these instances of local government overreach.

The superiority of liberty over local control as a governing principle is nothing new. It is firmly established in our nation's history and enshrined in our founding documents, most notably in the 14th Amendment to the U.S. Constitution.

My question for politicians trumpeting local control above all else is this: Do you oppose incorporation of the Bill of Rights to our state and local governments? Would you reverse the U.S. Supreme Court's 1925 decision in *Gitlow v. New York*, which ruled that state and local laws abridging freedom of speech are void? Would you reverse the court's 2010 *McDonald v. Chicago* ruling, which decided that the Second Amendment voided state and local laws banning handguns? Would you have stood with George Wallace in 1963 as he resisted the integration of public schools in the name of—you guessed it—local control? While bag bans and red-light cameras may not infringe on fundamental constitutional rights like freedom of speech, the right to bear arms or equal protection, they implicate important contractual and private property rights that the state has a duty to protect.

Meanwhile, the objections to alleged infringements of local control are selective and lack consistency. In reality, any law of statewide applicability enacted by the Legislature arguably infringes on "local control." For example, many municipalities in Texas ban texting while driving, while many more do not. The statewide texting-while-driving ban that has been proposed in the Legislature would effectively overrule the majority of municipalities in the state that have decided not to enact such a ban. Yet when legislators call for a statewide texting ban, advocates of local control are silent. Local control is never an issue when its supporters agree with a proposed state law restricting the scope of municipal authority.

Local control is an important principle that should guide lawmakers in their consideration of bills that affect local government. But surely no one would defend the ability of municipalities to allow warrantless searches, restrict political speech or seize private property without just compensation. When cities overreach and enact ordinances that infringe on individual rights, it is the duty of the Legislature to intervene. Liberty always trumps local control.

ARTICLE QUESTIONS

1) What are three criticisms of "local control" that the author makes?
2) Do you find his argument about liberty trumping local control convincing?
3) Why does the author argue that it is the legislature's authority to correct instances of overreach by municipal governments?

6.3) Who's Going to Pay for All of This?

County, July 13, 2016

JOEL NIHLEAN

State action has many unintended consequences for local governments, including fiscal effects. Joel Nihlean, writing for *County* magazine, an arm of the Texas Association of Counties, which lobbies on behalf of Texas counties in the legislature, highlights the case of Bell County, which will have to pay $2.5 million more for lawyers for financially indigent parents involved in Child Protective Services hearings because of changes to state mandates. Nihlean illustrates a long-running pattern of local government frustration with state government: "Decisions made at the state and federal level have meant increased spending at the local level." In some instances, raising taxes is the only solution for local governments required to comply with state laws.

Services provided by the state are often technically provided by the counties—while the state has a major say in how these services are provided (by setting rules), counties are on the hook for the bill. Consequently, according to Nihlean, local taxpayers often end up "bearing the financial brunt of these [state] directives." He points to two specific state mandates, one related to indigent legal defense and one to health care for jailed inmates in county jails, that require county governments to fund a significant percentage of the cost of these programs, with little state help. County budgets are often small, especially in less populated counties, and unfunded state mandates may "punch a hole" in their budgets. Legislative efforts to ban these unfunded mandates have failed.

Nihlean is critical of state policies that hamstring the ability of local governments to raise revenue. He specially points to state limitations on local governments' ability to raise property taxes (called revenue caps) that he argues choke counties' budgets and render them unable to meet the financial demands placed on them by the federal and state governments.

When he took a look at the numbers, Bell County Judge Jon Burrows realized the decision had all but been made for him. The county would need to raise taxes.

New legislation out of Austin that spring asked a lot of counties and, by extension, taxpayers. It required counties to appoint lawyers for financially indigent parents during all Child Protective Services (CPS) hearings, not just in cases where the parents' rights are possibly being terminated. With hundreds of CPS cases pending in Bell County and no funding accompanying the new mandate, Burrows realized they'd be on the hook for about $2.5 million more each year.

Raising taxes wasn't something anyone on the commissioners' court wanted to do, but the county's hand had been forced. They raised the tax rate by 1.5 cents per $100 of valuation.

That was 2005, and it wasn't the first time decisions in Austin ballooned the county's budget. The story was the same in 2007 and in 2013, and it has been much the same in each of Texas' 254 counties. As far back as many county officials can remember, decisions made at the state and federal level have meant increased spending at the local level.

Recently, the county has braced itself for possible new unfunded mandates by bumping up their reserve—usually covering three months of operations—to enough to cover a full five months of operating expenses.

Bell County is far from unique in this respect. Officials in counties across Texas have stories about the unpredictable spikes in costs and budgets that swell after each session. Even when the Texas Legislature holds the line on state-controlled taxes, well-intended and even essential bills they pass can bring local property tax increases.

These unfunded mandates put the tough choice of raising taxes or cutting services squarely in the laps of local officials who are far-removed from the committee hearing rooms, House and Senate chambers and general bustle of the Capitol. They're back in the real world—back where the rubber meets the road on all of the state's decisions.

Passing the Buck

Counties and the state are deeply connected by the services they both provide to Texans and the challenges those services aim to overcome. Most of the services provided and paid for by counties are actually state services. The state has a say in how these services are provided, and by extension, how much they will cost.

The state sets standards for indigent defense and jails, affecting the amount of money that must be spent there. It determines which crimes fall into what categories, affecting the courts and county jail systems. It provides some funding for Medicaid and mental health, which is connected to counties' mandated indigent health programs, the 1115 waiver programs and the judicial system. The list goes on.

Capitol insider Harvey Kronberg described the root of the problem for counties in a Feb. 16, 2015, edition of "The Quorum Report":

Perhaps the only thing that the Legislature consistently outperforms at is cost-shifting its responsibilities to downstream local governing entities. Sometimes the cost shifting is intentional, sometimes it is a bank shot of unfunded mandates that no one even realized was an unfunded mandate until implementation.

Just one example—one of the biggest problems facing sheriffs is that when the state cuts mental health funding, the direct and predictable result is that county jails fill up, costing local taxpayers. Sounds like a state induced local tax increase to this spectator.

While most unfunded mandates are the unintended consequences of legislation or agency regulations, not a plot to foist additional costs on local governments, the end result is the same—taxpayers end up bearing the financial brunt of these directives.

"Counties are a constitutional safety net government. They're there to make sure the basic functions of government are carried out. There's an impression out there, though, that if it isn't mandated, counties can cut it from their budget, and the reality is much more complicated than that," said TAC Legislative Director Paul Sugg.

Teasing apart what is mandatory and what is discretionary in a county budget is difficult. As creatures of the state, counties enact the will of the state on the local level. Counties provide the basic functions of government, like the judicial system and public safety, along with everything from essential record keeping and emergency preparedness, to elections for all levels of government and other must-haves like infrastructure and roads.

Many county officials estimate that providing these essential basic services takes up 50 to 75 percent of a county's budget. It varies from county to county and region to region depending on local conditions, where more criminal justice services might be needed or more road maintenance, but even that isn't the whole story.

"I quote 91 or 92 percent to the newspaper every time we set our tax rate. People need to know," said Denton County Judge Mary Horn.

Horn, who has been in office for 14 years—the longest serving judge in the county's history—spent almost a decade as the tax assessor-collector before becoming county judge. She says the situation is far more complex than just mandatory versus discretionary spending. Horn believes that to run a modern and efficient government, certain items labeled as discretionary are all but mandates.

In Denton County's 2016 budget, 59.5 percent is spoken for by state and federal mandates, essential items vital to the county's operation account for another 32.1 percent.

There's nothing in local government code mandating a human resources department for Denton County and its approximately 1,500 employees, according to Horn, but she believes it's essential to the efficient operation of a modern county government.

"No, HR isn't mandated, but we all better have one or we'd quickly be in serious trouble with state or federal law," she said.

The same is true of technology. As counties have transitioned from the pen and paper world of the past to the emailing and e-filing digital era, an IT department and information security have become unquestionable essentials.

"Big and small, these mandates and these vital, essential functions add up over time and drive the tax rate as much as anything does," said Sugg.

People often underestimate all of the things counties do, said Ector County Auditor David R. Austin. He estimates that state and federal mandates alone make up more than half his county's budget. This calculation includes some of the most basic services of government, like law enforcement and the judicial system.

From start to finish, counties cover about 75 percent of the costs for the judicial system in Texas. The recent creation of a new district court in Ector County illustrates the cascade of new costs a county agrees to take on as that system tries to meet the demands of a growing state.

"In our budget, the first rattle out of the box is judicial. Up until this current fiscal year we only had four district courts in Ector County. Then the state added another. So, the state pays the district judge, but then there's the local staff. That court's got to have a court reporter; it's going to have a court administrator; it's got to have a bailiff; it's going to have an actual court room; the judge has to have an office; and it's got to have equipment and office supplies," said Austin.

But it doesn't stop there.

"If you have another district court, then the district attorney says he'll need two more attorneys and two more secretaries to prosecute in that court. And then the district clerk's office says it needs more clerks that can record the actions of that court. All of that falls on the shoulders of the local taxpayer here," said Austin.

Stealth Tax Hikes

Indigent Defense

County officials often point to two state mandates—the Fair Defense Act of 2001 and the Indigent Health Care and Treatment Act of 1985—as two of the most onerous. Inmate health care and Blue Warrants also end up high on many lists. Holding inmates for the Texas Department of Criminal Justice is one of the largest costs counties bear.

Since the Fair Defense Act was passed, the cost of providing court-appointed attorneys has gone up 160 percent. However, state grants distributed by the Texas Indigent Defense Commission have covered only a small proportion of total costs. In 2015, counties paid more than $209 million. The state chipped in just $28.6 million.

During a March 2016 interim hearing of the House Committee on Criminal Jurisprudence, Rep. Abel Herrero expressed alarm over the expenditures of the state compared to those of the counties.

When asked why indigent defense costs were increasing, Executive Director of the Texas Indigent Defense Commission Jim Bethke testified to the committee that increases were driven primarily by the increasing number of defendants receiving court appointed counsel, as well as by an increase in fee schedules. He also pointed out that almost half of all states nationwide fully fund indigent defense, and about two-thirds of states provide slightly over 50 percent of the needed funding.

Texas is different. Here, the state only covers about 12 percent of the costs. The rest comes from property taxpayers.

The pressure it puts on taxpayers is one thing, but the real danger in underfunding indigent defense comes from the risk of inviting even more costly litigation. At least two Texas counties have been hit with lawsuits in recent years that claim deficiencies in the underfunded indigent defense system violate the Constitution.

Indigent Health Care

"Right now, indigent health care is an unfunded health care mandate from the state. The state said the county shall supply indigent health care—that is a cost that is paid by county taxpayers and we want to avoid that in the future," Rep. Matt Shaheen told the *McKinney Courier-Gazette* in 2011 when he served as a Collin County commissioner and on the Conference of Urban Counties Policy Committee.

In 1985, the Indigent Health Care and Treatment Act established counties as the payor of last resort, tasking them with providing health care for indigent residents of the county if there is no hospital district or other source that provides those services.

Federal law requires emergency room physicians to assess and stabilize any patient, regardless of their ability to pay. Many are ultimately covered by programs like Medicare, Medicaid, the Children's Health Insurance Program (CHIP) and other sources, but counties pick up where these programs stop—helping the least of the least in Texas.

Because there is no reporting requirement for expenditures under 6 percent of a county's general tax levy (GTL), it's unknown how much money counties are spending on indigent health care in Texas.

In theory the act does limit the financial responsibility of the county to 8 percent of the county's general tax levy. Once that threshold is reached, the state is supposed to step in at 90 percent of eligible expenses.

The problem here is that it only happens if state funding is available, and it isn't always available. Trinity County in East Texas, for example, runs their County Indigent Health Care Program for about four months each year before the money runs out. It then shuts down and waits for the next year and fresh funding.

According to the Department of State Health Services fiscal year 2015 report, counties that met the 6 percent of GTL reporting requirement spent nearly $20 million on indigent health. The state chipped in just $81,546.83 in matching funds—a 98.42 percent decrease in state assistance since 2005.

The money the state supplied to offset the cost of indigent health care in 2015 went to Hockley and Jones counties. Dozens of other counties received no matching funds.

Big Impacts on Small Budgets

Higher-dollar and headline grabbing mandates are passed down almost every session, but there are many more nickel-and-dime mandates that add up over time to major costs. The burden of these mandates might seem minimal at first glance, but they can have outsized impacts in rural Texas and introduce unpredictability to smaller county budgets.

A couple of years ago, Goliad County Judge Pat Calhoun found himself at the intersection of two unfunded mandates that had the potential to punch a big hole in his county's budget.

"We caught an individual doing a bad thing, and we put him jail. As it turns out, he had a Blue Warrant that we didn't exercise, and thank the good Lord we didn't exercise it," said Calhoun.

Blue Warrants act as an order from the state to arrest and hold parole violators in the county jail. They're held without bail and without reimbursement for the costs the county incurs until the state can retrieve them. Inmates sitting on a Blue Warrant can end up waiting in county jail for weeks or even months, all on the local taxpayers' dime.

The judge's trepidation about the Blue Warrant in this case was well warranted.

"This guy we caught was a bad hombre. He was from the Mexican Mafia, and it turns out he is also in Stage 4 renal failure," said Calhoun.

As of April 19, county jails were holding 1,543 people on Blue Warrant technical violations, with another 2,453 parole violators who also had new charges, according to a report on county jail population from the Texas Commission on Jail Standards. The feeding, clothing and health care of each of those inmates falls on the shoulders of local property taxpayers.

The cost of housing a person in the county jail can vary widely, particularly when health care costs are taken into account. TAC's County Information Program estimates that, statewide, counties spend more than $35 million on Blue Warrant inmates. In smaller counties, this mandate can take the budget for a real ride according to Calhoun.

Goliad County's "bad hombre" had been receiving dialysis three times a week, paid for through Medicaid before his arrest, but once he was taken in, the financial burden fell to the county—to the tune of approximately $50,000 a month.

"As soon as he became a guest of our local bed and breakfast here, he lost all of those benefits. I understand the intent was to try to incentivize people to be good so they can maintain benefits," said the judge. "But the truth is, all we're doing is trading one set of dollars for another. They know they'll get taken care of either way, but I'm a small county with a small budget. It throws us into turmoil pretty quick."

Calhoun's "guest" was quickly wearing out his welcome as he ate through the sheriff's budget with his dialysis costs. Because the county had not exercised the Blue Warrant, they had some room to find a solution. After some back and forth with the district attorney, the county agreed to put an ankle bracelet on the man and release him on a personal recognizance bond.

"I knew we'd only find him one of two places, dialysis or dead, and we went from spending $50,000 a month to $350. But that was only able to happen because we hadn't exercised that Blue Warrant," he said.

During the last legislative session Sen. Lois Kolkhorst worked with the Texas Association of Counties and the Sheriffs' Association of Texas to pass Senate Bill (SB) 790. The bill gives judges more discretion to release low-level parole violators on bail if they haven't committed a violent offense. But, because statute still requires the Board of Pardons and Paroles to certify that the parolee may be released on bond—a sometimes lengthy process itself—the relief it has offered to taxpayers has been limited.

The Buck Stops Where?

The buck stops with property taxpayers, and the financial burden put on them in recent decades has meant property tax hikes and reductions in services in many counties.

If public testimony before the lieutenant governor's Select Committee on Property Tax Reform and Relief is any indication, there is little appetite from the public to fund more of the state's business through property taxes.

In fact, the committee's existence seems to indicate that the Legislature has taken notice of the pile-on, or at least increasing property taxes these mandates fuel.

In November 2015, Lt. Gov. Dan Patrick appointed seven senators to serve on the new interim committee, tasking them with finding ways to "improve the property tax process, as well as reduce the burden on property owners." To that end, the committee, chaired by Sen. Paul Bettencourt, has been travelling around the state, hearing from the public and local officials.

County officials explained the burden of unfunded and underfunded mandates at every stop along the committee's tour, but they have been sounding the alarm for many years, and the message seemed to have been received by the Legislature in the past, too.

After the sticker shock many commissioners courts experienced with the 2001 Fair Defense Act, which more than doubled the cost of court-appointed attorneys, many counties were feeling pinched. In 2004, they sent a loud, clear message. That year, 253 of the state's 254 counties passed resolutions decrying the steady stream of new mandates. They called for a constitutional amendment to ban them.

Unlike the regularly proposed revenue caps, which take a top-down and one-size-fits-all approach, a ban on unfunded mandates gets to the root of the problem. It not only slows the growth of property taxes, but also the growth of county budgets.

Instead of a ban in 2005, counties got Senate Bill 6, which mandated counties to provide attorneys for indigent parents in CPS cases without a matching appropriation from the state to pay for the new costs. Bell County, like others around the state raised tax rates and cut services elsewhere.

But over the next couple of sessions, bills proposing bans on unfunded mandates were filed.

They all died quiet deaths in the shadows of bigger legislative battles

Then, in 2011 there was a flurry of activity. The state had a $27 billion budget hole to fill, and legislators were cost-conscious in the wake of the recent global financial crisis. Early that session, three resolutions cropped up, raising the eyebrows and hopes of county officials. All proposed constitutional amendments would ban unfunded mandates, and all seemed to have some legs.

The day before the Legislature gaveled in, Rep. Burt Solomons filed House Joint Resolution (HJR) 56, calling for a constitutional amendment banning unfunded mandates.

The legislative language read: "No bill enacted by the Legislature on or after January 1, 2012, requiring a local government to establish, expand or modify a duty or activity that requires the expenditure of revenue by the local government shall be effective until and unless the Legislature appropriates or otherwise provides for the payment or reimbursement, from a source other than the revenue of the local government, or the costs incurred for the biennium by the local government in complying with the requirement."

Solomons' bill had a head of steam. In a matter of two weeks it had 95 bipartisan authors and co-authors—just five shy of the two-thirds needed for the House to pass a constitutional amendment—and a Senate companion bill, Senate Joint Resolution (SJR) 17, filed by Sen. John Carona.

Both of the bills would have applied not just to cities and counties, but also community college districts, hospital districts, municipal utility districts and other special districts. The Chair of the County Affairs Committee, Rep. Garnet Coleman, narrowed the scope, filing HJR 89. It proposed that an unfunded mandate amendment apply only to counties.

The majority of Texas counties signaled their support for these bills by again passing resolutions in favor of curtailing unfunded mandates. Journalists wrote up stories about the groundswell of support and county officials penned op-eds for their local papers. But for all the bipartisan support and applause from county officials, the measures failed.

Carona's SJR 17 couldn't get a committee hearing on the Senate side. Coleman's and Solomons' bills each made it as far as the House Calendars Committee, but they never found their way to the floor.

Only time will tell if the lieutenant governor's property tax committee and 85th Legislature will pursue solutions that get at the root of the problem or not, but county officials should be prepared to speak with their representatives and senators about solutions that work, and proposals that don't.

"County officials want to be good partners in making government in Texas work," said Gene Terry, a former Marion County Judge and TAC's Executive Director.

"Right now, it's déjà vu all over again with the revenue caps. They come up every few sessions and they're a bumper sticker solution that doesn't really fix anything," he said. "The Legislature has a tough job, and as county officials, we're really all part of that same team. County officials are in the trenches, working hard to implement the state's decisions. We know what can work and what won't. So, it's our job to speak up next session."

ARTICLE QUESTIONS

1) What does the author mean when he argues that federal and state governments "pass the buck" to local governments?
2) What policies are the largest drivers of the costs federal and state governments impose on local governments?
3) Identify a solution to the problem of "unfunded mandates."

The Texas Legislature

Former Texas House Speaker "Gib" Lewis defended his fellow Texas legislators against accusations that they were mediocre by conceding that maybe they were, but he'd visited their districts, and it was "clear they represented the voters who sent them to Austin." Perhaps there was good reason for Speaker Lewis's lighthearted jest. In the past 100 years, the Texas legislature has erupted into fistfights and seen members wave around firearms (one shooting off blanks at the ceiling) and one member, frustrated by not being recognized by the Speaker, jump on the press table adjacent to the dais where the presiding officer stands to yell his questions at the Speaker.

Ann Richards once joked that politics in Texas is a contact sport, but the business of government under the Texas Capitol's pink dome is no joke. The legislature passes laws that affect every part of the lives of Texans, from how much sales tax they pay to the quality of their schools to the quality of their roads. With a budget that tops $200 billion every two years, everyone has a stake in the game.

Texas has a "part-time" legislature, in that the body meets every two years and its members receive low pay; in fact, the job of serving in the legislature is supposed to be part-time by constitutional design. As a result, how much to pay legislators in the Lone Star State is a debate that extends back decades. As Amelia Thomson-DeVeaux, writing for *FiveThirtyEight*, argues, legislators asking for a higher salary are often met with resistance from voters, even if objectively these legislators are deserving of high pay. After all, opponents argue, legislators are not supposed to be full time and are expected to have another source of income. This is an important point, because the rate of pay for legislators may affect who is attracted to those positions. Could you afford to run for election and then leave your job for six months (or more) every two years?

The process of creating legislation (or blocking it) is bound up with partisan and ideological struggles. The friction is both internal and external. External friction occurs as legislators strive to meet the demands of their voters and interest groups, who carefully watch their voting habits. Transitions in political culture and the racial and gender makeup of the polity also put pressure on the legislature to be more inclusive. Internal friction occurs as ideals collide and personalities clash over tactics and methods. When these dynamics are combined with the state's very short 140-day legislative session, the result is a biennial rush to meet the needs of Texas. As the state grows in size and scope, more oversight is needed to invest in state resources and protect its residents. The struggle to keep government small will inevitably conflict with efforts to meet the fast-developing needs of a growing state.

Several pressure points in the Texas legislature determine whether or not legislation is passed—the short duration of the session, the desires of the Speaker of the House and the lieutenant governor (who runs the Texas Senate), and partisan warfare. Is it supposed to be this way? Jon Cassidy, writing for *City Journal*, says yes—the Texas government is "broken by design." Small government limits the "scope of failure," and this is exactly the way the framers of the Texas Constitution wanted it to be. Cassidy also examines how politics, institutional rules, and the personalities of the "Big Three" (the governor, the lieutenant governor, and the Speaker) interact to make policy. Some clear friction exists between the branches of government. These fights can turn bitter and last beyond the legislative session as each individual or group jockeys for the dominant political position. Colliding political rivalries shape the outcome of the legislative process, pitting the parties against each other with an arsenal of rules that speed up or slow down the process. Which leader or chamber gets their way (or does not get their way) has important implications to what policies pass but also how the process itself functions. Abrasive relations between legislative chambers may dramatically slow the process and stunt progress on important legislation.

Colliding political rivalries also shape the outcome of the legislative process, pitting the parties against each other, with an arsenal of rules to speed up or slow down the process at their disposal, as Ross Ramsey's *Texas Tribune* dispatch from one particularly tense legislative session shows. Most observers don't see or particularly care about the making of the legislative sausage; they just want to eat the meal. Ramsey, however, who has over thirty years of experience watching the legislature in action, reports that which chamber gets its way has important implications for not only what policies pass but also how the legislative process itself functions. Abrasive relations between legislative chambers may dramatically slow the process and stunt progress on important legislation.

Deep ideological and political divisions on issues like sanctuary cities, voter identification laws, transgender bathrooms, the foster care system, and feral hogs highlight differences between the parties but also within the legislatively dominant Republican Party. How these issues are (or are not) resolved in Texas will signal how they might play out nationally.

CHAPTER QUESTIONS

1) On what issues are there ideological and policy differences *between* Republicans and Democrats in the Texas legislature?
2) On what issues are there ideological and policy differences *within* the Republican Party in the Texas legislature?
3) How do rules in the legislature (together or in the House or Senate) affect the kinds of policies lawmakers pass?
4) How do institutional frictions and personal rivalries change what kinds of legislation are debated and passed?

7.1) How Much Should State Legislators Get Paid?

Five Thirty Eight, April 7, 2016

AMELIA THOMSON-DEVEAUX

Despite the size of its economy and population, Texans' belief in small government keeps legislators' annual salary at $7,200—the lowest fixed salary for legislators in the nation. Legislators also receive a $190 per diem for meals [up from $150 when the article was written] and travel during the 140-day session every two years, a total of $26,600 for daily expenses for a regular session. Legislators are expected to have other jobs, because lawmaking is not designed to be a full-time occupation. As FiveThirtyEight's Amelia Thomson-DeVeaux finds in her thorough investigation, more professionalized (i.e., full-time, year-round) legislatures tend to pay more.

Should Texas pay its legislators more? As in other states where legislators have asked for a raise, the argument in favor of more pay is that the time and knowledge required to do the job well justify a higher salary. The arguments against suggest that higher pay could be out of step with the median family income in the state or could prevent otherwise qualified candidates from seeking the job, since most couldn't afford to take a major pay cut to serve as a legislator full-time. The public may also balk at increased legislative salaries, believing that government officials are already compensated enough. Ultimately, Thomson-DeVeaux suggests that states should either compensate legislators for a difficult job or avoid blaming them when things go wrong if they don't have the resources to succeed.

Earlier this year, a Republican state lawmaker in New Mexico proposed a constitutional amendment that would give his colleagues (and himself) something most workers take for granted: a paycheck. Since 1912, when New Mexico entered the union as a sparsely populated frontier settlement, its state legislators have worked without a salary, although lawmakers receive a per diem that amounts to approximately $7,000 for up to two months of work per year. Today, it's the only state with an unsalaried legislature. In an op-ed published in January, the amendment's sponsor, Terry McMillan, argued that a volunteer legislature has its limits. We tend to prefer a professional fire department to a squad of volunteers, he said—why don't we feel the same about the people in our government?

The amendment, which would have raised New Mexico legislators' salaries to match the state's median household income, around $45,000, died quietly when the session ended in February. But arguments like McMillan's raise a tricky question for American taxpayers: How much are our lawmakers really worth?

"The question of salaries has haunted American legislatures since the 1640s," said Peverill Squire, a professor of political science at the University of Missouri and an expert on state legislatures. "It has been a chronic issue where lawmakers generally ask for more pay and the public is almost always resistant."

When they ask for more money, lawmakers like McMillan try to make the case to voters that they deserve a pay raise because of the time and knowledge required to do their jobs well. It's a hard sell, because higher-compensated legislatures such as those in Illinois, Pennsylvania and New York, where lawmakers are paid well above the state's median income, routinely face accusations of incompetence or corruption. According to Squire and other political scientists, higher pay isn't a magic bullet for better governance—but there's evidence that when it comes to state legislatures, we get what we pay for.

Lawmaker salaries vary wildly across the country, from California, where legislators make nearly $100,000 a year, to New Hampshire, where they are compensated with $100 annually and no per diem. Overall, though, they tend to skew low. In 2014, according to research by Squire and Gary Moncrief, a political science professor at

Boise State University, the median base pay was $20,833.

Legislators in some states receive more money through per diems and expense allowances. Take Oklahoma, where legislators' base salary is $38,400. With the per diem of $153 per day, Oklahoma legislators took home an additional $10,404 in 2014, according to estimates by Squire and Moncrief. That put the lawmakers' total earnings close to the state's median household income.

Untangling just how much legislators take home is difficult, because at least in theory, any

per diem should go toward on-the-job expenses like meals and lodging. In about half of states, per diems are given without strings attached. This means that short of examining a legislator's tax return, it's impossible to know how much went toward actual expenses. But even with this extra cash, only 12 states (including Oklahoma) pay their state legislators a salary that matches or exceeds the state's median household income—and most compensate well below this marker.

In this varying landscape, figuring out whether pay raises are justified can be a struggle: Are

STATE	MEDIAN HOUSEHOLD INCOME (2014)	LEGISLATURE TYPE	LEGISLATOR SALARY + PER DIEM (2014)	LEGISLATOR PAY AS % OF MEDIAN HOUSEHOLD INCOME
California	$61,933	Full-time	$121,535	196.2%
Pennsylvania	$53,234	Full-time	$95,237	178.9%
Michigan	$49,847	Full-time	$82,485	165.5%
New York	$58,878	Full-time	$89,422	151.9%
Illinois	$57,444	Full-time	$75, 884	132.1%
Alabama	$42,830	Hybrid	$53,246	124.3%
Ohio	$49,308	Full-time	$60, 584	122.9%
Wisconsin	$52,622	Full-time	$55,663	105.8%
Oklahoma	$47,529	Hybrid	$48,804	102.7%
Alaska	$71,583	Full-time	$71,460	99.8%
Massachusetts	$69,160	Full-time	$68,193	98.6%
Hawaii	$69,592	Hybrid	$68,352	98.2%
Missouri	$48, 363	Hybrid	$44,790	92.6%
Delaware	$59,716	Hybrid	$51,375	86.0%
Colorado	$61,303	Hybrid	$51,960	84.8%
Washington	$61,366	Hybrid	$49,531	80.7%
Florida	$47,463	Full-time	$37,437	78.9%
Maryland	$73,971	Hybrid	$56,370	76.2%
Iowa	$53,712	Hybrid	$39,175	72.9%
Louisiana	$44,555	Hybrid	$31,980	71.8%
Kentucky	$42,958	Hybrid	$29,932	69.7%
New Jersey	$71,919	Hybrid	$49,000	68.1%
Minnesota (Senate)	$61,481	Hybrid	$41,805	68.0%
West Virginia	$41,059	Part-time	$27,860	67.9%
Tennessee	$44,361	Hybrid	$28,663	64.6%
Minnesota (House)	$61,481	Hybrid	$39,325	64.0%

Indiana	$49,446	Hybrid	$31,238	63.2%
Oregon	$51,075	Hybrid	$31,046	60.8%
Arizona	$50,068	Hybrid	$30,450	60.8%
Mississippi	$39,680	Part-time	$23,469	59.1%
North Carolina	$46,556	Hybrid	$27,523	59.1%
Arkansas	$41,262	Hybrid	$22,952	55.6%
Idaho	$47,861	Part-time	$25,344	53.0%
Kansas	$52,504	Part-time	$27,761	52.9%
Georgia	$49,321	Part-time	$24,262	49.2%
South Carolina	$45,238	Hybrid	$19,780	43.7%
Nebraska	S52,686	Hybrid	$21,482	40.8%
Connecticut	$70,048	Hybrid	$28,000	40.0%
Virginia (Senate)	$64,902	Hybrid	$24,840	38.3%
Virginia (House)	$64,902	Hybrid	$24,100	37.1%
Vermont	$54,166	Part-time	$19,086	35.2%
Texas	$53,035	Hybrid	$17,700	33.4%
Maine	$49,462	Part-time	$15,852	32.0%
Utah	$60,922	Part-time	$18,315	30.1%
Rhode Island	$54,891	Part-time	$14,947	27.2%
North Dakota	$59,029	Part-time	$15,591	26.4%
South Dakota	$50,979	Part-time	$10,400	20.4%
Montana	$46,328	Part-time	$8,659	18.7%
Nevada	$51,450	Part-time	$8,949	17.4%
New Mexico	$44,803	Part-time	$7,115	15.9%
Wyoming	$57,055	Part-time	$7,770	13.6%
New Hampshire	$66,532	Part-time	$100	0.2%

Sources: American Community Survey, National Council of State legislatures, Squire & Moncrief.

higher-paid legislators better at running their states? Squire and Moncrief, along with other political scientists, have worked over the years to measure the relationship between salary and legislative effectiveness, a slippery benchmark that can include a variety of measures, including efficiency (the number of bills passed), contact with constituents, and the innovativeness of a state's policies.

The researchers concluded that the best way to test the efficacy of a state legislature is through a concept called professionalism, which includes three components: salary, the number of days in a legislative session, and the size of the legislature's staff.

Most of the time, these factors align. Some big states like California and New York have "full-time" legislatures, as classified by the National Conference of State Legislatures; they meet for most of the year, and their legislators serve larger districts and receive relatively high salaries. Some states with smaller populations, like Montana and New Hampshire, are "part-time" legislatures, with short sessions and fewer constituents. Lawmaker pay in those states tends to be nominal.

About half the states, though, are classified as "hybrids"—they generally have low pay but might have a long session or larger staffs.

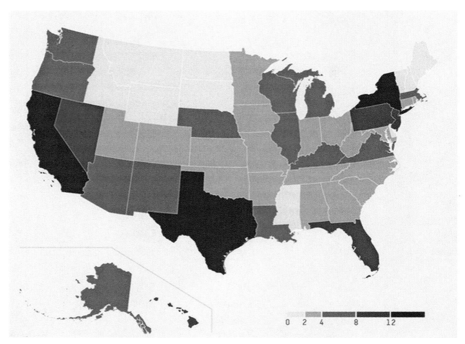

Figure 7.1   Which state legislatures are heavily staffed?
Number of staffers per state legislator by state, 2009
Source: National Conference of State Legislatures

Using the U.S. Congress as a benchmark, Squire created a scale to assess professionalism. With this scale, he and other political scientists found that the state legislatures that meet for longer and give their legislators more resources (both in terms of staff and salary) are more efficient, passing a greater percentage of bills overall and enacting more bills per legislative day. They have more contact with constituents and are more attentive to their concerns. They are also more independent, both from party leadership and the governor, and more likely to take on government reforms and enact complex and innovative policies. "When you compensate a legislator well and give them a staff, they're able to put more time into their work and actually develop some knowledge around different policies," Squire said.

Low pay also puts limits on who can realistically serve in a legislature. In states like New Mexico that have short legislative sessions, lawmakers must leave their day jobs for one or two months every year and travel to the state capital—in addition to dealing with year-round demands from constituents. Many lawmakers must be independently wealthy or have flexible jobs that allow them to juggle politics and everyday work. Part-time legislators are also more likely than full-time legislators to be retirees, Moncrief said. It's no surprise, then, that state lawmakers tend to be older than their constituents.

Lawmakers with less time to spare and no staff to guide them may rely more heavily on lobbyists to advise them about legislation, Squire said. A lawmaker in Missouri, a hybrid state, recently got into hot water when he declared that he sees lobbyists as "unpaid staff."

Thad Kousser, a professor of political science at the University of California, San Diego, worked in the New Mexico legislature when he was a graduate student. Although he was only a page, a grant he'd received for school meant that he was making more money than the House speaker. It was a stark contrast with the California legislature, where he'd worked for several years previously. There, legislators were not only paid more—but they also had access to highly trained staff. "In California, people with J.D.s and Ph.D.s are writing the bills and investigating the legislation," he said. "In New Mexico, you have the governor's analysis and a Xerox machine."

So when state legislators ask for more money, should voters listen? Neil Malhotra, a professor of political economy at Stanford University, said his research shows that when legislators ask for raises, they are responding to the demands of an increasingly complicated job. In his view, when lawmakers ask for more pay, they're not promising to work better or more efficiently—they're asking to be compensated adequately for what they're already doing.

"It's all relative, of course," Moncrief said. "Legislators in low-population states where the legislature only meets a couple of months do not need to be paid six figures. But virtually all political scientists who've looked at this issue would agree, I think, that most legislators are underpaid for the work they do." His co-author, Squire, suggested that at a minimum, legislative pay be pegged to the state's median household income.

Malhotra said Americans' suspicion of political institutions puts lawmakers in a bind. "It's really irrational," he said. "We don't want to equip politicians with the resources to do their jobs, and then we blame them when things don't work the way we want."

ARTICLE QUESTIONS
1) What is legislative "professionalism"? Does Texas have a "professional" legislature?
2) What is your view on whether or not Texas should increase its legislators' pay?
3) Would increasing legislative salaries draw more candidates to seek legislative office?
4) If legislators supplemented their travel or gift giving with campaign funds (from political donors) kept separate from their government account, would you favor that?

7.2) Broken by Design
City Journal, 2016

JON CASSIDY

The stately edifices and pristine marble columns that make up the Texas Capitol complex hide a dirty little secret: the structure of the system is designed to slow or stop legislation before it gets passed. Why? Jon Cassidy argues that Texas's lawmaking system is "broken by design"—that the state's small government limits the "scope of failure," and this is exactly the way Texans like it.

The legislature is divided into a House and a Senate, both run by different leaders. The executive, headed by the governor, has modest legislative power. These three institutions often engage in vicious battles over legislation. This is particularly true for the "Big Three"—the governor, the lieutenant governor, and the Speaker of the House—who act as the roller-coaster operators for the legislature's 140-day carnival. At the beginning of the 2017 session, all three leaders were Republicans, but this offered no guarantee of political cooperation. As Cassidy observes, each of the Big Three has a distinct style of politics, a unique temperament, and a different ideological bent, and each favors slightly different issues. The chambers and branches of government also have different schedules within the 140-day session.

Cassidy makes it clear that even though things look polished on the outside, the legislature is often much more fractious and complicated than it seems. This is by design, where a legislature run by "citizen-statesmen" is tasked with the enormous responsibility of running Texas government.

Texas is "wide open for business." That's the pitch that Rick Perry made around the country during his three terms as governor of the Lone Star State. It fit with the popular image of Texas: low tax, low regulation, business-friendly, superconservative—the state so antigovernment that it elects a legislature and sends it right back home. Texas's part-time legislature—it meets in 140-day sessions every other year—has been a key factor in its economic success. A 2000 study by Stephanie Owings of the U.S. Naval Academy and Rainald Borck of Berlin's Humboldt University found that states with part-time legislatures spend 12 percent less, on average, than states with full-time or hybrid legislatures. Lawmakers who don't see themselves as the center of the universe, it seems, are less likely to want to pay for everyone's health care, fret about fracking, or declare half the state environmentally protected. Texas's biennial legislature kills most big, economy-wrecking ideas before they gain momentum.

The system is not without its shortcomings. Cronyism is pervasive. Texas has fewer regulations than other states, but what regulations do exist often protect moneyed interests. Without reform, local debt and pension debt could one day swamp the state economy.

Despite these problems, Texas is thriving, in part because of the small-government ideals that its founders put at the heart of the state constitution and the political institutions that it established. The early Texans fully expected government to fail, so they did everything they could to limit the scope of that failure. Texas government is, in a sense, broken by design—leaving civil society free to flourish.

Texas is a one-party state, but for most of its history, the Democrats were in charge. From 1873 to 1978, no Republican was elected governor, but the Democratic governors from the 1940s through the 1970s were all fairly conservative. Factionalism has always dominated the legislature—with urban interests facing off against rural interests, and commerce against agriculture—but party membership has usually been an afterthought, with Democrats rarely vying with Republicans. Since the election of George W. Bush as governor in 1994, the GOP has come to dominate Texas politics. Bush won reelection in 1998, and he handed off power to fellow Republican Perry after winning the 2000 presidential race. Perry won election in his own right in 2002, and again in 2006 and 2010. Republican Greg Abbott took office in January 2015. The GOP won a majority in the state senate in 1996 and in the house in 2002.

For all his visibility on the national level, though, Texas's governor isn't the most powerful figure in state politics. That distinction belongs jointly to the lieutenant governor and the speaker of the Texas House of Representatives. As presiding officer of the state senate, the lieutenant governor appoints committee chairs and directs legislation and budgeting, just like the speaker of the house. The governor can veto legislation and use the bully pulpit, but that's about it. His "cabinet" is made up of elected officials with their own constituencies, and he has no real authority over them. More than 200 independent state agencies and commissions exist in Texas, and while the governor gets to appoint people to most of them, he generally can't remove them without senate consent, much less direct them, so they tend to do as they please.

Even as Texas has become overwhelmingly Republican, conservatives haven't held all the levers of power. From 2003 to 2009, the house was governed by a strict conservative, Tom Craddick, nicknamed "auto-Craddick" by Democrats, who chafed under opposition rule. This clean-living, solitary, authoritarian figure presiding over a chamber full of good ol' boys became vulnerable to a leadership coup when a cohort of Democrats swept into office on President Obama's coattails in 2008. With the GOP majority cut to just two seats, a group of centrist Republicans called the "Gang of 11" joined with Democrats to put Republican two-termer Joe Straus, whom critics called a RINO (Republican in name only), in the speaker's chair. Straus then doled out committee chairmanships to the Gang of 11 and several key Democrats. The senate was governed during the Perry years by Lieutenant Governor David Dewhurst, a moderate who deferred to senate traditions—a two-thirds rule, in particular—that allowed Democrats to block legislation. Talk-radio host Dan Patrick jettisoned the rule when he was elected lieutenant governor in 2014, establishing a new dynamic: a senate governed by Patrick, a Tea Party favorite, and a house run by Straus.

Patrick and Straus are the de facto heads of the Texas government, but they have just 80 calendar days to get their work done. The state constitution forbids the legislature from passing any bills, or even holding floor debates, during the first 60 days of the session, which are reserved for filing bills. By Day 120, any House bills still stuck in committee are dead. The House then faces a series of deadlines for floor approval of various bills. The Senate's rules are more flexible, but it still needs to get bills over to the House by Day 130 or so for any hope of passage. Unless the governor calls a special session to deal with a particular issue, the legislature adjourns on Day 140, known as *sine die*, and traditionally marked by drunkenness. Then the governor gets another three weeks to exercise vetoes. The legislature has formal authority to override a veto, but this power is meaningless after *sine die*. Everybody has gone home.

Texas's abbreviated legislative calendar affects the state's power dynamics in many ways. Individual members rarely challenge the decisions of the lieutenant governor or the House speaker about which bills to bring out of committee. Both officials have broad authority to appoint committee chairs, assign bills to committee, interpret rules, and otherwise direct proceedings. Straus

and Patrick have mastered all the usual tricks for making undesirable legislation disappear without embarrassing votes. For example, a 2015 measure known as "campus carry," letting university students bring guns to class, could have generated just the sort of political theater that the House leadership didn't want. So they buried debate on the bill on the final night of the session, and it cleared the floor a half-hour before a midnight deadline. Governor Abbott signed it into law on June 1 of that year.

The Texas Legislature passes a surprising number of bills in its short sessions. In 2015, it sent 1,322 bills to Governor Abbott's desk. California, by comparison, passed 807 bills all year. In *Roll Call*'s state-by-state comparison of bills and resolutions passed during the 2013–14 Congress, Texas was far and away the numerical leader. With this volume of legislation flowing past lawmakers, insiders can slip things through fairly easily. Yet the great majority of these bills are trifling, since there isn't much taxpayer money to play with. The state constitution requires that the two-year budget fit under the state comptroller's revenue projections, and since the popularly elected comptroller is invariably a Republican, those projections are usually quite conservative.

Not everything about Texas's minimalist government is praiseworthy. Short bursts of lawmaking produce the occasional embarrassing accident. In 2011, for example, lawmakers erroneously removed penalties for driving without license plates, and had to wait two years to reinstate them.

The part-time legislature is dominated by full-time lobbyists. Contribution limits are nonexistent. From about 1952 onward, you could call the factions Left, Right—and money. Money backed the Democrats until the 1990s, when it went Republican. The reason for the shift was the greed of a key Democratic constituency: trial lawyers. In the 1980s, trial lawyers had succeeded in getting several of their candidates elected to the state supreme court, which resulted in major rulings that opened the door to some astronomical court judgments over the next decade. In 1993, a few major homebuilders and other wealthy businessmen formed Texans for Lawsuit Reform, and started raising money to help elect Bush and other Republican reformers, who made the issue a priority. Over the next decade, Texas tort law was completely rewritten. Medical-malpractice suits, for one, have all but vanished. Texas's system of elected judges, however, virtually guarantees that the plaintiffs' bar will always have a friendly court somewhere in the state.

Political donations often correlate closely with government contracts. The owner of the state's biggest highway construction company wrote Straus a $100,000 check for his reelection during the last cycle. Not surprisingly, the speaker has shown a fondness for highway and water projects. Supermarket magnate Charles C. Butt opposes school choice; he donated $50,000 to Straus and millions more to others, so the legislature with the GOP supermajority has avoided the issue. The most influential contributor remains Texans for Lawsuit Reform, with more than $34 million in contributions over the years. The group spends much of its time now on keeping the trial lawyers from getting plaintiff-friendly Republicans elected to the bench.

All the influence-peddling has resulted in more corporate welfare and cronyism than one would imagine, given Texas's image as a free-market haven. A *New York Times* investigation three years ago tallied up $80 billion in tax abatements, subsidies, and other crony-capitalist goodies handed out each year. Texas gives away $19 billion in such deals annually, roughly as much as Michigan, Pennsylvania, New York, and California combined.

Texas also regulates more than one might think. Counterproductive policies such as price controls ensure that residents wind up paying some of the highest costs in the country for car and home insurance, not to mention closing costs on home purchases. Texas is famous for resisting Obamacare, but state law had already imposed expansive and expensive coverage minimums. Mercantilist regulatory schemes frustrate competition in several large industries, including alcohol and car sales, and occupational licensing does the same to small businesses. A part-time legislature rarely gets around to pruning the weeds of administrative law. It's been 20 years since lawmakers tried to ax a bureaucracy.

Texas's founders wanted a legislature run by citizen-statesmen—but these days, we've also got lawyers, lobbyists, bond salesmen, and assorted fixers as part-time solons, and they've formed an establishment culture that rewards insiders. Lawmakers once got elected and came to Austin for a session or two before returning to private life and handing their seats over to others. In the nineteenth century, two-thirds of each class would be freshmen. Up until the 1950s, it was half or more. Now it's about 20 percent.

Serving in the Texas legislature isn't a realistic job option for most working professionals. It only pays $600 per month, plus $150 per diem for expenses, but it's too time-consuming to be a side job. Some CEOs and a few small-business owners— accountants, salesmen, consultants— can adjust their schedules to accommodate service in Austin, but their ranks are thin. According to the National Conference of State Legislators, 26 percent of Texas legislators are lawyers—twice the national average. Most are the sort of attorneys who never see the inside of a courtroom. They work in "government affairs" for their firms. Or they collect whopping fees for underwriting billions of dollars in bonds for state-funded government agencies (the practice is illegal for members of Congress). Or they take advantage of a privilege that they've written into Texas law that gets any lawsuit involving a legislator postponed during session. They can make six figures employing the tactic for a client who needs to stall. One study found that Texas had the busiest revolving door in the nation, with more lawmakers-turned-lobbyists than any other state. Conflicts of interest are often blatant.

The Texas legislature is responsible, at least in part, for two big threats to the state economy. One is local debt, particularly school debt; the other is pension debt. The Constitution of 1876 dedicated some of Texas's wide-open spaces—and the rights to the minerals beneath—for the support of schools, and created the Permanent School Fund to guarantee school bonds. The result of guaranteeing so much cheap money is that Texas has the highest school debt per capita in the country, tied with South Carolina. The schools owe $72.4 billion in principal that will cost $117.1 billion to repay, according to the state Bond Review Board. That's Puerto Rico–size debt, just for schools (though, to be fair, the Texas economy is 15 times bigger than Puerto Rico's). Local debts in some areas are driving property-tax rates that push 4 percent. Texas now has the sixth-highest property-tax rates in the nation.

The legislature also funds teachers' pensions statewide, and it has seized control of some local police and fire pension funds. Here, Straus's alliance with the Democrats comes into play, but Patrick is also well funded by public-safety unions (who may, of course, write giant checks like anyone else). In a right-to-work state that bans almost all public-sector collective bargaining, nobody fears the unions. Even the far-right guys will take union checks.

No state's lawmakers are eager to tackle the unfunded pension problem, but Texas's lawmakers have an extra incentive to ignore it. They earn an annual salary of just $7,200, with the understanding that they'll eventually collect a decent state pension. Lawmakers with at least eight years of service can begin collecting their pensions at age 60; those with 12 years of service can begin collecting at 50. The pension amount gets calculated according to a formula that lawmakers devised themselves in 1981: every year of service is worth 2.3 percent of a district judge's salary—currently $125,000. A lawmaker who serves for 20 years is eligible for an annual pension of $57,500. The average state-employee pension, by contrast, is just $17,000 per year.

In 2012, federal election rules required Perry to disclose a $90,000 pension that he had already begun collecting as governor. Voters were outraged, but lawmakers have changed nothing since. They're keeping their pensions.

Those are some of the problems: the good news is that the benefits of the Texas model, overseen by its part-time legislature, are impossible to ignore. From 2000 to 2014, Texas created some 2.5 million nonfarm jobs, more than a quarter of the U.S. total for the period. In 2015, amid free-falling oil prices, Texas still managed to finish third among states in job growth, thanks to booming health care, education, professional services, manufacturing, hospitality, warehousing, and light industrial sectors. Construction is doing well, too. Wondrously cheap housing and pro-growth land-use policies draw people and business to the state. None of this diversification was centrally planned. It's the product of an economy that's wide open to foreign trade and immigration. Immigration has boosted native Texans' income by an aggregate $3.4 billion to $6.6 billion a year. Income inequality is up, too—but that's just another way of saying that high-paying jobs are growing fastest.

To a large degree, the Texas model has worked because the Austin governing establishment is penned in, limited in the damage that it can inflict by a state constitution that not only keeps lawmakers from enacting new laws for one out of every two years but also severely restricts taxation and imposes budget caps. Texas has no state income tax, and instituting one would require voter approval. The legislature makes do with a sales tax, a handful of excise taxes, and an onerous gross-receipts tax that penalizes high-volume businesses. The Texas state government simply never has the money for bold new expansions of government. So it stays small, just as the original Texans wanted it. It's not perfect and never will be, but the state is flourishing.

ARTICLE QUESTIONS

1) What does the author mean when he says that Texas government is "broken by design"?
2) Do you agree that the system of government should be inefficient on purpose?
3) Why does the author argue that friction may result from leaders' different perspectives?
4) In the opinion of the author, what are the good and bad aspects of the state's part-time legislature?

7.3) Legislative Dance Partners Stepping on Each Other's Toes

Texas Tribune, April 22, 2015

ROSS RAMSEY

In Texas, the compactness of every legislative session plus the necessity for legislators to get their pet bills passed multiplied by the pressing needs of the state on key issues (like the budget) together produce a formula for friction—or, as veteran political reporter Ross Ramsey of the *Texas Tribune* puts it, "tomfoolery." Ramsey pulls the curtain back on one tense week in the legislature in 2015 in an article that summarizes the inevitable delays, distraction, and disorder that come with almost every Texas legislative session. Amid all the tension built into the legislative process, the difficulty of resolving disputes between the two chambers of the legislature may be the most time-consuming.

Ramsey outlines the *Schoolhouse Rock* version of the legislative process: a clean and simple process in which each stage resolves disputes and ultimately leads to the passage of legislation. Politics certainly complicates the legislative process, as do chamber rules and bicameralism (the two-chamber system). Both the House and Senate chambers have fixed rules about when legislation can be considered, and both have their own preferences about what legislation on the same topic should look like. Retaliation for one issue or another may catch other innocent bills in the legislative crossfire—bills that may be important to the state or to the areas represented by legislators who brought them up.

Few normal people can tell you whether a piece of legislation started in the Senate or the House. It doesn't make much difference. The real measure of legislation is whether it becomes law.

But lawmakers are not like the rest of us: They might be the only people who care whether it is a Senate or a House bill that passes, but sometimes they care quite a bit. That can throw them off course.

On Monday, the House passed legislation that would permit licensed Texans to carry handguns in the open. The Senate did the same thing a month ago, sending an open carry bill to the House that has yet to be referred to a House committee for consideration. The two versions have some differences, as always, that might be reconciled in a meeting of lawmakers from each body. But there is one difference that cannot be reconciled: House Bill 910 and Senate Bill 17 don't have the same number.

Ignoring the Senate's version gummed up the works, and the Senate's answer to that slight was nearly simultaneous. The Senate voted out a border security bill, and instead of running with House Bill 11, which arrived in the Senate on March 23, senators went with Senate Bill 3, passing it and sending it to the House.

For any of this to get into the law books, someone must blink, agree to drop their own legislation and work with the bill sent over by the people on the other end of the building.

To become law, a piece of legislation is filed, gets through a committee in one chamber, passes that chamber, then gets sent over to make the same laps in the other chamber. Things that have passed the House go to the Senate for approval, and vice versa. Conference committees of House and Senate members meet to iron out differences in what the chambers have approved, and then those compromises go to each place for final approval. On everything but constitutional amendments, the resulting legislation goes to the governor for approval or veto.

That's the *Schoolhouse Rock* version. What's happening now is that the people in the Texas House and Senate are operating like Nebraskans. Nebraska, as you know from middle-school civics, has a unicameral Legislature. Only one chamber. Nobody has to phone a friend to succeed.

Read what the Senate did as you choose: They either fumbled a major piece of legislation that's on the governor's hot list and slowed it down, or they offered a bit of retaliation for the House's disregard of the Senate's open carry bill.

Maybe you saw some of the heated reaction from state Rep. Dennis Bonnen, R-Angleton, directed at Lt. Gov. Dan Patrick and the Senate?

"Had they chosen to do what historically happens and pass the House bill over with their changes, we could be quickly moving to a conference committee and getting this bill on the governor's desk much sooner rather than later," Bonnen said.

He might have said the same about the House and handguns.

Patrick and company declined to answer him, but the standoff has the makings of an Al Pacino–Robert De Niro movie—with actors cussing, yelling and otherwise chewing up the scenery.

Other bills, big and small, are caught in similar crossfire, including legislation that would move the ethics-enforcing public integrity unit from the Travis County district attorney's office to the Texas Rangers or someplace else; reauthorize the state's river authorities; regulate accidental spills from wastewater facilities; limit debit card surcharges; manage and collect disputed oil and gas royalties on state land; allow people with terminal diseases to opt for experimental or clinical drug treatments that have not been approved for general use; and one that would eliminate a tax on fireworks.

It's not that legislators don't know how this is done. The Senate waited for the House's budget and passed its version of that so that the two bodies can get to work on their differences. The chambers swap ownership of the budget each session to make sure no one monkeys with the only bill that absolutely has to pass.

And the tomfoolery on some of the other bills has some practical effect, believe it or not. The House and Senate are feeling each other out as they enter the end-of-session crunch, when negotiations, tactics and deadlines become critical. The major legislation tends to work out, and it gobbles up time that might otherwise be used for less important bills.

That Darwinian bottleneck keeps most proposals from becoming law and forces lawmakers to focus on what's important to the state. And on who gets credit.

ARTICLE QUESTIONS

1) What three primary stumbling blocks to the passage of legislation are outlined in the article?
2) What are some of the reasons why Republicans and Democrats in the Texas legislature are at odds?
3) Would the Texas legislature run more efficiently if it were unicameral (only one house instead of two)?
4) What are the implications of legislative fracas that slow the lawmaking process down?

Chapter 8

Governors of Texas

On paper, the governor of Texas is a "weak" governor, with restricted powers and limited control over other influential government offices, such as attorney general and state comptroller, many of which are elected separately. The legislative branch significantly checks the authority of the governor on appointment matters, and the branches share power on several other functions. So wary of gubernatorial power were the framers of the 1876 Texas Constitution that they engaged in no serious debates about the role of the chief executive. The effect was a discombobulated, decentralized position with a short term of office (originally set at two years, now four) and low pay.

However, the influence of the modern Texas governor is significant at several levels of government in ways that are both allowed by the Constitution and those opportunities that governors make themselves by force of their personalities. The office is more than the sum of its parts; if used properly, the governor's powers allow for significant expansion of executive authority. Texas governors have expanded their power through aggressive use of the veto power, the appointment power, and the power to call special sessions. But with less power explicitly granted them by the Constitution, governors must earn the powers they use. This is where Brian McCall, a former state representative and current chancellor of the Texas State University system, finds the critical intersection between a governor's personal influence and his or her personal powers. McCall argues in *The Powers of the Texas Governor* that the state's governors are only as strong as they make the office. The power of the governor is in his or her ability to leverage the "social game" of politics to get his or her way. This means that governors must be good people without a tendency to showboat and with a willingness to listen to their legislative partners. Governors who can do these things are more effective in office than those who can't, according to McCall.

The experience of Texas's current governor, Greg Abbott, demonstrates the importance of the governor's personality and skills. In his 2015 inaugural address, his first major speech as governor of Texas, Abbott set the tone for his next four years in office. The Governor's even-keeled approach has become his hallmark—one that has both served him well in dealing with the state's fractious politics and caused him to ignore potentially critical problems faced by the state. In his speech he highlighted issues like transportation, water, education, workforce readiness, and veterans' health care as agenda items for his term as governor. The power and reach of the Texas governor, then, is again determined by who holds the office.

The governor has the power to appoint individuals to specific boards and commissions but less power over administrative functions once that appointment is made, including limited removal power. Consequently, the selection of these individuals is critical to the governor's political agenda. Governors are not required to appoint individuals of any specific race or gender, although some, like Ann Richards, have vowed to make appointments that "looked like Texas." Abbott in his first two years was less successful at making appointments that reflect the diversity of the state, a fact pointed out by the *San Antonio Express-News* editorial board.

Although generally considered weak on paper, the powers of Texas governors can rise and fall depending on how willing the governor is to use these powers and how much authority other institutions (like the legislature or judiciary) are willing to cede to the executive.

CHAPTER QUESTIONS

1) Are the powers of the Texas governor too weak for this individual to successfully perform his or her job?
2) The limited constitutional powers of the Texas governor stem from the period following the Civil War. Is this approach to government outdated, and should the governor's powers be expanded to accommodate modern political interactions?
3) What characteristics do you most value in a Texas governor? Why?

8.1) Conclusion (Chapter 10)

The Power of the Texas Governor: Connally to Bush, 2009

BRIAN MCCALL

> Texas may have a weak governor on paper, but don't tell Texas governors that. Governors wield power through the bully pulpit (the ability to speak directly to Texans through social media and the news media), a large staff, and the ability to set the political agenda. Brian McCall, a former state representative and current chancellor of the Texas State University system, outlines how Texas governors have overcome their weak institutional limitations to achieve significant political power.
>
> Governors have several levers of power they can push and pull to get their way. McCall describes several: doing favors, working closely with key legislators, becoming an effective communicator, and acting in a pragmatic fashion. Undergirding all of these opportunities is McCall's main point: a governor is only as strong as he or she makes the office. The power of the governor is in his or her ability to leverage the "social game" of politics to get his or her way. Some governors, like Ann Richards and Bill Clements, have had these traits, but circumstances beyond their control have nonetheless interfered with their efforts. Economic troubles, conflicts with other executive officials, and legislative friction may minimize a governor's power. Above all, a governor must have the welfare of the citizens of Texas in his or her vision—this is what makes a truly great governor.

Governor Bush, as president-elect, told Lieutenant Governor Rick Perry that the governorship of Texas was the best job in the world. Months later, the new president of the United States called Governor Perry and asked, "Perry, do you remember what I told you about the governorship of Texas being the best job in the world?"

"Yes," replied the governor.

"Well, it's true!" said the leader of the free world.[1]

Indeed, those who have held the office tend to think highly of the experience. While serving, governors and their families live in a magnificent, mid-nineteenth-century Greek Revival mansion (the fourth-oldest governor's mansion in the nation). They can entertain legislators, supporters, and visiting dignitaries in one of the most historically significant residences in the nation. Overnight guests can sleep in Sam Houston's bed and pen a postcard telling friends about the experience while sitting at Stephen F. Austin's desk.

With a staff of approximately 150 people to work on policy and political matters, as well as to attend to personal concerns, a governor will have many needs and expectations covered without any second thought. The governor of Texas need not stand in lines. Pilots fly, drivers drive, personal chefs feed, and assistants fetch and deliver, while armed officers keep a constant vigil.

Typically, citizens are grateful when the governor of Texas cuts a ribbon to open a new public library in their town. Children are pleased when the governor recognizes their parents' fiftieth wedding anniversary by signing a resolution honoring the occasion. Graduates recall fondly that the governor delivered their commencement address. More than any other politician in the state, the governor can curry favor by doing favors.

As the personification of state government, a governor easily draws (and can generate) media attention. A former legislator decries that "the cacophony of legislator voices can rarely compete with a governor who can capitalize on the ability to command broad attention—which is surely one of the executive's principal strengths."[2] Staged events such as ceremonial bill signings and disaster proclamations ensure that a governor will receive credit for the ensuing good or relief (even though the governor may have had about as much to do with the bill's passage as with the occurrence of the disaster). Because a governor has no voting record, the disadvantaged can perceive the governor as sympathetic even if the governor never lifts a finger to address their concerns. Similarly, a skillful governor reads the movement of the legislature and gets out in front of its parade. The governor's ability to generate publicity can be a tremendously useful mechanism for advancing pet issues (since governors win their office—not mandates for their programs—with votes). To institute their programs, governors must persuade legislators, those who work in the news media, and members of the public.

Although the framers of the state constitution sought to limit—and succeeded in limiting—the influence of the governor's office, they overlooked one thing: power is a social game. Governors who are highly developed socially and who are driven to make changes can transcend the institutional limitations of the office. Paul Burka said of one governor that there were no benefits for being his friend and no consequences for being his enemy, yet this assertion is not true for every governor of Texas. Indeed, a strong governor creates those benefits and consequences and uses them to wield power effectively.

A collaborative governor who works with the legislature can realize numerous goals, often defying the naysayers, but an autocratic governor soon realizes the limitations of the power that he temporarily holds. As former Speaker Pete Laney says, "The power of the governor's office is dictated by how much the legislature wants to put up with."[3] To varying degrees, most governors of Texas have come to realize this. Clements realized this in his first term, while Smith learned this toward the end of his time in office. Most governors recover gracefully from the temporary illusion of self-importance that they may hold upon entering office. The smart ones realize: "The higher your station, the greater the need to remain attuned to the hearts and minds of those below you, creating a base of support to maintain you at the pinnacle. Without that base, your power will teeter, and at the slightest change of fortune, those below will gladly assist in your fall from grace."[4] Or as Mike McKinney, an aide to Governor Preston

Smith, suggests, "There is a day when it all just slams shut, and all of a sudden, you can't get your phone calls returned. Just like that! I guess one of the things that I realize is that every governor who takes office thinks that he is in charge of the state. But when the legislature convenes, that feeling is rocked. That's when the governor realizes that he's not really in charge of the state."[5]

Any elective office in a democracy lacks absolute power. The actual power of an elected official is largely the effective or ineffective use of potential or inherent power. Every position of leadership comes with potential power that may be augmented or limited by realistically assessing opportunities and skillfully exploiting them. However, in the case of the governorship of Texas, in large part, the lack of absolute power is due to the status of the office by law, so that the powers of the governor remain limited unless other officeholders, particularly in the legislature, give express consent otherwise. Every schoolchild learns of the checks and balances of the federal government, but there are many checks and balances upon the power of the governor of Texas. McKinney explains that the state constitution in effect makes the legislature the ruler of the state: "The governor has some real power, but it is always in connection with a legislative body. It's always that the governor *may* do something with the consent of the legislative budget board or with the consent of the speaker or lieutenant governor."[6]

Power is a social game. The successful governor will understand people and their motivations. He will possess attractive personal characteristics, a measure of persistence, and a degree of courage and independence. Further, the effective state chief executive will have both a vision and a plan to make that vision a reality. The effective governor will motivate others to want that vision and plan to succeed.

However, in the power game of legislative politics, governors are surrounded by people who, for the most part, have no interest in helping them unless it is in their clear interest to do so. Constituents tend to understand a legislator's reasons for voting against a governor's agenda more readily than they will accept a legislator's explanation for supporting a plan that does not benefit them directly.

Over time, if a governor has nothing to offer a legislator's own self-interest, that governor risks eventually incurring the wrath of the lawmaker. Like the state senator who busted Connally's appointee "just to let the governor know I exist," legislators—as far as governors are concerned—know that "there is no more infuriating feeling than having their individuality ignored, their own psychology unacknowledged."[7] Governor Richards and Governor Bush understood the significance of the individual legislator, and both governors treated each legislator with appropriate respect—unless or until a legislator burned his or her bridges with the governor. Governors Connally and Clements, to varying degrees, paid a price for their lack of attention to individual legislators. Legislators saw both governors as aloof. The price in Connally's case was the Senate bust; in Clements's case, it was the first veto override in thirty-eight years.

The effective governor cannot afford to overlook a legislator's broken promises or misrepresentations. The effective governor balances the reward of being the legislator's friend and the loss of being his enemy. Jack Martin concludes, "If you ever get to the point where the majority of people you are dealing with think that they have nothing to lose by going up against you—you're gone!"[8] Paul Burka writes, "These axioms are especially important for a Texas governor, who occupies an office with little inherent strength and who therefore must earn whatever power he hopes to exercise. A governor has little authority over the executive branch, which is run by other elected officials in some instances and independent boards in others; he has even less authority over the budget, which is the province of the Legislature. A governor has only one power, really—the power to persuade."[9]

It is often claimed that Henry Kissinger, upon becoming secretary of state, mused that the thing he liked best about the job was that when he bored people, they thought that it must be their fault. Once the governor-elect has assumed office, his or her jokes suddenly become funnier. A common temptation is for governors to overestimate their own charm, which may lead them to make less effort to charm, seduce, or gently persuade their constituents and colleagues.

In addition to a governor's own political instincts, the most effective chief executives suffer people who are not afraid to tell them what they do not wish to hear. Staffers who can only answer yes permit governors to make errors that lead to bad leadership. One wonders whether a forceful staffer working in the governor's self-interest could have prodded Briscoe out of the do-nothing image that became so ingrained in the voters' minds. Could anything have persuaded Richards to roll up her sleeves to do the necessary party building? Her failure to do so eventually helped doom her reelection efforts. Similarly, one wonders whether good staff work might have prevented Dolph Briscoe's constitution flip-flop or White's confusing and divergent economic forecasts.

Good governors realize what is going on and discern whom they can trust. In addition, they give their former enemies reasons to trust them, realizing that allies are generally more useful than enemies. Effective governors know that in many cases an empowered former enemy often turns out to be more loyal than a friend, inasmuch as a former enemy will have more to prove. Ann Richards lamented that there is often more to fear from friends than from enemies. As she put it, "I've always said that in politics, your enemies can't hurt you, but your friends will kill you."[10]

Mark Twain said, "You can take a starving dog and feed him—and he will not bite you. This is the principal difference between a man and a dog." The effective governor, when asking for help, will appeal to a legislator's self-interest, but never to the legislator's mercy or gratitude. As Robert Greene and Joost Elffers write in their examination of power, in words that seem to echo Machiavelli, "If you need to turn to an ally for help, do not bother to remind him of your past assistance and good deeds. He will find a way to ignore you. Instead, uncover something in your request or in your alliance with him that will benefit him, and emphasize that all out of proportion. He will respond enthusiastically when he sees something to be gained for himself."[11] The politically astute governor, in short, will appeal to a legislator's self-interest. Governor Preston Smith effectively used this strategy when telling the University of Texas advocates that he was eager to sign their legislation—and would do so—once he first was able to sign the legislation for Texas Tech University, which caused them to have an interest in helping him with *his* goals.

In addition, a governor with a sense of humor—particularly a governor who can deftly deflect tough issues with humor—has an advantage over a humorless governor, no matter how earnest, hardworking, and dedicated to the public's well-being. Both Richards and Bush capitalized deftly upon their talent for humor, receiving media coverage outside Texas which they used to their political advantage. The high-minded approach is not always best. Jane Hickie recalls a tense moment in the Richards campaign when the candidate was asked tough questions about the death penalty: "A reporter asked, 'What is your opinion on the death penalty?' Richards said, 'When I'm elected, I'm going to uphold the laws of the State of Texas.' The reporter asked, 'Well, what would you do if the Texas legislature gave you a bill to abolish the death penalty?' She said, 'I'd faint!'"[12]

In addition, effective governors are tireless activists for the causes that they have proclaimed. This was the case with Governor Bush. As Elton Bomer said of him, "When he made up his mind that something was the right thing to do for the state, he would put all of his energy and resources behind it, including his political capital, to accomplish those things. So he got the reputation around the state that all you have to do is listen, and you'll know what's likely to happen because he's going to do what he says he's going to do."[13]

When asked, "What makes a good governor?" Reggie Bashur, the press secretary to both Bill Clements and George Bush, says, "A clear sense of purpose, knowing what you want to achieve. You need to go into office with an agenda. Secondly, the ability to work with the legislature. It is an interactive process. The governor's office is only as good as the level of cooperation that he can solicit from the lieutenant governor, the speaker, and the members of the legislature. The governor must have that ability to interact in a constructive way. Third, a governor must have people around who can do the same—cooperate, communicate, and interact to move an agenda forward."[14] In addition, Bashur went on to say that Bush—in particular—had no patience for leaks. Bush demanded loyalty. Furthermore, he "had no patience for staff or anybody else posturing. He wanted everything to be fair and equal, on an open plane that was transparent, and for everybody to work together and cooperate."[15]

Pike Powers, the chief of staff to Governor White, offers a different answer to the question of what makes a good governor: "Oh, I think he, or she, has to be an effective communicator. I think they need to understand that the legislative interests are very diverse, and they need to be patient with that. They must be able to balance those diverse interests and be able to communicate with the media. White's great strength was that he'd walk into a room and within minutes he would sense the pulse of the room to know what was happening and how to respond to it. He just had a very significant intuitive sense."[16]

Former state senator Babe Schwartz believes that a good governor has "courage, vision, the ability to articulate a vision, and independence. I tell you, I guess money is responsible for this, but show me a guy today who will do something on his own when his chief political supporters happen to be on that issue on the other side. They don't have any courage if they don't!"[17]

Former lieutenant governor Bill Hobby believes that for a governor to be good, he first must be a good person. Accordingly, Hobby concludes that Briscoe, of the governors he served with, was "the best person, the most humane, the most understanding, and the most compassionate. Bill Clements was the worst."[18]

Former Speaker Gib Lewis has a different take. He believes that a good governor, above all, must be open-minded: "The worst thing that I have found over the years is for the governor to have a tendency to want to showboat. If they can refrain from doing that, they make a lot better governor. But when you—and I've seen them all do it to a degree—get out and sign some highway bill in the middle of a Houston freeway at five o'clock in the afternoon—or some crazy deal like that—to showboat it—that turns people off. I think it works against them."[19]

Jack Martin believes that both Ann Richards and Bill Clements were good governors because they inspired hope in people for positive change. Ann Richards, Martin says, was a good governor "first and foremost because Ann gave people the hope that here was going to be something other than the status quo, and that it was something that they could get excited about, and they could really have their lives improved by it. That's not a philosophical or a party thing. I think to some extent, Clements did that when he got elected governor. I think Clements gave people the hope that the status quo wasn't going to be the same."[20] Other reasons for their being good governors, in Martin's opinion, came down to their character and personality traits: Clements's candor and Richards's pragmatism: "Clements had this refreshing candor, so it's not a partisan thing. What was wonderful about Ann was that she was a pragmatist. Ann could wheel and deal with anybody, Republican or Democrat. If you were willing to get in the room with her and be objective about Ann and what Ann stood for, then she'd trade with you all day long. But if you were one of these people who decided that she was evil before the meeting began, which a lot of people did, there'd be no chance."[21]

However, no matter how much the officeholder may seem larger than life, the office is bigger than its holder. Mark White found that out. He had skills as sound as those of anyone else who had ever served in the office, but the times were against his success. The economy plummeted. The things beyond the control of the chief executive—whether good or bad—present the biggest challenges to any governor. As Greene and Elffers conclude, "Luck and circumstance always play a role in power. This is inevitable and actually makes the game more interesting. But, despite what you may think, good luck is always more dangerous than bad luck. Bad luck teaches valuable lessons about patience, timing, and the need to be prepared for the worst; good luck deludes you into the opposite lesson, making you think your brilliance will carry you through. Your fortune will inevitably turn, and when it does, you will be completely unprepared."[22]

White began his first legislative session not only by declaring that the budget was sound, but also by further advising legislators not to let anyone tell them otherwise. Two years later, the state was in a financial crisis, with the value of oil having plummeted by almost two-thirds. Knowing how to assume office in good times—and not bad times—makes a good governor good.

Because governance in Texas is designed to be carried out by several independently elected persons, an effective governor is ever aware of rivalries that the governor can create or work to prevent. Sometimes it is important to have and to make enemies. Often, however, it is not. Governor Clements made an enemy of his attorney general, Mark White. Governor Briscoe underestimated the ambition of Attorney General John Hill. Both governors ended up being challenged by their rivals. To be sure, the plurality of the executive branch can create rivalries, and those rivals can sometimes overtake the leadership of the governor. To a lesser degree, those rivalries can make the life of the governor difficult, as in the case of Lieutenant Governor Bullock and Governor Richards, whose personal differences created scars that never healed cleanly.

Notwithstanding all this, perhaps the most important characteristics of a good governor are a thick skin and personal vision. It has been said that legislative politics can be vicious because the stakes are so low. Every governor examined herein has been tough, relatively immune to criticism, and focused on doing work that is bigger than his or her own personal agendas. A good governor is interested in the welfare of the next generation. Each governor, to varying degrees, has taken this approach. Long may this approach continue in the State of Texas and its highest elective office.

NOTES

1. Perry, personal interview, July 6, 2006.

2. Rosenthal, *Governors and Legislatures' Contending Powers*, 25.

3. Laney, personal interview.

4. Greene and Elffers, *48 Laws of Power*, 370.

5. McKinney, personal interview.

6. Ibid.

7. Greene and Elffers, *48 Laws of Power*, 372.

8. Martin, personal interview.

9. Burka, "Strange Case of Mark White," 136.

10. Burka, "Sadder but Wiser," 59.

11. Greene and Elffers, *48 Laws of Power*, 95.

12. Hickie, personal interview.

13. Bomer, personal interview.

14. Bashur, personal interview.

15. Ibid.

16. Powers, personal interview.

17. Schwartz, personal interview.

18. Hobby, personal interview.

19. Lewis, personal interview, July 28, 2006.

20. Martin, personal interview.

21. Ibid.

22. Greene and Elffers, *48 Laws of Power*, 415.

ARTICLE QUESTIONS

1) What are three ways that a governor can use the office to maximize his or her influence?
2) Are you persuaded by the author's point – the relatively weak formal powers but strong personal powers – about the Texas governor?
3) What kids of mistakes do governors make in office that lead to failures of policy, politics, or persuasion?

8.2) 2015 Inaugural Address

Office of the Texas Governor, 2015

GREG ABBOTT

Before he was governor of Texas, Greg Abbott was a justice on the Texas Supreme Court and attorney general. Before all that, he withstood a personal tragedy that left him paralyzed from the waist down and in a wheelchair for the rest of his life. He was twenty-six then and an aspiring lawyer in Houston—now he is the de facto leader of the state Republican Party at a critical period in its history. Abbott's Republican Party is pushing ideologically further to the right, splitting moderates from conservatives on several policy matters.

The governor came to office with a unique perspective, one influenced by his disability, his wife's Latina identity, and his service as a judge. His exacting attention to detail, work ethic, and sense of urgency in moving his career forward have driven his approach to his office. How might this approach shift as Abbott faces an internally divided party, an increasingly polarized electorate, and a state that is slowly trending more Democratic?

In his inaugural address Abbott describes a state with promise but also problems. He highlights issues like transportation, water, education, workforce readiness, and veterans' health care as agenda items for his term as governor. As governor, he promises to push back against Washington if it regulates too much, spends too much, or violates state sovereignty. He argues against "cookie-cutter" approaches to teaching and that students should have great teachers who recognize their value and uniqueness. Finally, he pledges to make job growth a priority to keep Texas's economy on track.

Texas faces many challenges in the twenty-first century as the state continues to grow, its demographics change, and its economy hits rough patches. In your opinion, does Abbott outline an agenda that will meet the needs of the Lone Star State?

Thank you and welcome to your capitol of Texas.

Lieutenant Governor Patrick, Speaker Straus, elected officials, members of the judiciary and the legislature—and most especially, my fellow Texans.

Let me express my deep gratitude to the people of Texas for electing me governor of the greatest state in America.

For fourteen years we the people have placed our trust in a man I am humbled to succeed. Along with his wife, Anita, he has been a faithful steward of the miracle that is Texas. And I thank Rick Perry for his unwavering leadership.

The path that brought me here I could not have traveled alone. I share today with so many, starting with a woman of genuine warmth and character: My beautiful wife, Cecilia.

Texas has been the blending of cultures from across the globe even before we became our own nation. My wife represents that as she now has made Texas history as the first Hispanic First Lady in the history of our great state.

Cecilia and I share this day with our precious daughter, Audrey. Through your eyes we see the promise of the next generation of Texans.

I am honored to be Texas governor. But the title that matters most to me is Dad.

Family is everything to us, as shown by the legions of family members with us today. I won't name them all but I want all of them to know how grateful I am for their love and support.

I do want to recognize my father-in-law, Bill Phalen, and perhaps the most famous mother-in-law in Texas, *mi madrina*, Maria de la luz Segura Phalen.

I also want to recognize Gary Abbott. He's my big brother and a retired commander in the U.S. Navy where he served for 20 years.

Thanks to my brother Gary and to every man and woman who has ever worn the uniform of the United States military. Their extraordinary service has secured our freedom to celebrate events of democracy like this today.

But, let's face it, for me this moment was highly improbable. During this month 30 years ago I laid in a hospital bed recovering from injuries that broke my back and left me forever unable to walk.

The journey from that Houston hospital to the Texas governorship was possible because of two powerful forces.

First is the grace of God. The Book of Matthew reminds us that with God all things are possible.

I am reminded of this when I hear a song that often plays in churches. It's titled "You Raise Me Up":

> You raise me up so I can stand on mountains;
> You raise me up to walk on stormy seas;
> I am strong when I am on your shoulders;
> You raise me up to more than I can be.

As I begin my governorship I humbly ask for God's continued grace and guidance, and I assure you: We will never forget that we remain one nation under God.

The other powerful force that allowed me to go from that Houston hospital to this inauguration is that I had the good fortune to live in the great state of Texas.

Texas is the place where the improbable becomes the possible.

Many thought that it was improbable that Texans would overcome total devastation at the Alamo. And yet the unyielding drive for independence that has always filled the hearts of Texans led to victory at the battle of San Jacinto. And thus began the legend that Texas has become.

To this day Texas has been filled with legends who started humbly and succeeded spectacularly.

Where a boy like Dan Duncan who grew up dirt poor in East Texas started a business with two trucks and $10,000, but with hard work and true grit he went on to become one of the wealthiest Texans ever.

Where people like Colleen Barrett can climb the ladder from executive assistant to being listed as one of the most powerful women in America as president of Southwest Airlines.

Where a 13-year-old daughter of immigrants from Mexico worked nights in a drapery factory but never gave up on her dreams. Now Eva Guzman is the first Latina to serve as a justice on the Texas Supreme Court.

And where a mother from Wichita Falls who, like so many mothers, chose to stay at home with her children to raise them and instill in them the values she thought important.

Although she's now in heaven with my dad she's no doubt proud that her timeless love and devotion inspired her son to become the 48th governor of Texas.

These stories are the promise of Texas. These stories are not the exception because our state truly is exceptional.

I am living proof that we live in a state where a young man's life can literally be broken in half and yet he can still rise up and be governor of this great state.

As governor I will ensure Texas remains the state that provides that brand of opportunity for every Texan.

Texas truly is the land of opportunity, the place where anyone can achieve anything. But as great as Texas is there's more we must do.

More for the families stuck in traffic.

More for parched towns thirsty for water.

More for parents who fear their child is falling behind in school.

More for employers searching for skilled workers.

More for our veterans who return broken from battle.

And we must do more for the millions of Texans who are tired of seeing our state sovereignty and the rule of law ignored by a federal government that refuses to secure our border.

As governor, I will ensure that we build the roads needed to keep Texas growing. That taxes raised for roads will be spent on roads. I will speed up our needed water projects, and I will secure our border.

As governor I will continue my legacy of pushing back against Washington if they spend too much, regulate too much, or violate our state sovereignty.

Any government that uses the guise of fairness to rob us of our freedom will get a uniquely Texan response: "Come and take it."

We Texans aren't spoiling for a fight, but we won't shrink from one if the cause is right.

For too long Washington has tried to remake America in its image. In Texas, we offer a different approach: We don't put our trust in government; we put our trust in the people, and I will make sure we keep it that way.

We must never forget that government is the servant of the people—not the other way around.

I will also ensure that we keep Texas number one in the nation for job creation. We will promote policies that limit the growth of government—not the size of your dreams.

Yet we know too many still live on the fringe of opportunity. For them there is no solace in number one rankings that fail to touch their lives. I speak about children living in broken homes and struggling in broken schools.

On this point we cannot be captive to partisan arguments. Our children transcend politics. If Texas is to remain the leader at creating jobs we must become the leader at educating our children.

Countries sometimes excel because of their military might.

States are different. We excel by our mental might. Texas should be the source of the greatest minds the country has ever known.

These great minds will not be molded by a cookie-cutter approach to teaching. Instead they will be the product of great teachers who recognize the value and uniqueness of each student.

We will cultivate those teachers to educate those students to fill the growing job markets that will keep Texas the economic engine of America.

With us today is one of those teachers, my English teacher at Duncanville High School, Nancy Nickel.

She taught me more than how to read and write. She taught me to reach for my dreams.

Thank you, Mrs. Nickel, and thanks to all of our tremendous teachers.

There is no place like Texas. We will ensure that remains just as true for the next generation as it does for those here today.

So, take a moment. Look at where you're standing or sitting right now. The ground beneath your feet is more than just grass or pavement.

It's the soil that centuries ago bore the hopes and dreams of settlers who risked it all to come to a land that promised freedom and opportunity.

Scripture teaches us that tribulation produces perseverance, perseverance, character and character, hope.

Texans are filled with hope because our lives have been infused with the perseverance and character that sprang from the tribulations faced by those who came before us.

And we must make sure this hallowed ground stirs the hopes and dreams of those who come after us.

We must keep Texas on a path that ensures that years from now people will stand on this very ground as grateful to this generation as we are to past generations.

To do that we must do more than work to find common ground to solve our problems.

We must seek higher ground that will continue to elevate Texas, not just as a leader in this nation, but as a leader in this world.

Because as goes Texas, so goes America, and as goes America, so goes the world.

So we must take the lead here in Texas—from Amarillo to McAllen, from El Paso to Beaumont. We must work together to ensure that even the future is bigger in Texas.

May God bless each and every one of you, and may God forever bless the great state of Texas.

ARTICLE QUESTIONS

1) What are the key themes of Abbott's inaugural address?
2) How have the events of Abbott's life affected his governing philosophy?
3) What are the issues the governor outlines as the most important for the state? Do you agree?

8.3) Value in Diversity in Appointments

Express-News, April 25, 2016

EDITORIAL BOARD

Appointment powers are one of the most lasting that a governor has in his or her toolbox. Since these individuals are selected by the governor, he or she has the ability to shape the executive branch in a way that reflects the state's diversity. However, analysis from *San Antonio Express-News* Austin bureau chief Peggy Fikac and reporter David Saleh Rauf reveals that two years into Governor Abbott's tenure, three-fourths of his appointments have been Anglo individuals and 60 percent have been men. In contrast, the state's population is 43 percent Anglo and just over 50 percent female, making the governor's picks not reflective of the state's diversity.

Linking the importance of race and ethnicity in higher education to their importance in government, the *San Antonio Express-News* asks that the governor give careful thought to the impact of diversity on Texas's government. More fair representation provides for unique perspectives, the editorial argues, which help policymakers and bureaucrats successfully implement policies for a changing Texas. In an increasingly diverse state like Texas, what weight should diversity play in executive appointments?

Gov. Greg Abbott's appointments to date do not reflect the diversity of Texas' population. We urge him to consider the state's demographic composition in the future. It will make for fairer—and more knowledge-based—representation.

The U.S. Supreme Court is weighing, in the case of an alternate admissions process at the University of Texas at Austin, whether race can be used as one factor among many in admissions.

No matter how the court rules, the values driving UT's goal of a student body that looks like the state should be the same ones that Gov. Greg Abbott considers in appointments.

An analysis of the governor's appointments so far indicates he is falling short.

Peggy Fikac and David Saleh Rauf of Hearst Newspapers' Austin bureau looked at Abbott's appointments and found that three-fourths of his picks have been white and more than 60 percent have been men. This, in a state that is 43.5 percent white and a bit more than half female.

To be precise, among his 460 appointments, 72 percent have been white, 62 percent men, 45 percent white men, 27 percent white women, 15 percent Latino and 6 percent African-American.

UT and other universities defend race and ethnicity as factors among many in recognition of diversity's value. There is fairness inherent in giving access to quality education to a broader segment of the population, and creativity blooms when different experiences meet—as important in classrooms as it is in the workplace. The same applies to gender.

In workplaces in particular, different experiences mean an ability to strategize, plan and execute armed with broadened abilities to understand markets and constituencies, and it means an enhanced ability to communicate with them and to deliver what they need.

In the case of government, diversity potentially means fairer representation, an important concept even when positions aren't directly elected. And this includes regional representation. We note that 12.6 percent of the governor's appointments are from South Texas, an area that includes San Antonio. South Texas' population is 17.32 percent of the total state population.

One in 4 of his appointees has been a campaign contributor, but we're assuming that most are, in fact, qualified for their posts. And we know that this record of appointments that do not reflect the state's demographics is one shared by Abbott's predecessors, including the last Democratic governor, Ann Richards.

But we also know for a certainty that race and ethnicity—and gender and the region you live in—don't spell lack of qualification.

Fikac and Rauf explained that the governor has the potential to make as many as 3,000 appointments in a four-year term. We urge him to consider diversity—and the state's demographic composition. It will make for fairer—and more knowledge-based—representation.

ARTICLE QUESTIONS

1) Identify three reasons the editorial argues that diversity is positive for Texas's government.

2) Are you persuaded by the editorial's opinion about the importance of diversity in gubernatorial appointments?

3) In past legislative sessions, representatives have tried but failed to pass legislation requiring the governor to make a minimum number of appointments of racial or ethnic minorities and females. Should a governor be subject to such requirements, , or should all appointments be at the governor's discretion?

Chapter 9

The Plural Executive in Texas

Texas has a long history of distrust of executive power, reflecting anger at the dictatorship of the Mexican government before the Republic was born and dissatisfaction with the Union after the Civil War when Washington imposed a strict central government on the state. Subsequent Texas constitutions consequently minimized executive power in state government.

The resulting diffusion of authority and power throughout the executive branch is called the "plural executive." Offices wielding such power include the lieutenant governor (responsible for both executive and legislative duties in the Texas Senate), the attorney general (the chief legal officer for Texas), the comptroller of public accounts (the state's tax collector), the land commissioner (responsible for managing and leasing the state's land), and dozens of boards and commissions—some elected, some appointed—that shape the state's policy direction. How do all these offices get along?

This "plural executive" system forces governors to share power with other elected officials and checks the power of statewide executives. The implicit purpose of this arrangement is to ensure that no single state executive or legislative office becomes too powerful. It also ensures that multiple executive branch offices remain creative and nimble and opens up the possibility of greater democratic representation.

Former lieutenant governor Bill Hobby once remarked, "The only job of the lieutenant governor is to call the governor and ask about his or her health." Unlike lieutenant governors in most other states, Texas's has a strong and sizeable role with both executive and legislative duties. Because these duties span the most important parts of the state government, the lieutenant governor is Texas's most powerful governing force, at least on paper. In fact, *Texas Monthly* in 2017 featured the current lieutenant governor, Dan Patrick, on the cover of its February issue holding a giant gavel with the headline: "The Power Behind the Throne." Chief political writer R. G. Ratcliffe makes a good case for the speed and efficiency with which Patrick has amassed and used political power in his first few years in office. His actions have had profound implications for state politics and the policies produced by the legislature.

Although they are not as visible as the politicians who control them, the state is largely run by bureaucrats. A bureaucracy is a complex professional organization that administers government actions through routine tasks. Governments rely significantly on bureaucracies to function. Because of the state's enormous landmass, number of businesses, population, and economy, the bureaucracy in Texas is necessarily huge. Individual offices run these parts of the bureaucracy, and each plays a significant role in the functioning of Texas's government.

The attorney general is the state's lawyer, and his clients are the governor, state agencies, and government entities requesting rulings on public information requests. The attorney general's primary responsibility is to defend Texas's laws and constitution by representing the state in court. The Attorney General's Office is charged with enforcement of consumer regulations, protection of the rights of the elderly and disabled, and oversight of child support issues and widespread fraud, including deceptive business practices, car repair fraud, telemarketing scams, identity theft, and other consumer-related complaints. Ken Paxton, the current occupant of the office, has faced legal and ethical problems but has maintained his laser-like focus on the issues that drove him into office: stamping out voter fraud and enhancing Texans' religious liberty. *Texas Monthly*'s R. G. Ratcliffe writes that while Paxton's detractors argue that he is using the office for political purposes, this tension underscores the dual roles of attorney generals in Texas as servants of both the state's interests and their own political coalition.

The Texas land commissioner, the oldest continuously elected position in Texas, established in 1836, is the administrator of the state's public lands—an important role because these properties generate funds from oil and gas production that flow into the Permanent School Fund. The office is also in charge of the Veteran's Land Board, which makes low-interest loans available to veterans to purchase land and homes and oversees state veterans' cemeteries and skilled-care facilities for veterans. George P. Bush, nephew of former president George W. Bush and grandson of former president George H. W. Bush, is the current land commissioner, and although the office is an obscure one on a national scale, Commissioner Bush may play a central role in the future of the Republican Party in Texas. Christopher Hooks, writing for *Politico*, examines the friction between Bush's political positions and those of the rest of the Republican Party and what implications this tension will have for the future of state politics.

CHAPTER QUESTIONS

1) How do the personalities of executive officeholders heighten or detract from their influence in state government?
2) Members of the plural executive are elected to partisan offices. Should Texas elect or appoint these officials?
3) What traits do the individuals elected to executive office in Texas have in common?
4) How do partisan politics affect the roles and responsibilities of executive officers? Does this interaction change your perception of the offices these individuals hold?

9.1) The Power Behind the Throne (Selections)

Texas Monthly, February 2017

R. G. RATCLIFFE

> Lieutenant governors used to be like the "spare tire" of government—kept pumped up and ready to go with the hope that they would never be used. The office of lieutenant governor was initially designed to be a "backup" in times when a governor could not serve. Times have certainly changed, however—and nowhere more so than in the state of Texas, where the lieutenant governor wields significant political and institutional power. R. G. Ratcliffe investigates the growing political power of Texas Lieutenant Governor Dan Patrick, charting his journey from conservative radio show host to state senator to lieutenant governor. His trail has been punctuated by controversy, but there is no denying that, as *Texas Monthly* puts it, he's a powerful force in state government.
>
> Patrick's revamping of the lieutenant governorship starts in an unlikely place: rules. The Texas Constitution allows the lieutenant governor to serve as the head of the Texas Senate, and that chamber's rules allow the lieutenant governor to have almost complete say over the makeup of committees, the committees to which legislation is assigned, and which members are allowed to speak. Ratcliffe argues that Patrick grabbed the reins of state government by capitalizing on what he perceived as a lack of leadership by other Republican officials. This "gift for political maneuvering" has been evident not only in Texas politics but also in national politics, with Patrick becoming involved in the 2016 presidential election.
>
> At the heart of Patrick's conservative agenda is legislation that would require people in Texas to use the bathroom of their biological gender instead of the gender they identify with—a so-called "bathroom" bill. Ratcliffe charts the history of these laws and points out that they have always generated controversy. Despite opposition from many in the business community, Patrick has been adamant that the state's voters have signaled their support for this kind of law. Ratcliffe ends his article by suggesting that power is fleeting and challenges are likely. Does he anticipate there will be political change on this issue or institutional backlash?

One Thursday in late May, a cadre of lobbyists representing some of Texas's most powerful industries asked Dan Patrick, the state's lieutenant governor, to join them for a discussion of his agenda for the Legislature's 140-day session that would begin in January. They gathered in the second-floor ballroom of the Austin Club, a private, six-decade-old institution that sits a few blocks from the Capitol. The club occupies the historic Millett Opera House, which dates to 1878 and was where populist presidential candidate William Jennings Bryan once railed against the gold standard. With the possible exception of the Capitol itself, no other building in Texas has been the site of more deal making. Many club members are former legislators or past advisers to Democratic and Republican governors, and at lunchtime when the Legislature is in session, a parade of lawmakers often marches south on Congress Avenue, turns left at Ninth Street, passes through the club's grand entrance, and vanishes from public view into elegant rooms where they dine as lobbyists' guests. The walls are dark-wood paneling, the tables are covered in white linens, and fresh flowers are everywhere. In this cloistered environment, bonhomie, fine food, and wine create bonds of friendship between lobbyists and state officials—the lifeblood of policy making in Texas.

The group that had invited Patrick was the Texas Business Roundtable. It consists of more than two dozen lobby shops representing government contractors, petrochemical companies, hospitals, retailers, and restaurateurs, among others—the kinds of businesses that have traditionally dictated the direction of Texas politics.

And in the past, they would have considered a sitting lieutenant governor an ally, or at least an honest broker in resolving conflict. Patrick is a different breed, though. He's not an establishment Republican but rather a product of the party's fervent grass roots.

Patrick came to prominence as a right-wing talk-radio host in Houston and parlayed that notoriety into a seat in the Texas Senate. In his first session, in 2007, he was an outsider disdained by many of his colleagues. His first proposal on the floor—to change Senate rules to make it harder for Democrats to block bills, which senators of both parties considered a breach of protocol—was voted down thirty to one. But in the decade since, his brand of politics has become mainstream, and Patrick has gradually accumulated influence. By 2014, when he was elected lieutenant governor, the presiding officer of the Senate, his takeover was complete.

Patrick's legislative agenda for 2017 feels as if it could have once been programming for his talk show. He has 25 priorities, which appeal largely to social and fiscal conservatives. While some involve broad public policy, such as balancing the state budget and improving Child Protective Services, the majority are wedge issues. They include property tax restrictions on local governments, a First Amendment shield law for ministers who preach politics from the pulpit, and a crackdown on so-called sanctuary cities, where police do not actively enforce federal immigration laws. Patrick is also passionate about passing a voucher plan that would allow parents to spend public money to send their kids to private schools.

At the Austin Club, Patrick laid out the highlights of his agenda, building to his top priority, one that wasn't likely to go over well with some of the assembled business lobbyists: a bill that would require transgender people to use public restrooms that correspond to their gender at birth, not the gender they identify with. Patrick has said his intent is to keep men out of women's restrooms, and he has referred to the bill as the "women's privacy act." To Patrick's critics, though, the proposal is rank discrimination against transgender Texans.

It's the specter of that discrimination—or what people around the country might see as discrimination—that has business leaders spooked, and it's not a feeling they're accustomed to, especially on this topic. Restroom access was a nonstarter the last time the Legislature was in session, in 2015; a handful of House bills on the subject never even got committee hearings, and Patrick and the Senate ignored them. But in recent years, religious-right activists began promoting the idea that municipal antidiscrimination ordinances could allow a sexual predator to enter women's public restrooms merely by declaring that he was a female at heart—though there's no evidence that has ever occurred. North Carolina famously passed strident restroom restrictions, and business leaders in that state watched the backlash in horror: corporate relocations and expansions were halted, and major college and professional sporting events were moved out of state. The Texas Association of Business has estimated that similar restroom legislation, if passed in Texas, would cost the state economy up to $8.5 billion, including the possible loss of college basketball's 2018 Final Four, in San Antonio.

The association has used those estimates to justify its strong opposition to a restroom bill, and various power brokers, including Dallas Cowboys owner Jerry Jones, have tried to persuade Patrick to drop the notion. Such behind-the-scenes pressure from the business lobby has often proved decisive at the Capitol: the hidden government of lobbyists effectively murdered tax reform under Governor George W. Bush, and Governor Rick Perry succeeded only when he let the lobby write the bill. Faced with major opposition from big business, many politicians have acquiesced. But Patrick, with his political base in tea party groups and evangelical churches, is not so beholden to the business community, and at the Austin Club in May, he made it clear who was in charge.

Patrick told the business lobbyists that the women's privacy act is a passion for him, then offered a warning: "If you're not with me, I'm not with you." What the lobbyists heard was, oppose my restroom bill and your clients' legislation is dead in the Senate.

Patrick was culling the herd. He fully expected businesses with an interest in tourism, corporate relocations, and national employee recruitment to oppose him. What he wanted was to get the businesses not directly affected by the legislation to stand down. Patrick's veiled threat was about more than just a piece of conservative legislation, though. He was re-establishing the lieutenant governor as the most powerful politician in Texas and positioning himself as the state's culture warrior in chief.

Much of Patrick's clout comes from the reach of his office. The power stems from the state constitution and Senate rules, which make the lieutenant governor the ultimate authority on which bills come to the floor for debate. He appoints the committees and then decides which bills those committees will handle. The lieutenant governor also sets the Senate's daily agenda. If he dislikes a senator or the senator's legislation, he will simply never recognize him or her to bring a bill up for a vote. Controlling the flow of legislation to such a degree enables the office of lieutenant governor, in the right hands, to bend lawmakers, lobbyists, interest groups—or anyone who has business before the Legislature—to the occupant's will.

In the nineties, the irascible Democrat Bob Bullock was particularly effective. (Disclosure: Paul Hobby, *Texas Monthly*'s chairman, served as Bullock's chief of staff in 1991.) He was famous for using "drive-by ass-chewings" to get his way. Patrick has yet to reach Bullock's level, but he has several advantages over his predecessors. For one, he has a huge Republican majority in the Senate. And several of the body's longest-tenured members, some of whom had strident personalities—and who might have fought the lieutenant governor on certain issues—have retired over the past three sessions, leaving a crop of Republican newcomers more aligned with Patrick's ideology. In fact, about 15 of the 20 Republican senators are like-minded social conservatives. Finally, the Democrats are nearly powerless. In his first session as lieutenant governor, Patrick fulfilled a campaign promise by implementing a rule change—the same one he had first sought in 2007—that raised the number of votes required to block a bill from debate. That has effectively neutered Democrats' ability to halt the conservative

agenda. All of this allows Patrick to run the Senate with ease and leaves him free to pressure lobbyists into, say, staying neutral on his restroom proposal. Otherwise their bills have no chance.

Despite the power of the office, Patrick's predecessor, David Dewhurst, was viewed around the Capitol as fairly weak during his dozen years in office, from 2003 to 2015. As one senator told this magazine about Dewhurst in 2011, "I don't think he knows what power is." For much of that time, the force in state politics was Perry, who, by harshly punishing enemies and rewarding cronies and allies, managed to concentrate an unprecedented amount of power in the governor's office. When Perry stepped down after fourteen years, he left a leadership vacuum at the top of state government. The incoming governor, Greg Abbott, had a limited agenda in 2015. And House Speaker Joe Straus, supported by a coalition of Democratic and moderate Republican House members, has typically been focused on building compromise among various factions in his chamber. That left Patrick, who eagerly filled the void by setting out an aggressive agenda in 2015 and making himself the dominant figure at the Capitol.

The power dynamics between the big three state leaders appear roughly the same so far in 2017. If anything, Patrick seems even sturdier, having learned in his first session in statewide office how to effectively deploy his authority. Abbott, meanwhile, often looks more like a politician trying to avoid reelection mistakes than one set on creating a legacy. In a December meeting with reporters, Abbott responded to most policy questions by saying he wanted to either study a topic further or take a wait-and-see approach. Asked specifically about Patrick's restroom proposal, just weeks before the session, Abbott said, "As a general rule I don't think men should be in women's bathrooms. . . . We need to dig into the facts and find out who has been harmed or endangered or been compromised and how often that's happened." Asked bluntly if a transgender person who identifies as a woman should be considered a woman, Abbott said, "This isn't an issue that should be determined without a full evaluation, all the information. We are in the information-gathering stage right now." He did describe his "four pillars" for the session as the ever-controversial freedom, economic opportunity, educational advancement, and safety and security.

Abbott does have a few specific aims: He has been wrestling with fixing the troubled Child Protective Services department, he is pushing for rules requiring the burial or cremation of aborted fetuses, and he has proclaimed that he will cut off state funding to universities that declare themselves as sanctuary campuses for undocumented students. But his agenda for the session is thin, focused mainly on his call for a convention of states to propose amendments to the U.S. Constitution. Otherwise, he's largely left the field to Patrick. Moreover, the governor seems to lack Patrick's sharp political instincts for knowing where the base of his party is headed and when to take risks.

For all the news stories written about Patrick and all the controversy he's generated, his political savvy is rarely mentioned. During his years on talk radio, Patrick learned how to gauge his listeners, picking the topics—the red meat—that would animate his conservative audience. And who are voters if not an audience? He then turned them into his base, busing Houston residents to the Legislature in 2003 to protest their property taxes, for example. He leveled attacks not only on Democrats but also on Republicans, such as President George W. Bush, for being insufficiently conservative. He was a tea party politician before the tea party even existed.

But the best example of Patrick's gift for political maneuvering was his handling of U.S. senator Ted Cruz, who, until very recently, was the state's most prominent and popular elected official. Cruz had launched his bid for the presidency as a no-compromise politician who practiced poke-'em-in-the-eye brinkmanship against the Obama administration. Before Cruz even announced his candidacy for president, Patrick had endorsed him, declaring Cruz "the prescription for what is ailing the country and our party." Patrick was one of Cruz's most visible surrogates throughout the campaign, standing next to the candidate during Cruz's victory speech the night of the Texas primary.

But when it became obvious Trump would win the Republican nomination, Patrick deftly shifted to the winning side. After Cruz dropped out of the race, Patrick immediately endorsed and promoted Trump as the party nominee, and Trump reciprocated by naming him the campaign's state chairman, describing the lieutenant governor as "a passionate conservative who has been a good friend to our campaign." Meanwhile, other Texas politicians were either noncommittal on Trump or noticeably less enthused. Senior U.S. senator John Cornyn tried to ignore Trump. Abbott eventually, begrudgingly, gave his support but mostly stayed silent, except when he called on the nominee to show "true contrition" after video surfaced of Trump making insulting statements about women.

For his part, Cruz turned his endorsement—or lack thereof—into a saga. At the national party convention, in July, he delivered an awkward and self-destructive speech in which he pointedly refused to endorse Trump and urged Republicans to "vote your conscience." The reaction from delegates that night in the convention hall and from Cruz's constituents for weeks afterward was largely negative, and pressure built for him to endorse Trump, specifically in the form of rumors that he would face a primary challenge in 2018.

In the midst of this, Patrick took advantage. He went on Laura Ingraham's national radio talk show and, with a few well-chosen words, forced Cruz to kowtow to Trump. Patrick said he was "disappointed" in Cruz and said the senator risked being "left in the rearview mirror of the Republican party moving forward." He went on. "So I'm hoping Ted comes forward. I'm still visiting with him on that issue." By the end of the week, Cruz had endorsed Trump.

This is the bizarre modern world of politics and media, where a former talk-show host can use talk radio to compel a national politician to take a knee to a billionaire businessman who had his own televised reality show. Unfortunately for Cruz, his endorsement angered his hard-core supporters, and by backing Trump, a man he'd so forcefully opposed, he damaged his brand as the rare public official who puts conservative ideals above ambition. Instead, he looked like another craven politician. In the end, Cruz—through his own fumbling and with an assist from Patrick—ended up with the worst result: Trump supporters still detest him for his convention speech, and the anti-Trump Republicans feel betrayed too.

Patrick, by comparison, came out of the 2016 election as popular as ever among the party's grass roots—and with a new ally in Washington. When Trump won the presidency, Patrick declared that "Texans will now have a good friend in the White House." Patrick had walked tall down a path where others tiptoed. In that transcendent moment, Dan Patrick became the most influential politician in Texas. Now he's investing his significant political capital in a risky, divisive issue.

The history of public toilet controversies is long, dating back at least to the days of ancient Rome, but the women's room is a relatively new contrivance on the timeline of humanity. Even today some countries don't have public facilities for women. Historically, a woman's place was often considered to be at home, and that is where she was meant to use the restroom. (Some feminists have referred to this as the "urinary leash.") But in 1887, Massachusetts passed a law requiring workplaces that employed women to provide them with a restroom. When Selfridge's department store opened in London, in 1909, it was the first store in Britain to provide women's toilets. Harry Selfridge believed ladies were likely to shop longer and spend more of their husbands' money if they didn't have to run home for bladder relief. In the first half of the twentieth century, racial segregation laws in Southern states required that public facilities have separate restrooms for men, women, and nonwhite minorities, the latter being a restroom where adult men and women and children often used the same toilets. News accounts at the time reported no sexual assaults.2qwedx

In the nineties, Texas women were empowered by the election of Governor Ann Richards, who in 1993 signed the "potty parity" law, requiring certain new buildings and renovated sports facilities to have two toilets in women's restrooms for every one toilet in the men's room. "On behalf of all women in the state of Texas, and all women who visit the state of Texas, and all of us sports fans who go into those stadiums with those long, long lines, what a pleasure this is," Richards said at the bill-signing ceremony. Now the restroom parity of the Ann Richards era has given way to the restroom privacy of Dan Patrick's.

The lieutenant governor first seized on the issue during the 2015 referendum to overturn an antidiscrimination ordinance in Houston that gave protections to people in the lesbian, gay, bisexual, and transgender community. A pastor-led group had been fighting in court to overturn the Houston Equal Rights Ordinance, known as HERO, which was supported by then-mayor Annise Parker, one of the nation's first openly gay mayors. Patrick and Abbott threw themselves into what should have been a local issue, urging voters to reject the ordinance. Opponents of HERO made the threat of men entering women's restrooms the center of their campaign, running a controversial television spot of a man following a young girl into a stall. By Election Day, religious-right activists had boiled the HERO fight down to signs that read: "No Men in Women's Bathrooms."

In an interview on Fox News, Patrick was challenged by host Megyn Kelly on his claim that antidiscrimination ordinances "allow men in ladies' rooms." She asked whether it would allow men in ladies' rooms or "allow trans women in ladies' rooms." Patrick said she didn't get it. "They don't have to be dressed like a woman. They can be dressed like an ordinary man. What this creates is a great loophole for all the sexual predators and sex offenders," he said. "I don't want an eight-year-old granddaughter walking into a bathroom with a thirty-year-old man there."

Yet there are already state criminal laws against sexual predators and Peeping Toms. And there's never been a documented case in Texas of a transgender woman assaulting anyone in a restroom. But in the past year, anytime a perverted man committed a crime in a women's room in Texas, social conservatives claimed it was proof that equal rights for transgender Texans will protect such criminals. Patrick released a poll that found that 69 percent of Texas voters "believe it should be illegal for a man to enter a women's restroom."

The Williams Institute at the UCLA School of Law estimates that there are 125,000 transgender people living in Texas, less than one percent of the state's population. Many are men who have been living as women and dressing as women their entire adult lives. Some have undergone sex change operations, while others use hormone therapy to grow breasts. Forcing them to use a men's room could put them at risk of hate crimes.

More than 1,200 Texas businesses have joined with LGBT activists to form a group called Texas Competes as a show of solidarity against laws that allow discrimination, including American Airlines, Southwest Airlines, computer chip manufacturer AMD, Dow Chemical, La Quinta Inns & Suites, the Greater Houston Partnership, and the Dallas Mavericks. Breitbart Texas responded with a story titled "Texas Businesses Surrender to LGBT Agenda on Religious Liberty Issues." But harping by social conservatives has not prompted the business community to back down. The Texas Association of Business is leading a coalition called Keep Texas Open for Business to fight against Patrick's proposal. The group has cited reports that North Carolina lost $630 million in business in the first several months after the passage of its bill, and some experts predict that long-term losses could run as high as $5 billion. One study estimated that the Texas loss of economic activity from the restroom bill would range from $964 million to $8.5 billion, with the loss of as many as 185,000 jobs. "We do not want to be North Carolina or Indiana," said Chris Wallace, the president of the association. Patrick's aides dismissed the study as "fearmongering" and speculative. Jared Woodfill, the president of the Conservative Republicans of Texas, an advocacy group that promotes "Constitutional liberties based upon Biblical principles," went so far as to categorize the study as "fake news," because it analyzed a bill that, at the time, had not yet been filed.

Such fierce opposition recalls the strength demonstrated by the business lobby in successfully killing previous conservative proposals in the past decade, especially on immigration. When Perry called a special session in 2011 to ban sanctuary cities, late home builder Bob Perry (no relation) and grocery store magnate Charles Butt combined forces to snuff out the governor's anti-immigrant bill, because their businesses needed the workers. In 2015 the Texas Association of Business blocked

legislation to abolish the program of in-state college tuition for undocumented children who graduate from a Texas high school. If the business lobby unifies in opposition to the restroom bill, Patrick's proposal could be in trouble, hence his heavy hints at holding other business-friendly legislation hostage.

With Abbott waffling, the business lobby is relying on Speaker Straus to keep the legislation bottled up in the House. You could almost hear the collective sigh of relief when Straus told Evan Smith of the *Texas Tribune* last fall that Patrick's transgender restroom bill wasn't his "most urgent concern." Then Straus allowed the cold chill of fear to reemerge. "That doesn't mean the House [isn't] going to feel differently than I do." His message to the lobby seemed clear: God helps those who help themselves, and so does the House speaker. If big business wants to halt the restroom bill, it needs to win over House members. In other words, the lobby is on its own.

Patrick has been as defiant as ever. Shortly before the business roundtable in May at the Austin Club, he told the *Houston Chronicle* that there had been similar threats of business boycotts before the repeal of HERO, in 2015, and that those threats turned out to be just "bluff and bluster" that amounted to nothing. Since HERO's defeat, Houston has hosted the 2016 Final Four and this year's Super Bowl. "I think the handwriting is on the bathroom wall: Stay out of the ladies' room if you're a man," Patrick said. "If it costs me an election, if it costs me a lot of grief, then so be it. If we can't fight for something this basic, then we've lost our country."

In the end, the restroom bill isn't just about transgender rights or women's safety or whether San Antonio will lose the Final Four. It's also a rare showdown between two political heavyweights in Texas: the business lobby and the lieutenant governor. If Patrick prevails and brings big business to heel, he will not only solidify his power but also set himself up to fulfill whatever political ambitions he may have. But if the bill fails to pass, Patrick's standing in the Capitol may be diminished, and other interest groups and politicians may soon challenge him. That's the thing about great power, as Ted Cruz found out. It can be fleeting.

ARTICLE QUESTIONS

1) What impressions of Lieutenant Governor Dan Patrick do you have after reading this article?
2) What are three elements of the lieutenant governorship that make it a powerful force in Texas politics?
3) Why does the author argue that Patrick may encounter an unwelcome reaction to his use of power and his stance of the bathroom issue?

9.2) The Televangelism of Ken Paxton

Texas Monthly, December 2016

R. G. RATCLIFFE

Most Texas attorney generals are obscure figures who spend more time in court than in front of the television cameras. Texas's current attorney general, Ken Paxton, has other plans. Veteran journalist and senior political writer for *Texas Monthly* R. G. Ratcliffe offers an in-depth profile of a public official under scrutiny but maintaining his cause. The opening passage places Paxton square in the middle of the tragic aftermath of a shooting of five police officers in Dallas during a Black Lives Matter protest. More recent serial bombings in Austin have brought the attorney general back into the national media's sights.

Ratcliffe is critical of Paxton, claiming that he is more interested in "having the title of attorney general than being attorney general." In this account, his frequent television appearances are more for show than an attempt to govern—a way to advance his constituents' political agenda. At the same time, Paxton faces more challenges than political opponents. His legal troubles, including multiple criminal indictments for securities fraud, have haunted his tenure in office and have made him the first sitting attorney general in Texas to be indicted in thirty years. Other issues confronting the office include staff departures, internal confusion about controversial legal opinions, and concerns about the competence of the office.

Ratcliffe argues that being a visible fixture on the state and national political stage has helped to revive Ken Paxton's image—but has it gone far enough to restore the image of the Attorney General's Office?

The sun had not yet risen when Ken Paxton stationed himself in downtown Dallas. This was the July morning after a peaceful Black Lives Matter protest had ended with a sniper's killing five police officers and wounding nine others, and the city center had become one massive crime scene. Paxton stood inside the yellow police tape, but he wasn't there to investigate. The attorney general is often referred to as Texas's top law enforcement official, but that description is incorrect. While divisions within the agency do hunt down sexual predators and human traffickers and, when requested, assist local district attorneys in prosecuting criminal cases, the attorney general is actually the state's top lawyer. Paxton himself has no law enforcement background. As an attorney, he's specialized in estate planning as well as probate and corporate transactions. In fact, his most extensive experience with the criminal justice system has come on the wrong end of it. In July 2015, seven months after taking office, he'd been indicted for securities fraud, including two first-degree felonies. So that morning in Dallas, Paxton had no official role—the city's police and prosecutors were handling the case, and if they needed help, they could call upon the Texas Department of Public Safety, the Dallas County sheriff's office, and even the FBI. But Paxton had driven downtown for a specific purpose. He was there for the exposure.

With the crime scene as a backdrop, Paxton gave one television interview after another. What the reporters and anchors wanted in the confusing whirlwind of that early morning was information, but each interview revealed that Paxton was hopelessly out of the loop. On *CBS This Morning* at 7:09, Paxton had to answer questions with phrases like "I don't know," "I'm not sure of that," and "I have not gotten an update." Even by late morning, Paxton had to tell one reporter, "Actually, I don't know a lot of details yet." Perhaps no exchange was more revealing than the one with ABC's *Good Morning America* host George Stephanopoulos.

For that interview, Paxton stood in front of a police car, its flashing lights bouncing off the pavement in the dark morning. At age 53, Paxton has a receding hairline, and his appearance is soft, with the complexion of someone who doesn't spend much time outdoors. A sports injury in college left him with a sleepy right eyelid and a crooked smile that can look like a smirk.

"What more can you tell us about those injured officers now in the hospital?" Stephanopoulos asked.

"Let me just say, this is a sad day for Texas," Paxton replied. "It's a resilient state. But we're praying for the families as well. We're not going to forget these fallen heroes, and we want the families to know that we support them. I don't have a lot of details yet on the condition of some of the people who were injured, but I think we'll have that relatively soon."

Stephanopoulos pressed for details. "Do we know if it was two or if there were more [shooters]?" Paxton had a vague expression on his face. "There are still many, many policemen down here investigating that. I don't think they've made a final determination." Were all the suspects in custody, Stephanopoulos asked. "I'm not sure we totally know that," the attorney general said. Paxton, with a bang of hair falling down toward his eyes, resorted to stating the obvious. "This is still a

major crime scene," Paxton said. "It's the largest one I've ever seen. I used to work a couple of blocks from here. It's very surreal, and it's like nothing I've seen in downtown Dallas in the twenty-five years or so that I've been here."

Texas's top two elected officials were also in Dallas that day. Governor Greg Abbott had cancelled a family vacation and returned to Texas and offered up the resources of the Department of Public Safety to the city. Lieutenant Governor Dan Patrick consoled families of the fallen and wounded officers at Parkland and Baylor hospitals (later in the day, he made a controversial statement blaming protesters, in part, for inciting the shooting). As Abbott dealt with a serious injury—unbeknownst to the public, he had suffered severe burns to his legs and feet while on vacation—and Patrick comforted victims that morning, Paxton used the Dallas tragedy to appear as often as possible on television.

As the day wore on, there were more interviews: *Fox & Friends*, *CNN New Day*, *Morning Joe*, Glenn Beck TV. Paxton conducted eighteen television interviews before taking a break at 5 p.m. to stand behind Abbott at a news conference with Mayor Mike Rawlings, and then did four more appearances that evening. And he was back at it four days later. On the Tuesday after the shootings, Paxton sat for four morning interviews, then paused to attend a memorial service for the officers led by President Barack Obama. Forty minutes after the service ended, Paxton was back on CNN with host Jake Tapper.

Paxton's affinity for the spotlight was a recent development. In fact, two months before the shooting, he'd used state funds to hire a public relations firm to help burnish his image. But prior to that, Paxton had been an elusive figure for the media, especially the state's major newspapers. After securing the Republican nomination in 2014, he'd barely bothered to campaign in the general election, shunning media appearances and candidate forums. The *Houston Chronicle* described him as running a "shadow campaign." Even recently, while he frequently appears on television, he has offered few interviews to the mainstream print media. (Paxton refused numerous interview requests for this story over two months, though he answered a few questions submitted by email.)

But by watching hours of video of his speeches and interviews, by speaking with agency insiders, and by culling hundreds of pages of documents obtained through open-records requests, we saw a portrait emerge of Paxton's first two years in office.

He appears to be a politician more interested in having the title of attorney general than being attorney general. He has used his office as a cudgel in the culture wars for the Christian right. He's continued to live in McKinney, about thirty miles north of Dallas, rather than move to Austin for the daily duties of running his office. As a result of his absence from the office, he's grown jealous of aides, who have received the positive media attention that has eluded him, a feeling that apparently intensified after he was indicted. In March, he got rid of his top staffers, replacing them with religious-right activists, and hired two public relations firms that specialize in crisis management. Suddenly, the once-reclusive Paxton was often popping up on television and at press conferences, discussing lawsuits and events—like the Dallas sniper case—with which he had little direct involvement. With his own criminal trial now approaching, publicity, it seems, has become Paxton's affirmation.

If the attorney general's office were a private law firm, it would be among the largest in Texas, with more than seven hundred lawyers, 30,000 cases in progress, and a two-year budget of $1.15 billion. Its lawsuits range from enforcing mundane actions by state regulatory agencies to protecting the state's authority to carry out death sentences. The agency is also charged with collecting delinquent child support payments; it took in $3.8 billion last year that was owed to about 1.7 million children. And the state's new open carry law gives the office power to sue local governments that block the carrying of firearms on government property. The AG's office also offers legal opinions, represents state entities in court, determines which government documents can be released to the public, prosecutes political corruption and voter fraud, and protects Texas consumers from predatory businesses. In short, the office has broad authority. It could be argued that the attorney general has a greater influence on the daily lives of Texans than the governor.

In political philosophy, Paxton is similar to his two most recent predecessors, Abbott and current U.S. senator John Cornyn. Paxton has continued to fight the Obama administration on numerous fronts in court, picking up where Abbott left off. Paxton's lawyers won court rulings halting an Obama immigration order and lost in the defense of the state's anti-abortion law and the ban on same-sex marriage. Paxton noted, in a speech to Texas delegates at the Republican National Convention in July, that his office had filed a dozen suits against the federal government in his first eighteen months in office. "So we're on a really good pace," he said.

But while their ideologies may be similar, Paxton's predecessors had far more distinguished résumés. Before they became attorneys general, Cornyn and Abbott had been accomplished litigators, and both had served terms on the Texas Supreme Court. And once they were elected attorneys general, both had reputations in the office for making the final edits on the state's largest lawsuits, and Abbott confidently allowed his chief appellate lawyer, solicitor general Ted Cruz, to shine in public, putting Cruz on the path to winning election to the U.S. Senate.

Paxton, meanwhile, wasn't exactly a towering figure during almost a dozen years in the Legislature, as a representative and later a senator. He passed few bills of statewide importance. Perhaps the most notable piece of legislation that he passed was one requiring "Welcome to Texas" highway signs to include the phrase "Proud to Be the Home of President George W. Bush." (Paxton later amended the statute to remove the phrase after Bush left office.) Before the 2011 session, he ran against incumbent Joe Straus to become Speaker of the House, but he surrendered before the vote was taken because he'd failed to rally enough support in the Republican Caucus.

However, the bills Paxton didn't get passed were probably more important to his political ascension. He carried a bill to prevent school districts from obtaining sex-education materials from organizations like Planned Parenthood, and he co-authored a state constitutional amendment to protect from lawsuits individuals and businesses that refused to provide services because of religious objections. And he rallied support for legislation to require women to get a sonogram before an abortion. These proposals made Paxton a favorite of religious conservatives, and they aligned with his own fundamentalism.

Paxton has been married to his wife, Angela, for thirty years, and they have four children. They met as undergraduates at Baylor University, and she refers to June 1 as "I Love You Day," the anniversary of the first time Paxton spoke those words to her. They were among the founders of the nondenominational evangelical Stonebriar Community Church in Frisco, just west of McKinney, where Angela would mentor young women, teaching them how to dress modestly but with style. He's served on the board of the Prestonwood Pregnancy and Family Care Center, an agency dedicated to steering women away from abortion. The Paxtons later moved their worship to Prestonwood Baptist Church, a mega-congregation on two campuses in the northern Dallas suburbs, which is built on the "inerrant truth of the Bible." With the exception of the fraud indictments against him, Paxton is a pillar of his community, a fundamentalist who wears his Christianity on his sleeve.

Former law partner George Crumley said Paxton is one of the last people he would have expected to go into politics. "I can't say that he's shy, but he's certainly not the guy who is the life of the party," Crumley said. Paxton is "solid and trustworthy" but, if anything, spreads himself too thin. "If Ken had a fault in all of this it was that he had too much going on, too much on his plate. You need to make sure you don't let things slide. Ken is probably a victim of his own success and popularity."

When Abbott decided in 2013 to run for governor, an opportunity opened for Paxton. His main Republican primary opponent in the spring of 2014 was state representative Dan Branch, a respected Dallas lawyer with close ties to Speaker Straus. Both Branch and Straus were seen as insufficiently conservative by many Republican primary voters,

and Paxton had pastors, tea party groups, and the rigidly conservative Cruz on his side. "My strategy was very simple . . . get the church out to vote," Paxton told an audience at the First Baptist Church in Denison this past August. He was referring to his first run for the House, in 2002, but it's also exactly how Paxton defeated Branch in a runoff. More than two thirds of Republican voters in the primary and runoff attended church at least once a week, if not more, according to a survey by the Republican consulting firm Baselice & Associates. With Democrats perpetually overmatched, winning the Republican nomination was tantamount to capturing the office in November.

A dark specter lurked in the background during that election, though. Paxton conceded that he had failed to list all his business interests on a financial disclosure document. Even more damning, he admitted to the Texas State Securities Board that he hadn't registered as a securities dealer promoting investments. He received a reprimand and a $1,000 fine. Partisans, reporters, and political junkies knew of Paxton's transgressions before the election, but the allegations didn't sink in with the general public until after he was in office.

In July 2015 a Collin County grand jury indicted Paxton on two first-degree felony counts of securities fraud and a third-degree felony for failing to register as a securities dealer. The indictments charged Paxton with improperly encouraging investors in 2011 to invest more than $600,000 in a technology firm called Servergy Inc. Paxton allegedly didn't disclose to his clients that he was getting paid for steering investors to Servergy. The company also allegedly lied to potential investors about its funding sources; for example, its CEO told investors that Amazon was ordering Servergy's products, when, in fact, a single Amazon employee had merely wanted to test one product, according to Securities and Exchange Commission documents. (It's not clear if Paxton knew about these alleged misrepresentations.) Paxton's appeals and legal filings have delayed the case for more than a year, but the state's highest criminal court recently threw out his latest challenge, clearing the way for a trial in the coming months. "There is an indescribable peace in our family when, in the depths of our being, we know that I am innocent," Paxton wrote in response to questions from *Texas Monthly*.

Paxton is the first sitting Texas attorney general to be indicted in more than thirty years, and his fate may hinge on whether he was merely being sloppy or intentionally misleading clients. Two years ago, before his indictment, Paxton claimed it was the former, attributing his problems to legal ignorance. "Listen, there's no lawyer who's an expert on every area of the law," Paxton told KERA, the Dallas NPR affiliate, in 2014. "Securities laws are very complicated."

When Paxton took office in January 2015, there was concern among Austin's cadre of elected officials and lobbyists about whether he was prepared to handle one of the most important jobs in state government. But they were reassured when Paxton started surrounding himself with respected political and governmental veterans. The office, it seemed, would not be bumbling.

Paxton hired Chip Roy as his first assistant, Bernard McNamee as his chief of staff, and Scott Keller as his solicitor general. All three had been part of Cruz's Senate office staff; Roy had been Cruz's chief of staff and before that had worked for Cornyn and former governor Rick Perry. For communications director, Paxton hired Allison Castle, who had done the same job for Perry. It was an undeniably solid team with years of experience in state and federal government, the kind of staff Paxton would need, especially after deciding to continue to live in North Texas and visit the agency just a few days a week.

From his own campaign staff, Paxton hired Michelle Smith to oversee outreach to voters. Smith had previously been a member of the Rockwall City Council and the state director for Concerned Women for America. Her CWA biography states she has "worked hard to elect Christian conservative leaders." Though the rest of the team was based in the attorney general's headquarters, Smith was assigned to a Dallas office so she'd be readily available to Paxton.

While legal, Paxton's decision to live in McKinney instead of Austin has been costly to taxpayers. As with other statewide officials, Paxton receives personal security from DPS, but when the officers are outside Austin, they incur travel expenses. Through May 2016, the extra cost of providing security for Paxton at his Collin County home exceeded $57,000, according to records from DPS.

In written comments, Paxton defended his decision to stay at home in McKinney, arguing that with modern technology there was no reason for him to work most days in Austin. "I spend every day tirelessly defending, promoting, and serving our great state, whether in Austin, traveling around Texas, or close to home with my family."

The first major case facing Paxton after he took office was defending the state's ban on same-sex marriage before the U.S. Court of Appeals for the Fifth Circuit while a similar case was pending before the Supreme Court. When the nation's high court ruled that same-sex marriage was a constitutional right, Paxton's response created confusion. In an official opinion, he outlined how a county clerk who had religious objections to same-sex marriage could pass the duty off to another clerk or simply refuse to issue any marriage licenses. In a statement, Paxton called the ruling "lawless" and urged clerks to stand against it by refusing to issue licenses, saying private attorneys would represent them for free. This was a remarkable moment. Here was Texas's top lawyer advising his constituents to disregard a ruling from the Supreme Court. One clerk, in Hood County, followed Paxton's advice, and the county ended up paying almost $44,000 in legal fees when a lawsuit forced it to back down. Though Paxton's defiant stance on same-sex marriage was widely criticized by Democrats and progressives, his political base of social conservatives loved it.

And Paxton would draw on that goodwill later that summer when his felony indictments were handed down. After he was indicted, Paxton grew even more media-shy. His public speaking was limited to friendly audiences at churches and tea party events, and he withdrew from his office too, spending more and more time at his home in McKinney. Often he was unavailable for days, with his aides unable to find him for needed responses to questions. All elected officeholders travel the state to speak to civic groups and promote their policies, but the difference for Paxton was that he had disengaged, according to AG office sources. An unrelenting stream of news stories portrayed Paxton not as attorney general, defender of the unborn, individual religious liberty, and Second Amendment rights, but rather Ken Paxton, accused felon.

Paxton became concerned that—with his absence from agency headquarters—his aides were getting more positive attention than he was. Everything done by the attorney general's office occurs in Paxton's name, but after his indictments, that simply was not enough. While speaking at the Pflugerville First Baptist Church in September 2015, Paxton praised first assistant Roy as one of the "visionaries on this religious liberties issue," but Paxton prefaced it by self-consciously saying, "I get credit, sometimes not credit, for what happens in my office." The speculation circulating Austin was that with Paxton not around, Roy was the actual attorney general of Texas. Meanwhile, a frustrated McNamee resigned as chief of staff in November to return to private practice in Virginia. Then came two reports that prompted a crisis within the office. In February of this year, the *Texas Tribune* posted an interview with Roy and solicitor general Keller on the upcoming U.S. Supreme Court arguments challenging President Obama's executive order shielding some undocumented immigrants from deportation. When reporter Julián Aguilar went off topic to ask how Paxton's legal troubles were affecting the agency, Roy responded in a way that implied that the attorney general was often absent from the office: "We're in constant communication with the attorney general, and we're focused on doing our job every day to defend the state of Texas. . . . The first assistant attorney general, the solicitor general, our head of civil litigation, all of us are charged to manage the daily affairs of this agency, and that's what we're doing."

On March 1, the *New York Times* profiled Keller and Stephanie Toti, a lawyer for the Center for Reproductive Rights, as they prepared to face off before the U.S. Supreme Court over Texas's new restrictions on abortion clinics. The fight to preserve the anti-abortion law was one of Paxton's signature issues, but his name didn't even appear in the *Times* piece. Castle, the communications director, and her staff had contacted about fifty national news organizations but could not get Paxton any major interviews. Tension grew between his political aides and the agency staff. Agency insiders said that while sitting in the Supreme Court cafeteria, Smith, Paxton's political aide, pulled up a copy of the *Times* article on Keller, turned to a communications deputy, and complained that she was "sick and tired" of seeing other people's names in the papers. Smith denies the exchange occurred. (The Supreme Court would later overturn the law's most restrictive measures, saying it placed an undue burden on a woman's constitutional right to an abortion.)

Paxton had traveled to Washington for the oral arguments. He bought his own tickets on Southwest Airlines on a promotional "Wanna Get Away" fare, for a round-trip total of $450. And in what appears to have been a fit of petty pique, a handwritten note was included on a voucher submitted to the state that read, "Purchasing own airfare resulted in conservation of state funds." Attached to it was a copy of Roy's voucher, showing that his ticket had cost the state $1,176. "Comparison for what our agency would have incurred," another handwritten note says.

Eight days after the abortion hearing, Paxton called Roy and Castle individually into his office and gave them a choice of resigning or being fired. They resigned. And the departures set off a cascade of more bad publicity. There were repeated stories about how one senior staff member after another was fleeing an attorney general's office that appeared in turmoil. Even worse, Lauren McGaughy, of the Dallas Morning News, reported that several staffers, including Roy, were still receiving their salaries weeks after they'd left the agency. The agency said that Roy and Castle had been put on "emergency leave," a provision usually reserved for health and family emergencies. There were rumors that the emergency leave pay was used improperly as hush money for Roy and Castle, though both have told the Texas news media that they received only money that they were owed. The controversy prompted a legislative inquiry into the practice of using emergency leave as de facto severance pay, which isn't permitted for state employees. Paxton had bungled his way into another public relations disaster, and it wouldn't be the last.

Paxton gave his first major speech after he took office to the First Liberty Institute, a nonprofit that offers pro-bono legal support for Judeo-Christian groups or individuals who believe government has trampled on their religious liberties. This was fitting. Paxton has a long history with the Plano-based group, crediting First Liberty president Kelly Shackelford with convincing him to enter politics, in 2002. In that first speech, Paxton played to religious fundamentalists' fears of being victims of the tyranny of the majority and of a godless government. Paxton said those who believe in religious liberty should stand against "mob rule" and referred to a "pop culture noise machine" on issues like same-sex marriage. "Our Founding Fathers correctly understood that a government that mandates one opinion over another is tyrannical," Paxton said. The speech was also a bit of foreshadowing, because by the second year of Paxton's administration, the attorney general's office had started looking like a branch of First Liberty.

When more than 150 lawyers signed on to a grievance with the State Bar of Texas against Paxton because of the confusion he'd caused after the Supreme Court's same-sex marriage ruling, it was First Liberty general counsel Jeff Mateer who came to his aid, writing op-eds in the state's newspapers defending Paxton. (The grievance was eventually dismissed.) When Paxton was indicted, it was Midland oilman Tim Dunn—a member of the First Liberty board of directors—who wrote an editorial claiming Paxton was the victim of a conspiracy because he had once dared to challenge the reelection of Speaker Straus. Dunn had also helped Paxton win the attorney general's race by guaranteeing a $1 million loan to his campaign through Dunn's Empower Texans political action committee.

After the ouster of Roy and Castle, Paxton turned to First Liberty to fill the vacancies. He hired Mateer as his first assistant to replace Roy. Paxton initially employed First Liberty chief of litigation Hiram Sasser as his chief of staff in the position left open by McNamee's departure, but Sasser soon returned to his old job because of family health issues. As Castle's replacement as communications director, Paxton named management consultant Marc Rylander, who had until recently been a pastor at Prestonwood Baptist Church. (In 2003 Rylander wrote a letter to the *Morning News* chastising the paper for publishing same-sex commitment ceremonies, calling it a "journalistic compromise and tasteless submission to the homosexual agenda." Rylander went on to write, "The thought of a homosexual couple does not stir animosity in me. But the idea of that couple being recognized and honored in your paper is appalling.") It was unprecedented for a Texas attorney general to name the general counsel of a religious advocacy group as his top lieutenant and a pastor as his spokesperson.

"General Paxton has demonstrated antipathy toward the separation of church and state," said Kathy Miller, the president of the left-leaning Texas Freedom Network. Paxton is "charged with upholding the law"; instead, she said, he is trying to undermine it. But one of Paxton's longtime friends from the Legislature—Republican representative Dan Flynn, of Canton—said many people of faith in Texas agree with Paxton and his agenda. "We believe in protection of life. We believe in traditional family values, strong advocates of the Constitution," Flynn said. "We believe in states' rights, believe in the Second Amendment. All those issues that are important to Texans."

Probably nothing was more symbolic of Paxton's position on LGBT issues than the hiring of Mateer from First Liberty. The nonprofit pushed the idea that an individual's constitutional liberties trump what they see as society's changing morals and sensibilities. When Plano adopted its anti-discrimination ordinance, Mateer opposed it and threatened a First Liberty lawsuit against the city on behalf of any business fined under it. Before he became the top lawyer in Paxton's shop, Mateer had represented Sweet Cakes by Melissa, an Oregon bakery that had refused to make a wedding cake for a lesbian couple.

Miller said that Mateer doesn't believe in the separation of church and state. The Freedom Network has noted that at conferences Mateer often holds up a $100 bill and says he will give it to anyone who can find the words "separation of church and state" in the Constitution. "So a fundamental principle of our nation's founding is something he denies," Miller said.

At a basic level, Mateer is correct. The words do not appear in the Constitution but instead are drawn from an 1802 Thomas Jefferson letter, which the Supreme Court cited in 1878 to uphold laws against polygamy. "To permit this would be to make the professed doctrines of religious belief superior to the law of the land, and in effect to permit every citizen to become a law unto himself," the court wrote. Even the early Texans believed in the separation of church and state, mainly because of having lived under state-mandated Catholicism when a part of Mexico. As Texans prepared to join the Union, in 1845, the founder of Paxton's alma mater, R.E.B. Baylor, convinced his fellow Texans that the first state constitution should prohibit members of the clergy from serving in any executive or legislative office: "It seems to me further that it is calculated to keep clear and well defined the distinction between Church and State, so essentially necessary to human liberty and happiness." Mateer, however, said he draws on a U.S. Supreme Court dissent written by Justice William Rehnquist, "who said Jefferson's phrase separation of church and state is a misleading metaphor. . . . I want to keep minimal federal government out of religion."

The ties between Paxton and First Liberty are financial too. Because the criminal case against Paxton involves his private law practice, he cannot use campaign funds to pay for his defense, and any money he raises personally must be free of conflicts of interest with the attorney general's office. When Paxton accepted a $1,000 gift from First Liberty president Shackelford and his wife, it was listed on Paxton's public disclosure forms as "gift . . . from family friend who meets the independent relationship exception," although there is anything but an independent relationship between Paxton and Shackelford's institute.

Perhaps the most revealing examples of Paxton's close relationship with First Liberty are the five occasions in which he has used the prestige of his office to support the group, filing friend-of-the-court briefs in favor of First Liberty clients. While such amicus briefs are really more of a political statement, they can boost the chances a court will take a case seriously, especially when that brief comes from a state attorney general. Two of the briefs involved religious nonprofits that objected to filling out waiver forms so they would not have to pay for contraceptive insurance for employees under the Affordable Care Act. Though one pertained to Texas nonprofits, the other was on behalf of the Little Sisters of the Poor, a group of nuns located in Denver. On another occasion, Paxton filed an amicus on behalf of a Marine at Camp Lejeune, in North Carolina, who was receiving a bad-conduct discharge in part for posting a Bible verse in a work space she shared with another Marine and refusing an order to remove it. Closer to home, Paxton also supported First Liberty's challenge to the Kountze school district over a one-time ban on cheerleaders' putting Bible verses on banners at football games. A district judge was prepared to dismiss the case because Kountze ISD had dropped its objection to the Bible verses, but First Liberty and a private attorney representing the cheerleaders' families appealed to the Texas Supreme Court. A favorable Supreme Court ruling in the case not only set the stage for a permanent injunction against the school district but also opened the door to the possibility of First Liberty's obtaining attorneys' fees from the district's insurance policy.

But it's a case in El Paso that raises the most troubling questions about Mateer's presence in the attorney general's office. The suit began with Mayor John Cook's backing a nondiscrimination ordinance, which led to an effort to recall the mayor spearheaded by Bishop Tom Brown and his Tom Brown Ministries and Word of Life Church. The recall vote failed, and Cook turned around and filed a lawsuit alleging that Bishop Brown violated state campaign finance law during the recall election by utilizing forbidden corporate money.

Before joining Paxton's staff, Mateer represented Brown in the case on behalf of First Liberty.

And, in another interesting twist, the court had once asked then–attorney general Abbott's office whether it wanted to become involved in the case, and Abbott's staff declined.

But after Mateer joined the staff, Paxton's office suddenly got involved in the case, writing a letter to an El Paso court asking it to reconsider federal campaign finance laws before awarding damages. The case was settled in May. Mateer said he had nothing to do with the El Paso filing and that he had immediately recused himself once he learned about it. "I had no discussions with anyone, so I don't know how it came in," he said. But an email obtained through the Public Information Act shows that Dave Welch, the head of the U.S. Pastor Council, had contacted Mateer and another Paxton aide, asking them to intervene on Brown's behalf.

Cook's attorney, Mark Walker, said the filing was suspicious because of Mateer's previous involvement in the case. "It's outrageous. I don't care what your political leaning is, I just want you to follow the law," Walker said. "I'm concerned about over-politicization of the [attorney general's] office, and I'm a pretty conservative person."

By the time Mateer and Rylander joined the staff in early 2015, the public perception of Paxton couldn't have been much lower. Newspapers in Austin, Corpus Christi, Houston, and Longview had called for his resignation, while the *Morning News* and the *San Antonio Express-News* urged him to step aside until his criminal case could be resolved. Paxton, still backed by his core supporters, was unmoved. "Anybody remember how many papers endorsed me when I was running against a Democrat?" he asked a crowd of partisans. "The answer is none. So is it shocking to me that they're not helping me right now?"

Still, he hired not one but two crisis-management public relations firms in March, and slowly they began to work to rehabilitate his image.

One of the firms was the Dallas-based Spaeth Communications, which, according to agency documents, was paid $2,529 by the attorney general's office. The other was CRC Public Relations, an Alexandria, Virginia, company, which was paid $19,500 from Paxton's campaign account. The two

Republican firms were familiar with each other. They had worked together in 2004 to organize and promote the controversial Swift Boat Veterans for Truth group that attacked Democratic presidential nominee John Kerry.

The Dallas firm's owner, Merrie Spaeth, had been the director of media relations in the Reagan White House. She had also coached special prosecutor Ken Starr for his presentation to the House during the impeachment of President Bill Clinton. And most recently she had been advising Starr in his handling of the media in the rape scandal that occurred while he was president at Baylor University. (By coincidence, in January Paxton protected Baylor from having to release campus police reports on one of the rapes, citing common-law privacy even though the victim already had identified herself on ESPN.)

Paxton's PR investment soon showed results. Six weeks after Castle's staff had been unable to get Paxton any national media interviews, he suddenly had a flurry of exposure around the state's arguments to the Supreme Court against Obama's immigration policies, including interviews in New York with CNN and Fox News. Solicitor general Keller was again representing the state, but this time it was Paxton in the limelight.

In April Paxton shared the stage with Keller during an appearance on Greta Van Susteren's *On the Record*, on Fox. After throwing a softball question to Paxton, Van Susteren made a point of noting for her viewers that Keller was the lawyer arguing the case. She would do the same thing again in June, when the two men appeared on her show by satellite feed after Texas won a Supreme Court ruling that upheld an injunction against the Obama immigration plan. Paxton might not have been the lawyer arguing the case, but he was going to play one on TV.

Though Paxton's staff changes may have resulted in his receiving more positive press, they also weakened the barriers that traditionally separate state business from overtly partisan politics. For instance, Rick Perry's policy as governor—including when Castle was on his staff—was to use campaign or private funds for travel to avoid any chance that taxpayers would cover the cost of politicking. When Abbott took over the governor's office, he adopted the same policy. But after Castle left Paxton's office, things changed rapidly.

The most egregious blending of state business with politics at taxpayers' expense occurred on a June trip to the nation's capital. The dates of the trip coincided with the Faith and Freedom Coalition's Road to Majority conference, where Paxton spoke on the final day. Paxton made the trip with Mateer, Rylander, and Smith.

Paxton tried to work in some state business. On the first morning in Washington, he held a news conference on the steps of the Supreme Court to announce that Texas was joining a 21-state lawsuit against Delaware for keeping unclaimed funds from a national check-writing service. But that hadn't been the point of the trip. In fact, the news conference had been added to his schedule at the last minute, and Rylander admitted it was held in Washington only because Paxton was already going to be there on other state business. On the day after the news conference at the Supreme Court, Paxton gave a speech at the Heritage Foundation on climate change litigation involving Exxon. But besides that speech, Paxton's schedule had numerous undocumented hours.

The Road to Majority conference is a Christian conservative political gathering that featured speeches by various Republican candidates, including GOP presidential nominee Donald Trump. Also coinciding with the trip was a filing by his Washington-based lawyers challenging a civil suit—separate from the criminal prosecution—filed against him by the Securities and Exchange Commission over his Servergy work. Paxton's lawyers did not respond to inquiries about whether he met with them during the trip.

Paxton's own request for travel for the three days shows that the original reason for going to Washington was "for speaking event, 'Think Tank,' presented by Road to Majority." But when he tweaked his travel plans on June 1, all mention of Road to Majority vanished from the travel requests for him and his entourage, becoming instead a simple "speaking event," though the dates of travel continued to overlap with the political event. The Road to Majority organizers posted photographs on Facebook of Paxton speaking.

Mateer's expense report listed the speech as "state business." The total cost to Texas taxpayers for the four days of travel for Paxton and his three aides during the political gathering exceeded $7,800.

Paxton didn't use state funds to attend the July Republican National Convention, in Cleveland, but there too he took every opportunity to appear before an audience or a camera, even sitting for an interview with MSNBC.

Paxton spoke to Texas delegates in a hotel ballroom on the morning of the convention's third day. Angela, who has much more stage presence and charisma than her husband, introduced him, as she often does at events, by singing a ditty she'd written in which she declares herself a "pistol-packin' mama" whose "husband sues Obama."

The attorney general received a warm ovation from the party faithful. "I was on Fox News last night," Paxton gleefully told them. "I just wanted to see how many of y'all stayed up to watch me at 2:05 a.m. this morning." Everyone laughed, and Paxton seemed to be gently making fun of himself.

But then you do have to wonder: Who exactly goes on television in the middle of the night? In this case, a politician trying to beat an indictment. Part of his strategy seems to be appearing on television as often as possible, and it's hard to argue with the results. His indictment is barely even mentioned anymore during his TV appearances, and he's rarely asked about it.

When Paxton was first indicted, his political career seemed in shambles, and there was rampant speculation that he would resign, especially after he shrank from the spotlight. But his public reemergence and his television offensive make his political survival seem like a real possibility.

His trial in Collin County is expected to begin in the coming months. Even if he's convicted of the felonies, it's not clear that Paxton would immediately be forced from office. He would likely be disbarred, but he could still carry on; there's no requirement in the state constitution that the attorney general have a law license. Moreover, state law is murky on whether a convicted felon can remain in office. On the other hand, if Paxton is acquitted, he would once again be tough to beat in a Republican primary, and with Democrats offering only token resistance in the general election, he'd be likely to win another term, in 2018.

On that count, he can draw inspiration from the last sitting Texas attorney general to be indicted, from another time and another party:

In 1983 Democrat Jim Mattox was charged with abusing his office. As with Paxton, many Austin insiders thought his political career was over. But Mattox persevered. He was later acquitted, and in 1986 he won reelection.

ARTICLE QUESTIONS

1) What are your impressions of Ken Paxton from this article—do you believe that he is a politician advancing his cause or a public servant willing to put the voters' desires into practice?

2) The author is critical of the state's attorney general. Do you find this criticism convincing?

3) Should Texas elect (through partisan elections) or appoint its attorney general?

9.3) The Next George Bush: Can the Heir to America's Oldest Political Dynasty Save the GOP?

Politico, January 26, 2014

CHRISTOPHER HOOKS

Most statewide public officials toil in obscurity—that is, unless your last name is "Bush." The legacy of the Bush family in Texas is as storied as that of the Kennedys in Massachusetts and the Roosevelts in New York. Yet the youngest member of the Bush clan to win elected office has sought to distance himself from his family's more moderate politics. This is especially important as the political environment in Texas today is more conservative than the Texas of the 1970s, when Barbara Bush described herself and her husband as only two of three Republican voters in their precinct in Midland.

Christopher Hooks, a writer for the progressive *Texas Observer*, argues that reinvention is as much a Bush family tradition as running for office. George H. W. Bush reinvented himself as a more conservative Republican, George W. Bush worked to shed the image of the patrician Bush family, and George P. Bush has taken more conservative stands on policy issues. But George P. has another key difference from his family: he is Latino, the son of Jeb Bush and Mexico-born Columba Bush. His heritage has been strongly embraced by the Republican Party, which recognizes that changing state demographics favor (and potentially demand) Latino candidates for office. Will George P. Bush be the first Latino governor of Texas? Most Republicans hope so, but the tension between some Republicans' beliefs about immigration and Latino voters' preferences may complicate that scenario, even for a Bush.

It's an unseasonably warm midwinter day when a giant blue campaign bus arrives at a downscale strip mall in Pasadena, Texas, announcing the imminent return of a Republican dynasty. George Prescott Bush, the scion of arguably the most successful political family in American history, is launching a statewide bus tour that will introduce him to public prominence as he runs for commissioner of the Texas General Land Office, an important but generally obscure statewide position.

Bush is a lock: He faces no serious challengers, a fact attributable largely to the overwhelming advantages that accompany his name. Come

November, the handsome, studious and half-Hispanic 37-year-old George P. will walk into public office, and a choir of observers will begin a round of intense speculation about what his ascension means for his party, his state and his country.

One might think the Bushes had acclimatized themselves to public recognition by now. Yet there's Pierce Bush, another nephew of former President George W., fleece-jacketed and playful-seeming as he circles the giant bus emblazoned with a huge blowup of George P.'s face, taking pictures with his phone. "It's not every day you see your cousin on one of these," he tells me. He seems proud—and a bit incredulous.

Inside the strip mall, the small office of the San Jacinto Republican Women is packed. Older women stand around chatting about P.—his resemblance to different members of the Bush family and the well-being of Barbara Bush, George P.'s grandmother, who recently told the nation it should forget the dynasty thing and look outside of the "Kennedys, Clintons, Bushes" for a new generation of leaders. Her grandson seems not to have taken the message personally; asked about it at another campaign stop, George P. said that Barb was talking mostly about the presidency.

Bush has been campaigning with a calculatedly low profile for months, but this six-week, statewide bus tour, starting a month before early voting begins for the March primary, is something of a coming-out party. While land commissioner is an important post—the office oversees Texas's oil-rich public lands—campaign events for the position usually have as much pomp and circumstance as a rotary club meeting in a dry county. Today, though, there's a lot of enthusiasm, with even the manicurists at next-door Orchid Nails, who do not speak much English, recognizing the Bush name and coming over to have their picture taken with the candidate.

When George P. finally takes the microphone, he speaks for just over two minutes. It's a speedy pitch, laden with slabs of red meat for the GOP faithful—proof that he has adopted the rhetorical style of the state's Tea Party faction. "Our state's values and our future are under attack, and this attack is being led by one man and one man only, and that's Barack Obama. He wants to bring his liberal progressive agenda to the shores of Texas. And I think we sum up our message to him and Wendy Davis in just two words," he says. "No way." He goes on to speak about guns and the Second Amendment, partial-birth abortion and renewing the state's pride in its petrochemical industry—none of which falls even remotely under the purview of the land commissioner.

No one seems to mind. Afterward, P. poses for pictures and makes the rounds in the shopping center. Then he departs for well-heeled fundraisers in downtown Houston.

When people talk about George P.'s potential, they're talking about two things. First, there's his name. For those keeping score: George P. is son of Jeb Bush, governor of Florida; nephew of George W. Bush, former president and governor of Texas; grandson of George H. W. Bush, former president; great-grandson of Prescott Sheldon Bush, senator from Connecticut; and great-great-grandson of Samuel Prescott Bush, the patriarch.

Spend time with George P.'s campaign, and it quickly becomes apparent how impossible it is to separate his identity from his family background. Even the campaign photographer working the bus tour, David Valdez, has been shooting Bushes for three decades.

When it comes to the Bush legacy, George P. plays a balancing act. It's a huge asset, of course, and it lends excitement to what would otherwise be a dull campaign. But he attempts to differentiate himself from the family in ways large and small. For one, he describes Newt Gingrich as a political role model, and whereas his uncle branded himself a "compassionate conservative," George P. describes himself as a "movement conservative." He talks earnestly about how he's "been interested in politics from a very young age." A lot of people develop an early interest in politics, but few have led a political party's national convention in the Pledge of Allegiance at age 12, as P. did in 1988.

Born in Houston in 1976, George P. grew up in Florida but returned to the Lone Star State to attend Rice University (and play on the baseball team there) during his uncle's first term as governor. He then taught public school back in Florida and worked on W.'s presidential campaign before enrolling at the University of Texas School of Law. He practiced corporate law for a time and touts his experience with two investment firms, as well as his service in Afghanistan as an intelligence officer in the Naval Reserve.

In conversation, he deploys careful phrasing to distance himself from the family, while simultaneously keeping them close to mind. When I ask what the Bush name means to him in his current campaign, he replies that "they've provided their advice. Some pieces have been heeded, some pieces have not been heeded." Sometimes, though, his phrasing is less careful. On a number of occasions, he has used the royal "we" to refer to his campaign or his family or both, like when he recently told the Associated Press, "We're a mainstream conservative that appeals to all Republicans."

Despite that statement, Bush hasn't, in fact, asserted himself as a mainstream conservative, instead using the heated rhetoric of the Tea Party. At the Pasadena event, he closed by telling the crowd that they "deserve a future that springs from the wells of freedom dug deep under the ground by the founders of our great republic and the heroes of 1836"—a nod to the Texas revolution.

ARTICLE QUESTIONS

1) Why does the author indicate that George P. Bush must balance the more conservative politics of Texas today with his family's political legacy?
2) Name three issues that might stand in the way of George P. Bush winning a higher office.
3) What are three factors that might benefit George P. Bush if he seeks to win higher office?

The Texas Judiciary

Before the Texas Revolution, justice was difficult to administer in the territory. Under the Mexican constitutions of 1824 and 1827, the power of the judiciary was centralized in state courts. The weakness of the judicial system did not provide for the judiciary to act as a check on the executive or legislative powers—a fundamental tenant of English common law that the American settlers of Mexico expected—nor provided for practical appeal of local decisions to higher courts, which were located several hundred miles away in the state's capital.

These issues, when combined with widespread distrust of centralized government, put the Texas judiciary squarely in the hands of the people and produced an ordered system in which judicial power checks but is also checked by the other branches. The current Texas Constitution remedies the early frustrations in part by fragmenting the judiciary into many parts. Article 5 vests judicial power in "one Supreme Court, in one Court of Criminal Appeals, in District Courts, in County Courts, in Commissioners Courts, in Courts of Justices of the Peace, and in other such courts as may be provided by law." More courts fundamentally mean more access to justice, the theory goes.

The chief justice of the Texas Supreme Court does more than listen to arguments and write opinions. He or she also serves as an administrator and voice for the judiciary in Texas. In his 2017 "State of the Judiciary Address," Chief Justice Nathan Hecht outlines several requests to the legislature for funds for judicial safety efforts, compensation for judges, expanded access to justice for poor Texans, the reformation of the fee and bail systems, and measures to make the court system more fair for children, those with mental illness, and guardians of elderly or incapacitated Texans. Justice Hecht persuasively argues that the legislative, executive, and judicial branches need to work together, rather than in competition, to achieve justice for all Texans.

During the early years of the court system, many justices' careers in Texas were cut short by yellow fever, criminal investigations, or ambition. James Haley, author of a history of the Texas Supreme Court, calls the justices during this period "a potent galley of Frontier Texas manhood." Much has changed in the Texas judiciary since those chaotic early days, but justices still have a reputation for being old Anglo men with white hair and dark black robes. Nevertheless, the state judiciary is rapidly becoming more diverse, reflecting the growing diversity of the state.

How the state elects judges has become a point of controversy. The process of electing judges is unique to Texas and only a handful of other states. In a white paper, Rice University Baker Institute Fellow Mark P. Jones argues that Texans like to do things in a unique way but that its partisan judicial election process has had several negative consequences, such as removing otherwise qualified judges from the candidate pool based upon partisan preferences rather than individual characteristics. Jones further offers a balancing perspective on what reform of this process might look like.

Fundraising is another potential problem for incumbent judges and judicial candidates. As the *Texas Tribune*'s Ross Ramsey points out, those running for judicial office must raise money to compete in Texas's partisan elections, but this may create conflicts of interest for judges, who are in a position to make legal determinations related to issues advocated by political donors. Ramsey is not alone in this criticism— several former chief justices have attempted to change the system to make it less dependent on political fundraising. But can such reforms go far enough to address the problem without requiring a major overhaul of the existing process?

As Texans look to improve the quality of justice in the state, they will need to encourage greater legislative participation in such efforts, especially related to the issues of political fundraising, access to the justice system, and ensuring that the will of the people is carried out.

CHAPTER QUESTIONS

1) What are the major challenges facing the judiciary in Texas today?
2) Texas has many courts and judges for the purpose of making justice accessible to the public. Do you feel closely connected to the legal system, or is it still an abstract entity?
3) Should Texas elect its judges, or should it switch to alternative ways to select judges as other states have done?

10.1) The State of the Judiciary in Texas
Texas Judicial Branch, 2017

CHIEF JUSTICE NATHAN L. HECHT

In addition to hearing cases and writing opinions, the chief justice of the Texas Supreme Court is required by law to deliver to the legislature each session a "State of the Judiciary" address that evaluates the accessibility of the courts and discusses the courts' future directions and needs. The intention is that this message will promote understanding between the legislative and judicial branches. The address is also an opportunity for the judiciary to report on what the courts have done, especially the number of cases they have heard and the number of opinions that have been written. These annual addresses also offer important warnings about upcoming issues and requests for assistance.

Chief Justice Nathan Hecht's 2017 address delivered a sobering message for the legislature and all Texans: the state's justices, and the larger judicial system, are at risk from violence. He describes an incident in late 2015 in which Texas District Judge Julie Kocurek was shot by a former criminal defendant outside her home. Through Judge Kocurek's story, Justice Hecht personalizes his request for heightened security for the courts and asks for fundamental reform of the process of protecting the system.

Justice Hecht also reminds Texans that security is not the only issue facing the courts—low pay for judges is another important concern, one that may be pushing qualified individuals to leave the public arena and retreat to private practice, where the compensation is significantly better. Finally, Hecht reports on the judicial system's positions on bail reform, access to justice, and the need for a modern court records system. Of all of the items important to the judiciary he mentions, which do you think is the most important? Which issue does he see as the top priority?

Lieutenant Governor Patrick, Speaker Straus, Members of the 85th Legislature, former Chief Justice Phillips, former Chief Justice Jefferson, Members of the Judiciary, distinguished guests, ladies and gentlemen:

I have the honor to report to you on the state of the Judiciary. I begin with a story.

Late on a Friday evening, a young man—let's call him Will—drives his mom home from a high school football game—a Texas ritual in the fall. A trash bag blocks the driveway, so he gets out to move it. Suddenly, silently, a figure emerges from the darkness, raises a gun, then shoots through the car window at Will's mother. Glass explodes. Shrapnel and bullet fragments rip her body. Another blast. And another. And another. I'm going to die, she thinks; my life as a mom, wife, and sister is over because of what I do for a living, because I'm a judge.

The shooter flees into the darkness as quickly as he came. The judge is rushed to the emergency room.

Her condition, praise God, soon stabilizes; but healing—physical healing, family healing—takes awhile. She stays in the hospital 39 days, enduring 27 surgeries and losing a finger. All in all, it is a miracle she survives. At last, she goes home, at Christmas time.

The story is true, as most of you know from the news. The mother, wife, and sister shot outside her Austin home on November 6, 2015, was District Judge Julie Kocurek. Months later, after she felt stronger, I asked her to come by my chambers. She had wondered and prayed, she said, why me? Following an investigation, a man who had been a defendant in her court has been charged and is awaiting trial. But, she told me, God had given her a second chance. Faith and family had sustained her. "I don't know what the reason is," she said, "but I do believe God was waiting for me in that driveway. He prevailed. Evil did not."

I asked Julie about her plans. She could retire, she said. But if she left the bench, people would think you can threaten a judge and scare her off, maybe scare off other judges, intimidate them, show that justice cannot stand up to violence. She would not do that. Poised, courageous, determined, humble, faithful, she would prove that judges sworn to preserve, protect, and defend the constitution would not cower in the face of lawlessness. She would return to the courtroom—and she did, amidst great celebration.

She is here, with her son, Will, her daughter, Mary Frances, and her husband, Kelly. Ladies and gentlemen, it is my privilege to present to you one of the Texas Judiciary's heroes, Judge of the 390th District Court of Travis County, Julie Kocurek, and her family.

With judges like Judge Kocurek serving the people of Texas every day, I am proud to report to you that the state of the Texas Judiciary is strong.

Security

The attack on Judge Kocurek highlights the need for statewide improvements in judicial and courthouse security. Judges are not the only ones at risk; courthouses must be safe for staff, parties, lawyers, and jurors. Every threat must be taken seriously. Texas judges surveyed after the shooting reported four basic concerns: inadequate training, communication, and security protocols; inadequate resources; no state-level direction; and the ready availability of judges' personal information in publicly searchable government databases.

The Texas Judicial Council, which sets policy for the Judiciary and includes four members of the Legislature—Senator Zaffirini, Senator Creighton, Chairman Smithee, and Representative Murr—has made comprehensive recommendations to improve judicial security. One is to fund a new position, director of state judicial security, to oversee security plans and initiatives statewide. Another is to amend existing laws to ensure that personal information judges provide to government agencies is always, automatically, shielded from public access. Some protections exist already, but gaps should be closed. And state funding for local law enforcement and the Department of Public Safety should be increased to cover essential security costs, including personal protection for threatened judges.

The Judicial Council's recommendations are contained in Senate Bill 42 by Senator Zaffirini. I urge its passage, and I hope you will entitle it the Judge Julie Kocurek Judicial and Courthouse Security Act of 2017.

Compensation

Judge Kocurek reminds us again that judges serve at considerable personal sacrifice, including inadequate compensation. Judicial pay is a topic of almost every State of the Judiciary address. I would like to change that.

The problem of setting judicial compensation has vexed legislatures in every state and the national Congress for, well, seemingly, forever. Ten years ago, the 80th Legislature of Texas created the Judicial Compensation Commission—nine members appointed by the Governor—to take a new, data-based, fact-driven approach. The Commission is required to compare salaries of state and federal judges and officials, as well as private sector attorneys, assess changes in the cost of living, and report before each legislative session the proper salaries necessary to attract and keep the most highly qualified individuals, with diverse experiences.

The Commission has prepared five very thorough reports. No report has ever been faulted. None has been followed. The Commission has done all the Legislature asked, but the difficulties in setting judicial pay persist.

This year, judicial compensation must be increased merely to keep it on a par with 1991. We continue to fall further behind federal judges and judges in other states—27th overall, and last among the six largest states. The Commission also urges that its recommendations be part of the baseline budget, presumptively accepted unless rejected. The Judicial Council approves.

That would be progress, but I propose a better solution. We already agree that judicial salaries should be based on salaries of other judges, officials, and lawyers, and cost of living increases, all of which can all be quantified. Just look up the numbers. All we need is to agree on a simple mathematical formula to use from now on, then each session, just plug in the numbers. Tie legislative retirement to the formula, or not. None of it would ever have to be debated again. A formula now would settle the matter once and for all. I urge you to consider it.

Access to Justice

You have heard me say many times, the justice system must be accessible to all. Justice only for those who can afford it is neither justice for all nor justice at all. The rule of law, so revered in this country, has no integrity if its promises and protections extend only to the well-to-do.

The Texas Legislature's funding for access to justice has been critical. For veterans returning home to the freedoms they risked their lives to protect, basic legal services can help them manage their bills, stay in their homes, keep their jobs, and sadly, resolve family frictions. Last session, the Legislature appropriated $3 million for basic civil legal services specifically for veterans. Please do it again. It changed many lives. Last session, the Legislature appropriated $10 million from the Sexual Assault Program Fund for basic civil legal services for sexual assault victims. Please do it again. In only a very short time, these funds have helped more than 4,000 victims.

Legal aid providers handled over 100,000 cases last year. In addition, they helped direct cases to lawyers willing to handle them for free, *pro bono publico*—for the public good. Every dollar for legal aid thus provides many dollars in legal services. Every year, Texas lawyers donate millions of dollars and millions of hours. A million hours, by the way, is 500 work-years. Legal aid helps the poor be productive and adds to the economy's bottom line. That's why national CEOs and general counsel support access to justice initiatives—they're good for employees, good for customers, good for communities, and good for business. And besides all that, it's the right thing to do. As much as has been done, only 10% of the civil legal needs are actually being met. Access to justice still desperately needs your help.

Justice Gap Commission

Legal fees are also beyond the means of middle-income families and small businesses. There is a justice gap in this country: people who need legal services, lawyers who need jobs, and a market that cannot bring them together. More and more people try to represent themselves out of desperation. In 2015, the Supreme Court of Texas formed a commission, chaired by my predecessor, Wallace Jefferson, to examine ways to help lawyers provide legal services at lower cost. The commission has reported its recommendations, and we will work to implement them. One way is to continue support for the State Law Library, which makes resources available to lawyers and non-lawyers free of charge.

If justice were food, too many would be starving. If it were housing, too many would be homeless. If it were medicine, too many would be sick. If it were faith, too many houses of worship would be closed. The Texas Judiciary is committed to doing all it can to close the justice gap. We are grateful for the Legislature's support.

Electronic Filing and Access to Court Records

Access to justice is also improved by easier access to court records, but we must have a statewide system. The Supreme Court has ordered that all filings in civil cases in county, district, and appellate courts be sent to clerks electronically over the Internet. Last year, more than 8.5 million court documents were filed electronically. The savings to lawyers, parties, and clerks has been monumental. In a little over two years, electronic filing will also be required in criminal cases.

The 75th Legislature created the Judicial Committee on Information Technology to develop a statewide, electronic, court document system. The Committee has now recommended that judges, clerks, and lawyers have access to electronic filings through a portal called re:SearchTX, simply by pressing a button. This convenience will greatly reduce costs and delays in litigation. Soon, the Committee will make recommendations on public access to electronic filings, improving transparency for the justice system. The Committee will recommend ways for protecting privacy, preventing abusive data-mining, recovering costs, and providing counties revenue to establish and maintain a statewide system. A statewide system will also provide more information about how the work of courts is changing, what kinds of cases the courts handle [sic], and what improvements can be made. In planning for the future, this information is crucial.

Texas is a leader in technology. We have three of the world-recognized knowledge capitals: Austin, Dallas, and Houston. A 21st century statewide electronic court record system will save money, improve transparency, and increase efficiencies. The federal courts have used a similar system, PACER, throughout the country for 16 years. The Texas electronic filing and access system will be the largest in the country and will be the single most significant modernization of the Texas courts in history.

Bail Reform and Pretrial Release

In the past two sessions, the Judiciary has joined forces with the Legislature to decriminalize truancy and student misconduct at school. Children and families have been the beneficiaries. Now it is time for us to take up reform of the bail system and criminal pretrial release.

Twenty years ago, not quite one-third of the state's jail population was awaiting trial. Now the number is three-fourths. Liberty is precious to Americans, and any deprivation must be scrutinized. To protect public safety and ensure that those accused of a crime will appear at trial, persons charged with breaking the law may be detained before their guilt or innocence can be adjudicated, but that detention must not extend beyond its justifications. Many who are arrested cannot afford a bail bond and remain in jail awaiting a hearing. Though presumed innocent, they lose their jobs and families, and are more likely to re-offend. And if all this weren't bad enough, taxpayers must shoulder the cost—a staggering $1 billion per year.

Take a recent case in point, from the *Dallas Morning News*. A middle-aged woman arrested for shoplifting $105 worth of clothing for her grandchildren sat in jail almost two months because bail was set at $150,000—far more than all her worldly goods. Was she a threat to society? No. A flight risk? No. Cost to taxpayers? $3,300. Benefit: we punished grandma. Was it worth it? No. And to add to the nonsense, Texas law limits judges' power to detain high-risk defendants. High-risk

defendants, a threat to society, are freed; low-risk defendants sit in jail, a burden on taxpayers. This makes no sense.

Courts in five counties use readily available risk assessment tools to determine that the overwhelming majority of people charged with non-violent crimes can be released on their personal recognizance without danger to the public or risk of flight, and at less cost to the taxpayers. The Judicial Council recommends that this be standard practice throughout Texas. Liberty, and common sense, demand reform.

Mental Health

Many who enter the criminal justice system suffer from serious mental illness. Untreated, they are eight times more likely to be incarcerated, and if released, pose problems for the communities to which they return. Like the bail system, ineffective approaches to mental illness cost defendants, the courts, the government, and society. The Judicial Council recommends changes in the Code of Criminal Procedure to allow more effective management of mentally ill criminal defendants and better procedures for obtaining treatment, medication, and restoration. I urge you to consider them.

Fines, Fees, and Costs

Last year, Texas' 2,100 justices of the peace and municipal judges handled 7 million traffic, parking, and other minor offenses. Most people ticketed just paid the fine and court costs. Others needed a little time and were put on payment plans for an extra fee. Altogether, over $1 billion was collected. Some defendants said they couldn't pay at all. Judges believed them in about 100,000 cases, waiving the fines or sentencing them to community service. In 640,000 cases—16%—defendants went to jail for minor offenses.

Jailing criminal defendants who cannot pay their fines and court costs—commonly called debtors' prison—keeps them from jobs, hurts their families, makes them dependent on society, and costs the taxpayers money. Most importantly, it is illegal under the United States Constitution. Judges must determine whether a defendant is actually unable, not just unwilling, to pay a fine. A defendant whose liberty is at stake must be given a hearing and may be entitled to legal counsel. For the indigent, the fine must be waived and some alternative punishment arranged, such as community service or training. For those who can pay something but only by struggling, adding multiple fees threatens to drown the defendant in debt: there are extra fees for payment plans, for missed payments, for making payments—yes, there is even a fee for *making a payment*—pay to *pay*—warrant issuance fees, warrant service fees—the list goes on and on. And revoking a defendant's driver's license just keeps him from going to work to earn enough to pay the fines and fees.

A parent disciplining a child may say, this hurts me more than it hurts you. When taxpayers have to say to criminal defendants, this hurts us more than it hurts you, something's wrong. The Judicial Council has concluded that the system must be revamped. I urge you to adopt its recommendations.

Guardianship Reform and Funding

The population is aging, and the number of elderly and incapacitated Texans needing help managing their affairs is increasing. There are more than 50,000 active guardianships in Texas, involving an astounding $5 billion. To protect the people being cared for and their assets, the law requires guardians to report regularly. The Office of Court Administration's Guardianship Compliance Project, funded in the last session as a pilot, has reviewed more than 10,000 cases in 18 courts and 11 counties. In almost half the reviewed cases, guardians had not complied, and courts did not have the resources to monitor the cases. To protect the assets and quality of life for the elderly and incapacitated, the Judicial Council recommends that the Compliance Project be extended statewide.

Children's Commission

Working at the other end of the generational spectrum, the Supreme Court's Children's Commission has enlisted hundreds of professionals contributing thousands of hours to improve the foster care system. The Commission has provided training to judges and lawyers handling children's cases.

It has shown how to improve educational outcomes for children in foster care. It has advocated for changes in the law and developed tools and best practices to prevent child fatalities and end human trafficking. At Senator Kolkhorst's request, the Commission helped implement a bill to prevent the overuse of psychotropic medication with foster children. And the Commission is working with Senator Schwertner and others this session on legislation that will bring sweeping changes to the foster care system.

The Commission has always operated with federal grant funds. Until those grants are again funded, I must ask this Legislature to make up the difference. Any lack of support for the Commission now would be a sharp blow to improvements in the foster care system the Legislature is considering. Texas' greatest asset by far is her children. The Commission helps preserve that asset for us all.

Judicial Selection

I will say only a word about judicial selection, but it is a word of warning. In November, many good judges lost solely because voters in their districts preferred a presidential candidate in the other party. These kinds of partisan sweeps are common, with judicial candidates at the mercy of the top of the ticket. I do not disparage our new judges. I welcome them. My point is only that qualifications did not drive their election; partisan politics did. Such partisan sweeps are demoralizing to judges and disruptive to the legal system. But worse than that, when partisan politics is the driving force, and the political climate is as harsh as ours has become, judicial elections make judges more political, and judicial independence is the casualty.

There is no perfect alternative to judicial elections. But removing judges from straight-ticket voting would help some, and merit selection followed by nonpartisan retention elections would help more.

Beyond the Bench Summit on Law, Justice, and Communities

Judges across the country are concerned that recent tensions between law enforcement and communities, which have weakened our institutions, not erode public trust in the courts. Trust is the Judiciary's most important asset. People must not think the justice system is rigged. As the country works through its political and social differences, we want all to have utter confidence in the courts to be fair, to hear all sides, and to provide equal justice under law.

In December, the Supreme Court and the Court of Criminal Appeals convened a historic summit in Dallas to discuss law, justice, and communities. We invited all stakeholders to participate: judges, prosecutors, defense lawyers, civil rights lawyers, law enforcement, educators, community activists, and the clergy. We asked them to have an authentic, frank conversation about the courts and the justice system. And we did what judges do best: we listened.

An African-American college student body president told how her brother was killed by police when she was growing up. Moments later, sitting a few feet away, a white police officer, the widow of a police officer killed in the demonstrations in Dallas last July, told how she had filed their marriage certificate earlier that day, the happiest day of her life, only to be wakened in the middle of the night by a knock at the door and word that her husband was dead. For a few hours, 200 people with opposing passions tried to hear one another and understand what it means for there to be justice for all. And we and they left vowing to get closer to that goal, justice for all. Faith in the courts, just for inviting the dialogue, and listening, was strengthened.

The Rev. Dr. Tony Evans reminded us that cracks in society, like cracks in a house, mean the foundation is weak. Trust is the courts' foundation. The Judiciary's commitment is to strengthen that foundation. We ask the Legislature's help.

Efficiency

The Judiciary is committed to doing its work efficiently. The Supreme Court of Texas now decides all argued cases by the end of June, just as the United States Supreme Court does. Lawyers now expect all decisions by June. We are processing petitions faster. The Court of Criminal Appeals is still the busiest court in the country and still timely resolves its cases. The courts of appeals are staying caught up. Those courts have had the same number of justices for 36 years, but their work is up 35%. Last year, our more than 3,000 trial court judges disposed of nearly 9.5 million cases. The courts are doing an enormous amount of work timely and efficiently. We have not yet had to make bricks without straw, but we have certainly had to make the straw go further. Soon we will begin using technology to revamp processes in civil cases to bring public justice closer to the people.

Conclusion

As important as it is for courts to be efficient, it is more important for them to get every case right. We are committed to making all our processes serve the cause of justice. In that spirit, we ask your help with security and compensation, electronic access to court documents, and guardianship monitoring, and your continued help with access to justice for the poor and the middle class. We pledge to work with you to reform the bail system, the treatment of those with mental illness, and the imposition of fines, fees, and costs for minor offenses.

The framers of the Constitution divided the power of government among three branches, intending them to be competitive. They succeeded. But in this state, we have proved that the branches can work together for the people's good. That is the state of the Texas Judiciary.

God bless you, and may God bless Texas.

ARTICLE QUESTIONS

1) What policies does Hecht advocate for reforming the security of the justice system?
2) Why does Hecht argue that access to justice for all Texans is important?
3) What evidence does Hecht cite to claim that the court system was efficient in the prior year? Is this evidence persuasive?

10.2) The Selection of Judges in Texas: Analysis of the Current System and of the Principal Reform Options

Baker Institute for Public Policy, 2017

MARK P. JONES, PH.D.,

Texans brag that Texas is the most unique state in the Union. When it comes to selecting members of the state judiciary, that brag is true: Texas is one of only two states that elects (and then reelects) judges in partisan elections. These elections are primarily driven by straight-ticket voting, in which voters can simply select a party and then all the candidates affiliated with that party are automatically selected on the ballot. Mark Jones, a Rice University Baker Center Fellow and professor of political science, investigates the consequences of this mechanism in a report about the selection of judges in Texas.

Jones reports that most states select their judges through nonpartisan commissions or gubernatorial decisions. In addition, only ten states allow straight-ticket voting in judicial elections. Today in Texas, two out of every three voters in the state's largest counties now vote straight-ticket. The result is frequent "sweeps" of judges in and out of office, causing upheavals within the judicial system every few years and even removing judges considered superior candidates by the Texas Bar Association. Neither the process nor the reforms of it that have been proposed are perfect. Each potential reform has advantages and disadvantages. Jones identifies several avenues for reform, along with their costs and benefits, so you can decide for yourself what the proper course should be.

Executive Summary

Texas is one of only two states that initially elects and then re-elects its judges in partisan elections where voters have the option of casting a straight-ticket vote. A consequence of this rare combination of partisan elections and straight-ticket voting is extremely limited variation in the share of the vote received by judicial candidates and a concomitant tendency for judicial election sweeps whereby one party wins all of the judicial races within a jurisdiction, be it at the statewide, appeals court district, or county level. At present, an overwhelming majority of Texas judges are elected based not on their legal qualifications and judicial philosophy, or even on their own campaign efforts, but rather on the performance of their party (in the straight-ticket vote) and of their party's top-tier candidates (e.g., presidential, gubernatorial) within the jurisdiction where their race is being contested.

Approximately one-half of the 50 U.S. states select their supreme court and intermediate court judges via the use of a judicial nominating commission which proposes a slate of candidates to the governor who appoints the judges, either with or without confirmation by the state senate. A little more than two-fifths of the states select their supreme court and intermediate court judges via popular elections, nonpartisan in two-thirds and partisan in one-third. Almost three-fifths of the states select their trial court judges in popular elections, two-thirds in nonpartisan elections and one-third in partisan elections.

In 1992, 20 states provided voters with a straight-ticket voting option. Two dozen years later, that number had dropped by half to 10 in 2016. During this same time period the proportion of Texans who cast a straight-ticket vote steadily increased, with more than three-fifths of the state's voters casting a straight-ticket vote in the last three elections (2012, 2014, 2016). In many counties such as Harris, Dallas, Tarrant, Fort Bend, and Montgomery, two out of every three voters now vote straight-ticket.

Analysis of judicial elections between 2008 and 2016 reveals that a party's judicial candidates running in the same jurisdiction tend to receive shares of the popular vote that are extremely similar. The median difference in the vote share received by the majority party's candidates was 0.58 percent in statewide judicial races, 0.52 percent in court of appeals races, and 0.96 percent in county-level races in the 20 most populous counties. This limited variance underscores the reality that an overwhelming majority of voters are indirectly voting for a party's judicial candidates via their straight-ticket vote, often not even looking at the judicial races on their ballot.

The principal consequence of this limited vote-share variance is the prevalence of partisan sweeps at the statewide, appeals court district, and county levels where a single party wins all of the judicial races on the ballot within a jurisdiction. Between 2008 and 2016 an average of 100 percent of statewide, 94 percent of appeals court district, and 88 percent of county-level jurisdictions experienced partisan sweeps. And the trend is toward an increasing prevalence of sweeps, with 100 percent of the appeals courts and between 90 and 95 percent of the counties experiencing partisan sweeps during the two most recent electoral cycles.

Harris County elects more judges at the county level (district and county court) than any other county. It also is arguably the most competitive of the state's five most populous counties, with Democrats winning the largest share of the vote in three of the past five elections and Republicans winning the largest share in two. There exists very little variance in the share of the popular vote won by a party's county-level judicial candidates in Harris County, with more than half of a party's candidates having a share of the vote that is within one percent of their fellow judicial candidates. As a result of this limited variance, when a party wins the straight-ticket vote by more than a fraction in the county, it wins either all (100 percent in 2010, 2014, 2016) or most (85 percent in 2008) of the judicial races.

The partisan sweeps in Harris County often result in the defeat of the judicial candidate who the members of the Houston Bar Association (HBA) consider to be the superior candidate. The data suggest that the attorneys base their preferences more on a candidate's skills, experience, and philosophy as a jurist than on his or her partisan affiliation. In some elections, approximately two-thirds of the candidates preferred by HBA members lose, victims of the partisan sweep caused almost exclusively by their party's overall sub-par performance.

Every legislative session, bills are introduced to reform the methods by which Texas judges are selected. Here, four prominent potential reforms are presented, along with a summary of their principal advantages and disadvantages. These reforms could be implemented for the selection of all judges or of only a subset (e.g., trial court judges), in the latter case following the model of the dozen states that utilize different methods to select their appellate court and trial court judges.

The reforms vary in the extent to which they would deviate from the status quo in Texas, with the first two requiring the amendment of the Texas Constitution and the latter two possible to implement via statute alone. The most extreme reform utilizes a judicial nominating commission to draft a slate of candidates from which the governor appoints a judge, with the governor endowed with the power of reappointment. The second reform employs an identical initial appointment method via a judicial nominating commission, but reappointment is determined by a retention election whereby voters are given the option to retain or remove a judge.

The third reform maintains the popular election of judges, but removes the partisan label for judicial candidates along with the direct role of the parties (i.e., party primaries) in the candidate-selection process. The fourth reform is identical to the current selection method employed in Texas, with the exception that the straight-ticket option does not apply to judicial elections and the ballot is redesigned to ameliorate the effect of this reform on ballot roll-off (i.e., undervoting).

The Selection of Judges in Texas: Analysis of the Current System and of the Principal Reform Options

Texas is an outlier among U.S. states in regard to the manner in which it selects its appellate and trial court judges. The state combines partisan elections with straight-ticket voting, the result of which is an unusually strong tendency for partisan sweeps in statewide, appeals court district, and county-level judicial elections.

This report is divided into ten main sections. Section I provides a broad overview of the different methods (and their popularity) employed to select judges across the United States. Section II examines the evolution of the use of straight-ticket voting in the United States. Section III highlights the rarity of Texas's combination of the partisan election of judges with straight-ticket voting. Section IV details the organization of the Texas court system and the rules governing the selection of judges in the state. Section V provides an empirical analysis of straight-ticket voting trends in Texas and in the state's 20 most populous counties. Section VI underscores the limited variance that exists in the popular vote won by judicial candidates via a statistical analysis of district- and election-specific pairwise comparisons of the share of the vote received by the majority party's judicial candidates at the statewide, court of appeals district, and county levels. Section VII contains empirical analysis of the prevalence of judicial sweeps in Texas at the statewide, court of appeals district, and county levels. Section VIII contains a case study of the consequences of the combination of partisan elections and straight-ticket voting in Harris County, the state's most populous county (and the third most populous county in the nation). Section IX presents four leading reform options for the selection of Texas judges along with a discussion of the reforms' respective principal advantages and disadvantages. Section X concludes.

I. Judicial Selection Across the 50 States

The 50 U.S. states employ a wide variety of methods to select their state judges, with the methods often varying depending on whether the court in question in the state is an appellate court (supreme or intermediate) or a trial court. These selection methods can, however, be placed into two general categories (appointment and election), which in turn each have a set of subcategories.

The Selection of Supreme Court Judges

The most common method of judicial selection for supreme and intermediate courts is appointment via a judicial nominating commission. Among the 50 states, 48 have a single supreme court, while Oklahoma and Texas have two supreme courts (in Texas, the Texas Supreme Court and the Texas Court of Criminal Appeals). The most common method of judicial selection for trial courts is via a nonpartisan election.

As Figure 10.1 details, 23 states employ a judicial nominating commission for the selection of their supreme courts, while another five employ some other type of appointment method (gubernatorial or legislative), resulting in a majority of states (28) that select their supreme court judges via appointment. It should be noted that in the 23 states where a judicial nominating commission is employed, the commission provides a list of candidates from which the governor (or legislature, in South Carolina) makes the final appointment, in some states with the consent of the state senate. While the initial selection of judges in these states is done via appointment, in a majority of these states (16) retention elections are held to determine whether or not a judge should continue in office. In these retention elections, incumbent judges appear alone on the ballot and voters cast a yes or no vote on whether or not to retain them.

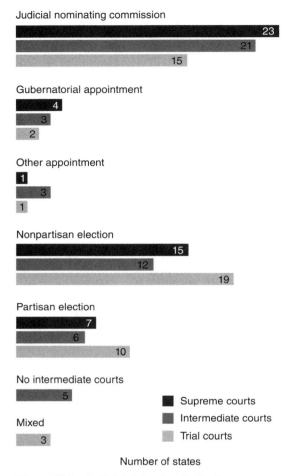

Judicial nominating commission

23
21
15

Gubernatorial appointment

4
3
2

Other appointment

1
3
1

Nonpartisan election

15
12
19

Partisan election

7
6
10

No intermediate courts

5

Mixed

3

■ Supreme courts
■ Intermediate courts
  Trial courts

Number of states

Figure 10.1   Judicial Selection Methods in the 50 States

Supreme court judges are selected via contested popular elections in 22 states, nonpartisan elections in 15 states, and partisan elections in seven states. In an overwhelming majority of these states, judges run for reelection by the same method of nonpartisan or partisan election, but in three cases judges originally elected in a nonpartisan (one state) or partisan (two states) election are retained via retention elections.

The Selection of Intermediate Court Judges

Five states do not have intermediate (appellate) courts. Among the remaining 45 states, appointment via either a judicial nominating commission (21) or some other form of appointment (six) is the most common method of judicial selection. As was the case for the supreme courts where judicial nominating commissions are used, the governor appoints a justice from a list provided by the nominating commission, sometimes with and sometimes without the confirmation of the state senate. Among the five states where appointment without a nominating commission is used to name intermediate judges, in two the appointment is made by the governor while in the others the appointment is made by the legislature, the chief justice of the supreme court, or the supreme court. Sixteen of these 26 states utilize retention elections for the reelection of intermediate court judges.

Eighteen states directly elect their intermediate judges via contested popular elections, with two-thirds of these elections nonpartisan and one-third partisan. In 15 of these states, judges run for reelection in the same type of election (nonpartisan or partisan) by which they were first elected, while in three (one with initial nonpartisan elections and two with initial partisan elections), they compete in retention elections.

The Selection of Trial Court Judges

Nonpartisan elections are the most common method utilized to select trial court judges, with 19 of the 50 states choosing their trial court judges via this method. An additional 10 states elect their trial court judges in partisan elections, for a total of 29 states that utilize contested popular elections to initially choose their trial court judges.

Judicial nominating commissions are used in 15 states to select trial court judges, while three other states employ another form of appointment (gubernatorial or legislative). As was the case with the supreme court and intermediate court judges selected via the former methodology, governors appoint trial court judges from a list of names provided by a judicial nominating commission, with this appointment often needing confirmation from the state senate. In all but a handful of these states, once initially selected, these appointed judges retain their position via retention elections.

Finally, in three states the methods employed to select trial court judges vary depending on either the specific type of trial judge being selected or the jurisdiction in which the election is being held. For instance, in some cases the more populous counties use one selection method while the less populous counties utilize another.

II. Straight-Ticket Voting Across the 50 States

In states with straight-ticket voting (also referred to as straight-party voting), voters are provided with an option by which they can cast a vote for all of a party's candidates on their ballot through a single action. In states where this straight-ticket option is not provided, voters must cast their votes race by race.

In the 1992 presidential election, voters in 20 states had the option of casting a straight-ticket ballot. Two dozen years later in the 2016 presidential election, voters in half as many states (10) had that option (see Figure 10.2), with straight-ticket voting retained in one state (Michigan) only because of an injunction that prevented a 2016 state law that abolished straight-ticket voting from being enforced.

Other than Michigan, nine states continue to use straight-ticket voting: Alabama, Indiana, Iowa, Kentucky, Oklahoma, Pennsylvania, South Carolina, Texas, and Utah. Indiana, however, no longer utilizes straight-ticket voting in at-large races where more than one officeholder is being elected. The states that abolished straight-ticket voting between 1992 and 2016 are Georgia, Illinois, Missouri, New Hampshire, New Mexico, North Carolina, Rhode Island, South Dakota, West Virginia, and Wisconsin.

III. Partisan Election of Judges and Straight-Ticket Voting: A Rare Combination

As detailed above, only a few states employ partisan elections to select their Supreme Court, intermediate, and trial court judges—seven, six, and 10, respectively. Of these states, only four also employ straight-ticket voting: Alabama, Indiana, Pennsylvania, and Texas. Indiana selects its Supreme Court and intermediate court judges via a judicial nominating commission but elects its trial court judges in partisan elections. Pennsylvania initially elects all of its judges in partisan elections, but once in office these judges are retained via retention elections.

Only Alabama and Texas simultaneously combine the initial partisan election and any subsequent reelection of supreme court, intermediate court, and trial court judges with straight-ticket voting. In sum, Texas is an outlier among U.S. states in its use of straight-ticket voting, its use of partisan elections to select its judges, and especially in its extremely rare combination of partisan election (and reelection) of judges with straight-ticket voting.

IV. The Texas Court System

The Texas court system can be divided into four general levels. At the apex are the state's dual superior appellate courts: the Texas Supreme Court, which has final appellate jurisdiction in civil and juvenile cases, and the Texas Court of Criminal Appeals, which has final jurisdiction in criminal cases. Each court has nine justices who are chosen in partisan elections for staggered terms of six years, with one-third renewed every three years

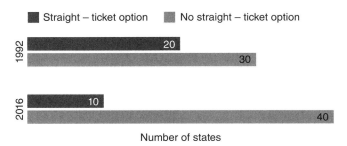

Figure 10.2 Straight-Ticket Voting in the 50 States (1992–2016)

except in the event of a vacancy, in which case an election is held to elect a justice to complete the unexpired term. In the interim, judicial vacancies are filled by gubernatorial appointment with the advice and consent of the Texas Senate.

In Texas, the intermediate position in the judicial structure is occupied by the state's courts of appeals. The state has 14 appeals court districts, which have a number of justices ranging from three to 13. Every county is located in a single court of appeals district, with three exceptions. A 10-county region in the Houston metropolitan area (Harris, Fort Bend, Montgomery, Brazoria, Galveston, Chambers, Waller, Grimes, Washington, and Colorado Counties) constitutes the geographic base for both the 1st and 14th Courts of Appeals. The boundaries of the 5th and 6th Courts of Appeals overlap in Hunt County, and the boundaries of the 6th and 12th Courts of Appeals overlap in Gregg, Rusk, Upshur, and Wood Counties. Appeals court justices are elected for six-year terms with an unbalanced staggering of terms.

The trial courts in Texas fall into four categories: district courts, statutory county courts, statutory probate courts, and constitutional county courts. According to the Texas Judicial Branch's Office of Court Administration, as of September 2016 there are 465 district courts (367 containing one county and 98 containing multiple counties), 243 statutory county courts (in 89 counties plus 1 multi-county court), 18 statutory probate courts (in 10 counties), and 254 constitutional county courts (1 in each county). All of these judges are chosen in partisan elections from a single district/place for four-year terms.

Every county has a constitutional county court presided over by a constitutional county judge. Because the county judge also has administrative responsibilities as the presiding officer of the county's commissioners court (the governing body for Texas counties), in the more populous counties the constitutional county judge's responsibilities for trials are assumed by the statutory county courts of law. Even in counties lacking a county court of law, the county judge's role as the county's chief executive is generally more prominent than his or her judicial role. As a result, the election of county judges is not examined in this report.

Finally, the state of Texas has 806 justice courts, with 806 judges (ranging from one to eight per county) chosen for four-year terms at the precinct level in partisan elections. The state's justice courts are responsible for minor civil matters, criminal misdemeanors punishable by fine only, evictions, and magistrate functions. In addition, throughout the state of Texas there are 933 municipal courts with 1,294 judges. These municipal judges can be either elected or appointed (the most common method) depending on the city charter, for terms that vary from two to four years. Municipal judges are the only judges in Texas who are not selected exclusively via partisan elections and are responsible for criminal misdemeanors punishable by fine only, municipal ordinance cases (primarily traffic violations), and magistrate functions. Neither the selection of justice court or municipal judges is examined in this report.

At present, when partisan elections for judicial positions are held, the judges are listed in the following order on the ballot (with state and county executive and legislative offices interspersed depending on the specific office): chief justice, supreme court; justice, supreme court; presiding judge, court of criminal appeals; judge, court of criminal appeals; chief justice, court of appeals; justice, court of appeals; district judge; criminal district judge; family district judge; judge, county court at law; judge, county criminal court; judge, county probate court; and justice of the peace.

V. Straight-Ticket Voting in Texas

Over the past twenty years, there has been a clear and relatively constant positive trend in the proportion of Texas voters casting a straight-ticket vote.[1] Data from the Austin Community College's Center for Public Policy and Political Studies displayed in Figure 10.3 underscore that with one exception (2006), the proportion of voters using the straight-ticket option has increased (or remained constant) compared to the preceding presidential (for the quadrennial presidential election cycle) and gubernatorial (for the quadrennial gubernatorial election cycle) election. The proportion of

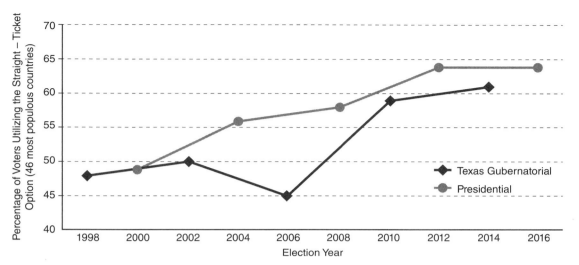

Figure 10.3   Straight-Ticket Voting in Texas Gubernational & Presidential Elections (1998–2016)

straight-ticket voters in gubernatorial elections has increased from 48 percent in 1998 to 61 percent in 2014. By the same token, the proportion of straight-ticket voters in presidential elections increased from 49 percent in 2000 to 64 percent in 2016. The one exception to this rising trend in straight-ticket voting was the 2006 gubernatorial election, where the presence of two high-profile independent gubernatorial candidates, Carole Keeton Strayhorn (at the time a Republican serving as the state's comptroller) and Kinky Friedman (who would in 2014 make a bid to be the Democratic Party's nominee for agriculture commissioner), who together won 31 percent of the gubernatorial vote, reduced the proportion of voters casting a straight ticket.

Within this context of rising straight-ticket voting over time, there nevertheless remains a considerable amount of inter-county variance in the popularity of straight-ticket voting. Table 10.1 lists the 20 most populous counties based on their mean proportion of voters casting a straight-ticket ballot during the 2008–2016 period.[2] In some counties (Fort Bend, Montgomery, Harris, and Dallas), on average more than two-thirds of those participating cast a straight-ticket vote, while in others the mean is either less than half (Nueces and Lubbock) or only slightly above half (Travis, Williamson, and Cameron).

VI. Limited Variance in the Judicial Vote: Pairwise Comparisons

This section analyzes the extent to which judicial candidates running in the same jurisdiction in the same year—be it statewide, appeals court district, or county (the same 20 most populous counties examined in the preceding section)—win a similar share of the vote within an identical partisan electoral context. An identical partisan electoral context is defined as a situation where both the Democratic and Republican parties presented candidates, and if minor parties (i.e., the Libertarian Party and the Green Party) ran candidates (which is quite rare outside of statewide contests), these minor parties also ran candidates in the elections being compared.

For every one of these judicial elections, the absolute value of the difference in the share of the vote won by every majority party candidate compared to the share won by every other majority party candidate was calculated.[3] The majority party is defined as the party that won the majority of the judicial races within the respective jurisdiction (i.e., statewide, appeals court district, or county [this includes district judges elected in a single county as well as county court elections, but excludes the constitutional county courts]).

Table 10.1 Percentage of Voters Casting a Straight-Ticket Ballot (2008–2016)

Texas County	2008	2010	2012	2014	2016	2008–2016
Fort Bend	67	66	75	74	77	72
Montgomery	66	62	73	70	71	68
Harris	63	68	69	69	68	67
Dallas	65	68	69	65	68	67
Tarrant	63	67	66	66	67	66
Hidalgo	63	62	69	63	69	65
Jefferson	63	62	66	61	67	64
Collin	58	62	65	65	65	63
Denton	55	61	65	63	65	62
Galveston	54	58	66	61	62	60
Webb	59	55	59	60	64	59
Bell	51	56	63	62	61	58
Brazoria	52	55	60	58	63	58
El Paso	55	53	52	56	63	56
Bexar	53	50	64	50	58	55
Cameron	57	51	59	47	56	53
Williamson	50	50	51	56	58	53
Travis	49	50	55	47	54	51
Lubbock	41	42	52	51	56	48
Nueces	47	43	47	44	56	47
20 County Mean	**57**	**57**	**62**	**59**	**63**	**60**
20 County Median	**56**	**57**	**65**	**61**	**64**	**61**

In the handful of cases where an equal number of Democratic and Republican judges were elected in a jurisdiction, the majority party was defined as the party whose candidate won the largest share of the two-party vote.[4]

The 2008 to 2016 period provides 29 pairwise comparisons for statewide judicial races, ranging from highs of 10 pairs in 2008 and 2016 to a low of zero pairs in 2012, when the Democratic Party only fielded candidates for two of the six state-wide judicial races, and one of those races also had a Green Party candidate and a Libertarian Party candidate while the other only had a Libertarian Party candidate. On average, the majority party statewide candidates varied very little in the share of the vote they received, with the median pair of candidates differing in their vote share by only 0.58 percent (see Table 10.2). Table 10.2 also provides the 25 percent (i.e., lower) and 75 percent (i.e., upper) quartile values for the pairwise differences in statewide races, which were 0.33 percent and 0.96 percent respectively, indicating that three out of every four statewide candidates won a percentage of the vote that differed by less than one percent from that of their fellow candidate(s).

The 2008 to 2016 period provides 85 pairwise comparisons for appeals court district races, ranging from a high of 41 in 2012 to a low of 7 in 2016. Similar to the case for statewide candidates, the median difference in the percentage of the vote won among the majority party appeals court candidates in the same district was 0.52 percent during this period. The 25 percent to 75 percent quartile range for the appeals court pairwise differences was 0.26 percent to 1.26 percent.

The 2008 to 2016 period provides 1,820 pairwise comparisons for county-level courts in the state's 20 most populous counties. The median pair of majority party candidates in the same county won a share of the vote that differed by slightly less than one percent (0.96 percent). The 25 percent to 75 percent range for the county-level courts was 0.46 percent to 1.65 percent. Overall, these numbers reveal a slightly greater level of variance in the share of the vote won by county-level candidates, which was in part the result of a couple of counties

Table 10.2 Pairwise Differences Among Judicial Candidates in the Same Jurisdiction

Year	Category	Statewide Courts	Appeals Courts	County-Level Courts
2008	Median	1.01%	0.81%	0.78%
	25–75%	0.65–1.47%	0.41–1.23%	0.38–1.31%
	# of Pairs	10	18	174
2010	Median	0.40%	0.30%	0.98%
	25–75%	0.14–0.47%	0.12–0.95%	0.46–1.66%
	# of Pairs	6	16	1143
2012	Median	—	0.48%	0.77%
	25–75%	—	0.26–1.59%	0.38–1.33%
	# of Pairs	—	41	187
2014	Median	0.47%	0.60%	1.04%
	25–75%	0.16–0.63%	0.51–1.11%	0.51–1.83%
	# of Pairs	3	3	636
2016	Median	0.56%	1.04%	1.00%
	25–75%	0.13–0.96%	0.34–1.26%	0.48–1.62%
	# of Pairs	10	7	180
2008–2016	**Median**	**0.58%**	**0.52%**	**0.96%**
	25–75%	**0.33–0.96%**	**0.26–1.26%**	**0.46–1.65%**
	# of Pairs	**29**	**85**	**1,820**

(Bexar County in particular) that featured notably higher pairwise differences than was the norm elsewhere in the state.

In all, these numbers underscore the very limited variance in the vote share won by judicial candidates from the same party, with median differences of approximately 0.5 percent in statewide and appeals court races and one percent in county-level contests. Even at the 75 percent (i.e., upper) quartile mark of the distributions, the candidates differed in the share of the vote won by less than two percent. The results of this limited variance in partisan performance are the near-universal sweeps analyzed in the next section (except in instances such as Harris County in 2012, where the majority party's average share of the two-party vote in the jurisdiction was extremely close to 50 percent).

VII. Sweeps and Splits: Statewide, Court of Appeals District, and County-Level Elections

In this section, elections from 2008, 2010, 2012, 2014, and 2016 are examined to assess the extent to which judicial positions in a set of defined jurisdictions were all won by candidates from the same party (a partisan sweep) and the extent to which the positions were won by candidates from different parties (a partisan split). The analysis

population consists of all statewide elections, all court of appeals district elections where more than one position was on the ballot, and all county-level judicial elections (district courts, statutory county courts, and statutory probate courts, but not constitutional county courts) in the state's 20 most populous counties where more than one judge was being elected.

Figure 10.4 provides information on the evolution of partisan sweeps over the past five elections for the statewide courts, appeals courts, and county level courts. All five elections featured statewide partisan sweeps. The proportion of appeals court district sweeps has largely trended upward over the past five elections, from 80 percent in 2008 to 100 percent in three of the past four elections (2010, 2014, and 2016) and 91 percent in the fourth (2012). A similar pattern is seen in the countywide judicial elections during the same time frame, with sweep rates of 90 percent in 2008, 84 and 83 percent in 2010 and 2012, and 90 and 95 percent during the two most recent election cycles. Figure 10.4 underscores the prevalence of judicial sweeps in Texas elections, where one party's candidates win all of the seats in play in the jurisdiction, be it Republicans statewide in 2014 and 2016 or Democrats countywide in Bexar County and Harris County in 2016.

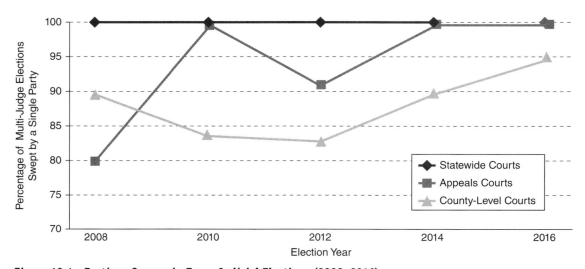

Figure 10.4   Partisan Sweeps in Texas Judicial Elections (2008–2016)

VIII. Straight-Ticket Voting and Judicial Elections: A Harris County Case Study

Year in and year out, no Texas county elects more judges at the county level (i.e., district and county judges) than Harris County. And among the state's five major urban counties (Bexar, Dallas, Harris, Tarrant, and Travis), Harris County is arguably the most competitive, with Democrats winning the largest share of the vote in three of the past five elections (2008, 2012, 2016) and Republicans winning the largest share of the vote in two of the past five elections (2010, 2014). Harris County's purple tint results in few uncontested judicial races (as are common in other counties), with both parties regularly able to field a full slate of candidates (the Democratic slate in 2014 is the partial exception).

In three of the past five elections (2010, 2014, and 2016), one party has won every single judicial election that took place in Harris County (see Table 10.3). And in 2008, one party won 85 percent of the judicial elections in play. In these four elections the respective party's success at the top of the ticket in the straight-ticket vote and in the contest for the highest profile office (president or governor) drove voter behavior, with judicial candidates winning or losing based almost exclusively on the strength of the party and presidential/gubernatorial coattails. The only election year that did not see a near or complete sweep was 2012, which resulted from the Democratic and Republican parties being so evenly matched at the top of the ticket, with the Democratic share of the two-party straight ticket vote only barely surpassing the Republican share (50.17 percent vs. 49.83 percent) in the county. This effective partisan deadlock left most judicial races on a knife's edge, with the outcome of half of the judicial races decided by less than one percent of the vote.

The data in Table 10.3 underscore the very limited variance in the share of the vote won by the judicial candidates in these elections; in all five election years, more than half of the majority party's judicial candidates did not differ in their share of the popular vote by more than one percent from that of their fellow judicial candidates on the ballot that year. Even the gap between the majority party candidate who won the lowest share of the vote and the majority candidate who won the highest share of the vote was never more than four percent across 179 contests spread over

Table 10.3   County-Level Judicial Elections in Harris County (2008–2016)

Category	2008	2010	2012	2014	2016
Majority Party	Democratic	Republican	Democratic	Republican	Democratic
Share of Races Won by Majority Party	85%	100%	56%	100%	100%
Median Majority Judicial Vote Share	51.10%	55.95%	50.18%	54.73%	52.19%
25 Percent Quartile Majority Judicial Vote Share	50.16%	55.18%	49.79%	54.03%	51.40%
75 Percent Quartile Majority Judicial Vote Share	51.31%	56.87%	50.78%	55.34%	52.92%
Highest Majority Judicial Vote Share	52.48%	57.41%	51.38%	56.36%	54.11%
Lowest Majority Judicial Vote Share	48.58%	53.87%	49.09%	52.84%	50.93%
Majority Party Share of Two-Party Straight-Ticket Vote	53.23%	54.70%	50.17%	54.74%	54.10%
Percentage of Voters Using Straight-Ticket Option	62%	67%	68%	68%	66%
Number of Contested Two-Party Judicial Races	27	59	25	42	26

five election years. In 2012, the largest pairwise gap between the best- and worst-performing candidates was 2.29 percent (51.38 percent vs. 49.09 percent), while in 2008 the largest gap was 3.90 percent (52.48 percent vs. 48.58 percent). During this time period, between three-fifths (62 percent) and two-thirds (68 percent) of Harris County voters cast a straight-ticket vote.[5]

Table 10.3 highlights the prevalence of judicial sweeps in Harris County, as the straight-ticket vote combined with the coattails of the candidates at the top of the ticket either carried judicial candidates into office or ensured their defeat. As a result, while many outstanding jurists were elected each cycle, it is also true that many judges, including those with considerable experience on the bench, were defeated not due to their judicial talents, but rather to the sub-par general popular support for their party and its marquee candidates.

If you asked 1,000 Harris County voters to name a candidate running for a district or county judicial post (other than that of the county judge) in a given election year, you would be lucky to find 100 who could name more than one, 10 who could name more than a dozen, and one who could name more than half. In fact, outside of a few diehard party activists, the only group of individuals who have a reasonably good handle on who is running for judge across the board in a given election year are a subset of attorneys belonging to the Houston Bar Association.

Every election year, these attorneys are polled by the Houston Bar Association on their preferences in the judicial races taking place in the county. While partisanship undoubtedly drives some of these preferences, the bipartisan nature of the Houston Bar Association's Judicial Preference Poll's results suggests that on average, the lawyers base their preferences more on the candidate's skills, experience, and philosophy as a jurist rather than on their partisan affiliation; a contrast to the general public whose vote is almost exclusively based on the candidate's partisan affiliation, with in a large majority of the cases even this support indirect via the straight-ticket vote rather than a race by race evaluation by the voter. For example, in 2016, a majority of the lawyers who participated in the Houston Bar Association's Judicial

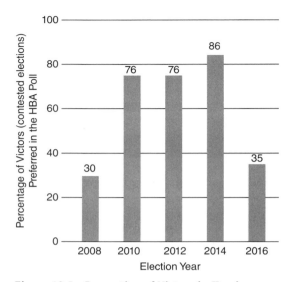

Figure 10.5   Proportion of Victors in Harris County Judicial Elections Preferred in the Harris County Bar Association's Judicial Preference Poll

Preferences Poll preferred the Republican candidate in 17 races and the Democratic candidate in nine races. Similarly, in 2012, the participating members of the Houston Bar Association favored Republicans in 15 races and Democrats in 10.

Figure 10.5 provides the proportion of Harris County judicial races (district and county) where the judicial candidate preferred by the attorneys participating in the Houston Bar Association's Judicial Preferences Poll was victorious in the November election. The proportions range from lows of 30 percent and 35 percent in 2008 and 2016 respectively to highs of 76 percent, 76 percent, and 86 percent in 2010, 2012, and 2014 respectively. The years of 2008 and 2016 in particular reveal a high level of disconnect between the opinions of the members of the Houston Bar Association and the choices made by the voting public (primarily through their straight-ticket votes).

IX. Four Options for Reforming the Selection of Judges in Texas

The review of judicial selection procedures and use of straight-ticket voting across the 50 states contained in Sections I and II reveals that Texas is an outlier in the country in regard to its combination of the use of partisan elections for judicial offices and the employment of straight-ticket voting. At the same time, Sections I and II provide the most prominent examples of reform options for Texas, should there be a desire to modify the current method by which judges in the state are chosen. These reform alternatives in turn can be roughly grouped into those that would require a constitutional reform and those that could be implemented via a statutory change. Some states utilize the same method to choose judges, from the supreme court down to the trial courts, while others use different selection methods depending on the specific office in question.

Four leading reform options are reviewed below with a description and a discussion of their principal advantages and disadvantages based on the extant literature. The first two would require the amendment of the Texas Constitution, while the latter two could be implemented without a constitutional reform via the passage of a statutory reform. The four reforms are presented in descending order with regard to their deviation from the current status quo in Texas. At the end of the section, a similar analysis of the advantages and disadvantages of the state's current judicial selection method is provided. It should be noted that these reforms could be implemented for the selection of all judges, or only for the selection of subsets of judges, for instance retaining the current selection method for the Texas Supreme Court and Texas Court of Criminal Appeals judges, but changing the way appeals court, district court, and county court judges (excluding the county judge) are selected.

The Texas Constitution prescribes that judges be elected for terms of four or six years, depending on the office. Any reform that would remove the popular election of judges would therefore require an amendment to the Texas Constitution, which in turn would need to be supported by at least two-thirds of the members of the Texas House of Representatives and of the Texas Senate as well as receive the support of a majority of voters in a subsequent constitutional amendment vote. Reform options that retain the popular election of judges

can be changed by a reform of the relevant portions of the Texas legal code. These reforms require only a majority vote in the Texas House of Representatives and in the Texas Senate, along with the governor's affirmation (explicit or implicit).

Reform Option 1. Judicial Nominating Commission

Under this general system, a judicial nominating commission provides the governor with a short list (i.e., a slate) of potential candidates for a judicial post. The governor then appoints a specific candidate either alone or (more commonly) with the advice and consent of the state senate. When the judge's initial term is up the governor has the option to re-nominate the justice either pending or not pending legislative ratification.

The principal advantages attributed to this selection method are:

- The selection of judges via a commission bolsters judicial independence by removing partisan politics, political patronage, and money from the equation to a greater degree than under the electoral alternatives;
- Political elites are better able to identify and evaluate the credentials and abilities of potential judicial candidates than are voters;
- Appointed judges may be less likely to be swayed by public opinion than judges who are either chosen or retained via popular elections.

The principal disadvantages attributed to this selection method are:

- It does not provide voters with any voice in the selection or retention of judges and is therefore undemocratic;
- It utilizes a process that is often opaque and deficient in terms of transparency;
- The process is not entirely divorced from partisan politics and patronage since the members of the commission are normally chosen by individuals with partisan and/or policy agendas;
- It may result in judges who are less willing to block or overturn executive orders or legislation;

- Judges within pure appointment systems are more likely to be perceived by the public as political cronies.

Reform Option 2. Judicial Nominating Commission with Retention Elections

Under this system, a judicial nominating commission provides the governor with a short list (i.e., a slate) of potential candidates for a judicial post. The governor then appoints a specific candidate either alone or (more commonly) with the advice and consent of the state senate. When a judge's initial term is up, he or she competes in a popular retention election, with voters given the option to retain or remove the judge. This methodology is often referred to as the "Missouri Plan," reflecting the Show Me State's status as the first state to adopt this particular methodology more than 75 years ago.

The principal advantages attributed to this selection method are:

- The selection of judges via a commission bolsters judicial independence by removing partisan politics, political patronage, and money from the equation to a greater degree than under the electoral alternatives;
- Political elites are better able to identify and evaluate the credentials and abilities of potential judicial candidates than are voters;
- Appointed judges may be less likely to be swayed by public opinion than judges who are initially selected in competitive nonpartisan or partisan elections;
- Compared to the prior option, where reappointment is not done via retention elections, it:
  - Allows voters to play a role in determining whether a judge should be retained or removed and is therefore more democratic and increases the popular accountability of judges;
  - Bolsters the independence of judges vis-à-vis the governor and legislature (compared to systems where reappointment is not done via retention elections).

The principal disadvantages attributed to this selection method are that it:

- Does not provide voters with a voice in the initial selection of judges and is therefore still in many ways undemocratic;
- Utilizes an initial appointment process that is often opaque and deficient in terms of transparency;
- Is not entirely divorced from partisan politics and patronage, since the members of the commission are normally chosen by individuals with partisan and/or policy agendas;
- May result in judges who are more easily swayed by public opinion than in an appointment system without retention elections;
- Results in a level of roll-off in retention elections that is higher than that which occurs in either nonpartisan or, especially, partisan elections (discussed below).[6]

Reform Option 3. Nonpartisan Judicial Elections

Under this system, judicial candidates compete in nonpartisan elections similar to those employed at the municipal level in Texas. No partisan label is included next to their names, and often they first compete in a nonpartisan primary from which the top two candidates advance to the general election.

The principal advantages attributed to this selection method are that it:

- Provides voters with a voice in the selection of their judges and is therefore more democratic and accountable than the appointment systems;
- Weakens the influence of the governor and legislature over the judiciary;
- Diminishes the role of partisan considerations in the judicial selection process;
- Requires (compared to the current method) voters to consider the judicial contests race by race instead of simply checking a partisan box at the top of the ballot.

The principal disadvantages attributed to this selection method are that it:

- Places the responsibility for selecting judges in the hands of a public that by and large is unfamiliar with the candidates competing and knows even less about their qualifications and judicial philosophy;

- Increases the public (i.e., visible) role of special interest groups in the selection of judges and can therefore erode public confidence in the independence and impartiality of the judiciary;
- Politicizes the judicial branch to a greater degree than when judges are appointed;
- Inserts campaign contributions and money openly into the judicial selection process;
- The principal disadvantages of this method's removal of partisanship from the ballot for judicial elections are that it:
  ○ Deprives voters of an important voting cue and source of information about the candidates;
  ○ Can lead to campaigns that tend to revolve around hot-button social issues;
  ○ Increases the amount of money spent in judicial elections and therefore the importance of campaign contributions;
  ○ Can require voters to choose between de facto partisan candidates without the benefit of party labels, since parties often still play a role in the recruitment of judicial candidates in nonpartisan elections;
  ○ Results in the highest level of ballot roll-off (i.e., under-voting) among the three principal forms of direct judicial election (nonpartisan elections, partisan elections with no straight-ticket option for judicial elections, partisan elections with straight-ticket voting).

Reform Option 4. Partisan Elections Without a Straight-Ticket Option for Judicial Elections

Under this system, judicial candidates compete in the general election in partisan elections, but unlike the case for other offices (e.g., president, state representative, county commissioner), the straight-ticket option does not apply to judicial elections.

The principal advantages attributed to this selection method are that it:

- Provides voters with a voice in the selection of their judges and is therefore more democratic and accountable than the appointment systems;

- Weakens the influence of the governor and legislature over the judiciary;
- Provides voters with the valuable informational voting cue represented by the candidates' partisan affiliation;
- Reduces (compared to the current method) the impact of high-profile races and pure party-line voting driving the election of judges (which concomitantly results in widespread partisan sweeps);
- Requires (compared to the current method) voters to consider the judicial contests race by race instead of checking a partisan box at the top of the ballot and never looking at the judicial contests on the ballot;
- Reduces (compared to nonpartisan elections) the role of money in the judicial election process.

The principal disadvantages of this selection method are that it:

- Places the responsibility for selecting judges in the hands of a public that by and large is unfamiliar with the candidates competing and knows even less about their qualifications and judicial philosophy;
- Politicizes the judicial branch to a greater degree than when judges are appointed;
- Inserts campaign contributions and money openly into the judicial selection process;
- Results in a greater amount of roll-off (i.e., the prevalence of undervotes) compared to the case when straight-ticket voting is employed for judicial elections.
  ○ Note: the increase in the extent of roll-off occasioned by a switch from partisan elections with a straight ticket to partisan elections without a straight-ticket option for judicial elections can be mitigated via a combination of optimal ballot design and voter education.

Current Method: Partisan Elections with a Straight-Ticket Option for Judicial Elections

All judges, from the Texas Supreme Court to county level courts, are selected in partisan elections where voters are provided with a straight-ticket option.

The principal advantages attributed to this selection method are that it:

- Provides voters with a voice in the selection of their judges and is therefore more democratic and accountable than the appointment systems;
- Weakens the influence of the governor and legislature over the judiciary (compared to the appointment systems);
- Provides voters with the valuable informational voting cue represented by the candidates' partisan affiliation;
- Limits the level of drop-off in judicial contests to a greater extent than any other method;
- Reduces the role of money in the judicial election process (compared to nonpartisan elections);
- Results in the least amount of ballot roll-off of any of the methods of popular election.

The principal disadvantages of this selection method are that it:

- Places the responsibility for selecting judges in the hands of a public that by and large is unfamiliar with the candidates competing and knows even less about their qualifications and judicial philosophy;
  - Exacerbates this disadvantage (compared to the method of partisan election without a straight-ticket option for judicial contests) by increasing the proportion of voters casting ballots in judicial races who are unfamiliar with the candidates and who do not review the judicial races they are voting in due to their use of the automatic straight-ticket option;
- Politicizes the judicial branch to a greater degree than when judges are appointed;
- Inserts campaign contributions and money openly into the judicial selection process;
- Decreases (compared to the method of partisan election without a straight-ticket option for judicial contests) the incentives for judges to campaign as individuals and for voters to research the judicial candidates.

Overall, Reform Options 1 and 2 represent the most dramatic departure from the current judicial selection process status quo. Both would require an amendment of the Texas Constitution to be implemented.

Reform Options 3 and 4 would represent less profound changes to the status quo of judicial selection in the Lone Star State, especially in the case of Option 4, where partisan elections would be retained with the reform centered on removing the election of some (e.g., appeals court district, district, and county level) or all judges from the straight-ticket mechanism. Compared to the status quo, both Reform Option 3 and Reform Option 4 would result in a significant amount of voter roll off in judicial races (especially Reform Option 3), but the extent of this roll off could be limited through ballot design and voter education efforts. Voters could for instance be alerted at the beginning of the ballot that the straight-ticket option does not apply to judicial elections as well as be reminded (where some form of electronic voting is employed) if they have not voted in some or all of the judicial elections when they first attempt to submit their ballot.

X. Conclusion

Texas is one of only two states that elects and re-elects its judges in partisan elections in combination with a straight-ticket voting option. The result is a powerful tendency for party-line voting and high-profile executive races to drive vote choices in down-ballot judicial races, resulting in limited variance in the vote shares received by judicial candidates and partisan sweeps at the state, appeals court district, and county levels.

Every recent biennial regular legislative session in Texas has featured multiple proposals to significantly modify the methods by which judges are selected in Texas. However, none of these bills ever reached the governor's desk, with most never even making it out of committee. Some of these proposals involved constitutional amendment, while others required only the passage of a statutory reform. This report provides an overview of four leading reform options, discussing both their advantages and disadvantages. These reforms range from dramatic changes to the status quo (e.g., the creation of a judicial nominating commission and retention elections) to relatively modest changes to the status quo (e.g., the elimination of the straight-ticket option for judicial races). During the 85th Legislative Session, Texas legislators once again have the opportunity to enact reforms to the process by which the state selects its judges, with the power, for instance, to adopt any of the four above-mentioned methods, either for all judicial contests or for only a select few (e.g., trial court judges).

NOTES

1. Under Texas law a voter casting a straight-ticket vote for a specific political party is casting a vote for all of that party's candidates on the remainder of the ballot. Voters who initially cast a straight-ticket vote do, however, have the option of subsequently going through the ballot race by race and changing their vote to support a candidate from a different party.

2. The 20 most populous counties (as of 2016) are, in descending order: Harris, Dallas, Tarrant, Bexar, Travis, Collin, Hidalgo, El Paso, Denton, Fort Bend, Montgomery, Williamson, Cameron, Nueces, Brazoria, Bell, Galveston, Lubbock, Webb, and Jefferson. Together, these 20 counties contain almost three-fourths (73 percent) of the state's population.

3. The use of the share of the vote won by the minority (second-place) party's candidates leads to similar findings.

4. Election data are drawn from the Texas Secretary of State's Elections Division and the respective elections offices of the 20 most populous counties either directly from their websites (or via e-mail in response to a data request) or indirectly from *Texas Election Source* publisher Jeff Blaylock.

5. The values for straight-ticket voting in Table 10.3 vary slightly from those in Table 10.1 as a result of minor differences in the denominator employed by the two sources.

6. Roll-off (or undervoting) occurs when a voter who has cast a ballot in one or more other races on the ballot does not cast a vote in a specific race.

REFERENCES

Ansolabehere, Stephen, and Charles S. Stewart III. 2005. "Residual Votes Attributable to Technology." *Journal of Politics* 67: 365–89.

Ballotpedia. 2016. "Judicial Selection in the States." http://www.ballotpedia.org/judicial_selection_in_the_states.

Baum, Lawrence. 2003. "Judicial Elections and Judicial Independence: The Voter's Perspective." *Ohio State Law Journal* 64(1): 13–41.

Becker, Daniel, and Malia Reddick. 2003. *Judicial Selection Reform: Examples from Six States.* Des Moines, IA: American Judicature Society.

Blaylock, Jeff. 2016. *Texas Election Source.* http://www.txelects.com.

Bonneau, Chris W., and Melinda Gann Hall. 2009. *In Defense of Judicial Elections.* New York: Routledge.

Bonneau, Chris W., and Eric Loepp. 2014. "Getting Things Straight: The Effect of Ballot Design and Electoral Structure on Voter Participation." *Electoral Studies* 34(2): 119–30.

Burden, Barry C., and David C. Kimball. 2002. *Why Americans Split Their Tickets: Campaigns, Competition, and Divided Government.* Ann Arbor, MI: University of Michigan Press.

Canes-Wrone, Brandice, and Tom S. Clark. 2009. "Judicial Independence and Nonpartisan Elections." *Wisconsin Law Review* 2009(1): 21–65.

Canes-Wrone, Brandice, Tom S. Clark, and Jee-Kwang Park. 2012. "Judicial Independence and

Retention Elections." *Journal of Law, Economics, and Organization* 28(2): 211–34.

Champagne, Anthony. 2008. "Judicial Reform in Texas: A Look Back After Two Decades." *Court Review* 43(2): 68–79.

Cheek, Kyle, and Anthony Champagne. 2004. *Judicial Politics in Texas: Partisanship, Money, and Politics in State Courts.* New York: Peter Lang.

Council of State Governments. 2003. *Judicial Democracy.* Lexington, KY: Council of State Governments.

Failinger, Marie A. 2005. "Can a Good Judge Be a Good Politician? Judicial Elections from a Virtue Ethics Approach." *Missouri Law Review* 70: 433–518.

Fortson, Ryan, and Kristin S. Knudsen. 2015. "A Survey of Studies of Judicial Selection." *Alaska Justice Forum* 32(2–3): 1–12.

Geyh, Charles Gardner. 2008. "The Endless Judicial Selection Debate and Why It Matters for Judicial Independence." *Georgetown Journal of Legal Ethics* 21: 1259–81.

Gilbert, Michael D. 2014. "Judicial Independence and Social Welfare." *Michigan Law Review* 112: 575–625.

Golezhauser, Greg, and Damon M. Cann. 2014. "Judicial Independence and Opinion Clarity on State Supreme Courts." *State Politics & Policy Quarterly* 14(2): 123–41.

Haag, Stefan. 2014. "Report #9: Straight-Ticket Voting in Texas 1998–2014." Austin, Texas: Center for Public Policy and Political Studies, Austin Community College District.

Haag, Stefan. 2016. "Report #11: Straight-Ticket Voting in Texas 1998–2016." Austin, Texas: Center for Public Policy and Political Studies, Austin Community College District.

Hall, Melinda Gann. 2001. "State Supreme Courts in American Democracy: Probing the Myths of Judicial Reform." *American Political Science Review* 95: 315–30.

Hernson, Paul S., Richard G. Niemi, Michael J. Hanmer, Benjamin B. Bederson, Frederick G. Conrad, and Michael W. Traugott. 2007. *Voting Technology: The Not-So-Simple Act of Casting a Ballot.* Washington, D.C.: Brookings Institution Press.

Hojnacki, Marie, and Lawrence Baum. 1992. "'New Style' Judicial Campaigns and the Voters: Economic Issues and Union Members in Ohio." *Western Political Quarterly* 45: 921–48.

Houston Bar Association. 2016. Judicial Preference Polls, 2008, 2010, 2012, 2014, 2016. http://www.hba.org/judicial-poll-results.

Iaryczower, Matías, Garrett Lewis, and Matthew Shum. 2013. "To Elect or Appoint? Bias, Information, and Responsiveness of Bureaucrats and Politicians." *Journal of Public Economics* 97: 230–44.

Jefferson, Wallace B. 2016. "Choosing Judges: My View from the Inside." In *Texas Politics Today 2017–2018 Edition,* Mark P. Jones, William Earl Maxwell, Ernest Crain, Morhea Lynn Davis, Christopher Wlezien, and Elizabeth N. Flores, 256–57. Boston: Cengage Learning.

Jones, Mark P., William Earl Maxwell, Ernest Crain, Morhea Lynn Davis, Christopher Wlezien, and Elizabeth N. Flores. 2016. *Texas Politics Today 2017–2018 Edition.* Boston: Cengage Learning.

Kimball, David C., and Martha Kropf. 2005. "Ballot Design and Unrecorded Votes on Paper-Based Ballots." *Public Opinion Quarterly* 69: 508–29.

Klein, David, and Lawrence Baum. 2001. "Ballot Information and Voting Decisions in Judicial Elections." *Political Research Quarterly* 54: 161–80.

Kritzer, Herbert M. 2007. "Law Is the Mere Continuation of Politics by Different Means: American Judicial Selection in the Twenty-First Century." *DePaul Law Review* 56: 423–67.

Kritzer, Herbert M. 2016. "Impact of Judicial Elections on Judicial Decisions." *Annual Review of Law and Social Science* 12: 353–71.

Miller, Michael G., Michelle D. Tuma, and Logan Woods. 2015. "Revisiting Roll-Off in Alerted Optical Scan Precincts: Evidence from Illinois General Elections." *Election Law Journal* 14: 382–91.

National Center for State Courts. 2016. "Judicial Selection in the States." http://www.judicial-selection.com.

National Conference of State Legislatures. 2016. "Straight Ticket Voting States." http://www.ncsl.org/research/elections-and-campaigns/straight-ticket-voting.aspx.

Schotland, Roy A. 2007. "New Challenges to States' Judicial Selection." *Georgetown Law Journal* 95: 1077–1105.

Stein, Robert M., Greg Vonnahme, Michael Byrne, and Daniel Wallach. 2008. "Voting Technology, Election Administration, and Voter Performance." *Election Law Journal* 7(2): 123–35.

Streb, Matthew J., ed. 2009. *Running for Judge: The Rising Political, Financial, and Legal Stakes of Judicial Elections*. New York: New York University Press.

Texas Judicial Branch. 2016. "2016 Annual Statistical Report." Austin, Texas: Office of Court Administration.

Texas Secretary of State. 2016. "Election Results." Austin, Texas: Elections Division.

Tomz, Michael, and Robert P. Van Houweling. 2003. "How Does Voting Equipment Affect the Racial Gap in Voided Ballots?" *American Journal of Political Science* 47: 46–60.

United States Census Bureau. 2016. "Population Estimates, July 1, 2016." Washington, D.C.: United States Department of Commerce.

Willoughby, Larry. 2012. "Report #8: Straight Ticket Voting in Texas 1998–2012." Austin, Texas: Center for Public Policy and Political Studies, Austin Community College District.

ARTICLE QUESTIONS

1) What are three consequences of partisan judicial elections in Texas?
2) In what years did a party "sweep" (win 100 percent) of the judicial elections in Harris County?
3) Identify three reforms to Texas's system of judicial selection described by the author.
4) Do you believe Texas should move to a new system of selecting judges? Should judges be elected or selected by a nonpartisan panel?

10.3) Should We Take Judges Out of the Fundraising Business?

Texas Tribune, May 15, 2015

ROSS RAMSEY

In the wake of fundraising scandals involving judges taking bribes, Texas passed legislation in 1995 that capped contributions to judicial candidates, although the limits differ depending on the type of judicial race and the population of the district. These changes allowed the state to ensure the integrity of the system by making the process more transparent and less able to be influenced by campaign funds, but it also required judges to fundraise for their own elections.

Texas Tribune executive editor and longtime Texas political reporter Ross Ramsey argues that judges should be taken out of the fundraising "business," as has happened several other states. Quoting former justices who worry about paid personal relationships seeping into judicial decisions, Ramsey attempts to make the case that justices should be banned from taking campaign contributions. Justices aren't supposed to represent the people who elect them or their donors specifically, he contends—they are supposed to uphold the rule of law. Ramsey argues that this position may be compromised if campaign donations are used to curry favor with judges, even if there is not any specific wrongdoing intended.

On the other hand, he acknowledges that the First Amendment's provisions guaranteeing free speech could be compromised if limits are placed on an individual office seeker's ability to fundraise on his or her own behalf, since such funds help get the candidate's message out. The state requires judges to run for election, so taking away their ability to communicate with voters is like sending them into a football game without a helmet.

It might seem silly to elect people who promise they won't represent you, their political party or their donors, but that's what we expect judges to do. They're supposed to apply the law, and if they do any of those other things, they're probably out of line.

Florida elects judges but bars them from raising their own campaign money. Lots of Texas judges—and Texas lawyers—would love to see similar restraints here.

"If you are an incumbent judge and you call a lawyer and ask for money, what is that lawyer going to say? No?" asks Wallace Jefferson, a former chief justice of the Texas Supreme Court who now practices law in Austin. "That incumbent judge is going to raise more money. But no one should feel pressured to contribute."

Better, he says, to take the judges out of the fundraising business and leave the transactional part of politics to campaign committees and others.

It could happen: The U.S. Supreme Court upheld Florida's law last month after challengers said it violated their First Amendment rights. That court was also concerned with whether asking for money sullied the impartiality of the elected judges. The court decided that was a serious enough public interest to justify the fundraising restriction.

"Simply put, the public may lack confidence in a judge's ability to administer justice without fear or favor if he comes to office by asking for favors," Chief Justice John Roberts wrote in the majority opinion.

It's hard to keep politics out of the law when judges have to stand for election. Nathan Hecht, the current chief justice of the Texas Supreme Court, touched briefly on that in his State of the Judiciary speech earlier in the legislative session. "I have not spoken to the problems of judicial selection because I have no consensus solution," he said.

Hecht went on to say that Texans want accountable judges but said voters know so little about them that "election results are usually the product of campaign spending, familiar names, political swings and blind luck."

The first two of those—the controllable variables—have to do with money, which is required by campaigns to make unfamiliar names familiar.

In its purest form, raising money for a political campaign is simply a way of asking for support and a kind of endorsement all at once. The donor offers the candidate a little of what's needed to proceed and the candidate who gathers the most support—in the form of money and votes—wins.

It smells just fine in the civics textbooks, but in practice, it can carry a strong scent, especially in judicial races. For one thing, judges aren't supposed to represent the people who elect them. "Unlike a politician, who is expected to be appropriately responsive to the preferences of supporters, a judge in deciding cases may not follow the preferences of his supporters or provide any special consideration to his campaign donors," Roberts wrote.

Some states have dumped judicial elections altogether, and others have opted for hybrid forms, such as one where voters decide whether to retain judges who initially are appointed to office.

Judges here have asked for changes in how Texas gets its jurists, but legislation has never gone far. Neither have other changes.

This legislative session, state Rep. Rafael Anchia, D-Dallas, filed a bill that would start public financing of campaigns for appellate judges in Texas. It was sent to the House Elections Committee on March 9 and never heard from again.

Sen. and former state District Judge Joan Huffman, R-Houston, has a bill that would eliminate straight-ticket voting in judicial races—the idea is to free judges from the slings and arrows of party politics. That one is stalled, as is its identical twin in the House, filed by Rep. Kenneth Sheets, R-Dallas.

Jefferson and Tom Phillips, who preceded him as the Texas high court's chief justice, wrote an amicus brief in the federal case, along with a couple of former chiefs of Alabama's Supreme Court. "As former Chief Justices who have observed countless elections in our own States, and run as candidates for judicial office, we are well-acquainted with the genuine dangers—and sometimes actual abuse—present when judicial candidates personally solicit campaign contributions from parties and lawyers," they wrote.

Now that the Florida law has been upheld, Jefferson thinks "it would be a step in the right direction" for Texas to take judges out of the campaign fundraising business.

"To me, money is not in the center except to the extent that the public believes, if a judge is accepting money from a lawyer or litigant, that they'll be more likely to favor that lawyer or litigant," Jefferson says. "I don't believe that is generally true, but the public believes it. And I understand that belief. It undermines the ideal of impartial justice."

ARTICLE QUESTIONS

1) What are some of the reasons given for banning judges from accepting campaign contributions?

2) Should Texas continue to have partisan elections for judges? What are the pros and cons of this approach?

3) What is your opinion on whether or not judges should be barred from asking for campaign funds?

Chapter 11

Elections

Party and powerful financial interests still hold significant sway in who gets elected in Texas today. Contributing to this phenomenon is Texas voters' decreasing likelihood of voting, a trend that complicates rule by the people. How district lines are drawn, how Texans register to vote, and who is excluded from voting for various reasons all shape the politics of the state. The road to voting rights has been long and difficult for several groups, including women, African Americans, and Latinos, whose struggles have been punctuated by demographic changes, social changes, and judicial interventions. These changes (and reactions to these changes) will frame the politics of the state for decades to come.

Court challenges to established election processes often come from unusual places. Pasadena, Texas, famous for being the location of the 1980s John Travolta movie *Urban Cowboy* and home of an annual strawberry festival that boasts the largest strawberry shortcake in the world, is also famous for its role in the struggle for voting rights. When the mayor of Pasadena moved to change the how city council members were elected and diluted minority voting strength in the process, the case served as a spark that touched off an explosion. Writing for the *Texas Tribune*, journalist and voting rights expert Alexa Ura describes the battle for voting rights in a Texas city that is truly divided: one side of Pasadena is growing more Hispanic and more Democratic, while the other side remains older, Anglo, and more Republican. This divide has created political friction that has framed the debate about the importance and long-term relevance of the Voting Rights Act.

At the center of voting rights is the process of registering to vote. The struggle for voting rights has increasingly focused on challenges in representation, access to the ballot box, and opportunities to participate in parties and as candidates. Change in Texas politics has been slow, but transformations are occurring. A trio of researchers at the Hobby School of Public Affairs at the University of Houston argue that Texas's voter identification law (which requires voters to show one of several approved photo identification documents at the polls before voting) has led to confusion among Texans, especially nonvoters and Latinos. They find that the photo ID law may have kept some nonvoters from voting in two key Texas battleground elections, but that it was not the only or the primary factor. The voters who were least likely to vote because of confusion were more likely to vote for Democratic candidates.

The process of voting itself is challenging, Bryan Jones argues in an editorial in *TribTalk*, because the state is still using "pen and paper" to register voters. Why can't Texas register voters online? Texas is a large and diverse state—and also a young and mobile one. These attributes tend to produce poor turnout among registered voters, a challenge for interested groups, parties, and campaigns seeking to motivate voters to register to vote, let alone come out to vote. Would online registration change all that? Jones identifies several reasons why online registration (digital voter registration, or DVR) is a good fit for Texas. Cost is the first benefit: it would be cheaper than the current system. Access is another: with technology available, Jones argues that the state, known for its bold action in other spheres, should embrace the digital convenience of online registration.

Change or continuity in Texas hinges on voters exercising their right to vote, but not all Texans are eligible to do so, for a variety of reasons. One significant collateral consequence of a criminal conviction in Texas is the loss of voting rights, a measure called felony disenfranchisement. Most states, including Texas, ban felons from exercising their right to vote for the duration of their prison sentence and while on probation or parole. Eleven states extend the voting restriction beyond the offender's completion of his or her sentence. The harshest postincarceration voting restrictions can be found in the South (e.g., Texas, Florida, Mississippi, Alabama), which has embraced the political value of being tough on crime and has a cultural history of keeping lawbreakers separated from the rest of society. Brandon Sams, a student at Texas State University and an opinion writer for the *University Star*, makes a case for more leniency in restoring ex-felons' right to vote. What implications would the lifting of these restrictions have for state politics?

Demographic changes portend a more Democratic Texas, so the theory goes, but this shift has been slow, partly because Texans' conservative politics are deeply entrenched. The state has seen intensely partisan battles over redistricting in the past and will definitely see more in the future as a growing Texas is set to receive several new congressional districts after the 2020 census. Why has there been so much contention? Small changes may matter, and how lines are drawn often dictates who wins that seat, making redistricting the heart of elections in Texas.

CHAPTER QUESTIONS

1) Does Texas make it difficult for residents to register to vote and to vote?
2) What are three challenges of increasing voter registration and turnout in Texas elections?
3) How can the state improve its voter registration process? How could these changes improve voter turnout?

11.1) The Texas Voter ID Law and the 2016 Election: A Study of Harris County and Congressional District 23

University of Houston Hobby School of Public Affairs, 2016

MARK P. JONES, RENÉE CROSS, AND JIM GRANATO

In Texas, a prospective voter must register to vote at least thirty days before an election and must be a U.S. citizen, a resident of the county where the individual intends to vote, at least eighteen years old, not a convicted felon, and not judged to be mentally incapacitated. This all seems simple enough, but other policies make voting more complicated. Voters must show photo identification in order to vote, something most but not all of Texas's prospective voters have. Taken together, such requirements impose greater costs on less educated individuals and those less attentive to politics. Are these requirements reducing voting?

University of Houston Hobby School of Public Affairs researchers Mark P. Jones, Renée Cross and Jim Granato investigate how Texas voter ID rules affect voting outcomes in two key areas: the 23rd Congressional District, which spans much of the Texas border from El Paso to San Antonio and is one of the few competitive districts in Texas, and Harris County, the state's largest county. Confusion about the law was widespread during the 2016 elections, with the authors claiming that nonvoters did not have a good understanding of the rules. They found that only one in five Texans could correctly identify the photo ID rules, and most were unaware that they could still vote without their ID if they signed an affidavit and showed the ID at a later time.

In terms of electoral outcomes, Jones, Cross, and Granato find that between 15 and 17 percent of nonvoters did not vote because they did not possess an official voter identification, and two-thirds of those voters would have voted for a Democratic candidate if they had voted. Lack of voter ID was not the principle reason nonvoters didn't vote, but it was a factor for some. The authors conclude that the photo ID law may have partially discouraged some from voting, but a lack of state-approved photo ID kept few from actually voting. However, Latinos were more likely to be misinformed about photo ID rules, potentially causing divergent racial impacts.

Executive Summary

In 2016, voter photo ID regulations were once again in force in Texas. This study examines the impact of those regulations on voter participation in the state's two highest profile battleground jurisdictions during the 2016 electoral cycle: Harris County and Congressional District 23 (CD-23). It also explores familiarity among non-voters with the 2016 photo ID rules, rules that have served as the foundation for revised photo ID legislation presently being considered in the Texas Legislature during the 85th legislative session (e.g., Senate Bill 5 and House Bill 2481).

The data employed in the study are drawn from two separate representative surveys of registered voters who were eligible to participate in the November 8, 2016 election but did not cast a ballot (i.e., non-voters). The surveys were conducted in English and Spanish in February and March of 2017, with 424 and 395 interviews completed in Harris County and CD-23 respectively.

Virtually all registered voters in Harris County and CD-23 who did not participate in the November 2016 election possessed one of the state approved forms of photo ID needed to cast a vote in person. All together, 97.4% and 97.8% of non-voters in Harris County and CD-23 possessed an unexpired state-approved photo ID, with these proportions rising to 98.5% and 97.9% when photo IDs that had expired within the previous four years were considered (in 2016 IDs that had expired within four years of the voting date could be used to vote in person). The most common photo ID held by non-voters was a Texas driver license, with 82.9% and 84.1% of Harris County and CD-23 non-voters possessing an unexpired Texas driver license. Among those between the ages of 18 and 25 (who in theory would be the principal beneficiaries of an expansion of the forms of state approved ID to include public college and university IDs), 97.4% and 97.5% of Harris County and CD-23 non-voters possessed an unexpired state approved photo ID, rising to 100% in Harris County (and remaining at 97.5% in CD-23) when expired IDs were considered.

Approximately three-fifths of non-voters in Harris County (58.8%) and CD-23 (63.6%) agreed that one of the reasons they did not vote was because they didn't like the candidates or the issues, making it the reason for not voting with the highest level of agreement in both locales. At the other end of the continuum, approximately one in seven non-voters in Harris County (16.5%) and CD-23 (14.8%) signaled a lack of possession of a state approved photo ID as one of the reasons they did not participate in the 2016 election. Among this sub-set of non-voters whose nonparticipation was attributed at least in part to the photo ID requirements, approximately two-thirds of those with a preference would have voted for the Democratic candidates in the Harris County District Attorney and Sheriff races and in the CD-23 race. This suggests that had these individuals participated, the Democratic candidates in the former two contests would have enjoyed even larger margins of victory and the Democratic candidate in CD-23, Pete Gallego, would have defeated his Republican rival, Will Hurd, instead of losing to Hurd by 1.3% of the vote.

However, when pressed to give the principal reason why they did not cast a ballot in 2016, only 1.5% and 0.5% of non-voters in Harris County and CD-23 identified a lack of a state-approved photo ID as the principal reason they did not vote. Among this handful of non-voters, 86% actually possessed an approved form of photo ID, while 14% did not. While the photo ID law at least partially discouraged some people from voting, an actual lack of a state approved photo ID kept virtually no one (only one non-voter among the 819 surveyed) from turning out to vote in 2016.

Only one in five non-voters in Harris County (21.1%) and CD-23 (17.9%) could accurately identify the photo ID rules in effect for the 2016 election. Three in five non-voters in both jurisdictions (58.4% and 59.7%) incorrectly believed that all voters were required to provide a state approved form of photo ID to vote in person, unaware that voters who did not possess a photo ID could still vote if they signed an affidavit and provided one of several supporting documents. In both Harris County and CD-23, Latino non-voters (15.1% and 14.8%) were significantly less likely than Anglo non-voters (24.3% and 27.6%) and, in Harris County, than African American non-voters (27.9%), to accurately understand the photo ID rules governing the 2016 election. Latino non-voters in both locales also were significantly more likely than Anglo (and in Harris County, African American) non-voters to believe that the 2016 photo ID rules were more restrictive than they actually were.

Three out of four Harris County (74.2%) and CD-23 (75.1%) non-voters incorrectly believed that only an unexpired Texas driver license qualified as a state approved form of photo ID to vote in person in 2016. A mere 14.4% and 13.8% of non-voters in these two jurisdictions were aware that in 2016 an expired Texas driver license could also be used as long as it had expired within the past four years. In Harris County, Latinos (82.4%) were significantly more likely than Anglos (72.3%) to believe they could only use an unexpired Texas driver license as a form of photo ID to vote in person in 2016. In CD-23 there were however no significant differences between Latino (75.4%) and Anglo (76.8%) non-voters.

The survey data clearly indicate that non-voters in Harris County and CD-23 did not have a good understanding of the voter photo ID rules in force for the 2016 election. Only one in five non-voters were aware that it was possible for registered voters who did not possess one of the seven state approved forms of photo ID to still vote in person by signing an affidavit and providing one of many easily obtainable supporting documents. And, only one in seven non-voters knew that an expired (within four years) Texas driver license qualified as a state approved photo ID for the purposes of voting in person in 2016.

The uninformed and misinformed state of the Texas non-voting electorate in 2016 highlights the need for a more robust state-sponsored voter education campaign to increase public knowledge regarding the photo ID rules that will be in effect in 2018 when Texans vote in races to choose elected officials for positions ranging from U.S. senator and governor to county judge and constable.

I. The Texas Voter ID Law and the 2016 Election: A Study of Harris County and Congressional District 23

The 2016 election represented the second general election in Texas where voter photo ID rules were in force. In an effort to better understand the impact of the state's photo ID rules on voter participation, we conducted surveys of non-voters in the Lone Star State's two highest profile battleground jurisdictions: Harris County and U.S. Congressional District 23 (CD-23).

This report contains nine sections. Section II reviews the history of voter photo ID regulations in Texas over the past half dozen years. Section III briefly discusses the two jurisdictions examined in the study, Harris County and CD-23. Section IV provides basic details on the survey methodology. Section V describes the non-voter population in regard to ethnicity/race, partisanship, and voting preferences. Section VI details the extent to which these non-voters possessed one or more of the state-approved forms of photo ID required to cast a vote in person in 2016 (without completing an affidavit) as well as the level of approved photo ID possession across ethnic/racial groups and age cohorts. Section VII analyzes the reasons why these non-voters did not participate in the 2016 electoral process, both in general as well as in regard to the principal reason these non-voters listed as the reason they did not cast a ballot in the fall of 2016, while at the same time exploring what the hypothetical electoral consequences of this non-participation were for the outcome of several high profile competitive races. Section VIII assesses non-voter knowledge regarding the photo ID rules that were in effect for the November 8, 2016 election as well as the extent to which

knowledge levels differed across ethnic/racial groups. Section IX concludes.

II. Voter ID in Texas: 2011–2016

In 2011, the Texas Legislature passed Senate Bill 14 (SB 14) that created a new requirement for voters to show *photo* identification when voting in person (Hobby et al. 2015).[1] Initially, the U.S. Department of Justice (DOJ) argued that Texas's voter photo ID law disproportionately placed an undue burden on minority voters and thus rejected the Texas law, a decision upheld by the U.S. District Court for the District of Columbia on August 30, 2012. However, on June 25, 2013, the U.S. Supreme Court decision in *Shelby County v. Holder* removed for the present time the requirement that Texas seek federal approval for election law related changes, and subsequently the 2011 voter ID law immediately took effect. While a U.S. District Judge (Judge Nelva Gonzales Ramos of the United States District Court for the Southern District of Texas based in Corpus Christi) struck down Texas's voter ID law on October 9, 2014, a panel for the U.S. 5th Circuit Court of Appeals issued a preliminary injunction against the ruling of the U.S. District Court, which then was confirmed 6-3 by the U.S. Supreme Court on October 18, 2014. As a result, Texas's photo ID law was in force for the November 2014 election, requiring a state-approved form of photo identification in order to vote in person. The approved forms of photo identification were as follows:

- Texas driver license issued by the Texas Department of Public Safety (DPS);
- Texas Election Identification Certificate (EIC) issued by DPS;
- Texas personal identification (ID) card issued by DPS;
- Texas concealed handgun license (CHL) issued by DPS;
- United States military identification card containing the person's photograph;
- United States citizenship certificate containing the person's photograph;
- United States Passport.

Photo identification was not required to cast an absentee/mail ballot in Texas, but no-excuse absentee voting is almost exclusively limited to those 65 and older. All other voters must either be disabled, in jail (but otherwise eligible to vote), or out of town on election day and during the entire early voting period (October 20 to October 31 in 2014) in order to cast an absentee ballot.

On July 20, 2016, the U.S. 5th Circuit Court of Appeals concurred with Judge Gonzales Ramos that the Texas photo ID law had a discriminatory effect and did not comply with the Voting Rights Act. As a result, an interim set of rules issued by the judge and accepted by the plaintiffs and the state of Texas was in force for the November 2016 election (Jones et al. 2016). The approved forms of photo identification were as follows:

- Texas driver license issued by the Texas Department of Public Safety (DPS);
- Texas Election Identification Certificate (EIC) issued by DPS;
- Texas personal identification (ID) card issued by DPS;
- Texas concealed handgun license (CHL) issued by DPS;
- United States military identification card containing the person's photograph;
- United States citizenship certificate containing the person's photograph;
- United States Passport.

In contrast to 2014 when the photo IDs above had to either be unexpired or to have expired no more than 60 days prior to the date they were being presented at the polling place, under the court-ordered agreement in force for 2016, all of the photo identification was considered valid if it had expired no more than four years prior to the date it was being presented at the polling place.[2]

As in 2014, photo identification was not required to cast an absentee/mail ballot in Texas, but no-excuse absentee voting was still limited to those 65 and older. All other voters had to either be disabled, in jail (but otherwise eligible to vote), or out of town on election day and during the entire early voting period (October 24 to November 4 in 2016) to vote absentee.

And, also in contrast to 2014, registered voters who did not possess, and could not reasonably

obtain, one of the above-mentioned seven forms of photo ID could vote as long as they completed an affidavit at the polling place explaining why and also presented one of the following supporting documents[3]:

- Valid voter registration certificate;
- Certified birth certificate (original);
- Copy of or original current utility bill;
- Copy of or original bank statement;
- Copy of or original government check;
- Copy of or original paycheck;
- Copy of or original government document with name and an address (original required if it contains a photograph).

At present, proceedings are underway in the U.S. District Court to assess whether or not the 2011 voter photo ID was passed with discriminatory intent. At the same time, legislation is currently under consideration in the Texas Legislature that would modify the original legislation passed in 2011 to make it closer in form and impact to that which was temporarily in force for the 2016 general election.

Hobby et al. (2015) examined the impact of Texas's voter photo identification regulation in the November 2014 election using a case study of voter behavior, preferences and attitudes in CD-23. A survey of 400 CD-23 registered voters who did not vote in the November 2014 election indicated that for 5.8% of these non-voters the principal reason given for why they did not vote was because they did not possess any of the seven forms of photo identification required by the state to cast a vote in person. More than twice that many (12.8%) agreed that their lack of any one of these seven photo IDs was a reason they did not vote.

However, when further queried about the different forms of photo identification in their possession, the survey revealed that a much lower proportion (2.7%) of CD-23 non-voters in fact lacked one of the seven needed to vote in person. In all, while 12.8% and 5.8% of these non-voters cited a lack of a photo ID as a reason or the principal reason they did not vote, only 1.0% and 0.5% of the respondents both respectively attributed their non-voting in part or primarily to a lack of photo ID and actually did not possess an approved form of photo ID.

The 2015 study suggested that the most significant impact of the Texas voter photo ID law on voter participation in CD-23 in November 2014 was to discourage turnout among registered voters who did indeed possess an approved form of photo ID, but through some combination of misunderstanding, doubt or lack of knowledge, believed that they did not possess the necessary photo identification. The disjuncture between the proportion of voters who listed a lack of an ID as a reason or the principal reason they did not vote and the proportion of these individuals who actually did not have an ID highlighted the potential for voter education campaigns to clearly explain the types of photo identification required to cast a vote in person in Texas. The study also examined the potential impact of the Texas voter photo ID law on the outcome of the 2014 election in CD-23 between Pete Gallego and Will Hurd in which Hurd narrowly defeated Gallego. It suggested that the presence of the law kept far more Gallego than Hurd supporters away from the polls, quite possibly costing Gallego the election.

III. Purple Texas: Harris County and Congressional District 23

In Texas in November 2016, there existed a notable dearth of high profile competitive electoral contests, with an overwhelming majority of congressional, state legislative, and county offices either safely Republican or Democrat, with all statewide seats in the state safely in the Republican column at the present time. Texas Democrats last won a statewide race more than twenty years ago in 1994.

For this study we scoured Texas for high-profile and consequential races whose outcome had not been effectively pre-determined well before November by the partisan composition of the jurisdiction's voters. In November 2016 the three highest profile competitive races in "purple" jurisdictions were held in CD-23 (the only one of Texas's 36 U.S. House districts that is neither safely Republican nor Democrat) and in Harris County for the offices of district attorney and sheriff. These three races represent excellent test cases for the potential impact of Texas's voter photo ID legislation on electoral outcomes, since if the legislation does

have an effect in highly salient contests, it would be most likely observed in CD-23 and Harris County.[4]

With a population of 4.6 million, Harris County is far and away the most populous county in Texas as well as the third most populous county in the United States. The county's population is greater than that of 25 of the 50 U.S. states. Unlike Texas's other mega-counties which are either dominated by Democrats (Dallas, El Paso, Travis, and, to a lesser extent, Bexar) or Republicans (Tarrant), Harris County remains competitive with candidates from both parties having a realistic chance of victory in any given election (with Democrats enjoying a slight edge in presidential election years and Republicans enjoying a slight edge in gubernatorial election years).

Over the past three election cycles held under the current district boundaries created in 2011, CD-23 has been the only one of the state's 36 U.S. House districts that was not either safely Republican or safely Democrat. In the first election held using the current district boundaries (2012), the Democratic challenger, Pete Gallego, narrowly defeated the Republican incumbent, Francisco "Quico" Canseco, 50.3% to 45.6%. In 2014, Republican Will Hurd even more narrowly defeated Gallego, 49.8% to 47.7%, and in a 2016 rematch, Hurd defeated Gallego again, by the even narrower margin of 48.3% to 47.0%. CD-23 encompasses 26 complete counties and portions of three others, stretching from San Antonio (Bexar County) to Eagle Pass (Maverick County) on the U.S.-Mexico border, and out to the lower El Paso valley (El Paso County) on the outskirts of El Paso.

In Harris County, 1,388,898 (61.3%) of the county's 2,182,980 registered voters turned out to vote in 2016 while 794,082 (36.4%) did not cast a ballot on election day, early in person or by mail. In CD-23, 234,779 (54.9%) of the district's 427,676 registered voters turned out to vote in 2016 while 192,897 (45.1%) did not cast a ballot on election day, early in person or by mail.

IV. Survey Methodology

Two random samples were drawn from lists provided by Opinion Analysts Inc. (Austin, Texas) of registered voters in Harris County and CD-23 who were eligible to vote on November 8, 2016, but who did not vote early, on election day, or by mail (throughout this report these individuals are referred to as non-voters). Customer Research International (San Marcos, Texas) conducted the survey in English and Spanish using live operators between February 6 and March 9, 2017. A total of 424 and 395 interviews were completed for Harris County and CD-23 respectively in rough proportion to the sex, age and ethnicity of the population of non-voters (based on the voter files), with the final data weighted for analysis in proportion to the sex, age, and ethnicity of the non-voter population in Harris County and CD-23 respectively. The margin of error for both survey populations was +/− 4.8% in Harris County and +/− 4.9% in CD-23.

V. Non-Voters: Ethnicity/Race, Partisanship, Voting Preferences

Tables 11.1 and 11.2 provide the ethnic/racial distribution of the survey population of non-voters in Harris County and CD-23. Reflective of Harris County's ethnic/racial diversity, no ethnic/racial group accounted for more than a third of the non-voters, with Latinos at 32.8%, Anglos at 31.0%, African Americans at 20.2%, Asian Americans at 9.5%, and Native Americans at 1.1%. CD-23 is one of only eight (out of 435) U.S. congressional districts where Latinos account for an absolute majority of eligible voters (Pew 2016), and this large proportion of eligible Latino voters (52.8% in CD-23) is also reflected in the ethnic/racial distribution of non-voters: 72.2% Latino, 19.1% Anglo, 3.8% African American, 1.7% Native American and 0.8% Asian American.

Close to a majority of non-voters in Harris County and CD-23 self-identified as Democrats (48.4% and 48.8% respectively) while a little more than a third self-identified as Republicans (36.9%

Table 11.1   Ethnicity/Race of Non-Voters in Harris County

Ethnic/Racial Group	Proportion of Non-Voters
Latino/Hispanic	32.8
Anglo/White	31.0
African American/Black	20.2
Asian American	9.5
Native American	1.1
Other (volunteered)	5.4

Table 11.2   Ethnicity/Race of Non-Voters in CD-23

Ethnic/Racial Group	Proportion of Non-Voters
Latino/Hispanic	72.2
Anglo/White	19.1
African American/Black	3.8
Native American	1.7
Asian American	0.8
Other (volunteered)	2.3

and 36.2%). The remainder of the non-voter population was accounted for by true independents (14.7% and 15.0%).

In Harris County, a majority of Anglo non-voters (59.2%) self-identified as Republicans while slightly more than a quarter (25.5%) self-identified as Democrats (see Table 11.3). Latino non-voters provided a mirror image of Anglo non-voters, with 56.8% self-identifying as Democrats and 30.4% as Republicans. In CD-23 (see Table 11.4) Anglo and Latino non-voters also represent mirror images of each other, with 53.3% and 32.2% of Latinos self-identifying as Democrats and Republicans respectively and 53.2% and 32.8% of Anglos self-identifying as Republicans and Democrats.

Table 11.3   Ethnicity/Race and Partisan ID of Non-Voters in Harris County (in Percentages)

Partisanship	All Non-Voters	Latino	Anglo	African American	Asian American
Democrat	48.4	56.8	25.5	73.5	47.9
Republican	36.9	30.4	59.2	13.4	42.2
Independent	14.7	12.8	15.4	13.1	9.9

Table 11.4 Ethnicity/Race and Partisan ID of Non-Voters in CD-23 (in Percentages)

Partisanship	All Non-Voters	Latino	Anglo	All Others
Democrat	48.8	53.3	32.8	54.5
Republican	36.2	32.2	53.2	29.3
Independent	15.0	14.5	14.0	16.2

Had they actually turned out to cast a vote in 2016, in the presidential race more non-voters in Harris County and CD-23 (see Tables 11.5 and 11.6) would have supported Hillary Clinton (37.9% and 33.1%) than Donald Trump (25.8% and 22.5%), with a large proportion indicating that they would not have voted for any of the presidential candidates on the ballot in 2016 (25.5% and 35.1%). When the respondents are restricted to those with a preference among the four candidates who were on the Texas ballot, Clinton would have received the respective support of 50.9% and 51.1% in Harris County and CD-23 and Trump the support of 34.7% and 34.8%.

In the highest profile down-ballot races in Harris County, the Democratic candidates for Harris County District Attorney (Kim Ogg) and Harris County Sheriff (Ed Gonzalez) would have received more support from these non-voters than their respective Republican rivals, Devon Anderson and Ron Hickman (see Table 11.7 and Table 11.8). More than a third of the non-voters

Table 11.5 Harris County Vote Preferences for President (in Percentages)

Presidential Candidate	All Respondents	Respondents with a Preference	Actual Election Result*
Hillary Clinton (D)	37.9	50.9	54.0
Donald Trump (R)	25.8	34.7	41.6
Gary Johnson (L)	6.1	8.2	3.0
Jill Stein (G)	4.7	6.3	0.9
Would Not Have Cast Vote	25.5		

* Write-in candidates won 0.5% of the presidential vote.

Table 11.6 CD-23 Vote Preferences for President (in Percentages)

Presidential Candidate	All Respondents	Respondents with a Preference	Actual Election Result*
Hillary Clinton (D)	33.1	51.1	49.4
Donald Trump (R)	22.5	34.8	46.0
Gary Johnson (L)	6.8	10.5	3.0
Jill Stein (G)	2.4	3.7	0.8
Would Not Have Cast Vote	35.1		

* Write-in candidates won 0.8% of the presidential vote.

Table 11.7 Harris County Vote Preference for District Attorney (in Percentages)

District Attorney Candidate	All Respondents	Respondents with a Preference	Actual Election Result
Kim Ogg (D)	37.2	59.0	54.2
Devon Anderson (R)	25.8	41.0	45.8
Would Not Have Cast Vote	37.1		

Table 11.8 Harris County Vote Preference for Sheriff (in Percentages)

Sheriff Candidate	All Respondents	Respondents with a Preference	Actual Election Result
Ed Gonzalez (D)	39.6	63.7	52.9
Ron Hickman (R)	22.6	36.3	47.2
Would Not Have Cast Vote	37.8		

would not have cast a ballot for any of the district attorney or sheriff candidates however.[5] It suffices to say however that had all of these non-voters turned out to vote in the 2016 election, the margins of victory of Democrats Kim Ogg and

Ed Gonzalez would have been even larger than the 8.4% and 5.7% margins they achieved on November 8, 2016.

In CD-23, more non-voters would have voted for Democrat Pete Gallego (36.0%) than for Republican Will Hurd (23.2%), with the largest group of non-voters (38.5%) indicating they would not have voted in the race (see Table 11.9). Had all of these non-voters turned out to vote in the 2016 election, it is likely that Pete Gallego would have defeated Will Hurd, the opposite of what occurred on November 8, 2016 when Hurd narrowly defeated Gallego 110,577 to 107,526, or 48.3% to 47.0%.[6] It should be noted however that a majority of CD-23 non-voters with an opinion have a favorable opinion (very or somewhat favorable) of both Hurd (61.4%) and Gallego (61.1%) (see Table 11.10).

Table 11.9 CD-23 Vote Preference for U.S. House (in Percentages)

U.S. House Candidate	All Respondents	Respondents with a Preference	Actual Election Result
Pete Gallego (D)	36.0	58.5	47.0
Will Hurd (R)	23.2	37.6	48.3
Ruben Corvalon (L)	2.4	3.9	4.7
Would Not Have Cast Vote	38.5		

Table 11.10 CD-23 Non-Voter Evaluations of Will Hurd and Pete Gallego (Evaluations Excluding Non- Voters Who Didn't Know Enough to Have an Opinion in Parentheses) (in Percentages)

Evaluation	Will Hurd	Pete Gallego
Very Favorable	10.8 (16.8)	9.5 (15.2)
Somewhat Favorable	28.8 (44.6)	28.6 (45.9)
Somewhat Unfavorable	16.0 (24.8)	15.2 (24.4)
Very Unfavorable	8.9 (13.8)	9.1 (14.6)
Don't Know Enough to Have an Opinion	35.4	37.6

VI. Approved Photo ID Possession by Non-Voters

Non-voters were queried in the surveys if they possessed any of six approved forms of unexpired photo ID required to be able to vote in person in 2016. If the respondent indicated they did not possess a current (unexpired) form of the three most common forms of photo ID (Texas driver license, U.S. Passport, Texas Personal Identification Card), they were asked if they had a photo ID of that type which had expired within the past four years.

In our 2015 survey of CD-23 registered voters who did not cast a ballot in the 2014 general election we included a question asking if voters possessed a Texas Election Identification Certificate (EIC). We determined that an overwhelming majority of non-voters are unfamiliar with the EIC and frequently mistakenly indicated they had one (often confusing it with the voter registration card they receive in the mail from their county clerk). We therefore did not include a question about EIC possession in this year's surveys due to this confusion and the reality that only a miniscule fraction of Harris County and CD-23 residents possess an EIC. Data from the Texas Department of Public Safety (2017) indicate that between July of 2013 (the first month in which EICs were issued) and the end of 2016, a total of 879 EICs had been issued in the entire state of Texas (which has a total of 15,101,087 registered voters). Of these 879 EICs, 126 were issued in Harris County (2,182,980 registered voters) and 142 in CD-23 (427,676 registered voters).

Tables 11.11 and 11.12 underscore that an overwhelming majority of non-voters in Harris County and CD-23 possess at least one of these six state approved photo IDs needed to vote in person in Texas elections. In all, 97.4% of Harris County non-voters and 97.8% of CD-23 non-voters possess at least one form of valid (i.e., unexpired) photo ID. When the restrictions on the three most popular forms of photo ID (Texas driver license, U.S. Passport, Texas Personal Identification Card) are loosened to allow photo IDs that had expired within the past four years, the percentages of non-voters with an acceptable form of photo ID rise to 98.5% and 97.9% in Harris County and CD-23. More than four-fifths of non-voters in both Harris County and CD-23 possess

Table 11.11   Harris County ID Possession by Non-Voters and Three Most Common Forms of Photo ID (in Percentages)

Form of Identification	Possesses	Does Not Possess
1 or More of 6 Valid Forms of ID	97.4	2.6
1 or More of 6 Valid Forms of ID (Expired Within 4 Years)	98.5	1.5
Texas Driver License	82.9	17.1
U.S. Passport	47.8	52.2
Texas Personal Identification Card	34.5	65.5

Table 11.12   CD-23 ID Possession by Non-Voters and Three Most Common Forms of Photo ID (in Percentages)

Form of Identification	Possesses	Does Not Possess
1 or More of 6 Valid Forms of ID	97.8	2.2
1 or More of 6 Valid Forms of ID (Expired Within 4 Years)	97.9	2.1
Texas Driver License	84.1	15.9
U.S. Passport	52.2	47.8
Texas Personal Identification Card	31.5	68.5

Table 11.13   Ethnicity/Race and Proportion of Group That Possesses and Does Not Possess One or More of Six Valid Unexpired Forms of Photo ID in Harris County (Proportion Including Expired IDs in Parentheses) (in Percentages)

Ethnic/Racial Group	Possesses	Does Not Possess
Anglo	99.5 (100)	0.5 (0.0)
Latino	97.4 (99.1)	2.6 (0.9)
African American	95.2 (97.3)	4.8 (2.7)
Asian American	97.4 (97.4)	2.6 (2.6)

Table 11.14   Ethnicity/Race and Proportion of Group That Possesses and Does Not Possess One or More of Six Valid Unexpired Forms of Photo ID in CD-23 (Proportion Including Expired IDs in Parentheses) (in Percentages)

Ethnic/Racial Group	Possesses	Does Not Possess
Anglo	98.2 (98.2)	1.8 (1.8)
Latino	98.5 (98.7)	1.5 (1.3)
All Others	94.5 (94.5)	5.5 (5.5)

an unexpired driver license (82.9% and 84.1%) while approximately one-half of non-voters possess an unexpired U.S. Passport (47.8% and 52.2%).

Tables 11.13 and 11.14 examine the relationship between a non-voter's ethnicity/race and their possession of at least one of the six forms of state-approved photo ID, both unexpired and for the three IDs mentioned in the preceding paragraph that expired within the past four years (with these latter proportions in parentheses).

In Harris County virtually every Anglo non-voter possessed a valid ID (99.5%) and all (100%) possessed a photo ID that could have been used to vote in person in the 2016 elections. Conversely, 95.2% of African Americans possessed a valid form of photo ID, a percentage that rose to 97.3% when expired IDs were considered. In an intermediate position were Latinos, with 97.4% possessing a valid form of unexpired photo ID and 99.1% in possession of an acceptable form of photo ID when expired documents were included. These modest ethnic/racial differences in photo ID possession are not statistically significant. In CD-23 virtually equal shares of Anglo (98.2%) and Latino (98.5%) non-voters possessed a valid photo ID, percentages that either stayed the same (for Anglos) or rose slightly to 98.7% (for Latinos) when expired IDs were accounted for.

Tables 11.15 and 11.16 provide comparable information for four age cohorts: those 18 to 25, 26 to 45, 46–64, and 65 and over. Registered voters in the 18 to 25 cohort are those who would be the most likely beneficiaries were the forms of acceptable photo ID to be expanded to include photo IDs issued by state colleges and universities. In Harris County 97.4%/100% of non-voters between the ages of 18 and 25 possessed a valid/expired photo ID,

Table 11.15 Age and Proportion of Cohort That Possesses and Does Not Possess One or More of Six Unexpired Valid Forms of Photo ID in Harris County (Proportion Including Expired IDs in Parentheses) (in Percentages)

Age Cohort	Possesses	Does Not Possess
18–25	97.4 (100)	2.6 (0.0)
26–45	99.3 (99.3)	0.7 (0.7)
46–64	95.6 (96.5)	4.4 (3.5)
65+	95.6 (98.5)	4.4 (1.5)

Table 11.16 Age and Proportion of Cohort That Possesses and Does Not Possess One or More of Six Unexpired Valid Forms of Photo ID in CD-23 (Proportion Including Expired IDs in Parentheses) (in Percentages)

Age Cohort	Possesses	Does Not Possess
18–25	97.5 (97.5)	2.5 (2.5)
26–45	96.8 (96.8)	3.2 (3.2)
46–64	100 (100)	0.0 (0.0)
65+	96.1 (97.5)	3.9 (2.5)

while the comparable percentages in CD-23 were 97.5%/97.5%. Also recall that voters ages 65 and over are eligible to vote by mail where a photo ID is not required to cast a ballot.[7] In Harris County 95.6%/98.5% of non-voters age 65 and over possessed a valid/expired photo ID, while the comparable percentages in CD-23 were 96.1%/97.5%. None of the age differences among the four age cohorts in Tables 11.15 and 11.16 are statistically significant.

VII. Why Non-Voters Did Not Participate

In the survey the non-voters were read eight common reasons why people do not vote and asked whether they strongly agreed, agreed, disagreed, or strongly disagreed that it was a reason why they did not vote in the November 2016 election. The eight reasons were: 1) "You or a family member was ill," 2) "You were out of town," 3) "You were not interested or felt your vote wouldn't make a difference," 4) "You had transportation problems," 5) "You were too busy, with conflicting work, family or school schedules," 6) "You didn't like the candidates or the issues," 7) "You did not possess any of the state approved forms of photo identification needed to cast a vote in person," 8) "You went to vote but the line at the polling place was too long."

Tables 11.17 and 11.18 detail the proportion of non-voters in Harris County and CD-23 who strongly agreed, agreed, disagreed, and strongly disagreed with each of these eight statements. The highest level of agreement with a reason in both populations of non-voters was with the statement that they didn't vote because they didn't like the candidates or the issues, with approximately three-fifths of non-voters in both Harris County (58.8%) and CD-23 (63.6%) either strongly agreeing or agreeing with the statement. The next highest level of agreement was, in both populations, with the reason that the non-voter was too busy (with work, family or school), with approximately one-half of Harris County (46.2%) and CD-23 (52.9%) non-voters either strongly agreeing or agreeing with this reason for their not casting a ballot in 2016. The third highest level of agreement was, in both populations, with the reason that the non-voter

Table 11.17 Level of Harris County Non-Voter Agreement with Reasons Why They Did Not Vote (in Percentages)

Reasons Why They Might Not Have Voted	Strongly Agree	Agree	Disagree	Strongly Disagree
Didn't Like the Candidates or the Issues	43.4	15.4	12.7	28.5
Too Busy (Work, Family, School)	35.4	10.8	10.1	43.8
No Interest/Vote Wouldn't Make Difference	28.3	16.7	13.1	41.8
Out of Town	21.1	3.0	5.0	71.0
Illness (Self or Family Member)	17.3	3.6	6.5	72.6
Went, But Line at Polling Place Too Long	12.7	5.7	8.3	73.4
Didn't Have Required Photo ID	12.5	4.0	6.7	76.9
Transportation Problems	10.0	5.5	6.1	78.4

Table 11.18 Level of CD-23 Non-Voter Agreement with Reasons Why They Did Not Vote (in Percentages)

Reasons Why They Might Not Have Voted	Strongly Agree	Agree	Disagree	Strongly Disagree
Didn't Like the Candidates or the Issues	47.1	16.5	12.0	24.4
Too Busy (Work, Family, School)	34.4	18.5	8.9	38.3
No Interest/Vote Wouldn't Make Difference	32.1	16.0	15.1	36.8
Out of Town	19.1	3.1	9.3	68.5
Illness (Self or Family Member)	14.9	2.6	7.5	74.9
Went, But Line at Polling Place Too Long	12.6	4.9	11.5	71.1
Transportation Problems	10.9	3.9	9.6	75.7
Didn't Have Required Photo ID	9.8	5.0	11.9	73.4

was not interested or felt their vote wouldn't make a difference, with close to half of Harris County (45.0%) and CD-23 (48.1%) non-voters either strongly agreeing or agreeing with the statement.

The three reasons for non-voting that had the lowest level of agreement in the two populations were long lines at the polls, transportation problems and not having any of the state approved forms of photo ID required to vote in person. In both populations the third lowest level of agreement was with the statement that voters went to vote but (did not vote because) the line at the polling place was too long. In Harris County 18.4% of the non-voters either strongly agreed or agreed with this statement, with the comparable percentage in CD-23 a similar 17.5%. Transportation problems had the lowest level of agreement among Harris County non-voters (15.5%) and the penultimate level of agreement among CD-23 non-voters (14.8%). Conversely, a lack of required photo ID had the lowest level of agreement in CD-23 (14.8%) and the penultimate level of agreement among Harris County non-voters (16.5%).

In Harris County 95.0% of those non-voters who strongly agreed or agreed that a reason they did not vote was because of their lack of a required photo ID actually possessed one of the required forms of photo ID, with a nearly identical 95.3% of similar CD-23 non-voters also possessing at least one of the required forms of photo ID needed to cast a vote in person in 2016.

Tables 11.19 and 11.20 provide a breakdown of the ethnic/racial distribution of non-voters in Harris County and CD-23 who either strongly agreed or agreed that a reason why they did not vote was that they did not possess any of the state approved forms of photo identification needed to cast a vote in person. While Anglos were slightly less likely to express agreement with this reason than Latinos, African Americans, and Asian Americans in Harris

Table 11.19 Ethnicity/Race and Agreement That Not Having a Required ID Was a Reason They Might Not Have Voted in Harris County

Ethnic/Racial Group	Percentage Strongly Agreeing or Agreeing
Anglo	12.5
Latino	19.3
African American	20.4
Asian American	14.3
All Respondents	16.5

Table 11.20 Ethnicity/Race and Agreement That Not Having a Required ID Was a Reason They Might Not Have Voted in CD-23

Ethnic/Racial Group	Percentage Strongly Agreeing or Agreeing
Anglo	8.6
Latino	16.3
All Others	7.5
All Respondents	14.8

County and than Latinos in CD-23, none of these differences are statistically significant, meaning that we cannot rule out that they exist purely by chance.

Tables 11.21 and 11.22 provide the presidential vote preference of non-voters in Harris County and CD-23 who either strongly agreed or agreed that a reason they didn't vote was because they didn't have the required photo ID to vote in person. Tables 11.23, 11.24, and 11.25 provide comparable data for the Harris County District Attorney and Sheriff's races and for the CD-23 race. In the three competitive races featured in Tables 11.23, 11.24 and 11.25, among those with a preference, more than two-thirds of non-voters whose lack of participation was due at least in part to a belief that they did not possess a required photo ID would have cast a ballot for the respective Democratic candidate (Kim Ogg: 67.9%; Ed Gonzalez: 69.9%; Pete Gallego: 71.8%) compared to less than a third for the respective Republican candidate (Devon Anderson: 32.1%; Ron Hickman, 30.1%; Will Hurd: 28.2%). Had this subset of non-voters participated in the 2016 election, in Harris County Ogg and Gonzalez would have enjoyed larger margins of victory while Gallego would have most likely defeated Hurd in CD-23.

Table 11.21 Harris County Presidential Vote Preference Among Those Strongly Agreeing or Agreeing That the Voter ID Requirements Were a Reason They Did Not Vote (in Percentages)

Presidential Candidate	Actual Vote Result*	All Respondents Agreeing	Respondents Agreeing with a Preference
Hillary Clinton (D)	54.0	52.6	63.1
Donald Trump (R)	41.6	26.0	31.2
Gary Johnson (L)	3.0	4.8	5.8
Jill Stein (G)	0.9	0.0	0.0
Would Not Have Cast Vote		16.6	

* Write-in candidates won 0.5% of the presidential vote.

Table 11.22 CD-23 Presidential Vote Preference Among Those Strongly Agreeing or Agreeing That the Voter ID Requirements Were a Reason They Did Not Vote (in Percentages)

Presidential Candidate	Actual Vote Result*	All Respondents Agreeing	Respondents Agreeing with a Preference
Hillary Clinton (D)	49.4	35.2	48.4
Donald Trump (R)	46.0	21.6	29.7
Gary Johnson (L)	3.0	12.0	16.5
Jill Stein (G)	0.8	3.9	5.4
Would Not Have Cast Vote		27.3	

* Write-in candidates won 0.8% of the presidential vote.

Table 11.23 Harris County District Attorney Vote Preference Among Those Strongly Agreeing or Agreeing That the Voter ID Requirements Were a Reason They Did Not Vote (in Percentages)

District Attorney Candidate	Actual Vote Result	All Respondents Agreeing	Respondents Agreeing with a Preference
Kim Ogg (D)	54.2	47.4	67.9
Devon Anderson (R)	45.8	22.5	32.1
Would Not Have Cast Vote		30.2	

Table 11.24 Harris County Sheriff Vote Preference Among Those Strongly Agreeing or Agreeing That the Voter ID Requirements Were a Reason They Did Not Vote (in Percentages)

Sheriff Candidate	Actual Vote Result	All Respondents Agreeing	Respondents Agreeing with a Preference
Ed Gonzalez (D)	52.9	48.9	69.9
Ron Hickman (R)	47.2	21.0	30.1
Would Not Have Cast Vote		30.1	

Table 11.25   CD-23 U.S. House Vote Preference Among Those Strongly Agreeing or Agreeing That the Voter ID Requirements Were a Reason They Did Not Vote (in Percentages)

U.S. House Candidate	Actual Vote Result	All Respondents Agreeing	Respondents Agreeing with a Preference
Pete Gallego (D)	47.0	37.9	71.8
Will Hurd (R)	48.3	14.9	28.2
Ruben Corvalon (L)	4.7	0.0	0.0
Would Not Have Cast Vote		47.2	

After expressing their level of agreement or disagreement with these eight reasons for not participating, the non-voters were asked which among the reasons with which they either strongly agreed or agreed was the single reason that best explained why they did not vote in the November 2016 election (see Tables 11.26 and 11.27). When pressed to identify the principal reason they did not vote, a plurality of non-voters in both Harris County and CD-23 stated that it was because they did not like the candidates or the issues (31.9% and 37.7% respectively). The next most common response in both populations was

Table 11.26   The Principal Reason Why Harris County Non-Voters Did Not Vote in 2016

Principal Reason Why Person Didn't Vote	Percentage Listing as the Principal Reason
Didn't Like the Candidates or the Issues	31.9
Too Busy (with Work, Family, or School)	18.6
Out of Town	16.0
No Interest/Vote Wouldn't Make Difference	14.7
Illness (Self or Family Member)	9.5
Went, But Line at Polling Place Too Long	5.9
Transportation Problems	1.8
Didn't Have Required Photo ID to Vote in Person	1.5

Table 11.27   The Principal Reason Why CD-23 Non-Voters Did Not Vote in 2016

Principal Reason Why Person Didn't Vote	Percentage Listing as the Principal Reason
Didn't Like the Candidates or the Issues	37.7
Too Busy (Work, Family, School)	19.8
No Interest/Vote Wouldn't Make Difference	12.7
Illness (Self or Family Member)	10.7
Out of Town	10.5
Transportation Problems	4.6
Went, But Line at Polling Place Too Long	3.6
Didn't Have Required Photo ID to Vote in Person	0.5

that the person was too busy, with close to a fifth (18.6% and 19.8%) of both populations listing this as the principal reason they did not vote.

The least common principal reason why non-voters did not participate was because they did not have a required photo ID, with 1.5% of Harris County non-voters and 0.5% of CD-23 non-voters listing this as the principal reason they did not turn out to vote. Among this miniscule share of non-voters who listed not possessing a photo ID as the principal reason they did not participate in the 2016 election, 86% actually possessed an approved form of photo ID while 14% did not.

VIII. Non-Voter Knowledge of the 2016 Voter ID Rules

Section II detailed the evolution of the rules governing the photo ID requirements to vote in Texas between 2013 and 2016. Given the change in the rules between the 2014 and 2016 general elections, non-voters were queried regarding their knowledge of two key components of the photo ID rules in force for the November 2016 election.

First, the non-voters were asked: "Which of the following statements most accurately describes the photo ID requirements for Texans casting a vote in person in the November 2016 presidential election?"

The respondents were presented with the three statements below, and could also volunteer that they didn't know or were unsure which statement most accurately described the photo ID requirements.

A. All voters were required to provide a state approved form of photo ID.
B. No voters were required to provide any form of photo ID.
C. Voters who possessed one of the state approved forms of photo ID were required to provide it, but voters who didn't possess one could vote as long as they signed a declaration explaining why and provided one of several non-photo supporting documents.
D. Don't know/Unsure (only if volunteered).

Table 11.28 and Table 11.29 provide the responses to this question by Harris County and CD-23 non-voters. In both cases only around one-fifth of non-voters (21.1% in Harris County and 17.9% in CD-23) correctly answered that "Voters who possessed one of the state approved forms of photo ID were required to provide it, but voters who didn't possess one could vote as long as they signed a declaration explaining why and provided one of several non-photo supporting documents." The most common answer (58.4% in Harris County and 59.7% in CD-23) was the most accurate characterization of the photo ID rules in 2014, but not in 2016, following the agreement brokered by U.S. District Court Judge Nelda Gonzales Ramos that provided a route for registered voters who lacked an approved photo ID to still cast a ballot. Only a small handful of non-voters (3.5% in Harris County and 4.4% in CD-23) believed that anyone could vote in person without a photo ID (as, for example, is the case in states such as California and New York).

In both Harris County and CD-23, Latino non-voters (15.1% and 14.8%) were significantly less likely than Anglo non-voters (24.3% and 27.6%) and, in Harris County, than African American non-voters (27.9%) to accurately understand the details of the rules governing photo ID requirements in 2016 (see Tables 11.28 and 11.29). There were no other significant ethnic/racial differences in non-voter knowledge regarding the photo ID rules in force in 2016 in either Harris County or CD-23.

Table 11.28 Ethnicity/Race and Knowledge of Voter ID Rules to Vote in Person in Harris County (in Percentages)

Rules Governing In-Person Voting	All Non-Voters	Latinos	Anglos	African Americans	Asian Americans
Photo ID Required to Vote	58.4	68.3	53.2	52.6	59.6
No Photo ID Required to Vote	3.5	2.8	5.8	4.5	0.0
Actual Rules in Force	21.2	15.1	24.3	27.9	14.2
Don't Know/Unsure	17.0	13.8	16.8	15.0	26.3

Table 11.29 Ethnicity/Race and Knowledge of Voter ID Rules to Vote in Person in CD-23 (in Percentages)

Rules Governing In-Person Voting	All Non-Voters	Latinos	Anglos	All Others
Photo ID Required to Vote	59.7 pt	66.9	39.3	50.3
No Photo ID Required to Vote	4.4	3.8	6.7	1.2
Actual Rules in Force	17.9	14.8	27.6	23.8
Don't Know/Unsure	18.0	14.6	26.4	24.7

Latino non-voters were also significantly more likely than Anglo non-voters in both Harris County and CD-23 (and than African American non-voters in Harris County) to believe that the photo ID rules in force in 2016 were more strict than they actually were. In Harris County, 68.3% of Latinos believed that everyone needed to provide a photo ID to be able to vote in person, compared to 53.2% of Anglos and 52.6% of African Americans. In CD-23, 66.9% of Latinos believed that everyone needed to provide a photo ID to be able to vote in person, compared to 39.3% of Anglos.

In contrast to 2014, when a Texas driver license had to be unexpired (or have expired no more than 60 days prior to being presented for voter qualification) in order to qualify as an approved form of photo ID, in 2016 a Texas driver license that had expired within the previous four years was an acceptable form of state-approved photo ID. To assess the non-voters' understanding of the rules in force for 2016, they were asked: "Which of the following statements most accurately describes photo ID requirements for Texans casting a vote in person in the November 2016 presidential election if they were using their Texas driver license as their form of photo ID?"

A. The driver license had to be current; that is, unexpired.
B. The driver license had to be current, or have expired within the past four years.
C. Don't Know/Unsure (only if volunteered).

As Tables 11.30 and 11.31 underscore, an overwhelming majority of these non-voters (74.2% in Harris County and 75.1% in CD-23) incorrectly believed that only an unexpired Texas driver license could be used to vote in person in 2016. Only one in seven non-voters in Harris County (14.4%) and CD-23 (13.8%) were aware that a Texas driver license that had expired within the previous four years was an acceptable form of state approved photo ID to be able to vote in person in 2016.

In Harris County, Latino non-voters were significantly more likely than Anglo non-voters to believe that they could not use an expired (within four years) Texas driver license as their state-approved

form of photo ID in the 2016 elections. No other significant ethnic/racial group differences in mistaken belief existed in Harris County, or in CD-23, where Anglo and Latino non-voters were equally mistaken about the rules governing their ability to use an expired Texas driver license as a form of state-approved photo ID in 2016 (see Tables 11.30 and 11.31).

The data reviewed in this section underscore the limited, and most commonly erroneous, information that non-voters had regarding key components of the voter photo ID regulations in force for the 2016 election. Only around one in five non-voters were able to correctly identify the rules governing in-person voting that were in force in 2016 and an even smaller number were aware that an expired Texas driver license was a state-approved form of photo ID in 2016.

It is clear that the public education campaign carried out by the Texas Secretary of State in 2016 was not successful in its goal of educating Texas registered voters about the 2016 voter photo ID requirements. In retrospect, this is not surprising given the comparatively modest amount of funding ($2.5 million) allocated for this public education campaign.[8] As a case in point, in CD-23 alone, the candidates and their supporters combined to spend $15.4 million during the 2016 electoral cycle, more than six times the amount devoted to all voter photo ID education efforts across Texas's 36 congressional districts.[9] It also would appear that this ineffective public education campaign was significantly less effective in educating Latino non-voters than in educating Anglo non-voters.

IX. Conclusion

The 2016 election marked the second general election cycle in Texas in which photo ID requirements to vote in person were in force. In order to better understand the impact of these requirements on voter participation, non-voters (registered voters who did not vote) in the key Texas battleground jurisdictions of Harris County and CD-23 were surveyed.

The data from these representative surveys indicate that the presence of the voter ID rules at least partially discouraged some non-voters from turning out to vote, but that the photo ID rules at the same time only represented the principal reason why a small handful of registered voters did not participate in the

Table 11.30   Harris County Non-Voter Ethnicity/Race and Knowledge of Driver License Rules (in Percentages)

Driver License Rules	All Non-Voters	Latinos	Anglos	African Americans	Asian Americans
Unexpired Only	74.2	82.4	72.3	73.7	64.3
Unexpired or Expired Within Past 4 years	14.4	9.4	20.9	11.8	15.7
Don't Know/Unsure	11.4	8.3	6.8	14.4	20.0

Table 11.31   CD-23 Non-Voter Ethnicity/Race and Knowledge of Driver License Rules (in Percentages)

Driver License Rules	All Non-Voters	Latinos	Anglos	All Others
Unexpired Only	75.1	75.4	76.8	68.6
Unexpired or Expired Within Past 4 years	13.8	15.5	9.8	9.1
Don't Know/Unsure	11.1	9.0	13.4	22.4

2016 election. The data also underscore that virtually all non-voters possessed one of the approved forms of photo ID needed to cast a vote in person in 2016.

Finally, the results of this study reveal that non-voters were very poorly informed about the details of the photo ID regulations in force in 2016. Furthermore, in several instances Latino non-voters were significantly less likely than Anglo non-voters to have an accurate understanding of the photo ID rules and significantly more likely to believe the rules were more restrictive than they actually were. These latter findings suggest that a much more robust and well-funded public education campaign will be needed if Texas is to avoid a similar level of voter confusion and misunderstanding of the photo ID regulations that will be in force in 2018 when the state elects a wide range of public officials ranging from U.S. senator, governor and lieutenant governor to county judge, county commissioner, and constable.

NOTES

1. Texas enacted a voter identification requirement in 1971. However, it did not require a photo ID.

2. An exception to this four-year window existed for the U.S. citizenship certificate containing a photograph. A copy of a Texas Secretary of State public education poster on the 2016 rules is contained in Appendix I.

3. In the 2016 election more than 16,400 Texas voters, out of a total of 8,969,226 voters overall (or 0.2%), signed an affidavit that they had a reasonable impediment that kept them from obtaining an approved photo ID (Malewitz 2017).

4. A map of CD-23 is provided in Appendix II.

5. Of course given the presence of the straight-ticket option on Texas ballots, it is likely that many of these non-voters would have indirectly (and perhaps unwittingly) voted in these races by choosing the straight-ticket option for either the Democratic Party or the Republican Party.

6. Libertarian Party candidate Ruben Corvalan won 10,862 votes (or 4.7%).

7. Voters under 65 may vote by mail only under extraordinary circumstances (see Section II), whereas those 65 and older benefit from "no-excuse" absentee voting.

8. The Texas Secretary of State has refused to release complete details of how these limited funds were allocated and where (Saleh Rauf 2016).

9. Hurd spent $4.1m and his supporters $4.3m while Gallego spent $2.1m and his supporters $4.9m (Center for Responsive Politics 2017).

REFERENCES

Center for Responsive Politics. 2017. "Texas District 23 Race." Washington, D.C.: Center for Responsive Politics. www.opensecrets.org.

Hobby, Bill, Mark P. Jones, Jim Granato, and Renée Cross. 2016. "The Texas Voter ID Law and the 2014 Election: A Study of Texas's 23rd Congressional District." University of Houston Hobby School of Public Affairs White Paper No. 7.

Jones, Mark P., William Earl Maxwell, and Ernest Crain (with Morhea Lynn Davis, Christopher Wlezien, and Elizabeth N. Flores). 2016. *Texas Politics Today: 2017–2018 Edition*. Boston: Cengage Learning.

Malewitz, Jim. 2017. "Texas Republicans Pitch New Voter ID Law," *Texas Tribune*, February 21, 2017.

Pew Research Center. 2016. "Mapping the Latino Electorate by Congressional District" (January 19, 2016).

Saleh Rauf, David. 2016. "Texas Withholds Details of $2.5M Voter Education Effort," *Houston Chronicle*, August 26, 2016.

Texas Department of Public Safety. 2017. "Election Identification Certificates Issued by County and Month Between July 2013 and December 2016." Austin: Texas Department of Public Safety.

Appendix I

ID required for Texas Voters

You must present one of the following forms of photo ID when voting in person:*

★ Texas driver license issued by the Texas Department of Public Safety (DPS)
★ Texas Election Identification Certificate issued by DPS
★ Texas personal identification card issued by DPS
★ Texas license to carry a handgun issued by DPS
★ United States military identification card containing your photograph
★ United States citizenship certificate containing your photograph
★ United States passport

Do not possess and cannot reasonably obtain one of these IDs? Fill out a declaration at the polls explaining why and bring one of the following supporting documents:

★ Valid voter registration certificate
★ Certified birth certificate (must be an original)
★ Copy of or original current utility bill
★ Copy of or original bank statement
★ Copy of or original government check
★ Copy of or original paycheck
★ Copy of or original government document with your name and an address (original required if it contains a photograph)

*With the exception of the U.S. citizenship certificate, the identification must be current or have expired no more than 4 years before being presented for voter qualification at the polling place.

Exemptions: Voters with a disability may apply with the county voter registrar for a permanent exemption to showing ID at the polls. Voters with a religious objection to being photographed or voters who do not have a ID due to certain natural disasters may apply for a temporary exemption to showing ID at the polls. Please contact your voter registrar for more details.

VOTETEXAS.GOV

Appendix II

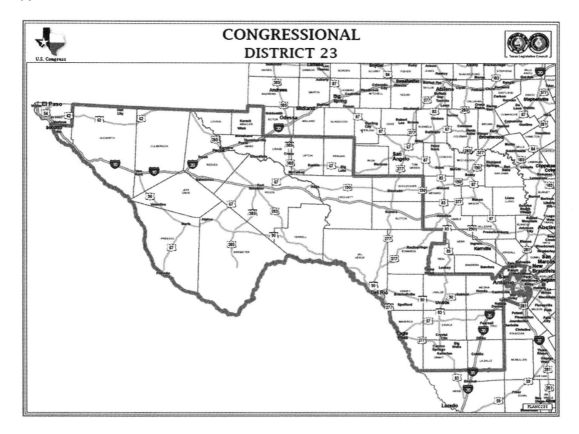

ARTICLE QUESTIONS

1) What is the intent of the photo ID law?
2) What was the primary reason why nonvoters chose not to vote? How much of a factor was the lack of photo ID?
3) What steps might be taken to resolve the confusion about the photo ID requirement in Texas?
4) Do you believe that the photo ID provision is necessary? Why?

11.2) Voting Rights Battle in Pasadena Could Have Texas-Wide Legal Ramifications

Texas Tribune, July 11, 2017

ALEXA URA

Texas has a history of excluding individuals from the franchise—the right to vote—often based upon race. Eventually, the state ran smack into federal laws that prohibited such practices, most notably the Voting Rights Act of 1965 (VRA), which prohibits racial discrimination in voting. Drawing on his own experiences of witnessing racial prejudice in Texas, President Lyndon Johnson signed the VRA into law to outlaw unconstitutional practices that discriminated against racial minorities. The fight over voting rights has played out across the nation, and even in the former "honkytonk" capital of Texas: Pasadena.

The Voting Rights Act continues to protect voters' rights to vote, but as of June 2013, the Supreme Court struck down its provision requiring certain states to "preclear" changes to voting policies before implementing them. *Texas Tribune* reporter Alexa Ura describes how events in Pasadena led to reinterpretation of the Voting Rights Act. Shortly after this provision was removed, efforts were undertaken in Pasadena to restructure the election of city officers from eight single-member districts to six single-member districts and two citywide at-large seats, a move that eliminated one majority-Hispanic district in the process.

Ura describes a city divided by race and income and identifies several implications of these divisions for city politics. As the demographics of other Texas cities similarly change, will there be more legal challenges of voting laws? As Ura points out, the outcomes of these cases will have consequences for voting rights in Texas and beyond for years to come.

Cody Ray Wheeler has a cowboy's name.

It's a product, he says, of being born the son of a North Texas refinery worker. In some ways it's emblematic of a changing Texas: Wheeler, who is Hispanic, represents a city council district with a majority-white voting constituency in this Houston suburb.

It's also a name that has put him at the center of a voting rights battle over whether city leaders here pushed changes to the council map to undercut the electoral power of a booming Hispanic majority.

"A Hispanic wasn't supposed to win that seat," Wheeler said over barbecue on a recent steamy afternoon. He's convinced his non-Hispanic last name made the difference in his narrow 33-vote margin of victory in 2013.

"I could not run as a Hispanic candidate," he said. "I would've lost."

His victory marked a milestone for a city with a racially acrimonious past. Though most Pasadenans are Hispanic, it was the first time two Hispanics served together on the eight-member council.

Wheeler's election also brought longtime Mayor Johnny Isbell's majority on the council down to one vote. Joined by two white city council members who represented majority-Hispanic districts on the north side of town, the two Hispanic members fell into a voting bloc that often pitted them against Isbell and the four council members who represented the southern, mostly white side of Pasadena.

After the 2013 elections, many Pasadenans believed the balance of power was about to shift, with hopes hinging on one of the districts represented by an Isbell ally that was predominantly made up of Hispanic voters. But that summer, the U.S. Supreme Court gutted the portion of the federal Voting Rights Act that had prevented dozens of jurisdictions with a history of discrimination against voters of color—including Texas and its municipalities—from changing their election laws without federal approval.

Texas had been subject to those federal controls for decades. About a month after the state was freed from that electoral guardianship, Isbell introduced a proposal to redraw the city council map—and replace two of the districts with at-large seats elected by the entire city.

A group of Hispanic voters challenged the new map in court, setting into motion a case that could have implications across Texas—and could even become a test of whether the federal Voting Rights Act can still serve as a safeguard for minority voters nationwide.

But that's only if parties on both sides of the case keep it alive in court.
Pasadena's voting rights fight is largely a result of changing demographic winds and the political tide that comes with them.

Lined by refineries to its north, the city of nearly 154,000 residents is a sprawling stretch of suburbia southeast of Houston in Harris County. Decades ago, the city charter imposed segregation and banned Spanish-language instruction. In the 1980s, it was home to the Ku Klux Klan's Texas headquarters.

But by the time the 2010 census rolled around, white residents were in the minority and almost two out of every three residents were Hispanic. Carnicerias, panaderias and quinceañera party stores followed; in one pocket of town, two dozen businesses catering mostly to Hispanics filled an entire shopping center.

This population boom among Hispanics was largely confined to the older north end of town where many residents have long pointed to deteriorating streets and shoddy drainage systems as evidence that the city neglects their neighborhoods in favor of the newer neighborhoods south of Spencer Highway where wealthier, white residents predominantly reside. "Seventy percent of the (city's) money is spent south of Spencer," Wheeler says.

As older, white voters die off and young Hispanics reach voting age, Pasadena's electorate has been changing even faster than Harris County as a whole, said Bob Stein, a Rice University political scientist who monitors elections in Harris County.

Hispanics' growth was translating to political clout on the city council, and their representatives saw the 2015 city election as their best chance to achieve a majority on the council that could help push for improved conditions on the north side.

Then came the Supreme Court decision that wiped clean the list of states and localities needing federal "preclearance" to change election laws and Isbell's "6-2 map" proposal. In addition to turning two council seats into at-large seats, it merged two council districts with Hispanic majorities into one.

Isbell, who did not respond to the *Tribune*'s request for comment, told voters at the time that the proposal was meant to make the council more representative and responsive to the concerns of all residents. In late 2013, Isbell told *SCOTUSblog* he pushed for the change "because the Justice Department can no longer tell us what to do."

Wheeler and the other Hispanic-backed council members fiercely opposed Isbell's proposal, which required voter approval. Historically, turnout among Pasadena's Hispanic residents has been lower than white residents, particularly in local elections. Because voting blocs are often aligned along racial lines, Pasadena Hispanics would likely be outvoted by whites when it came to electing the new at-large council members.

When the map proposal went before the council, Isbell cast the deciding vote to break a 4-4 tie, and the issue was placed on the November ballot. Pasadena voters approved the new map by a 79-vote margin out of 6,500 votes cast.

Then came the lawsuit. Civil rights attorneys representing Hispanic voters sued the city, claiming the new council districts unlawfully diluted the voting strength of Hispanics and intentionally discriminated against them.

After a seven-day trial in Houston, a federal judge earlier this year found that Pasadena had violated the Voting Rights Act and ordered the city back under federal supervision under a different section of the law—the first ruling of its kind since the Supreme Court's 2013 decision.

"In Pasadena, Texas, Latino voters under the current 6-2 map and plan do not have the same right to vote as their Anglo neighbors," Judge Lee H. Rosenthal wrote in a scathing opinion, which reinstated the city's eight single-member districts.

Rosenthal invoked Texas' dark, discriminatory legacy against voters of color—poll taxes, all-white primaries, eliminating interpreters at the polls— and outlined how it has endured through modern day-elections in a town where voters told a Hispanic candidate campaigning for a council seat that they "weren't going to vote for a wetback."

The judge also wrote there was credible evidence that Pasadena changed its map "precisely because Pasadena Latinos were successfully mobilizing and recently electing more of their candidates of choice."

The city has since appealed the case to the U.S. 5th Circuit Court of Appeals, contending that the city had no intent to dilute Hispanic votes and that the 6-2 map had no discriminatory effect.

Bob Heath, the city's lead lawyer in the case, contends that Rosenthal's consideration of the number of majority-minority districts in Pasadena and whether that's proportional to the city's voting age Hispanic population runs contrary to two recent opinions by the U.S. Supreme Court.

And that's where the case comes back to Wheeler's name.

Heath points out that four candidates preferred by Hispanic voters prevailed in the 2015 elections— the only contests held under the 6-2 map. Among them was Wheeler, who was re-elected in a district that's not majority-minority but is still "effective for Hispanics," Heath said.

"That's 50 percent (of the council seats) and Hispanics made up about 50 percent of the citizen voting-age population, so that was proportional representation," Heath added.

But Nina Perales of the Mexican American Legal Defense and Educational Fund—the attorney representing the Hispanic plaintiffs against the city— has repeatedly pointed out in court that Wheeler was assisted in his 2015 victory by "special circumstances"—his incumbency and his last name. Meanwhile, the number of Hispanic-majority districts was reduced to three under the 6-2 map.

The case could reverberate beyond Pasadena's city limits. Legal experts contend that a decision by the 5th Circuit could guide other courts around the country that are considering similar voting rights cases.

The Pasadena ruling also has the potential to help build a case against the state, which faces its own voting rights challenges in court, said Richard Murray, a political science professor at the University of Houston who has studied voting rights cases for decades.

In lifting federal electoral oversight for Texas and other jurisdictions in 2013, the U.S. Supreme Court noted that conditions for minority voters had "dramatically improved," but the justices left open the possibility that political jurisdictions could be placed back under preclearance if they committed new discriminatory actions.

Earlier this year, Texas faced a barrage of federal court rulings that found the 2011 Legislature intentionally discriminated against voters of color by passing a stringent voter ID law and redrawing the state's political maps. Those cases are still making their way through federal courts in Corpus Christi and San Antonio.

The Pasadena ruling—"particularly because it was so thoroughly stated and so strong and by a judge that has no history of favoring blacks or Latinos in redistricting cases"—could serve as "another brick in building this case that Texas has a recent history of discriminatory action," Murray said.

In a sign that Texas leaders also see Pasadena as a potential problem for its own cases, state attorneys filed an amicus brief in support of the city's appeal, arguing that preclearance "must be sparingly and cautiously applied" to avoid reimposing "unwarranted federal intrusion."

Judge Rosenthal's preclearance ruling in the Pasadena case was improper, the state contends, because it was imposed for a single incident of discrimination instead of pervasive and rampant discrimination.

If the results of the May election are any proof, the city's voters seem unwilling to upend the status quo in Pasadena.

Even with court-ordered single-member districts back in place, Pasadena voters elected a city council that's expected to generally break the same way it did before the redistricting fight.

The Hispanic-voter backed voting bloc lost their coveted fifth city council seat by just seven votes. With Isbell stepping down because of term limits, voters elected council member Jeff Wagner—considered an Isbell ally on the council—as the new mayor.

With the city's new slate of leaders sworn in last week, the future of the city's appeal of Rosenthal's order remains unclear.

Wagner was the only mayoral candidate who would not vow to drop the city's appeal, Wheeler pointed out over lunch.

Wagner, who did not respond to a request for an interview, previously told the *Tribune* he would consult with council members about the appeal and make a decision based on whatever consensus emerged.

Dropping the appeal and letting the lower court ruling stand would prevent an appeals court ruling that could set a precedent for the state—and eliminate the chance that it could reach the Supreme Court and become a test of the strength of the Voting Rights Act.

Perales, the MALDEF lawyer, said the plaintiffs are focused on eliminating voting discrimination in Pasadena. "That's what this case is about, and that's what we care about," she said.

Pasadena's Hispanic leaders also know that higher courts could rule against them and wipe out their victory that overturned the 6-2 map and put the city back under federal preclearance. Wheeler also points out that the city has already spent more than $2 million defending the case.

He will have a few more years on the council before term limits require him to step aside, but he wonders what the power balance will look like when someone else represents his district.

Wheeler wants to make sure his time on city council helps ensure that the system won't be rigged against Hispanic voters in the future—and pursuing the appeal puts that at risk.

"Why take the chance?" he says.

ARTICLE QUESTIONS

1) Why does the author argue that the changes to Pasadena's voting structure diluted the influence of minority votes?
2) Should Texas be required to "preclear" changes to its voting policies with the federal government, or does the state know best how to handle its voting process?
3) If changes to the structure of voting (e.g., reducing the number of districts) unintentionally create racial discrimination, should they be illegal?

11.3) Why Can't Texans Register to Vote Online?

TribTalk, March 6, 2017

BRYAN JONES

Texans can order pizza, pay bills, and watch their favorite football team on Sunday online—so why can't they register to vote online? Bryan Jones argues in his editorial that Texas should find a way to embrace online voter registration because it increases registration rates, decreases the likelihood of voter fraud, and saves money. Texas is still relying on "pen and paper" methods of registering citizens to vote, he points out—an inconsistency in a state that prides itself on doing everything best. A state that is demographically young like Texas should make an effort to try online registration, Jones suggests.

Jones also outlines some challenges to online voter registration, however. Change tends to occur slowly, and it is difficult to get 254 counties to uniformly switch to a new system.

Too, fraud is always a concern for the state's political leadership, and some worry that an online voter registration system would be at risk of being infiltrated by an outside person or group with nefarious interests. Jones takes each objection and argues that the costs of online registration outweigh the benefits and concerns can be addressed with some technological innovation.

As a native-born Texan, it's easy to be proud of my home state. We are, simply put, living in the greatest state of the greatest country on Earth. In the words of the great Sam Houston, ". . . no country upon the globe can compare with it in natural advantages."

Yet, there are places where Texas is, unfortunately, falling behind. One example is that Texas has not implemented electronic and/or online registration. There are 38 states using or preparing to use Digital Voter Registration, or DVR. Texas is not one of them.

Who cares? Texans do. In a 2014 survey, 61 percent supported the initiative. Sadly, 34 percent incorrectly believe DVR currently exists in Texas.

Texas currently uses a paper-and-pen process for voter registration. These forms are not only expensive, but introduce errors and limit the ability to find fraud.

Research studies have found that "modernization of voter registration boosts registration rates, increases voter roll accuracy [(i.e. decreases possibilities for fraud)], and saves money."

DVR fits Texas's needs for several reasons. First, as the second-largest home to active and reserve members of the military, it provides a convenience that would allow these heroes to register even when deployed. Second, over 50 percent of Texans are Millennials and GenXers, groups accustomed to digital convenience in every aspect of their lives. Finally, rural Texans, representing 20 percent of our state's population, would benefit from a digital system, as they are often miles away from election offices.

DVR produces a higher integrity voter registration roll. In the current process, election officers receive forms with handwritten answers that are often illegible, and must manually enter voter information data. That two-step process inherently introduces errors and results in incomplete applications. With accurate data entered into the process digitally by the voter, it is easier to identify issues related to voter roll accuracy.

Finally, Texas will realize savings by moving to a DVR. It can significantly reduce the Secretary of State's budget for the printing and postal return of forms. This digital option would require fewer temporary employees who perform manual data entry, saving counties considerable money. According to a research study, the average cost savings for switching from paper to online registration is between $0.50 and $2.34—a sizeable potential savings, given the population of Texas.

Concerns raised during the 2015 legislative session focused on a few major issues: impact from potential changes, technical capabilities, and the potential for fraud. However no fraud or security breaches are known to date in the growing list of states using the system.

First, the current process would not be eliminated with the adoption of DVR. The implementation would not eliminate the ability to print and fill out a voter registration request by hand. Nor would it weaken existing requirements for voter eligibility.

Officials from the Texas Department of Public Safety, the Secretary of State, and the Department of Information Resources all testified in 2015 that DVR would be secure and reliable. The technologies required to implement it are straightforward and have been vetted by states that have successfully implemented DVR.

To date, no state using DVR has reported a security breach since moving to digital voter registration. DVR reduces the number of third parties (volunteers, etc.) with access to sensitive personal data. In Texas, digital registration would be available only to individuals with driver licenses, using DPS data to match or reject applications. Standard digital technologies, including the use of encryption, automated hacking detection, routine audit logs, secure networks, and unique identifiers would impede unauthorized access. Digital voter rolls would be easy to quickly compare and audit. We already entrust our state government to store our voter data digitally in other settings within databases shared between and among the Secretary of State, DPS and most of the 254 counties.

Texans deserve to be able to digitally register to vote. Bills are already filed in both the House and the Senate to allow it. Your representatives and your senators, particularly those on the committees that will review the bills, need to hear your demands so DVR doesn't die like it did in 2013 and 2015.

Texans want DVR. Texans deserve DVR. Let's make sure Texans get digital voter registration.

ARTICLE QUESTIONS

1) What advantages does the author claim that online voter registration would have for the state?
2) What challenges would the state face in switching to an online voter registration system?
3) Weighing the costs and benefits of such a shift, do you believe that an online system of voter registration should be implemented in Texas?

11.4) Convicted Felons Deserve the Right to Vote

University Star, 2013

BRANDON SAMS

Texans convicted of certain felonies lose their voting rights, an act often referred to as felony disenfranchisement. More than half a million Texans and more than 5 million U.S. residents are prohibited from voting because of a past criminal conviction. Brandon Sams, a Texas State University student and reporter for the college's newspaper, the *University Star,* chronicles the racial and political impacts of criminal disenfranchisement laws in Texas and argues that ex-felons suffer from unjust and inequitable treatment

Texas's laws are not as severe as those of other states in this regard. In Texas, as in nineteen other states, after a convicted individual has completed his or her punishment (including parole or probation), his or her voting rights are automatically restored. The trouble is that many convicted felons do not realize this. Sams' editorial thus touches on the linked issues of voting rights, the nature of democracy, and the collateral consequences of criminal convictions.

Sams summarizes his point as: "It is inhumane to take away one of the core tenants of a democracy—voting." Furthermore, this system hits ex-felons who are African Americans the hardest, with 7.7 percent of African Americans disenfranchised by these laws compared to 1.8 percent of the population in general.

It is inhumane to take away one of the core tenets of a democracy—voting.

No matter the offense, suffrage should never be infringed upon. Laws preventing or restricting convicted felons from voting are unbalanced, unfair and, frankly, unjust.

While Texas is not the best when it comes to these things, it isn't one of the worst either. In Texas, after serving a term of incarceration, parole, supervision and probation, felons can register to vote once again. For once, Texas is not moving backwards or sliding towards its long-held conservative tenets.

While Texas' model is not ideal, it is the most common one in America, with 19 other states applying the same system of registration for their populations of convicted felons. However, any denial of universal suffrage is an affront to democracy, egalitarianism and long-established American beliefs.

According to the National Conference of State Legislatures, in many states ex-offenders have to apply to get their voting rights back or they simply lose their right to vote permanently. Only two states, Vermont and Maine, do not restrict felons from voting at all.

Talk about hitting a horse while it's down. People convicted of felonious crimes not only face restrictions from government funds, access to jobs and housing and suffer from overall public shame, but also they are forced out of universal suffrage.

The collateral consequences that felons face are inequitable and unjust, especially in a country that proclaims to be the "land of the free." Stripping someone of the right to vote is not only an affront to civil liberties, but it is also a slap in the face to people who have served their time to society, or at least so they thought.

Speaking of civil liberties, according to the American Civil Liberties Union, felony conviction disenfranchisement laws across the nation restrict approximately 5.85 million Americans from voting. That is equivalent to about 2.5 percent of the voting population.

Of course, as with all things having to do with the unbalanced beams of the United States' justice system, these felony conviction laws disproportionately restrict the rights of African-Americans. According to the Sentencing Project, 7.7 percent of African-Americans are disenfranchised by these laws compared to only 1.8 percent of the general population.

In the three states with the harshest laws, the statistics regarding the African-American population are even more disheartening. Over 20 percent of the African-American populations of Florida, Virginia and Kentucky have their voting rights permanently stripped away from them.

It is extremely inaccurate to tell people that if they do the crime, then they must do the time when the system currently in place seeks to marginalize and disenfranchise them for the rest of their lives. Even once felons pay their debt to society, they are constantly bombarded with obstacles to prevent them from getting back their "inalienable rights" to life, liberty and the pursuit of happiness.

America is proclaimed to be the land of the free and home of the brave. Yet, I wonder—free for whom? A country cannot truly be deemed free when there are over 5 million residents who have served their penance to society and are still being subjugated, suppressed and penalized. This land is not free for them and it will not be until these undue laws have been reformed.

ARTICLE QUESTIONS

1) If the almost 3 percent of the voting population who are prohibited from voting because of felony disenfranchisement voted, would there be an effect? What type of effect?
2) Should Texas strip convicted felons of their voting rights? For how long? Under what circumstances?
3) Does Texas's position of not allowing felons to vote risk damaging its reputation?

Chapter 12

Political Parties:
Texas in Blue and Red

The Lone Star State's political history has largely been shaped by political parties. Although never a competitive two-party state for long (the state was dominated by Republicans during the Civil War, then by Democrats until the 1980s, and then by Republicans from the 2000s to the present), party government has been the foundation of the state's politics. What does the history of Texas's political parties tell us about the future of its politics?

The prospect of a blue (Democratic) Texas has been threatened or promised, depending on your perspective, for years. Texas Democrats, aided by external organizations like Battleground Texas, headed by former Obama campaign staff, have argued that Texas is ripe for political change. John B. Judis, writing for the *New Republic*, zeroes in on the long-shot strategy of some political operatives who have had success in past presidential campaigns and hope to bring that success to Texas Democrats. Will the same tactics that have helped elect a Democrat to the White House elect a Democrat to statewide position in Texas?

The apparent shift toward the Democrats hasn't always been inevitable. The years following Franklin Roosevelt's New Deal cemented Texas as a Democratic (but not necessarily liberal) state. As time passed, the Republican Party took advantage of changing demographics, conservative sentiments about low taxes and minimal government, a booming population, and Democratic Party infighting to slowly accumulate power. The result, according to Texas Tech historian Sean Cunningham in his book *Cowboy Conservativism*, was a Republican Party takeover of state government that has largely continued to the present. Are there lessons for the Democratic Party in this history? Cunningham argues that the arc of progress that brought the Republicans to power could also work for the Democrats.

There are several reasons why Texas is likely to migrate from a solid red state to one characterized by a more robust two-party system. Texas is already a majority-minority state. If current trends continue, Hispanics and Anglos will eventually each account for 41 percent of the state's population. With more voter registration and more robust turnout, Hispanics, who lean Democratic, could tilt the state blue.

Organizations like the Texas Organizing Project hope to get more minority voters to the polls. Such an outcome requires proper organization. It also necessitates finding the right candidates, reaching white voters and those in other racial and ethnic groups, showcasing Republican Party extremism, and funneling political donations to Democrats in Texas.

That Texas will turn blue is inevitable for some observers, but how Democrats can achieve this is in some dispute. In the face of a national loss for Democrats in 2016 and only scattered wins in Texas, observers have suggested that the party should shift to a more moderate message, make inroads with Anglo suburban voters, or more aggressively court Latinos. Max Krochmal of Texas Christian University's Department of History in *Blue Texas: The Making of a Multiracial Democratic Coalition in the Civil Rights Era* argues that the Democrats should embrace an "unabashedly liberal, multiracial coalition" that connects politics with social justice movements. Following this recipe, he argues, will make Texas more Democratic.

However, arguments that say Texas will become a Democratic-majority state discount the counter trends that have emerged as Republicans have reacted and adapted to Democrat-friendly changes and ignore the glacially slow process of demographic and political change. Further, although Hispanic voters in particular favor Democratic candidates, Texas Democrats face a more serious deficit in Anglo votes than Republicans do with Hispanic votes. According to observers quoted in Judis's *New Republic* article, Republicans should be cautious but not panicky about Texas Democrats' electoral prospects.

Democrats do well in most of Texas's urban areas but do not dominate all of them. A trio of reporters from the *Texas Tribune*, Brandon Formby, Christopher Connelly, and Alexa Ura, find that Tarrant County in north Texas is the state's largest and most urban Republican-dominated county. Most of the county's representatives are Republican, and its voters supported Donald Trump by an almost 9 percent margin in 2016. Why is Tarrant County so different from other large metropolitan areas? Formby, Connelly, and Ura report that Tarrant County is less diverse, more rural, and more suburban than its counterparts, all characteristics prompting more Republican votes. Partisanship aside, leaders in Tarrant County say they put policy over politics. Is such an approach a model for the rest of the state?

CHAPTER QUESTIONS

1) How have the state's political parties adapted to Texas's changing demographics, economics, and politics?
2) Do you see the state changing politically in your neighborhood or among your family or friends?
3) Is there room in either party for moderates, or have the moderates been expunged from both?
4) Extremism in politics is now the norm. Is there a way to reduce party extremism, or is extremism a way that parties present clear differences to voters?

12.1) Yes, Texas Could Turn Blue

New Republic, October 2014

JOHN B. JUDIS

Texans haven't elected a Democrat to statewide office since 1994 or voted for a Democrat for president since 1976. So is there really a chance Texas could go Democratic? If so, what would cause such a shift? John B. Judis, writing for the *New Republic*, investigates several reasons why Texas may come to favor Democrats, breaking the more than twenty-year Republican streak. The first reason is demographic: the state is a majority-minority state. Although minority populations do not always translate into Democratic votes, as minority populations age, their propensity to vote increases. Judis outlines four scenarios—differing in their level of registration and turnout—for the political future of Texas.

Enthusiasm among Democrats to register to vote and turn out to vote is also contingent on having quality Democratic candidates who can inspire voters. While Texas has a thin bench from which to pull such candidates, there are some superstars, like Julian Castro, former mayor of San Antonio and secretary of housing and urban development. Quality candidates with good ideas for the future of Texas may even be able to convince moderate Texans or those recently emigrated from other states to side with the Democrats, especially in the "ideopolises," the large urban areas where most of the state's voters live.

Democrats do not determine their fate alone—ironically, Republicans have a significant say in the matter too. The Texas Republican Party has an enthusiastic base and a tremendous network of activists, and its candidates have traditionally received about 40 percent of the Hispanic vote. Republicans can expand these advantages by not committing such errors as backing away from immigration reform or demonizing Hispanics.

"Do you really think Wendy Davis is going to win?" I asked Jenn Brown, the executive director of Battleground Texas. "I sure do," she replied. Brown and her top staff may be the only people in Texas who think that Democrat Davis, who is running for governor, can defeat Republican Greg Abbott next week. But the larger question is whether Battleground Texas's strategy of turning Texas blue, which is currently married to Davis's candidacy, can over the next two, four, or six years make Texas, which hasn't elected a Democrat to statewide office since 1994, or voted for a Democratic presidential candidate since 1976, competitive again.

Battleground's strategy, as it was presented to me during a recent visit to Texas, relies primarily on demographic trends within the state. Texas has already become a majority-minority state like California. According to 2013 census figures, only 44 percent of Texans are "Anglos," or whites; 38.4 percent are Hispanic; 12.4 percent

African-American; and the remainder Asian-American and native American. By 2020, Hispanics are projected by the Texas State Data Center to account for 40.5 percent of Texans and African-Americans for 11.3 percent compared to 41.1 percent of Anglos. Texas's minorities generally favor Democrats over Republicans, but they don't vote in as great a proportion as Anglos who have favored Republicans by similar percentages. Battleground's strategy assumes that if it and other organizations like the Texas Organizing Project can get many more minorities, and particularly Hispanics, to the polls, then, as minorities increasingly come to outnumber Anglos, Democrats can take back the state.

Battleground's strategy has met with skepticism in some quarters. My former colleague Nate Cohn has argued that the numbers don't add up. Former Republican Party executive director Wayne Thorburn argues in *Red State* that the "Texas Democratic Party may have a more serious deficit with

Anglo voters than Republicans do with Hispanics." Indeed, there are grounds for skepticism. If you take the numbers, but keep the turnout and the degree of party support consistent with the most recent election in 2012, then it is unlikely the Democrats could achieve a majority by 2020, and perhaps not in the following decade. But if you take politics into account—if you assume that developments in both parties could alter baseline projections—then the Battleground strategy looks far more plausible.

Let's first look at how the population figures translate into votes. While the overall number of minorities already surpass that of Anglos, the numbers of voters have not. Who votes depends on how many in each group are eligible to vote. In 2014, about 46 percent of Hispanics are eligible to vote. The rest are not citizens or are under 18. By contrast, voter eligibility among whites is in the high seventy percent and among African Americans is in the low seventy percent range. The other factor is turnout. In 2012, only about 39 percent of eligible Hispanics voted compared to a little over sixty percent of Anglos and African-Americans. So in the 2012 election, and most likely in the 2014 election, in spite of Battleground's considerable efforts, Anglo voters, who are likely to favor Republican candidates, will outnumber minority voters.

In 2020, a presidential election year, the numbers should look different. Minorities' population edge should have increased, and eligibility among Hispanic voters, which has been growing, should be around 50 percent. I have tallied four scenarios for 2020. They show the conditions that would finally lead to a Democratic victory in 2020. (In each of these, I am keeping black turnout and support constant, and assuming that Asian and Native American eligibility and turnout increase slightly, and support for Democrats remains at about 60 percent. To be safe, I am also using the conservative Texas State Data Center figures, which some political scientists believe understate Hispanic growth.)

Scenario one: Hispanic turnout increases to 45 percent (which is still less than the national average for Hispanic voters) and support for the Democratic presidential candidate remains at 65 percent, and only 25 percent of whites

back the Democratic candidate. In that case, the Republican candidate would get almost 54 percent of the vote.

Scenario two: Hispanic turnout increases to 50 percent (which is still less than neighboring New Mexico), and support for the Democratic candidate climbs to 72 percent (which is still less than Hispanic support for Democrats in Colorado), but white support for the Democrat remains at 25 percent. In this case, the Republican squeaks by with a little over 51 percent of the vote.

Scenario three: Hispanic turnout only increases to 45 percent and support remains at 65 percent, but the Democrat gets 30 percent of the white vote. The Republican squeaks by with a little over 50 percent of the vote.

Scenario four: Hispanic turnout remains at 50 percent and support at 72 percent, but white support for the Democrat climbs to 30 percent. Then the Democrat gets 51.5 percent of the vote.

In other words, a Democratic presidential candidate could carry Texas in 2020 if Hispanic turnout grows, support for the Democratic candidate nears or exceeds 70 percent, *and* Democrats gather 30 percent of the Anglo vote. If the Democrats can't attract more than 25 percent of the Anglo vote, then even the most energetic efforts at Hispanic mobilization won't get their candidate across the finish line.

Raising Hispanic turnout and support for Democratic candidates obviously requires the kind of voter mobilization that Battleground and other groups are undertaking. This year, Battleground claims to have recruited 32,000 volunteers to register voters and get them to the polls. Registration in the state's five largest counties is up two percent, even though registration often goes down between presidential and mid-term elections. But success among Hispanics also depends on building organizations that function between elections. Battleground, which is an out-of-state creation, may not be best suited for this task. "Organizations come in for the election, and then they are gone," Jorge Montiel, the lead organizer for San Antonio's Metro Alliance, laments.

Success in mobilizing the Hispanic vote also depends on nominating candidates in Texas (and also nationally) who can appeal to these voters. According to several Democrats I talked to, Davis hasn't "connected" to these voters. In the primaries, she even lost several small counties to a token Hispanic opponent. She is principally known in the state for her stand on behalf of abortion rights—whereas many of Texas's Hispanics oppose abortion. Democrats urged San Antonio's former mayor Julian Castro, now the secretary of Housing and Urban Development, to run, but he declined, probably one San Antonio political leader speculated, because he feared certain defeat.

Finally, success in increasing Hispanic support for Democrats will depend on what Republicans in Texas and nationally do. In Texas, Republican governors have steered clear of the harsh rhetoric about "illegal aliens" that proliferates among many other Republicans. Abbott boasts a Latina wife. As a result, Texas Republican candidates for state office have gotten about 40 percent of the Hispanic vote, which has virtually assured their victory. This year, the Hispanic Bush, George P. Bush, is currently running for Land Commissioner, and if he becomes a leader of party, could keep many Hispanics voting for Republicans in state races.

But there are Tea Party Republicans, including Senator Ted Cruz, who decry efforts at immigration reform. In Arlington this year, a suburb of Dallas-Fort Worth, a Tea Party favorite Tony Tinderholt, who ousted a moderate incumbent in the primary, has warned that "people are going to die" to protect the border from people "with plans to do horrible disgusting things to American citizens." If Cruz and Tea Party types take over the Texas party, then it will become easier for Democrats to win votes in high state office, which are held between presidential elections.

Texas Democrats are likely to have an easier time painting the national party and its candidates as being hostile to Hispanics. In 2012, Obama got 71 percent of the Hispanic vote nationally against Mitt Romney, who used his opposition to immigration reform to win the nomination. Last year, Florida Senator Marco Rubio's support for immigration reform appeared to doom his presidential prospects. So even if Texas's Republicans foil Democratic efforts to boost their Hispanic support

in state elections, national Republicans might help Democrats increase Hispanic support for a Democratic presidential candidate.

In Texas, white voters have blended the anti-government ethos of the West and the deep South. Many Texas white voters began changing their party allegiance from Democrat to Republican after 1980 without changing their ideology. But Texans' bedrock conservatism among whites has been mitigated by in-migration from less Republican states and by the development of what Ruy Teixeira and I called "ideopolises"—large metro areas dominated by professionals who produce ideas. By garnering support in the Dallas, Austin, San Antonio, Houston, and El Paso metro areas, the Democrats might be able to get the 30 percent or more of the vote they need in presidential elections, and eventually the 35 percent they need in state elections.

In these metro areas, Texas Democrats can attract the same white voters who boosted Democrat hopes in states like Virginia and North Carolina: younger voters, who came of age after the Reagan-Bush era, professionals, and women. Davis's candidacy has probably helped among these voters. In a late September poll that showed Davis behind Abbott by fourteen points, she still had an edge among women and voters 18 to 44, while getting trounced among male and older voters. (In the same poll, Davis only got 50 percent of the Hispanic vote.) Mustafa Tameez, a Houston Democratic consultant, says that the Texas state legislature's lurch to the right, which spawned Davis's candidacy, will win over many of these voters. "The urban vote and women are the key to Democrats winning Texas," Tameez says.

Texas Democrats' ability to win over white voters will also depend on what happens to the national party. Obama remains deeply unpopular in Texas—identified with whatever failures white Texans ascribe to the federal government. There were no exit polls in the 2012 election, but Nate Cohn has estimated that Obama only got 20 percent of the white vote. Whites need to feel comfortable voting for a candidate identified with the national party. Tameez and other Democrats believe that Hillary Clinton, who defeated Obama in the 2008 Texas primary, will fare far better among the state's Anglos than Obama did. But even if they nominate a candidate more palatable to urban whites, the Democrats may have to wait until 2020 to have a good shot at winning Texas in a presidential vote.

Of course, Texas Republican politicians understand the threat that the state's demographic changes pose. Last year, Abbott warned that with the formation of Battleground, Texas was "coming under a new assault, an assault far more dangerous than when the leader of North Korea threatened when he said he was going to add Austin, Texas, as one of the recipients of his nuclear weapons." Abbott and the Texas Republicans have responded to the threat with new restrictions on voting and on registering voters that are designed to make it more difficult for minorities to get to the polls. But these restrictions are double edged. They will make it more difficult to vote, but they can also provide a rallying cry for Battleground and other groups trying to get out the vote. They can give the lie to Republican claims that they are sympathetic to the state's Hispanics and in so doing, speed the day of reckoning for Texas Republicanism.

ARTICLE QUESTIONS

1) What are three reasons identified by the author that suggest Texas may become a more Democratic state in the future?
2) Why does the author argue that Texas turning blue is a long shot?
3) Do you think Texas will turn blue? If so, when do you think this will happen?

12.2) Introduction

Cowboy Conservatism: Texas and the Rise of the Modern Right, 2010

SEAN P. CUNNINGHAM

How did a state that was solidly and unabashedly Democratic after the Great Depression and New Deal become so solidly and unabashedly Republican? Texas native and Democratic president Lyndon Johnson was among those asking this question as he held the tattered remains of his presidency in his hands in 1968. Texas Tech historian Sean Cunningham opens his investigation of the rise of conservatism in Texas at the end of Johnson's presidency, an administration that many consider the high-water mark of progressivism in the 1960s. Fast-forward to early 2000, when the Republican Party dominated statewide elections and pushed the state's policies in a more conservative direction. What caused this change in just a little over three decades?

Cunningham wrote his book Cowboy Conservatism to explain the historical decline of the Democrats and the rise of the Republican Party in Texas. Texas has always been conservative, even when electing Democrats who were generally conservative. Democratic Party infighting after the New Deal led many Democrats to switch their allegiance to the Republicans, robbing the party of its rising stars and leaving it more easily labeled as too liberal, a perception that hurt its ability to attract new voters. Demographics were also a major factor in Texas's shift: as the state's suburban areas exploded, Republicans appealed to their desire for smaller government and their fears of the "radical" Democratic Party, whose image was linked to "acid, amnesty, and abortion," according to Cunningham. Finally, as the 1970s and 1980s progressed, the Democratic Party came to be associated less with populism and working-class Texans and more with rising crime and failing government. Over the years, Republicans slowly cultivated their image and built a strong party that still dominates the state's politics today.

In May 1968, less than two months after announcing to the world that he would not run for reelection, Lyndon Johnson remained desperate to understand the convergence of political events that had so decisively unraveled his presidency. Surprisingly, no state puzzled Johnson more than his home state of Texas. In seeking to understand the changing political climate of the state that had sent him to Washington first as a representative, then as a senator, Lyndon Johnson charged George Reedy, his former press secretary and recently rehired special counsel, to prepare an analysis of Texas politics that could be used to benefit the Democratic Party in the upcoming general election. Reedy titled his report "Forces at Work in Texas."

"The political problems of Texas are complicated by the vast amount of territory that is covered," Reedy wrote. "The state ranges over so much of the nation that it comprises areas which differ in their geography, economy, history, and social outlook. The treaty of annexation authorizes Texas to divide itself into five states and the problems of Texas political leaders would be greatly simplified if this should happen as they could then deal with relatively homogenous populations." Reedy went on to detail the demographic, social, and economic nuances across the various regions of the state. He also discussed the impact of urbanization as well as the growing disconnect between Texas liberalism—which he said was actually populism confused with liberalism—and the evolving national liberal establishment. Among his many conclusions, Reedy warned that Texas, affected by numerous circumstances unique to most other southern states, could potentially become a bastion of conservative Republicanism in the coming decades.

Fast-forward almost four decades to 2004. That year, the platform of the Texas Republican Party reaffirmed the United States of America as a "Christian nation," denounced the "myth of the separation of church and state," demanded the inclusion of abstinence-only sex education for public schools, and called for the elimination of, among other things, the Department of Energy, the Environmental Protection Agency, the Internal Revenue Service, the income tax, the gift tax, the inheritance tax, the capital gains tax, the payroll tax, and various state and local property taxes. That same year, as Texas Republicans held all twenty-seven statewide elected offices, the Republican and former Texas governor George W. Bush won his second term as president of the United States, carrying more than 61 percent of his home state's vote—the seventh straight GOP presidential nominee to carry Texas. At the dawn of the twenty-first century, it seemed that George Reedy had been correct; Texas—once among the most yellow of "yellow-dog Democratic" states—was a bastion of conservative Republicanism.

This book is about political change as it evolved in one of the nation's largest and most important states during the tumultuous seventeen-year period between John F. Kennedy's assassination in Dallas and Ronald Reagan's ascension to the presidency in 1980. Certainly, partisan realignment is the most obvious aspect of that change. Texas was once as solidly Democratic as any state in the nation. By the end of the twentieth century, it was among the most solidly Republican. A simplistic analysis of this transformation, based in large part on the perception that Texas has always been a conservative place, might suggest that—as Ronald Reagan, the preeminent icon of modern conservatism, once similarly quipped—Texas didn't leave the Democratic Party; the Democratic Party left Texas. Yet the political changes that gripped Texas during the last decades of the twentieth century resulted from a far more complex mélange.

To be sure, more than mere partisan affiliation changed in Texas during the 1960s and 1970s. The state's economy changed. Cities grew larger and more industrial. Farms became larger and more consolidated. Suburban populations exploded. The oil and natural gas industries grew wealthier and more powerful. State demographics changed, as a flood of men and women from all parts of the country—Rust Belt to Sun Belt and all parts in between—converged in places like Dallas, Houston, Austin, and San Antonio, hoping that the Lone Star State's surging economic tide would carry them to a safer and more secure life. Most of these changes did not originate in the 1960s and 1970s, but they matured during this period and contributed to an evolving political context. All the while, growing national discord perpetuated fears, hostility, distrust, and disillusionment, forcing Texans—as all other Americans were forced—to reconcile their vision of what America was supposed to be with what America had actually become.

In Texas, the reconciliations of this discord were primarily debated and constructed in the political arena, broadly defined. As a result, the Democratic Party changed at both the state and national levels. The Republican Party changed as well. As the issues upon which America's postwar liberal consensus had been built grew increasingly complicated, both parties struggled to adjust. Both parties experienced periods of factional discord and ideological readjustment, even as they attracted new voters while alienating longtime party loyalists along the way. Both parties struggled to define themselves in the tumultuous context of war, domestic unrest, race riots, a sagging national economy, and the debate over government's role in each issue. America's liberal consensus collapsed in the 1960s, taking the New Deal coalition with it. This collapse profoundly undermined Texas's traditional party structure, even as the genesis of a new political culture was found in the rubble.

Yet, in a related—and perhaps more important—development, Texans' fundamental concept of party politics—their impressions, interpretations, and attitudes—changed in dramatic ways during the 1960s and 1970s. This change, more than any other, hastened the collapse of the traditional political order in Texas. As older issues were seen in new contexts, new issues emerged to threaten tradition, and party leaders warred with one another, the perceived meanings that Texans had of what it meant to be a liberal and what it meant to be a conservative also changed. In fact, the change in the perceived meaning of these two terms, and especially the possible consequences that Texans associated with each of these ideologies, explains—as much as does anything else—the transformations

that ultimately led to the ascendancy of a new conservative coalition, born in the wake of a sinking New Deal coalition undermined by wars both foreign and domestic, hot and cold, real and unreal.

To study the political transformations that shaped Texas during the last decades of the twentieth century is to see that the issues, events, and personalities that defined Texas politics coalesced in the 1960s and 1970s into a new political culture, the interpretive battle over which ultimately explains the state's partisan realignment. In other words, the battle to redefine Texas political culture through either a conservative or a liberal worldview, rather than through partisan loyalties, explains why it was not until the 1960s and 1970s that the Republican Party was successful in asserting itself in ways never before seen in the state's history.

At the root of this shift in Texans' perceptions of partisanship and political ideology were the construction of, magnification of, and capitalization upon certain images and icons. What and whom Texans associated with liberalism in 1980 was different than what and whom they had associated with liberalism twenty years earlier. The same can be said of conservatism. More important was that Texans associated their reconstituted images of liberalism with the Democratic Party, and their reconstituted images of conservatism with the Republican Party. This change was born out of a new era in American political history, one dominated by target marketing, public relations, advertising, and the projection of emotion-evoking images and messages mass-communicated for political purposes. More simply, Texas politics in the 1960s and 1970s was defined by public perceptions that were shaped by the purposeful use of specific images and icons that, collectively, transformed the state's political culture and led to partisan realignment. The formation of a significant Republican Party in Texas coincided with and was informed by these transformations in public perceptions.

One such icon was Barry Goldwater, who failed in his bid for the presidency in 1964 in large part because his brand of conservatism was perceived by a majority of Americans to be dangerous and extreme, even in Texas. Yet within a decade the political philosophy most commonly identified as dangerous and extreme, especially in Texas, was not conservatism but liberalism. As the national Democratic Party unraveled during the 1960s due to political assassinations, rising crime rates, civil disobedience, racial militancy, and intensified factionalism, the state Democratic establishment tried but failed to insulate itself against the national onslaught, using a banner of conservatism as its shield. Instead, beset by its own warring factions of conservatives and liberals, the Texas Democratic Party slowly crumbled while the national Republican Party assumed the mantle of a redefined conservatism strengthened by a revived coalition of fiscal libertarians and social moralists tied together by an evolving but never wholly new brand of anticommunism.

Within this context, conservatives in the Republican Party convinced a majority of Texans by the close of the 1970s that liberalism was the philosophy of "acid, amnesty, and abortion" and that the Democratic Party was the party of liberalism. The argument proceeded in that order. The reconstitution of political ideologies (as publicly perceived) preceded partisan realignment. Complicating matters, conservative state Democrats did not always fight against these reconstituted perceptions and, in many cases, unintentionally contributed to partisan realignment even as they fought to protect the established monopolistic power structure from which they benefited. Even more complex was the common practice of Texas liberals voting for conservative Republicans as a protest against the conservative hegemony within their own party, but also with the hope of forcing realignment. In this sense, the story of modern Texas conservatism cannot and should not be told strictly as a story of Texas Republicanism, for without the actions of Texas Democrats, the conservative Republican ascendancy in Texas might have had a very different look. And it was indeed the "look"— the image of a conservative philosophy, personified in Ronald Reagan, championing "law and order," "plain folks Americanism," and "God-fearing patriotism"—that both state and national conservatives benefited from and used to build a viable and ultimately dominant Texas Republican Party. This was "cowboy conservatism."

The Democratic Party dominated Texas politics until the 1960s and 1970s in large part because it was seen as the party of populist cowboy conservatism. In contrast to the perception of a Republican Party dominated by a wealthy and elitist establishment whose power was based in the country clubs of the northeast, most Texans had long believed that the Democratic Party best represented the values of hard-working, patriotic, Christian Americans. For decades, most Texans had viewed the Democratic Party as the party of states' rights, the party of limited and responsible government, and the party that had won two world wars and overcome a great depression. This perception fomented loyalty and loyalty evolved into tradition; Texans trusted the Democratic Party. Yet even beyond the overwhelmingly important matters of trust, tradition, and loyalty—and to be certain Texans had been loyally trusting the Democratic Party since before the first Confederate shots were fired at Fort Sumter in 1861—the vast majority of white Texans supported the Democratic Party simply because they believed the Democratic Party supported them.

Those perceptions unraveled in the 1960s and 1970s under the weight of national issues that seemed to reflect a decline in family values, an impotent military, and an incompetent and untrustworthy federal government. The prevalence of broadcast media in the 1960s and 1970s brought national images into Texans' homes. National problems became local problems, and local problems created local fears that demanded new solutions. As Texas became more industrialized, more suburban, more middle class, and more influential in shaping national political discourse, a majority of Texans began to lose confidence in the Democratic Party and increasingly questioned their partisan loyalties. Which party would fight the hardest to protect states' rights? Which party would be toughest on crime? Which party wanted to protect the traditions and values to which families and Texans had long subscribed? Which party best represented the families whose sons had sacrificed their lives to fight a war that so many scorned and some had even dodged? Which party understood what it would take to make America great once again? That the answers to these questions were necessarily vague and ambiguous mattered little, for simplicity of message was also at the heart of image formation and the conservative worldview.

Interestingly, the Republican Party did not easily or quickly emerge as the automatic answer to these and similar questions, at least not in Texas. The GOP was not predestined to assume dominance in Texas. Throughout the 1960s and 1970s, as liberal Texas Democrats fought for their party by voting for another, conservative Texas Democrats increasingly campaigned by promoting not their partisan identification but their philosophical convictions. Because of the widening disconnect between the state and national party, however, those campaigns were increasingly difficult to sustain. By the end of the 1970s, most white Texans—and a good many Mexican American Texans—began to find solace in a national Republican Party that, philosophically if not practically, seemed better prepared to handle the series of national crises that combined to paint a portrait of national decline. By the time of Reagan's election in 1980, most Texans (no longer a "Silent Majority") supported the Republican Party—at least in national campaigns—because they believed the Republican Party supported them. As Democrats were increasingly associated with a liberalism perceived as elitist, weak, and unpatriotic, it was clear that public perceptions were driving partisan realignment in Texas.

Beyond the importance of understanding the political transformations within Texas as a gateway to a fuller understanding of that state's history, it is equally or more important to recognize Texas's significance in the history of postwar American politics more broadly. Put another way, the story of modern American politics, and in particular the rise of modern American conservatism and the crisis of modern American liberalism, cannot be told without understanding the central role played by Texas. There are two key reasons why the exploration of Texas is vital to moving historians closer to a more complete understanding of postwar politics and modern conservatism. First, Texas, through its sheer size and presence, has commanded a national stage and exerted national influence for decades. Yet, this influence has dramatically increased since the early 1960s. Its most visible manifestation has been the persistence of Texas political leaders operating with national power. From Lyndon Johnson to John Connally and Lloyd Bentsen, from John Tower to James Baker and Tom DeLay, from George Bush to Dick Cheney to George W. Bush, few states, if any, have contributed as heavily to postwar American politics as has Texas.

Second, situated centrally in what the former conservative political strategist Kevin Phillips called in the late 1960s the new American "Sun Belt," Texas has not only stood at the heart of postwar America's ideological, economic, demographic, and social development, but has also existed as a bridge connecting the political traditions of the South with the rugged frontierism and individualistic ethos of the American West. Texas has been at the forefront of national urbanization, suburbanization, and even exurbanization. During the last decades of the twentieth century, Texas was home to four of the nation's top-ten largest and fastest-growing cities, embraced and benefited from the Rust Belt to Sun Belt migration of industrial workers, and established itself as the nation's energy nucleus—particularly through the emergence of the ever-expanding and influential 1970s oil industry. Texas was also central to the rise of the military-industrial complex, boasted the most vibrant economy in the country for much of the 1970s, and became an operations hub for the emerging evangelical Christian Right.

Furthermore, Texas offers a multifaceted setting that mirrors yet simultaneously contradicts traditional interpretations of race in the 1960s. Texas was, generally, a less heated front for the African American civil rights movement and yet fierce racism and segregation was palpable in several sections of the state. At the same time, however, Texas's demographics reflect a racial dynamic far more complicated than most areas of the South, where racism was focused more directly on blacks seeking integration and a political voice. In Texas, a significant Mexican American population—one that was larger than the black population of the state—altered political sensibilities pertinent to broader notions of white supremacy and even definitions of whiteness itself.

This book will frequently distinguish between Texas's various regions. Most typically, references will be made to four regions: East Texas, South Texas, Central Texas, and West Texas. Several basic assumptions can be gleaned simply from these geographic distinctions, but much more can still be said about the unique characteristics, demographics, and socioeconomics of each section. Such an understanding is necessary for any study of the state's political culture. For instance, only in East Texas—the region bordering Louisiana and extending not quite to present-day Interstate 45—did the presence of a large concentration of African Americans contribute to a political climate similar to that in much of the Deep South. Yet, as V. O. Key's classic work, Southern Politics in State and Nation, illustrates, East Texas did not mirror the "black belt" voting blocs of other southern states, where race was a far more salient issue in elections. At the same time, racial diversity was by no means limited to East Texas. In fact, far greater racial diversity existed in South Texas, where high concentrations of Mexican Americans (and Mexican migrants) created a very different sociopolitical dynamic. Class tensions ran high in these regions, particularly in South Texas, where a small but powerful number of conservative landowners typically controlled the economy in which large numbers of Spanish-speaking peoples attempted to forge a living. In this economic context, the political culture of South Texas has been most aptly compared to the system of "bossism" and ward politics that characterized northeastern politics for much of the late nineteenth and early twentieth century. Central Texas, on the other hand, was settled predominantly by German immigrants and was an early bastion of western frontierism and rugged individualism. Much of Central Texas arguably still embraces the state's heritage of independence and tradition more tenaciously than does any other section, as historically evidenced by the region's Union loyalties preceding the Civil War as well as by a consistent willingness to do what virtually no other region of the state was willing to do, at least

until the 1960s and 1970s: vote Republican. West Texas has long provided a base for the state's energy industry, with much of the state's wealth pumped out from the oil fields of the Permian Basin and the natural gas deposits of the Texas Panhandle. This region, which has a rich history of ranching and, therefore, a strong western regional identification, is also the largest cotton-producing area of the state—and one of the largest in the nation. The abundance of West Texas counties boasting little to no politically significant African American population long offset the political significance of East Texas counties concerned with race and also mirrors, demographically, the American Southwest far more than it does the American South. Variations also existed within each of these regions. Major urban metropolises like Dallas and Houston complicated the political culture of North and East Texas, while San Antonio and Austin became eclectic hubs for sources of political conservatism, moderation, and liberalism in South and Central Texas. Austin, in particular, forged an identity as one of the nation's fastest-growing and most dynamic cities, welcoming the relocation of numerous industrial, technological, and even entertainment enterprises. As the state capital, Austin has also obviously been the seat of state political power while simultaneously being home to the state's flagship (and probably most liberal) public university, the University of Texas. The religious makeup of the state also varies by region. The state's heavy Baptist influence and traditional anti-Catholic impulses have, for instance, necessitated a political reckoning with the overwhelmingly Catholic and Hispanic population of South and far West Texas. Beyond that, white dispensational Protestantism in Texas has long reinforced notions of independence, self-determination, free will, and a resistance to change and reform.

To understand the political and social culture of Texas is to see that demographic, economic, cultural, racial, and religious distinctions combined with the vast expanse of its land to create a state that defies easy regional identification. Many historians have long debated the question of whether Texas is a southern state, a western state, or something else—something unique. As much

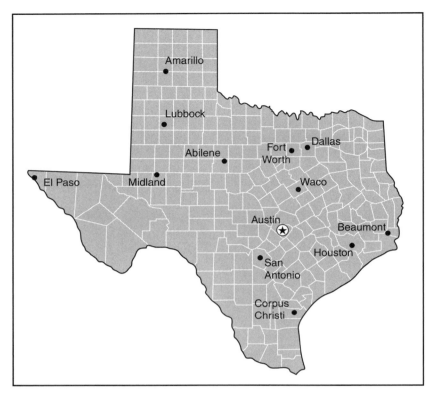

Figure 12.1   Texas's major cities and county boundaries

as anything else, Texas has long fashioned itself, to one degree or another, as a populist state. Having been the birthplace of the Farmers' Alliance that eventually evolved into the short-lived Populist Party of the 1890s, Texas was at the epicenter of a political movement that fused economic interests and political worldviews common in both the South and the West in the late nineteenth century. At a fundamental level, populism reflected, as historian Richard White puts it, "a political challenge to the dominant Northeast." While the enemy populists blamed for the country's problems changed over time, the impulse to fight against an established elite has persisted throughout Texas's history and helps to explain both the state's political culture and its regional identity. As Donald Critchlow has argued, conservatism by the end of the twentieth century mirrored the tenets of the populist tradition by implying "opposition to the

status quo, rebellion against the establishment, a democratic faith in the people, and a deep suspicion of the wisdom of the liberal elites in government, the media, and academia." The answer, then, to the question of whether Texas is a southern state or a western state may very well be that Texas—like the populist philosophy that has informed so much of its political culture—was and is concurrently southern, western, and altogether unique—and is therefore as complicatedly American as it is anything else.

In addition to the historical literature that addresses the question of Texas's regional identity, this book has also been heavily influenced by a growing list of recent studies on modern conservatism and postwar American politics. Historians such as Dan Carter, Joseph Crespino, Donald Critchlow, Matthew Dallek, Michael Flamm, Kevin Kruse, Matthew Lassiter, William Link,

Lisa McGirr, and Jonathan Schoenwald have influenced and inspired the explorations and arguments advanced in this book. These historians have individually and collectively pursued answers to the question of why electoral politics in the United States took the course that it did during the last half of the twentieth century.

Certainly, nuances and complications exist. Historians have debated the regional genesis of modern conservatism, some proposing that it was born in the South, others proposing the West. Some historians have emphasized modern conservatism's origins in the suburbs, the farms, or even the working-class enclaves of the Rust Belt. Various personalities have been identified—Ronald Reagan, Barry Goldwater, George Wallace, Jesse Helms, Phyllis Schlafly. Different issues have been explored—crime and the emergence of "law and order" as a political issue, civil rights and the role of race, a slumping national economy, the war in Vietnam, the rise of a politically active Christian Right. These and other answers proposed by the aforementioned historians and others have each added to our understanding of national political transformations in the postwar era.

Yet as the popular saying goes, everything is bigger in Texas. Certainly the story of modern conservatism's ascendancy is no different. As such, the overall picture of political change described in the following pages can be grasped only via a limited selection of carefully chosen historical fragments. Therefore, this book merely reflects a portrait of the exhaustive body of records that serves to further our understanding of the political transformations that shaped Texas during this critical period. Perhaps Texas, as complicated as it is, might be the perfect setting in which to build the bridge that connects each of these perspectives.

ARTICLE QUESTIONS

1) What are three reasons why the Democratic Party declined in power during the last half of the twentieth century?
2) What role did the economy play in the rise of the Republican Party in Texas?
3) How important was race in the changing politics of the state?
4) Do you find the author's arguments about the causes of the changes in state politics convincing?

12.3) Texas Democrats Must Get Back to Their Progressive Roots

TribTalk, November 21, 2016

MAX KROCHMAL

Texans assume that Democrats have always been the liberal party and Republicans the conservative party. This characterization historically isn't true. Texas Democrats, even during their period of power from the post–Civil War era until the 1980s, were a mix of conservatives and liberals. Conservative Texas Democrats were against civil rights reform, with many in favor of segregation, since Texas had a strong southern mindset. Max Krochmal, drawing on such history in a *TribTalk* editorial, argues that the struggle liberal Democrats had from the 1930s to the 1960s to unite and wrest control of the party from the conservative wing mirrors the quandary the party finds itself in today.

Krochmal argues that the Democratic Party in Texas was at its strongest when a coalition of African Americans, Mexican Americans, organized labor, and white liberals engaged in a grassroots struggle for the future of the party. This coalition prioritized civil rights and workers rights and brought activists of the party together. The strategy worked—the coalition conducted the state's largest voter registration drive and elected (and reelected) progressive Ralph Yarborough to the U.S. Senate. The party subsequently shifted away from this staunchly liberal perspective, much to the detriment of its success, Krochmal argues. Returning to these roots, he claims, is the way to turn Texas blue again.

As the results rolled in Tuesday night, one fact became clear: Contrary to many polls, Texas remains red as ever. Republican Donald Trump defeated Democrat Hillary Clinton by more than 9 percentage points in the state, a margin that shrank compared to 2012 but remained far from competitive.

Pundits will parse the data for months to come, but for the Texas Democratic Party, the results already present an opportunity for reflection. Many political operatives will look at exit polling and conclude that the party must moderate its message to make inroads among white voters in suburbs and rural areas, particularly among the white working class. Others will look at the ongoing demographic changes and conclude that Latinos will inevitably turn Texas blue.

Yet a hidden chapter of the state's history invites a third interpretation that, in turn, suggests a different road forward. Looking to the past reveals that the present Democratic Party already possesses a path to victory in Texas, but only if it assembles an unabashedly liberal, *multiracial* coalition that connects high politics with robust social movements.

Throughout most of the 20th century, Texas remained part of the Democratic Solid South and was therefore already blue. Still, the battle lines were clear. New Deal liberals of all colors fought to wrest the party away from conservative segregationists who had dominated it since Reconstruction.

It was in that context that between the 1930s and the 1960s, African Americans, Mexican Americans, organized labor, and white liberals gradually came together to form the Democratic Coalition, a group that paired electoral politics with grassroots struggles for racial and economic justice. Bringing in protestors and politicians alike, the coalition was deliberately democratic, led by four co-chairs elected from each of its four legs. After struggling to bring activists together across the color line, the Democratic Coalition took off in the mid-1960s because its members talked openly about their internal disagreements, prioritized the struggles for civil rights (broadly defined), supported union organizing, and combined rhetoric with action—most boldly, by organizing mass demonstrations and the state's largest ever voter registration and get-out-the-vote campaigns among black and brown Texans.

And their strategy worked. The coalition elected and re-elected the liberal Ralph W. Yarborough to the U.S. Senate, marched together in the streets to win and then implement the Civil Rights Act of 1964, and launched the first revolts of the Chicano Movement for self-determination in South Texas. The diverse activists forever expanded the Texas electorate and transformed its political map, providing Lyndon B. Johnson with a constituency as he and his party grew more liberal and more committed to civil rights. In the process, coalition leaders trained a generation of rank and file activists at both the ballot box and in the streets. Their work underwrote the left wing of the state's Democratic Party for the next half-century, up to the present.

Yet beginning in the 1970s—when Hillary and Bill Clinton famously came to Texas to work on the McGovern campaign—Texas Democratic Party officials responded to the threat of an ascendant Republican Party by turning away from the civil rights movements and the stalwart local leaders recruited by the coalition. Instead, they muted their commitment to social justice in an attempt to retain white swing voters in the state's rural areas and ballooning suburbs. And they lost.

It is clear that Democrats have thus far failed to learn from this history. In 2016, Clinton made only token appeals to Texas voters, and like her predecessors, she focused on cultivating donors rather than the grassroots. The party struggles to field credible candidates for statewide office. Turning Texas blue remains a distant dream. At this critical juncture, the party will again be confronted with calls to retreat from present-day struggles for racial and economic justice, to become the centrist alternative to the GOP. Such an approach is doomed to failure.

The Democratic Party will return to relevancy in the state—and nation—only when it recommits to an unflinching progressive agenda, to frank and open discussions about race, to prioritizing present-day civil rights and labor issues, and to forging a broad, multiracial coalition at the grassroots. Texas Democrats must do the hard work of door-to-door, precinct-level organizing and of forming uneasy alliances with diverse social movements.

In short, they must return to their roots.

ARTICLE QUESTIONS

1) What are the reasons the author argues that the Democratic Party was strong in the 1960s?
2) What are three events that he says caused the Democratic Party to drift away from its liberal roots?
3) Are you persuaded by the author's argument about the necessary direction of the Democratic Party?

12.4) Can Texas Republicans Hold America's Reddest Large Urban County?

Texas Tribune, January 17, 2017

BRANDON FORMBY, CHRISTOPHER CONNELLY, AND ALEXA URA

Despite its iconic frontier past, Texas today is an urban state, with a vast majority of its residents living in three major cities (Houston, Dallas, and San Antonio). An urban Texas increasingly means a Democratic Texas, although there are deviations from that trend. Fort Worth, often connected with Dallas in the eponymous "DFW," is itself the state's forth-largest city. *Texas Tribune* reporters Brandon Formby, Christopher Connelly, and Alexa Ura, however, note that unlike Texas's other major urban areas, Tarrant County, where Fort Worth is located, is the only major urban area that hasn't backed a Democratic presidential candidate in the past decade; furthermore, all four of the county's state senate districts and eight of its eleven state House seats are represented by Republicans.

Why is Tarrant County so different from other metropolitan areas in Texas? Although Fort Worth has largely shed its "Cowtown" past and has become more urban, the surrounding Tarrant County is more rural, and residents in these areas largely back Republicans for elected office. Tea Party Republicans, an active and conservative segment of the Republican Party, have a strong presence in these rural areas. Tarrant County also includes sprawling suburbs that tend to vote for Republicans and is significantly less demographically diverse than other large metropolitan areas.

Despite the pitched political battles happening all over Texas and North Texas, leaders in Tarrant County stress that good government should be prioritized over partisan fights. Fort Worth mayor Betsy Price commented, "Potholes don't care if you're a Democrat or a Republican. A crime spree doesn't care where you are." In today's polarized climate, is there room for bipartisan action on issues important to Texans?

Even though he can openly carry a handgun in Texas with the right permit, Jonathan Grummer thinks that still doesn't allow him enough freedom in a country where firearms rights are enshrined in the Constitution.

"Within reason, I want to be able to open carry everywhere in the United States because I'm a law-abiding citizen," he said.

While his stance plays into a stereotype of Texas being a rural, gun-loving bastion of conservative politics, Grummer lives in the third-largest county in the state. Sprawling out from Fort Worth, Tarrant County helps co-anchor the nation's fourth-largest metropolitan area along with Dallas.

But unlike other population centers in Texas, Tarrant's urban status hasn't flipped the county's conservative leanings.

Among the state's five biggest counties, Tarrant is the only one that hasn't backed a Democratic presidential candidate in the past decade. The 2016 presidential election heightened Tarrant's status as an outlier. Even as the rest of the state's big-city territories moved deeper into the Democratic column, Tarrant steadfastly emerged as America's most conservative large urban county.

President-elect Donald Trump, who takes office this week, won the county by an 8.6-point margin.

It was the narrowest win for a GOP presidential nominee in decades in Tarrant. But among the country's 20 largest counties, Tarrant was only one of two that swung Trump's way in November—and it had the wider margin.

Across Tarrant County, Democratic pockets are fewer and less powerful than their Republican counterparts. All four of the state senate districts that fall in Tarrant County are represented by Republicans. The GOP also holds eight of the county's 11 state House seats. Four of the five county commissioner court seats are held by Republicans.

Residents, elected officials and experts here point to a nuanced union of demographic, cultural and political forces to explain why.

"There's just all kinds of interesting numbers out there that make Tarrant County a lot different," said U.S. Rep. Marc Veasey of Fort Worth, the only Democrat holding one of the county's five congressional seats.

Tarrant's minority population, which tends to lean Democratic, hasn't caught up to the state's other big urban counties. At the same time, many Tarrant voters have a storied history of preferring practical governance to partisanship, according to officials and political observers. They say that helps support the moderate faction

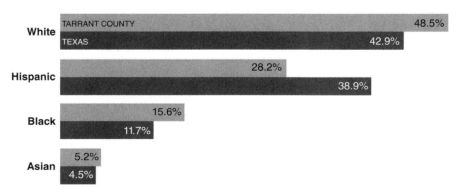

Figure 12.2   Tarrant County is less diverse than Texas   Almost half of Tarrant County's population is white, with a larger share of white residents than the state of Texas. The county actually has a slightly higher share of black and Asian residents than the state, but Hispanics are underrepresented.
Whites, blacks, and Asians only include those categorized as non-Hispanic.
Source: U.S. Census Bureau, 2015 American Community Survey 1-Year Estimates, Credit: Jolie McCullough

of the GOP, especially in Fort Worth, the nation's 16th-largest city.

Then there's the county's development pattern. A lot of Tarrant remains rural. And, unlike Harris, Dallas and Travis counties, many of Tarrant's affluent suburbs and conservative bedroom communities lie within its borders, not outside them. That's helped give rise to the NE Tarrant Tea Party, a passionate and organized group that simultaneously supports far-right local candidates and serves as a powerful base for statewide Republicans.

"We get a lot of credit for doing a lot of things, but I think it's because everything fell into place for us," said Julie McCarty, the group's president. "It's not because we had some grand strategy and this was our goal, was to take over Texas, you know, as the conservative wing of the party. It's just happened."

Fringes of Urban America

Tarrant's 1.9 million residents are spread out across Fort Worth, its bevy of suburbs and large stretches of rural land even farther out from the city center. Tarrant is also home to Arlington, the state's seventh-largest city and the place where the Dallas Cowboys and the Texas Rangers play. Like many precincts in Fort Worth's urban core, large parts of that town also went for Democratic presidential candidate Hillary Clinton.

To Tarrant's east is Dallas, a bustling county of 2.6 million people that went Democratic more than a decade ago. But on the other side is Parker, a county of 126,000 whose voters supported President-elect Donald Trump with a margin more than 7 times larger than what he received in Tarrant.

"I think Tarrant County is at the very fringes of urban America," said Jim Riddlesperger, a professor of political science at Fort Worth's Texas Christian University. "Obviously, if you go 30 miles west of here, you're in rural country."

Fort Worth locals say the county seat is the "biggest little town" in America. For tourists, its most well-known attraction is the Stockyards, a living throwback to the area's Western heritage. Cattle are herded through the historic district twice a day. The area also hosts the weeks-long Fort Worth Stock Show and Rodeo, a livestock and cowboy extravaganza that kicked off this month.

"It really is a city where everyone knows everyone else, and so it has less of an urban feel than you would find in other urban areas in the country," said Riddlesperger.

Fort Worth Mayor Betsy Price won election as mayor, a nonpartisan position, in 2011 after she had previously been the county's tax assessor-collector, a post she held as a Republican. The previous mayor, Mike Moncrief, was familiar to the city's voters from his time as a Democratic state senator.

Price said that for decades, Fort Worth voters have cared more about electing moderate, effective, business-minded officials rather than candidates from a particular party. When the Fort Worth native attended her first U.S. Conference of Mayors shortly after her election, she was shocked to learn that most of her counterparts in the country were Democrats.

"Potholes don't care if you're a Democrat or a Republican," she said. "A crime spree doesn't care where you are. Your citizens don't care. They just want their garbage picked up. They want to turn their tap on and have fresh water."

A Statewide Powerhouse in the Suburbs

Things are much different in Fort Worth's suburbs, especially those in the northeast corner of the county, where tiny but affluent towns surround Dallas/Fort Worth International Airport.

This is where one of more than a dozen chapters of the Tea Party took hold across the state around the time President Obama took office. Yet as the group grew to include more than a dozen cities, so did its influence and the number of lawmakers it propelled to office. McCarty, the NE Tarrant Tea Party's president, said as the group succeeded in getting their candidates elected, the organization has drawn more attention across Texas. Statewide candidates now request to come speak to the group. Big-name headliners draw more people to events.

"It's just this wonderful cycle," she said.

Konni Burton, the group's former vice president, was elected to the state senate in 2014. The Colleyville Republican said many suburban residents in her district have grown tired of electing GOP officials who only pay lip service to conservative tenets such as limited government and fiscal restraint.

"It's part of why I ran for office," she said. "I'm very aggravated that we have to constantly watch our Republican legislators."

That sentiment is what drew Grummer, the gun rights proponent, to the group. He first got involved after Congress and President Bush approved huge bailouts of the financial industry in 2008.

"We don't need to have the government taking our money and putting it into something that doesn't work," he said.

As Tarrant Grows, Demographics Change

Part of what has helped Tarrant become the state's lone Republican urban county is that its minority populations, which largely and traditionally tend to lean Democratic, haven't caught up to the state's other big urban counties.

White residents' share of the Tarrant population is falling, but it hasn't declined as quickly as it has in Harris, Dallas, Travis and Bexar, said state demographer Lloyd Potter. The county's Hispanic population is growing quickly, but it still lags behind the other big counties in terms of raw numbers, Potter added.

But that's likely to change.

While Tarrant remains more white than Texas as a whole, it's experienced a more significant drop in its share of white residents in the past 10 years compared to the state. In 2015, the county's white population dropped to 48.5 percent—down from 56.4 percent in 2005.

Whites' falling numbers in the county aren't limited to its urban core in Fort Worth. In fact, the white population experienced a bigger drop in its share of the population in the suburbs from 2005 to 2015.

Meanwhile, minorities' share of the population has increased steadily, growing both inside and outside of Fort Worth. Some of the largest concentrations of black and Hispanic residents still live near the urban core in neighborhoods north, southwest and southeast of downtown.

Growth among the county's Hispanic residents has yet to reach statewide levels, but black and Asian Texans make up a larger share of the county's population compared to their statewide numbers.

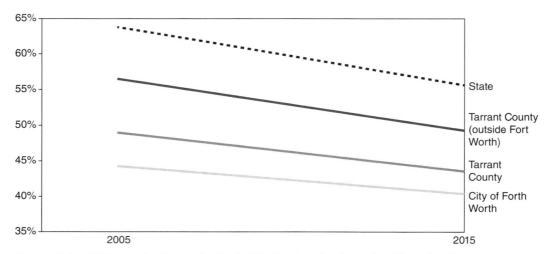

Figure 12.3 Whites a suburban majority, but that's changing fast Non-Hispanic whites remain a majority in the parts of Tarrant outside Fort Worth, but their share is falling at a faster rate than in Fort Worth, the county as a whole or the entire state.
Source: U.S. Census Bureau, 2015 American Community Survey 1-Year Estimates, Credit: Annie Daniel

"It's a pattern that's likely to set in in Tarrant as it has in Dallas and Harris," Potter said. "And that's likely to result in some shifts in the political orientation of the general population."

Reading the Tea Leaves

Veasey, the Democratic congressman, thinks the changing population could soon help give his party a boost at the polls.

"I'm not saying we're going to win Tarrant County yet," he said. "But I do think that we are going to be in the best position we've been in in a long, long time."

Others aren't convinced that demographics necessarily determine political affiliation. Riddlesperger, the political science professor, said Americans' political leanings these days largely come down to a voter's specific place of residence.

"The reason is because the issues that confront people living in urban areas are very, very different from the issues confronting people in suburban and rural areas," Riddlesperger said. "So their views of life, their views of necessities of life, are inherently different."

And even though Tarrant continues to grow, a lot of that is occurring on Fort Worth's north side, an area of new developments that look more like a typical suburb than a stereotypical urban core. Burton, the state senator, said she thinks the county's status as a Republican urban stronghold portends a national shift in her party's direction—and that Tarrant will only move more to the right.

Burton said many of the county's newcomers are attracted by the conservative political leanings.

"We're all very independent-minded Texans that truly believe in us doing things for ourselves, keeping government out for the most part," she said.

But Price, the mayor, said Tarrant's political future likely hinges on two things: how much this year's state legislative session is dominated by politics instead of governance and whether a bombastic incoming president can maintain voters' support once his administration is in power.

"People are tired of too much partisanship," Price said. "They're looking for things that help drive their life and make their life better."

ARTICLE QUESTIONS

1) What are the reasons that the authors suggest keep Tarrant County voting Republican?
2) How do elected officials in Tarrant County describe why they ran for office or how they act while in office? Do you find these statements persuasive?
3) Tarrant County, like the rest of Texas, is rapidly changing. Will these changes lead to political power shifts in the state?

Chapter 13

Taxes and Budget

Nobody likes paying taxes, especially Texans—to such a degree that the state has verged on bankruptcy at various points in its history. During the Republic years, President Mirabeau B. Lamar's administration almost went broke because of a desire for meager import fees and few luxury taxes. Texas's reputation for being a "low-tax, low-service" state limits the strain on residents' pocketbooks and is attractive to business but makes it hard for residents to get needed services and may require them to look elsewhere for help. The political struggle over the state's budget and tax policies stems from persistent questions about the role of state government, the obligations of the state to the residents of Texas, and public expectations for services.

Although it collects billions of dollars in multiple types of taxes, Texas is really a two-tax state: property tax and sales tax. Property taxes (called *ad valorem*, meaning "according to value") are assessed based upon the value of the property the taxpayer owns. From assessment to collection, they are locally based. If you own a home, you can get a property tax exemption to rebate some of the taxes you would otherwise pay. The state's sales tax since 1967 has been the state's largest single source of tax income, constituting more than 50 percent of the total in 2017. Both individual Texans and businesses pay these taxes. The state sets the rate at 6.25 percent, and local governments can add up to 2 percent to this (most do).

Former Lieutenant Governor Bob Bullock—as colorful a character as Texas politics has seen—declared that Texas would get an income tax when a "Russian submarine sailed up the Houston Ship Channel." Some politicians have floated the idea of a statewide income or property tax, but Ann Richards' biographer Jan Reid noted that for Texas politicians, "calling for an income tax was tantamount to throwing open the doors to vampires and werewolves. The only thing as bad was to oppose the death penalty."[1] Avoiding a statewide income or property tax maintains the state's economic edge, opponents of these taxes argue. Supporters claim that these taxes would provide a more consistent funding source than sales taxes or local property taxes which may deflate in sour economic times. In a concise "explainer" article for the *Texas Tribune*, Alex Samuels describes why Texas can't create a statewide property tax. The short answer: Texans don't want it and voted to make it unconstitutional. The longer answer involves a prioritization of local control over school funding and policies. But is this model sustainable for the long term?

Texas, like many people, regularly socks away a little extra payday cash for the future. In 1988, the state was coming out of a major recession that had rocked its economy. Fearing that future budget shortfalls would damage the economy, Texas established the Economic Stabilization Fund (ESF), almost always referred to as the "Rainy Day Fund," to save money for economic emergencies. Half of 75 percent of oil and natural gas production tax revenue (called "severance" taxes) every year flows into the Rainy Day Fund. Leftover (surplus) unspent funds at the end of each year and interest on the balance of the fund are also channeled into the Rainy Day Fund. As of 2017, the fund holds north of $12 billion.

Budget expert Eva DeLuna Castro from the left-leaning Center for Public Policy Priorities argues that the state has saved for too long and that anemic funding for multiple state priorities demands that legislators use these funds. In short, it's raining in Texas, and the Rainy Day Fund can help alleviate some of the pain caused by tight budgets. Standing in the way are conservatives, most of whom are Republicans but a few of whom are Democrats, who argue that the fund should be as robust as possible to demonstrate the state's fiscal strength and to save for a true economic disaster. Castro makes the case in her editorial that the state faces critical decisions on public education, higher education, and health care that could use funds from the ESF to keep Texas in step with other states.

The revenue the state takes in shapes the state's biennial (two-year) budget. The battle over the budget is always a battle over priorities. Mixed up in these battles are the politics of generating revenue and meeting demands for state services. These political struggles stem from persistent questions about the role of state government, the obligations of the state to the residents of Texas, and public expectations. Flush financial times make for easier decisions. Tough financial times require hard choices and strong political leadership.

The 85th session of the Texas legislature saw hundreds of issues addressed, and, as in every legislative session, conservatives and liberals disagreed about these issues' appropriate resolution. The conservative-leaning Texas Public Policy Foundation argues that the session was a success because of lean budget spending and the passage of measures such as limits on local government abuses of the legal system. On the other end of the political spectrum is Ann Beeson of the left-leaning Center for Public Policy Priorities who argues that the legislature missed opportunities to invest in critical state needs. She argues that tight budgets are the fault of the legislature itself, which imposed tax cuts that restrained overall spending, and that legislators avoided the pressing needs of the state's public school system.

Both sides agree that there were high points and low points to the 85th legislative session—an understandable conclusion, since the state's fiscal and budgetary choices reveal its priorities. Where do you stand on the session's fiscal and policy changes?

NOTE

1. Jan Ried, *Let the People In: The Life and Times of Ann Richards* (Austin: University of Texas Press, 2012), 386.

CHAPTER QUESTIONS

1) What makes a fiscal policy conservative or liberal?
2) What alternatives to current fiscal, taxing, revenue, or budgetary choices are offered by the authors and why?
3) Do the criticisms leveled by the authors signal a need for fundamental change, or are minor changes also an option?
4) Can you discern a central theme to the authors' criticisms of current policies?

13.1) Why Can't We Create a Statewide Property Tax to Fund Public Education?

Texas Tribune, August 4, 2017

ALEX SAMUELS

Texas is only one of seven states that does not have a statewide tax on income or property. Alex Samuels, writing for the *Texas Tribune*'s "Texplainer," describes the politics behind the resistance to establish a statewide tax on property even in the face of what some analysts suggest is a better economic model for funding public education. According to this argument, a statewide property tax could be fairer to local taxpayers because it would standardize the various local rates into one statewide rate, with the state then able to distribute these payments to all public schools.

However, the politics are more complicated than the economics, as Samuels makes clear. A statewide property tax would be unconstitutional, thanks to a provision added to the constitution by voters in 1982. Consequently, lawmakers and voters would have to overturn this provision before instituting such a tax. The state's "Robin Hood" system of funding public education, in which funds from property tax–rich areas are redistributed to property tax–poor areas, would also have to change.

Fiscally conservative Republicans embrace small government, which often means collecting minimal revenue and opposing taxes of almost any kind. Taxes are unpopular among all voters, regardless of party, so politicians are loath to institute a new tax, even if it does make good fiscal sense. So ingrained is this antitax sentiment that some states like Florida have written a ban on income tax into the state constitution. A statewide property tax does not fit with the culture of a state that generally values low taxes and low services. It may not be part of Texas's culture, but is it part of its future?

Today's Texplainer is inspired by a question from Texas Tribune *reader, Milton.*

Hey, Texplainer: Why can't we create a Texas-wide property tax to fund public education?

The short answer is because it's unconstitutional and only the Legislature can begin the process of changing that, according to a spokesperson from the Texas Comptroller's office.

If they decided to go that route, it would require the approval of two-thirds of each legislative chamber—and then Texas voters. The voters are the ones who approved of abolishing the statewide property tax in the first place—72 percent of them voted for Proposition 1 to repeal the tax in 1982.

"The predisposition of Texans . . . was against a statewide property tax because they thought, among other things, that it would lead to an income tax eventually," state Sen. Paul Bettencourt, R-Houston, told the *Texas Tribune*.

Texas school districts currently collect about $22 billion in property taxes, and bringing back a statewide property tax to fund public education—without replacing other local property taxes levied by cities, counties and other entities—would come with some challenges.

If Texas had a statewide property tax for schools, it would no longer need to use recapture, better known as the "Robin Hood" system, to help pay for public schools because the state would be in charge of distributing money equally across districts. Under recapture, the state takes money from school districts with more valuable property and re-distributes it to districts that have less valuable property.

"A statewide property tax is the mother of all recapture because the state would levy a tax and bring in all the property taxes and then distribute them out through the school funding formulas," said Sheryl Pace, a senior analyst for the Texas Taxpayers and Research Association.

Lawmakers would have a lot of things to sort out to make a statewide property tax work. For starters, school districts routinely borrow against their future property tax revenue, a practice that would need to be reconfigured if property tax collections were transferred to the state. Many school districts also offer property owners an additional local homestead exemption—something that would have to be equalized and regulated at the state level if local school property taxes disappeared.

However, enacting a statewide property tax wouldn't completely undermine local control, according to Chandra Villanueva, a senior policy analyst at the Center for Public Policy Priorities.

It would all depend on how the state set up its tax system, Villanueva added. For example, she said, the statewide tax could cover base-level funding for schools, but could allow an "enrichment tier" that would allow districts to impose local taxes on top of that for anything above and beyond the Texas Essential Knowledge and Skills (TEKS). That would include things like art and music, or professional development for teachers.

Replacing the local tax with a statewide property tax wouldn't solve the underlying problems with the state's school finance system, Villanueva said. That's because replacing local taxes with a statewide tax doesn't equal more money for schools.

Essentially, the state would be taxing the same property as local districts, so unless the state imposed a higher rate than what local taxpayers are currently paying, it would raise the same amount of money—just at the state level rather than the local level.

"Some people would think that would solve the revenue side of it . . . but unless they change the formulas, the inequities between school districts stay exactly the same," Pace said.

The bottom line: We can't create a statewide property tax unless lawmakers and voters approve one. It might solve some (but not all) of the structural issues with the state's school finance system, but it wouldn't necessarily cut your taxes.

ARTICLE QUESTIONS

1) Weighing the advantages and disadvantages of such a move, do you believe Texas should institute a statewide property tax?
2) Would a statewide property tax system take away school districts' power to tax and spend? Why or why not?
3) Would you support the move to a statewide property tax system?

13.2) If Needed, Rainy Day Fund Is There for Texas

TribTalk, January 5, 2017

EVA DELUNA CASTRO

Spending from the Rainy Day Fund has become a hot-button political issue in Texas. The Rainy Day Fund was set up to squirrel away funds for hard times but also serves as a check on spending, since it siphons some funds away from general revenue legislators would otherwise have to play with. Journalist R. G. Ratcliffe has argued that the Rainy Day Fund was originally created as a "gimmick by lawmakers fending off angry taxpayers." Leaving the Rainy Day Fund untouched has become a badge of political honor, and spending monies from it may provoke outcry from budget-conscious primary voters. Many argue the state has underfunded transportation and education in the name of fiscal conservatism and should use these funds to better address the state's fast-growing needs.

Budget expert Eva DeLuna Castro from the left-leaning Center for Public Policy Priorities argues that the Rainy Day Fund should serve as a "blessing during hard times," acting like a savings account. Tax cuts in recent legislative sessions have trimmed the funds available for fundamental state needs like public schools, higher education, health, and other services, Castro points out. It would not be unprecedented to use these funds to make up the difference, she argues, as past legislators have voted for withdrawals from the fund for similar issues.

However, the hurdle to access the funds is higher than that associated with other budget caps: tapping the fund requires a two-thirds vote by the legislature, which is difficult to achieve when Republicans, who control the body, fear backlash from conservative voters. Castro implores these members to consider this "common sense" measure to help Texans and limit the impact of painful budget cuts.

If you're fortunate enough to have a savings account, then you know it's a blessing during hard times. Texas is lucky to have a large savings account in its so-called Rainy Day Fund, created to prevent or reduce sudden massive cuts to schools, health care and other services Texans need. That is exactly why its actual name is the Economic Stabilization Fund.

Short-sighted tax cuts and diversions in recent legislative sessions mean that lawmakers may have reduced the General Revenue available to write the next state budget by at least $10.5 billion—independent of the drop in oil and gas prices.

Next week, we will learn from the comptroller's estimate exactly how much General Revenue will be available for schools, higher education, health and other services in the 2018–19 state budget. So this is a good time to get clear on the Rainy Day Fund itself and the proper uses of its $10 billion balance.

Since 1989, the Texas Constitution has required that a portion of oil and gas production taxes go into the Rainy Day Fund. Many states have a cash reserve, but Texas has the largest in the country. Our constitution authorizes the comptroller to make temporary transfers out of the Fund to make up for a General Revenue deficit. With a supermajority vote, the Legislature can also use the Rainy Day Fund as General Revenue in the current or next budget cycle.

State law requires the Legislature to set a minimum balance for the Fund every two years. This "sufficient balance" is $7.5 billion for 2018–19. The balance requirement was created in response to fears that too small a reserve would hurt the state's credit ratings. But in 2005, before the sufficient balance requirement existed, the Fund balance dropped to almost zero, with no harm done to the state's credit ratings.

As Comptroller Glenn Hegar noted in June 2016, "An ESF balance provides a flexible alternative, in addition to budgetary and revenue tools, to manage through challenging economic cycles. An ESF balance demonstrates fiscal strength and flexibility, but balances are not the only factor rating agencies consider."

So, when does it make sense to use the Fund? The Legislature has used the Fund frequently, for both one-time and ongoing budget items. Legislative approval by a two-thirds vote in the House and Senate is required to spend money from the Fund in most circumstances.

In the past, the Legislature has tapped the Fund for everything from public schools to criminal justice to closing shortfalls in Medicaid and the Children's Health Insurance Program. The Fund has been used for new budget items such as the State Water Plan or the Enterprise Fund.

It would be common sense for legislators to use the Fund when the only other choice would be state budget cuts that further destabilize the economy by, for example, triggering teacher layoffs or nursing home closures. Strategic, one-time uses of the Rainy Day Fund could also prevent larger costs in the future, such as those caused by underfunded state pensions.

Just as many households would do, dipping into savings can be part of a plan to get the state through a temporary shortfall. That's why the Rainy Day Fund was created. It is not designed to correct chronic underfunding of state services, and we don't advocate for such uses. If something needs additional funding in general, the Legislature should devise a way to provide permanent additional funding.

As the rhetoric heats up, let's remember that the Rainy Day Fund should be used as originally intended: to prevent sudden, massive cuts to schools, health care, higher education and other services on which Texans rely.

ARTICLE QUESTIONS

1) What legislative vote is required to take funds from the Rainy Day Fund?
2) For what purposes does the author argue that this fund could be used in the current policy environment?
3) Do you find the author's argument about the appropriate use of the fund convincing?

13.3) A Review of the 85th Texas Legislature

Texas Public Policy Foundation, 2017

In this overview, the conservative-leaning Texas Public Policy Foundation praises the "conservative successes" of the 85th legislature's budget and priorities, noting that the body continued the Lone Star State's "leadership on economic growth and the advance of liberty" while also setting the state on a path for future successes. At the heart of the session was what the Foundation argues was a conservative budget (Senate Bill 1), which included spending less money on prisons and extending pediatric telemedicine to rural Texas to cut down on costs. The group also praises the passage of a joint resolution (Senate Joint Resolution 2) requesting a convention of states to amend the U.S. Constitution—a measure that the Foundation believes would return more authority to the state to enact more fiscal restraint. Overall, the Foundation identifies "liberty" as the watchword of the session, celebrating the legislature's shift from prioritizing "local control" to prioritizing "local liberty" and its promotion of more public choice in public education.

A Conservative Texas Budget, major changes to our beleaguered foster care system, and significant criminal justice reform highlighted conservative successes in the 85th Texas Legislature. The following describe how the Texas Legislature made progress continuing Texas' leadership on economic growth and the advance of liberty while setting the stage for more to come.

Fiscal Policy

The Legislature made progress in limiting the size and scope of government by passing what could be two consecutive Conservative Texas Budgets, meaning increases in spending of no more than population growth plus inflation. The Legislature passed the second half of the 2016–17 budget with the passage of the supplemental budget, HB 2, finalizing what will likely be the first true Conservative Texas Budget in years. Moreover, it passed SB 1, the 2018–19 state budget, providing what could be a huge win for Texans if the Legislature in 2019 can follow up by completing the second straight Conservative Texas Budget.

Families and Children

Steps taken by the Legislature represented a monumental step forward for Texas foster children. Coming on the heels of a federal court decision finding that "rape, abuse, psychotropic medication, and instability are the norm" in the state's foster care system, intense pressure existed to throw more money at the problem. However, rather than just follow past practices, SB 11 draws on the success of a pilot program in Tarrant County and ensures the transfer of much of the responsibility for foster care from the state to communities—increasing the role of local agencies, community non-profits, and houses of worship in caring for children who are unable to remain safely at home. SB 11 serves as a pivot point in fulfilling the state's obligation to foster children.

Effective Justice

Criminal justice reform made significant advances during the regular session of the Texas Legislature. Owing to the successes of conservative criminal justice reform in previous sessions, the budget adopted by the Legislature calls for the closure of four unnecessary prison units. Adding to the four prisons closed since 2007, lawmakers took over 2,000 beds offline, all while saving taxpayers $50 million. Texas also enhanced its nondisclosure statute with the passage of HB 3016 that includes a Mothers Against Drunk Driving supported measure allowing nondisclosure, which prohibits public disclosure of a criminal record for first-time, low-level DUIs.

Local Governance

When it comes to local governance, the conversation at the Texas Legislature is shifting from how best to respect "local control" to how best to protect "local liberty." A number of bills demonstrate the shift toward local liberty. HB 100 preempts burdensome municipal ordinances regulating transportation network companies. SB 1248 limits city authority

over manufactured homes in designated manufactured home parks. Even the imperfect Houston pension reform bill illustrates the changing terms of debate when it comes to local control. A key plank of the reform is that the issuance of $1 billion of general obligation debt as pension obligation bonds must be subject to voter approval.

Public Education

Education freedom made its greatest progress to date in the recent legislative session. Though no school choice legislation finally passed, the issue remained a top focus throughout the session. SB 3, the most expansive vehicle of school choice (creating a near-universal statewide Education Savings Account, or ESA, program), passed the Texas Senate after a strong showing of public support in the earlier Senate Education Committee hearing. Public support in favor of school choice through the legislative debate heavily outweighed the opposition—a true first for this issue in Texas. Furthermore, two bills did increase education freedom this session. SB 1480 increases charter schools' access to the lower interest rates for building facilities that are currently available to traditional schools, while the passage of SB 587 ensures that military children will be able to access virtual schools.

Federalism and the Tenth Amendment

Key principles of federalism were preserved, protected, and advanced during the recently concluded regular session. SJR 2 is Texas' application to Congress for a convention of states. If 33 other states pass the same resolution, Congress must call the convention of states, where delegates would propose structural reform amendments in three areas: 1) fiscal restraint, 2) term limits, and 3) restraining the power and authority of the federal government. Texas is now 1 of 12 states to have passed this resolution. SB 21 lays out the process for selecting delegates to such a convention and the guidelines for governing the delegates' actions.

Economic Freedom

Economic freedom improved this legislative session. Major tort reform in HB 1774 puts to a stop abuses by trial lawyers in hail storm claims.

SB 277 reverses years of growth of renewable energy subsidies by making wind turbines built near military aviation bases ineligible for local tax abatements. Two bills reduce restrictions on work imposed through occupational licensing: SB 1503 abolishes the shampoo apprentice license, and HB 3329 prevents cities from charging electricians licensed with the state additional licensing or permitting fees.

Health Care

When it comes to increasing access to medical care through telemedicine, four bills stand out from the session. HB 1697 extends pediatric telemedicine to rural Texas. SB 1107 expands the types of telemedicine allowed. SB 1633 allows remote telepharmacy. SB 922 facilitates telemedicine within Texas schools. The net effect, especially in view of the resolution of recent lawsuits, will be greater access to health care in places within Texas where care is currently limited or not available at all. Additionally, passage of SB 1148 will prevent insurance carriers from withholding payments for lack of federal Maintenance of Certification.

Energy & Environment

A prudent perspective on the environment marked action by the Legislature. Noteworthy success can be seen in the session's water policy reform, including a handful of bills passed that reduce barriers keeping water right applicants from being granted a permit. SB 1009 and HB 3735 narrow the scope of factors that the Texas Commission on Environmental Quality (TCEQ) may examine when considering permit applications. SB 1430 encourages water portfolio diversification by creating specific value for the development of seawater desalination, uplifting the market of up-basin benefits.

Higher Education

The Legislature's regular session was relatively quiet when it came to higher education, despite significant debate during the preceding interim. One of the best aspects of this legislative inaction is that none of the major bills that would have significantly increased the cost of higher education were passed. Worst among these defeated bills was HB 1498, which would have allocated half a billion dollars from the Rainy Day Fund for campus construction that universities already have the ability to finance. The Legislature did do well in passing a bill strengthening career and technical education (SB 2105). This bill looks to help fill the middle-skills gap by increasing the focus of education in this area. Employers have been hard-pressed to find middle-skills applicants for some time.

ARTICLE QUESTIONS

1) Why does the Foundation believe the 85th legislative session was "conservative"?
2) What are three examples of successful legislative outcomes identified in this article?
3) On balance, do you agree or disagree with the Foundation's perspective on the session?

13.4) A Legislative Session Marked by Bruised Egos and Missed Opportunities

TribTalk, June 1, 2017

ANN BEESON

In contrast to the rosy picture conservative groups painted of the 85th legislative session, liberal groups were dismayed about several of the policy outcomes. Ann Beeson, executive director of the left-leaning Center for Public Policy Priorities, characterizes the session as full of "missed opportunities" and "bruised egos." Why the difference in perspective? Liberal groups had demanded more from state government than a "tight" budget, looking instead for investment in specific programs that they believed could help Texas be economically competitive. Beeson argues that the state created the tight budget problem by passing "short-sighted" tax cuts and revenue diversions in past sessions that made it impossible for the 85th session to address critical state needs. She also argues that the state choked the "engines of our economy"—local governments—from acting by cutting revenue that would have flowed to the governments closest to the voters.

Beyond the financial issues, Beeson argues that the passage of policies perceived to be anti-immigrant and missed opportunities to pass much-needed public school reform made Texas worse off after the session than before it began. Other such policies did not pass thanks to "sensible leadership," but Beeson ranks the session overall as a low for the state. Bright spots, she contends, can be found in the areas of mental health funding and protections against "surprise" emergency room medical bills. Moments of consensus were rare, however, and in her account, the session left hard-working families behind and immigrants "terrified."

That was by far one of the ugliest and least productive legislative sessions in recent memory.

Why was the session so vicious this year? The acrimony and hate didn't take place in a vacuum. Federal proposals from school vouchers to the effort to repeal the Affordable Care Act gave fuel to ultra-conservative Texas lawmakers. Then there were the fireworks between the Texas Senate and House. Finally, too many state lawmakers spent the session fighting Texas cities and counties, instead of working with local leaders to advance policies that could benefit all Texans.

Lawmakers had plenty of opportunities to adopt solutions that would have improved the lives of Texans. But instead of focusing on the real challenges facing our state, they were busy crafting discriminatory responses to manufactured problems. Thanks to the sheer determination and smart strategies of some leaders, a few sensible policies did manage to get through. But overall, the session exploited divisions between Texans and their neighbors while failing to make investments where they count.

Emboldened by Trump-inspired xenophobia, Texas lawmakers targeted immigrants and abandoned Texas' long-held reputation for sensible immigration policies. Despite hours of testimony against Senate Bill 4 from law enforcement, local officials, educators and faith leaders, the Legislature passed a damaging "show me your papers" law that requires local law enforcement to comply with all federal immigration detainer requests and bars local police—including campus police—from refusing to cooperate with federal immigration authorities.

Another blown opportunity this session was the failure to enact school finance reform. The 5.3 million students in Texas public schools deserve a quality education, regardless of where they live or their background. The House crafted a reasonable plan, but zealots in the Senate stripped most of the funding and attached a school voucher proposal that would have used state dollars to subsidize private school tuition—a "compromise" the House wisely and soundly rejected.

At the same time the Senate was refusing to pay the state's fair share of public school funding—the real way to control property taxes—it was pushing hard to limit the ability of local governments to raise the revenue they need. That was one of many state efforts to usurp local control from Texas cities—the engines of our economy. Though the scheme to cut revenue from local governments failed to pass during the regular session, we're watching to see whether Gov. Greg Abbott adds it to the agenda if he brings lawmakers back for a special session.

Speaking of funding, I wish I had a nickel for every time a lawmaker complained of what a "tight budget" we had. Remember that this session's budget situation was mostly created by the Legislature's own short-sighted tax cuts and revenue diversions last session. And the state budget they passed this session foolishly leaves billions of dollars in the Rainy Day Fund despite the growing population and changing needs of our state. Texans will suffer from these state cuts, especially compounded by looming federal cuts to health care, food and education programs.

There were some silver linings, and I'm grateful to the sponsors of those efforts. Mental health in Texas got a big boost when both houses passed bills that make coverage more accessible and equal, and bolstered programs that help people living with mental illness get the treatment they need and stay out of jail. Texans who receive surprise medical bills after visits to emergency rooms will now have better protections, and grandparents and other kinship caregivers will receive some additional financial support to help children stay with family.

As a proud Texan, I expected our elected leaders to come together and enact policies that would make Texas the best state for hard-working people and their families. Instead we're left with terrified immigrants, bruised egos and missed opportunities.

ARTICLE QUESTIONS

1) Why does the author believe the 85th legislative session represented missed opportunities for Texans?
2) What are three examples of legislative outcomes the author claims were missed opportunities?
3) Why does the author argue that the session left "immigrants terrified"?
4) On balance, do you agree or disagree with the author's perspective on the legislative session?

Chapter 14

Interest Groups and Political Power in Texas

Texas is not unique in having interest groups that attempt to obtain influence over the political and policy process. "For virtue, try Minnesota," joked journalist Molly Ivins in a 1988 column. Lobbying and political contributions are highly influential in state government, but their influence is restrained by other active groups and by legislators who sift through the advocacy on all sides to achieve quality outcomes for Texas. Fights between interest groups produce confrontations in the political arena, while the scuffle between advocates of disclosure and those opposed to it shapes state accountability and disclosure policies. Major brawls break out when political scandals shock the state, but they are almost always followed by reforms that seek to bring the system back into alignment.

Interest groups are not inherently bad—they represent key interests of businesses, trade groups, hundreds of occupations, and individual citizens. The activities in which these groups engage are varied and range from participating in elections to providing civic education to lobbying in the halls of the Capitol in Austin. As the state has grown and the number of interests has expanded, interest groups too have expanded their activities and grown in number. At different times interest groups in Texas have been deemed too influential, requiring oversight of their activities through various state agencies and rules. Moments of crisis, as in the creation of the Texas Ethics Commission, as explained by the *Texas Tribune*'s Ross Ramsey, reveal the state's ongoing struggle to police interest groups.

"Lobbying" is a term that originated during Andrew Jackson's first presidential term in office. Since individuals attempting to persuade members of Congress to engage in some action were not allowed on the floor of the House or Senate chambers, they hung around in the lobby—hence their name: "lobbyists." Lobbyists in Texas are often called the "Third House," the other two being the House and the Senate. According to Texas law, lobbying consists of "direct communications" with members of the legislative or executive branch of government with the aim of influencing legislation or administrative action.

In practice, anyone can consider him- or herself a lobbyist, but Texas law regulates some specific lobbying activities. Lobbyists are required to register with the Texas Ethics Commission and pay a fee of $750 per year within five days of signing that contact. According to Ethics Commission rules, an individual who engages in lobbying activities and receives more than $1,000 in salary from a firm or organization must register as a lobbyist. Likewise, an individual who spends more than $500 in a calendar year for the purposes of lobbying must also register as a lobbyist. These expenditures include payments, loans, gifts, meals, awards, and other entertainment.

After the Sharpstown stock scandal, which ensnared several elected officials in Texas, the process of lobbying in the state significantly and permanently changed. Lobbying is more sophisticated (and more regulated) today than it was back then: the "bourbon, beefsteaks and blondes" that were powerful weapons in the lobbyist's arsenal then are now forbidden. The Texas Ethics Commission (TEC) opened its doors in 1991 as the state's primary agency for regulating and enforcing laws related to interest group lobbying and campaign disclosure, setting disclosures, regulating lobbyists, and requiring public access to donor information. The Commission also hears complaints related to these disclosure requirements and has the authority to issue fines for violations.

New rules and cultural norms established new practices, but these changes don't necessarily mean the rules are enforced consistently. The *Texas Tribune*'s Ross Ramsey argues that the TEC is a "toothless" agency, "a dog that doesn't bite." The primary reason for this alleged impotence is political—commissioners are appointed by the very politicians they are supposed to be watching, leaving little incentive to be tough on lawmakers. Internal political strife also complicates the situation. State law requires that appointments to the Commission be balanced by party, making agreement about violations and punishments a challenge. Unless and until the legislature reforms the Commission, Ramsey is doubtful that the agency can fully carry out its mission.

The number of lobbyists has increased over time as Texas lawmakers deal with increasingly complicated and diverse issues. The size of the state economy has grown, and along with it the role of lobbyists to stake their claim to some of those funds. State government has also grown, as more laws are passed to regulate activities in the state. These trends reflect the increasing importance that lobbyists have on the political system. When these groups conflict for policy outcomes, which group wins?

The days of lobbyists brazenly buying off politicians may be past us, but concerns about the oversight and accountability of the system remain. Disclosure of financial information still remains a particular issue in the Lone Star State, and Texas still lags behind many others in responsible laws regarding public transparency. Like Ross Ramsey, James Drew, writing for the *Dallas Morning News*, argues that lobbying takes place in the "shadows" of Texas government. Because many of the state's rules are not enforced or are unclear, interest groups and lobbyists are able to skirt public reporting requirements.

Lobbying is done from outside of government, but interest groups may find ways inside it. An alarming report entitled "Rigged" from Texans for Public Justice claims that some executive agencies (like the Texas Railroad Commission) are too "cozy" with the industries they regulate. For instance, industry executives donate significant funds to the commissioners who regulate them. The danger of this system is the perception that it gives rise to of collusion between government and industry groups. The public wants the government to be responsive to its needs, not those of allied interests. Confidence in government is diminished if there is a perception that insiders are using personal connections to benefit themselves.

CHAPTER QUESTIONS

1) What major scandals in Texas political history have precipitated significant changes in the regulation of interest groups?
2) What are some of the ways that the influence of interest groups is limited? In what ways have interest groups been successful?
3) Are interest groups too "cozy" with the industries they regulate?
4) What kinds of reforms are identified by the authors to remedy flaws in the current system of holding interest groups and government accountable?

14.1) The Long and Winding Road to the Texas Ethics Commission

Texas Tribune, July 22, 2016

ROSS RAMSEY

> To the *Texas Tribune*'s Ross Ramsey, the Texas Ethics Commission is "a dog that doesn't bite"—and it is that way on purpose. But how can the state's primary agency charged with ethics enforcement have no teeth? Ramsey argues that the agency protects its own kin—the politicians and legislators who appoint members to the Commission. Put simply: a dog doesn't bite the hand that feeds it.
>
> The primary reason for the TEC's lack of enforcement is that the individuals appointed to it feel obligated to protect those in office. It would be politically hazardous for commissioners to come down hard on those politicians who appointed (and reappointed) them to their positions. Furthermore, enforcement actions are difficult for the TEC to pursue, requiring agreement by six of the Commission's eight members. This means that a supermajority has to agree to fine or punish any individual thought to have violated the law. Even if they do come to some agreement, the appointees are, by law, split by party: four Republicans, four Democrats. That divide may generate gridlock.
>
> Ramsey argues that the TEC needs some teeth to do its job properly and thoroughly. Legislators have been unwilling to give it such power, despite a push from Governor Greg Abbott. Ramsey is not optimistic about such prospects, however. The incentives built into the system make reform difficult.

The Texas Ethics Commission is a dog that doesn't bite.

It's designed that way.

It's the regulatory agency in charge of politicians and legislators. You think those folks want to give it real teeth?

That said, it's also a strange place when it comes to appointing commissioners.

Most executive branch agencies in Texas are overseen by elected officials or appointed boards and executives. The elected leaders are your own fault, assuming you're a voter. The appointments are mostly made by the governor, with a handful assigned to the lieutenant governor or the speaker of the House.

The eight-member ethics panel, however, is unique.

The governor appoints four members, and the lite guv and the speaker appoint two each. But wait, there's more. Each of them chooses from lists of potential appointees provided by legislators in the House and the Senate. Not done with the rules yet: Those lists are split by party.

In practice, that means the political caucuses in the House and Senate have the first cull when it comes to who serves on the state commission that regulates the political activities of candidates, officeholders and lobbyists.

Here's one example. Houston businessman Paul Hobby, whose term actually expired last November, has handed in his resignation. So has Tom Harrison, whose current term was over, technically, in November 2011—that's not a typo—and who has also sent in a letter saying he would like to move on.

House Speaker Joe Straus will replace Hobby, who was appointed from a list submitted by House Democrats and who would have to be replaced from a list provided by House Democrats. Harrison's appointment is similar, except that the appointing official in his case is Gov. Greg Abbott, who will pick from a list provided by Senate Democrats.

Harrison and Hobby aren't the only two holdovers on the commission. Wilhelmina Delco, a former state representative from Austin, was appointed by the lieutenant governor; her term expired in November 2015. The same is true of Bob Long, a gubernatorial appointee from Bastrop.

The commission is balanced politically, with half of the commissioners selected from Republican lists and half from Democratic lists.

Why? Because everyone was scared to death that one of the political parties would gain control and use the commission to terrorize its enemies.

Gotta admit, that sounds plausible.

The commission, like most of the state's ethics laws, was born in scandal. Unlike some of the others, it was created by amending the state Constitution.

Even the gray-haired folks don't remember much about putting the Texas Ethics Commission into the Texas Constitution. It was November 1991. It was one of 13 proposed amendments. And only one amendment—the one creating a state lottery in Texas—was getting any attention.

Even if they were thinking about the commission and even though they were doing it in the midst of nasty headlines about then-Speaker Gib Lewis, D-Fort Worth, and other state leaders, they were probably casting their vote based on legislative pay. Here's how it read: "The constitutional amendment creating the Texas Ethics Commission and authorizing the commission to recommend the salary for members of the legislature and the lieutenant governor, subject to voter approval, and to set the per diem for those officials, subject to a limit."

For the average voter, the thought process was even simpler: Ethics, schmethics. When can I get a lotto ticket?

They did approve that year's Proposition 6, along with its peculiar directions for appointing the new commission's members.

But the creators of this particular agency left out any incentive for the state's top officials to make new appointments to the commission. It's interesting work for the commissioners, but not a political plum. Whatever the commission does is politically hazardous, almost by definition. No governor or lieutenant governor or speaker is eager to jump into a controversy if there's no political gain to compensate for it.

It's easier just to leave things alone. The party caucuses in the House and Senate have been relatively content with the current commissioners, and the three officials whose job it is to appoint replacements haven't pressed for change.

Until recently, the commissioners themselves were willing to serve until well after their terms were supposed to end. Naming some new people could raise some attention, depending on who they are. If the state's leaders are provocative about their appointments, they could even restart Gov. Abbott's legislative push for stronger ethics laws after his first try produced mixed results.

Maybe lawmakers will give the ethics commission some teeth.

ARTICLE QUESTIONS

1) What were the political circumstances that brought about the establishment of the Texas Ethics Commission?
2) Why does the author argue the Texas Ethics Commission is "toothless"?
3) What can be done to strengthen the Texas Ethics Commission?

14.2) State Law Allows for Lobbying Deep in the Shadows of Texas

Dallas Morning News, February 2015

JAMES DREW

Lobbyists do their business in plain sight, but *Dallas Morning News* investigative journalist James Drew argues that they operate in the shadows of Texas government. How so? Drew points to one prominent example: Lobbyists are required to detail any expenditure on behalf of state officers or employees, their spouses, or their children. If a lobbyist spends more than $114 (as of 2018) on entertainment, food and beverages, lodging, or transportation, this information must be recorded. But despite these laws, lobbyists have found loopholes to avoid disclosure. One way this happens is by splitting restaurant checks. After a pricy steak dinner with cocktails and expensive wine, lobbyists can skirt disclosure requirements by splitting the bill to stay under the dollar limit that would require naming the specific lawmaker wined and dined.

These and other "lax" loopholes open the possibility for interest groups to exert an outsized influence on government and illustrate the "powerful alliance between lobbyists and lawmakers." Drew lays out these rules, which he describes as "gray and complicated," and then shows how difficult it is to comply with them and how easy it is to avoid full and accurate disclosure. In some instances, it is simply a matter of a "lobbyist" calling him- or herself a "consultant." The Texas Ethics Commission, as we learned in the prior reading, is only of marginal help in sorting through these complaints and punishing offenders.

Drew claims that Texas is fairly lax about disclosure requirements compared to other states. The implications of such laxity are dramatic—lobbyists and interest groups have become a major part of state government, but tracking their interconnections to see the course of policymaking is difficult.

Like many at the Texas Capitol, James "Trey" Trainor III has been on both sides of the desk, first as a legislative staffer and then as a lobbyist.

He learned how lobbyists paid for expensive things for legislators, all the while trying to keep the public in the dark about the perks provided.

For example, by splitting bills, lobbyists legally can hide which legislators and staffers get high-price meals, gifts, entertainment, transportation and hotels.

When details of such expenses go undisclosed, it becomes difficult to figure out whether someone is exercising undue influence over a lawmaker.

"I guess they always will find a way to game that system," said Trainor, an attorney who specializes in election and government law.

Texas' lobby law has significant loopholes and weaknesses that make it difficult for the public to track the powerful alliance between lobbyists and lawmakers.

People lobby legislators without registering with the state. The rules are so complex that even lobbyists can get confused. There's a lack of transparency about the legislation that lobbyists are trying to influence. And the state oversight agency routinely does not aggressively pursue alleged violators.

Legislators dictate the rules of the game.

Lobbyists say they do their best to comply with those rules.

But both camps do little to improve the regulations and many privately thrive on a game they say is played without referees.

Many legislators and lobbyists say they don't have a problem with how the law is working. The public hasn't pressured them to change the game anytime soon, they add.

Veteran lobbyist Don McFarlin said he has split legislators' food and beverage checks with other lobbyists, but said he has no problem if the Legislature requires more public disclosure.

"If you look at other states, they have some pretty stringent ethics laws. Texas is pretty lax," McFarlin said.

Looser Rules

Nearly 25 years ago, reacting to scandals, legislators restricted how much lobbyists could spend on them for gifts and entertainment, such as tickets to sports events and concerts.

But the regulations on how much lobbyists can spend on food and drinks for legislators are a bit looser: There is no limit.

Instead, the brake on spending is supposed to be disclosure. If the voters know which lawmakers are getting food and drinks from lobbyists, maybe public pressure would keep it in check.

In the good government world, here's how it would work:

A lobbyist takes a legislator to a steakhouse. The legislator orders an appetizer, a rib-eye with potatoes Lyonnaise, a bottle of red wine and slice of Chocolate Sin Cake for dessert.

The bill for the legislator alone totals $200. Because the amount spent by the lobbyist on the legislator is more than $90, state law requires the lobbyist to fill out a report.

That form, filed with the Texas Ethics Commission and available to the public, names the legislator along with the place and the date of the meal. It also names the exact amount spent or a range of amounts—such as "$200 but less than $250." It's called a "detailed report."

But for many legislators, the detailed report is the equivalent of toxic waste. It can be used by foes during the legislative session and at the ballot box to accuse legislators—fairly or not—of being in the pocket of lobbyists.

So in the real world of Austin, here's what often happens to that legislator's $200 tab:

The lobbyist takes two fellow lobbyists to the dinner. The lawmaker's tab is divided by three credit cards, cutting the amount each lobbyist spent on him to $66 and change. The detailed form no longer has to be filled out.

Besides, if the goal is to convince the legislator to follow their client's wishes, three lobbyist voices are better than one.

The $90 maximum amount that a lobbyist can spend on food and beverages for a legislator per day without having to file a detailed report is tied to the legislative per diem.

That's the amount that legislators get for their daily expenses in Austin. Since they are paid only $7,200 a year, legislators can supplement their salaries by not spending a big chunk of the per diem. Being fed by lobbyists lowers their costs.

This week, the Ethics Commission is scheduled to vote to boost the per diem from $150 to $190.

If so, the amount that a lobbyist can spend on food and beverages for a legislator per day without filing a detailed report would also rise, from $90 to $114.

But Rep. Charlie Geren, R-Fort Worth, has filed a bill that would lower that threshold to $50 per day. That would make it harder for lobbyists to split tabs to avoid filing detailed reports.

Jack Gullahorn heads a trade group for Texas lobbyists. He is the lobbyist for lobbyists.

He said that lobbyists splitting tabs is legal in Texas as a "joint expenditure." Lobbyists also must disclose a running total of every penny they spend on legislators or staff members, Gullahorn said.

"Today's legislature is made up of members that are basing their decisions on the best information available, not the best wine available," he said.

In Wisconsin, state law bans lobbyists from wining and dining legislators at all.

"You can't even accept a cup of coffee from a registered lobbyist, let alone anything that is expensive," said Mike Buelow, research director for the Wisconsin Democracy Campaign, a nonprofit watchdog group.

State officials say the law is easy to understand and administer.

Being Registered

Texas' lobby law sits atop a cracked slab.

The law can work well only if people who are lobbying register with the state.

There are two ways to trigger that requirement.

The first is if a person spends more than $500 over three months on lobbying.

The second is if someone does three things:

- Receives compensation, or expects to receive it, totaling more than $1,000 over three months.
- Devotes more than 5 percent of their paid time over three months to lobbying.
- Directly communicates with a legislator.

How do you know what 5 percent of your paid time is? Do you count 9-to-5 hours, or 24/7? What about the two-page list, in the code, of exemptions to the registration requirement?

And that is only part of lobby regulations that some say are too gray and complicated.

"It's the type of complexity that is ripe for exploitation by those who intend to not comply or minimally comply," said Vincent Johnson, a professor at St. Mary's University School of Law in San Antonio. "It is fraught with the potential for loopholes."

Lobbyists, for example, say they sometimes see people who have registered as lobbyists in the past chatting it up with legislators or staffers, even though they aren't currently registered.

Why aren't they registered? Are they under the 5 percent rule? Are they being paid less than $1,000 over three months?

Or have they decided to try to fly under the radar, knowing it's hard for anyone to get those answers, and it's unlikely a fellow lobbyist is going to tattle to the Ethics Commission?

It's a murky situation.

And the consequences are huge.

Registered lobbyists provide a lot of information that is public record.

That data includes who hired them and how much they get paid.

Without that information, it is extremely difficult for the public to track the various interests swirling around a controversial issue.

And it also can be dangerous to lawmakers.

People who lobby without registering as a lobbyist leave themselves and the legislators vulnerable to prosecution under the bribery statute if they offer or give something of value to a legislator.

The same applies if a legislator solicits a benefit from an unregistered lobbyist in exchange for action.

Tom "Smitty" Smith, director of the Texas office of Public Citizen, a nonprofit consumer and environmental group, said lawmakers should make it more clear how a lobbyist is defined in state law.

The issue is a hot one because the Ethics Commission last year fined conservative activist Michael Quinn Sullivan $10,000 for failing to register as a lobbyist in 2010 and 2011. He had registered in the past.

It was the first time a complaint alleging that a lobbyist failed to register has gone through the entire five-layer Ethics Commission process in the agency's 24-year history.

That last step is a rare instance in which the agency hears a complaint in public. (The commission routinely fines lobbyists for things like filing late reports, but only the outcome is public, not the deliberations.)

Sullivan has appealed the decision to Denton County District Court, saying the state lobby law is unconstitutional.

The Ethics Commission said part of Sullivan's job was to send emails to legislators and their staff members to influence the outcome of bills.

But Sullivan and his allies say he's not a lobbyist. They say he's petitioning his government, publishes a scorecard that rates how lawmakers vote on the issues and also is a reporter.

Tony McDonald, the general counsel for Empower Texans, the nonprofit group led by Sullivan, said the law is used to cast a wide net to force people to register as lobbyists.

"The worry is if we are lobbyists, the tea party groups are lobbyists and all the grassroots people are lobbyists," he said.

Washington state has lobbyist registration requirements that backers say are easy to understand.

Lobbyists generally are defined as those who are paid to influence state legislation. They are required to register with the state within 30 days of being hired or before they start lobbying, whichever comes first.

Texas lobbyists are also required to disclose their clients to the Ethics Commission. Those records are available on the agency's website.

The commission's rules require lobbyists to disclose what subjects they're lobbying about for their clients. There are dozens of categories, such as utilities and energy.

But that information is so general, it might not always be helpful to the public. Texas used to require lobbyists to list bill numbers, but scrapped that practice because of the large number of bills filed.

A more precise requirement is in California, where outside groups are required to disclose if they are behind legislation. The provision, known as "sponsored bills," enables the public to track bills shepherded by lobbyists.

It's transparent, but some say it has only increased the influence of major lobbying groups.

Call It Consulting

In some cases, the Texas lobby law isn't enforced aggressively.

Sometimes, campaign consultants appear to be lobbying without registering.

Without doing so, they can urge their campaign clients in the Legislature to vote a certain way—and their lobbying clients would benefit.

And the public wouldn't know about those entanglements. In fact, the legislator might not know, either.

"You end up with some people who say, 'Heck, I'm just going to call it all consulting and none of it lobbying,'" said Allen Blakemore, a Houston-based campaign consultant. "They don't make a disclosure. That is clearly not what the law intended."

His firm's clients include 10 legislators, the most powerful being the new lieutenant governor, Dan Patrick.

Blakemore also is a lobbyist and he registers. So far this year, he has racked up six clients, including Tesla Motors and the Wholesale Beer Distributors of Texas.

He said it's easy to find out who is a political consultant. Candidates are required to list them on their campaign finance reports. But Blakemore said he doesn't know how the Ethics Commission would identify political consultants who also lobby without registering, even if they wanted to do so.

"Consultant X is active in campaigns. Does he lobby? I don't know. How am I supposed to know? How in the world is the Ethics Commission supposed to know?" he said.

Paul Hobby, the Ethics Commission chairman, said lobbyists often complain that the agency beats up on people who register and doesn't target those who don't.

But it's tough for a small agency with a "meager budget" to pursue those who flout the lobby registration law, he said.

Blakemore said it's not difficult for him to do political consulting work for a legislator at the same time he is lobbying.

Other states are examining whether political consultants doubling as lobbyists is a conflict of interest.

In New York, a legislator has pushed a bill to prohibit campaign consultants from lobbying the officials they help elect. That battle is ongoing.

Honor System

Sandie Haverlah is a veteran lobbyist.

But with two environmental and consumer groups as clients so far this session, she said she doesn't have the budget to take legislators out to big meals. She said she registers even when the law doesn't require her to do so.

She said the lobby law is based on the honor system.

"On the busy days of the legislative session, there are over 1,000 scenarios where the law could be broken. Who is going to track all of that? The system is really built on those of us who want to be honest about it," Haverlah said.

The state Ethics Commission oversees the lobby law.

The eight-member commission needs at least six votes to move forward with an enforcement action.

That means a super majority has to agree to any fine or punishment for any lobbyist, although the commission recently has delegated minor matters to the staff.

Four members of the commission are appointed by the lieutenant governor and House speaker; the other four by the governor.

That means the state's top three elected officials control who calls the shots.

Reform plans, which have gone nowhere, have called for a simple majority to replace the super majority and for the governor to appoint all commission members so it would be more independent of the Legislature.

The Ethics Commission's enforcement hearings are rarely open to the public.

Hobby, the Ethics Commission chairman, said the agency has hired an enforcement director, but the agency's lack of investigative power limits what it can do.

The system is primarily designed to respond to third-party complaints, he said.

New Jersey has received high marks from good-government groups for how it audits lobbyists' disclosure records and imposes penalties on those who violate the law.

Trainor, the former legislative staffer and lobbyist, said a major purpose of the lobby law—to inform the public about how much lobbyists are spending on legislators or staff members—is not working.

He is a member of the legal team representing Sullivan in his battle against the Ethics Commission.

"You have a system where the lobbyist reports, there is no check on the system, and there is no way to know," Trainor said.

"You are the legislator and I am the lobbyist. I say, 'Hey, we are going to go out and have dinner tonight. It is going to cost $800. If you don't tell anybody, I don't tell anybody and nobody knows,'" he said.

At a Glance: Inside Texas' Lobby Law

Lobbyists are required to make detailed disclosures to the Texas Ethics Commission if they spend more than a certain amount on legislators or their staff members. Those forms, referred to as "detailed reports," are public records.

Food and Beverage

- Lobbyists must disclose details when they spend more than $90 in one day on a legislator or a staff member. Lobbyists are required to disclose the names of legislators or their staff members, the place, date and the amount, either an exact dollar figure or within a range.
- There is no cap on how much a lobbyist can spend on food and beverages for legislators or their staff members.

Entertainment

- Lobbyists must disclose details when they spend more than $90 in one day on a legislator or staff members, or on the spouse or dependent child of a legislator or staff member. The details are the same as the food and beverage rule: names of legislators or their staff members, the place, date and the amount, either an exact dollar figure or within a range.

- There is a $500 per year cap on how much lobbyists can spend for each legislator, staff member, or immediate family or guests.

Gifts

- Lobbyists must disclose details when they buy a gift valued at more than $50 and give it to legislators or staff members. The details are the names of legislators or their staff members, a description of the gift and the amount of the expenditure, either an exact dollar figure or a range.
- There is a $500 cap on how much lobbyists can spend per year on gifts for legislators or their staff members, or their immediate family and guests.

Transportation and Lodging

- Lobbyists must disclose details when they spend more than $90 per day on transportation or lodging for legislators or staff members. The details are the names of the legislators or staff members, the place, date and the purpose—but not the dollar amount or a range.
- There is no cap on how much a lobbyist can spend on transportation or lodging for legislators or their staff members per year.

Political Fundraisers or Charity Events

- Lobbyists are required to disclose details for any amount they spend so a legislator or their staff members can attend a political fundraiser or charity event. The details are the names of the legislators or staff members, the name of the charity or candidate or officeholder for whom the fundraiser was held, and the date.
- Lobbyists cannot pay for transportation and lodging for a legislator or staff members, or their immediate family or guests, for a "ceremonial event" or a "pleasure trip."
- Lobbyists can pay for transportation and lodging only if it's to "explore matters related" to a legislator's or staff members' duties, such as a

"fact-finding trip" or a conference where the legislator or staff members do something, such as giving a speech or taking part in a panel.

SOURCES: Texas Government Code, Texas Ethics Commission rules and Texas lobbyist handbook published by the Ethics Commission.

ARTICLE QUESTIONS

1) Why is Texas an outlier when it comes to ethics and lobbying reporting?
2) Identify three major problems with the enforcement of ethics rules in Texas, as identified by the author.
3) What are three things that the author argues or implies might be changed to remedy some of the problems identified?

14.3) Rigged: How the Texas Oil and Gas Industry Bankrolls Its Own Regulators

Texans for Public Justice, November 2016

Government agencies established to regulate an industry often end up being "controlled" by the very industries that they were designed to regulate. The Texas Railroad Commission, which contrary to its name sets rules about the production of natural resources and referees ownership of petroleum wells, is a classic example of agency capture, according to a scathing report from Texans for Public Justice. The report finds that the three members of the Railroad Commission took 60 percent of the more than $11 million in campaign funds they raised from the oil and gas industry they regulate. Several of the largest donors were individuals or firms directly regulated by the Railroad Commission, a connection the report's authors argue is a conflict of interest.

These "cozy" ties between the oil and gas industry and the Texas Railroad Commission led the Texas Sunset Advisory Commission to recommend major changes to the agency. These include changing the name to more accurately reflect the scope of the agency's mission, increasing transparency of case hearings, and banning Commission members from engaging in political fundraising from firms that have contested cases being considered by the Commission. The goal of these recommendations was to remove industry pressure from the agency. Do you think that the state will take these recommendations and reform the agency, or will the Railroad Commission continue moving down the same tracks?

The three sitting members of the misnamed Texas Railroad Commission conservatively took 60 percent of the more than $11 million that they raised in recent years from the oil and gas industry that they regulate. The No. 2 source of political funding for these commissioners was the Lawyers & Lobbyists sector, which accounts for another 7 percent of the commissioners' cash. With many of these attorneys representing clients before the agency, the two industries pressing the most business before the commissioners supply 67 percent of their funding. Oil and gas interests also supplied 65 percent of the money reported by Railroad Commission-elect Wayne Christian, whom voters just selected to replace retiring Commissioner David Porter.

Table 14.1   Money Raised by Current Commissioners (Since January 2010)

Commissioner (Party)	Year Elected	Itemized Contributions	Oil and Gas Amount	Oil and Gas Percent	Fundraising Period
Christi Craddick (R)	2012	$4,874,193	$2,718,624	56%	7/2011 thru 6/2016
Ryan Sitton (R)	2014	$3,688,668	$2,179,302	59%	9/2013 thru 6/2016
David Porter (R)	2010	$2,558,551	$1,752,526	68%	1/2010 thru 6/2016
Totals		$11,121,412	$6,650,452	60%	

This report analyzes the itemized campaign contributions of the three sitting commissioners and of the four finalists who vied for Commissioner Porter's open seat in November 2016. Where appropriate, this study tracks money raised as far back as 2010, when Porter first ran for the commission. Long a major player in Texas politics, the energy industry has an especially outsized role in bankrolling its own regulators. During the 2014 cycle, the energy industry accounted for 17 cents of every dollar raised by Texas' non-judicial state candidates. During that gubernatorial election cycle, Governor Greg Abbott raised more than $45 million—taking 22 percent of it from oil and gas interests. That industry clearly secured a major voice in the Governor's Mansion. Yet Commissioner-elect Christian is *three times* more dependent on the oil and gas industry than Abbott (this study also includes the money that Christian raised for the race that he lost to Commissioner Ryan Sitton in 2014).

When an industry pays from 56 percent to 65 percent of its regulators' prodigious political bills, who's regulating whom?

Top Contributors

The "Top Contributors" table further illustrates the industry's grip on the agency. It lists the 44 top contributors to the seven Railroad Commission candidates analyzed here. Note that just nine of these donors (20 percent) are not ostensibly regulated by the commission.

Yet several big donors classified in other industries also have oil running in their veins. The campaign of state Rep. Tom Craddick, R-Midland, became this study's No. 1 contributor by spending $625,937 to help daughter Christi Craddick win a 2012 Railroad Commission race. Although not classified in the energy industry, Tom Craddick worked for an oil-supply company, represents an energy district and tapped that industry for 35 percent of his political funding. The law firm Parsley Coffin Renner also invested $107,000 in Railroad Commission candidates. That firm specializes in representing energy clients before the Public Utility Commission and the Railroad Commission.[1]

Identifying the true source of Railroad Commission funds can be like prospecting for oil deep beneath the earth's surface. Commissioner Ryan Sitton's No. 1 contributor, for example, is the

Table 14.2   Money Raised by Four Party Nominees Seeking David Porter's Open Seat in 2016

Candidate (Party)	Itemized Contributions	Oil and Gas Amount	Oil and Gas Percent	Fundraising Period
"Wayne" Christian (R)	$1,110,887	$722,728	65%	9/2013 thru 10/2016
Mark Miller (L)	$126,007	$1,050	1%	6/2014 thru 10/2016
Martina Salinas (G)	$4,862	$0	0%	6/2014 thru 10/2016
Grady Yarbrough (D)	$0	$0	NA	7/2015 thru 10/2016
Totals	$1,241,756	$723,778	58%	

Conservative Republicans of Texas PAC (CROT), which gave Sitton almost $400,000 for his 2014 primary runoff against Wayne Christian. CROT is tied to Houston physician and conservative activist Dr. Steven Hotze, who is better known for his concerns about gay marriage and transgender toilets than for oil and gas rules. So why did ideological CROT go all in for Sitton against the arguably more socially conservative Wayne Christian in a race for an office that has little to do with CROT's social issues? And where did CROT get the money? The bizarre answer is that the money that CROT gave to Sitton's campaign came from . . . Sitton's campaign!

CROT PAC raised $1.4 million during the extended 2014 primary season. Its No. 1 donor was the Sitton campaign. Another top CROT donor was the campaign of then-retiring Railroad Commissioner Barry Smitherman (whom Sitton replaced). These Railroad Commission campaigns, which were overwhelmingly bankrolled by the oil and gas industry, supplied 38 percent of CROT's money in that period.

During the 2014 GOP primary runoff, Sitton's campaign moved a total of $430,000 to CROT PAC, which spent $396,687 promoting Sitton to voters (and that Sitton reported as in-kind contributions to his campaign). The money flowing between Sitton and CROT PAC was essentially a wash, with CROT taking an extra $33,000 or so, perhaps for overhead expenses. Those expenses included payments to the political consulting firms Blakemore & Associates and Baselice & Associates, firms that advised both CROT and Sitton. These lawful transactions effectively laundered the source of a pile of the Sitton campaign's petro dollars. They created the appearance that Sitton's top campaign contributor was the ideological Conservative Republicans of Texas PAC.[2]

As such major contributors as CROT PAC, the Parsley Coffin Renner firm and the Tom Craddick campaign demonstrate, this report dramatically undercounts the true extent to which Railroad Commissioners are financially dependent on the oil and gas industry that they regulate.

Another notable contributor is Kelcy Warren. When not running Energy Transfer Partners, which is building pipelines near Big Bend National Park and across sacred indigenous burial grounds in the

Table 14.3 Exchanges Between Sitton's Campaign and Conservative Republicans of Texas (CROT) PAC

Sitton to CROT PAC	Date	CROT PAC to Sitton
$20,000	3/26/14	
$40,000	4/30/14	
	5/1/14	$36,994
$140,000	5/9/14	$142,137
	5/12/14	$16,801
$230,000	5/15/14	$200,755
$430,000	**Totals**	**$396,687**

Dakotas, Warren serves as an Abbott-appointed Texas Parks and Wildlife commissioner.

By contrast, petroleum engineer and Libertarian candidate Mark Miller, whom several newspapers are endorsing as the most qualified current candidate, took just 1 percent of his $126,007 war chest from oil and gas interests. Miller's top support comes from Libertarian-leaning tech contributors.

Industry domination is not the Railroad Commission's only chronic, serious problem. Another is that voters select the leaders of this low profile yet powerful and misnamed agency. The Railroad Commission's 1891 founder, populist Governor Jim Hogg, specifically put it under the direction of gubernatorial appointees for fear that wealthy railroad barons would buy too much influence with elected commissioners. Three years later, lawmakers turned the commission into the elected office that Hogg rejected. As the agency's role morphed from overseeing railroads to regulating the energy industry, the industry bankrolling the commissioners changed—but the agency's name didn't. As a result, commissioners are picked by voters who think the agency does something with trains. These confused voters base their selections on little more than party labels and candidate names.

Voter reliance on candidate names can be disconcerting. By besting two better-funded candidates in the 2016 Democratic primary, Grady Yarbrough fed rumors that voters simply associated his surname with that of the late populist Democratic Congressman Ralph Yarbrough. Similarly, some insiders wondered if Railroad Commission staff scientist Lance Christian was recruited to run in the 2016

Table 14.4 Top Contributors to the Three Commissioners and Four Candidates

Amount	Contributor (Affiliation)	City	Industry
$625,937	Tom Craddick Campaign	Midland	Other
$396,687	Conservative Republicans of TX	Houston	Ideological/Single Issue
$297,890	Syed Javaid & Vicky Anwar (Midland Energy)	Midland	Energy/Nat'l Resources
$271,000	James L. Davis (West TX Gas/J. L. Davis Gas)	Midland	Energy/Nat'l Resources
$256,133	Mickey L. & R. Renee Long (Westex Well Services)	Midland	Energy/Nat'l Resources
$215,000	Terry G. & Pam Bailey (High Roller Wells)	Center	Energy/Nat'l Resources
$190,115	Kelcy L. & Amy Warren (Energy Transfer Partners)	Dallas	Energy/Nat'l Resources
$140,000	Trammell S. & Margaret Crow (Crow Holdings)	Dallas	Real Estate
$134,500	Good Government Fund	Fort Worth	Energy/Nat'l Resources
$125,000	Trevor & Janice Rees-Jones (Chief Oil & Gas)	Dallas	Energy/Nat'l Resources
$120,646	Texas Oil & Gas Assn.	Austin	Energy/Nat'l Resources
$112,000	James C. & Paula Henry (Henry Petroleum)	Midland	Energy/Nat'l Resources
$110,148	Julia Jones Matthews (Dodge Jones Foundation)	Abilene	Energy/Nat'l Resources
$109,500	Dian Owen Graves Stai (Owen Healthcare)	Abilene	Health
$107,184	Chris Faulkner (Breitling Energy)	Dallas	Energy/Nat'l Resources
$107,000	Parsley Coffin Renner LLP	Austin	Lawyers & Lobbyists
$105,500	Robert R. Beecherl (Piedra Resources/Verdad Oil)	Midland	Energy/Nat'l Resources
$101,000	Atmos Energy Corp.	Dallas	Energy/Nat'l Resources
$97,380	Donald E. & Lynne Wood (Permian Enterprises)	Odessa	Energy/Nat'l Resources
$91,937	James D. & Charlotte Finley (Finley Resources)	Fort Worth	Energy/Nat'l Resources
$85,000	Jeffery D. & Mindy Hildebrand (Hilcorp Energy Co.)	Houston	Energy/Nat'l Resources
$80,500	Frosty & Rhonda Gilliam (Aghorn Energy)	Odessa	Energy/Nat'l Resources
$80,000	Jack Wood (Western National Bank)	Odessa	Finance
$77,500	Cody & Tara Campbell (Double Eagle Dev.)	Fort Worth	Energy/Nat'l Resources
$75,000	Stephen & Patricia Chazen (Occidental Petroleum)	Pac. Pal.	Energy/Nat'l Resources
$75,000	Grass Roots Institute of Texas	Arlington	Ideological/Single Issue
$70,000	Timothy & Terri Dunn (CrownQuest/Enerquest Oil)	Midland	Energy/Nat'l Resources
$68,445	Loyd W Powell (Cholla Petroleum)	Dallas	Energy/Nat'l Resources
$65,000	Anne W. & John L. Marion (Burnett Oil Co.)	Fort Worth	Energy/Nat'l Resources
$63,000	Rosalind R. & Arden Grover (Grover McKinney Oil)	Midland	Energy/Nat'l Resources
$62,500	Charles "Dick" Saulsbury (Saulsbury Industries)	Odessa	Energy/Nat'l Resources
$61,145	T. Chris Cooper (Oilfield Water Logistics)	Dallas	Energy/Nat'l Resources
$60,500	Andrew Leslie Ballard (Ballard Exploration Co.)	Houston	Energy/Nat'l Resources
$60,000	Chesapeake Energy Corp.	OK City	Energy/Nat'l Resources
$55,000	Ray & Nancy Ann Hunt (Hunt Consolidated)	Dallas	Energy/Nat'l Resources
$55,000	Mackie McCrea (Energy Transfer Partners)	San Antonio	Energy/Nat'l Resources
$53,000	Blackridge Consulting	Austin	Lawyers & Lobbyists
$52,800	Energy Transfer Partners	Dallas	Energy/Nat'l Resources
$51,500	Fasken Oil & Ranch	Midland	Energy/Nat'l Resources

$50,000	Dustin Bailey (CenTex Frac-Tanks)	Center	Energy/Nat'l Resources
$50,000	Courtney & Margaret Cowden (KC Operating)	Midland	Energy/Nat'l Resources
$50,000	Patrick J. Moran (Moran Exploration)	Houston	Energy/Nat'l Resources
$50,000	Scott Douglas & Kim Sheffield (Pioneer Nat'l Res.)	Irving	Energy/Nat'l Resources
$50,000	Harold C. Simmons (Contran Corp)	Dallas	Finance

Note: Above contributors gave $5,215,447, or 42 percent of what the seven politicians raised.

GOP primary to confuse voters at the expense of Wayne Christian (Gary Gates beat Wayne Christian by 9 percentage points in the seven-person primary but Wayne Christian narrowly beat Gates in a two-man runoff). Many observers also believe that ethnic bias alone led GOP primary voters to replace incumbent Commissioner Victor Carrillo in 2010 with now-retiring Commissioner David Porter. Is this any way to run a railroad?

Will the Sun Set on Commission Conflicts?

Ordinary voters who elect the commissioners have a negligible role in bankrolling their campaigns. More than 90 percent of the money raised by the three sitting commissioners and by Commissioner-elect Wayne Christian came in checks of $1,000 or more. Horse-choking checks of $10,000 or more accounted for anywhere from one-third to two-thirds of the money that these four politicians raised.

These and other structural problems have given the Railroad Commission bad marks with the Texas Sunset Advisory Commission. It typically reviews state agencies every 12 years to determine if they return good taxpayer value, need reform or should

be abolished altogether. The Railroad Commission has received such poor reviews that it is currently undergoing its third Sunset review since 2010.

The latest Sunset staff report again slams the agency's deceptive name, calling for its rechristening as the "Texas Energy Resources Commission." It also suggests that the agency's case hearings and gas-utility rate cases could be done more professionally and transparently by the State Office of Administrative Hearings and the Public Utility Commission, respectively. Sunset staff argue that spinning off these functions would allow the commission to focus scarce resources on core functions such as enforcement, plugging abandoned wells and ensuring pipeline safety. Sunset staff argue that major agency changes are needed to improve pipeline safety, increase bonding requirements for new oil and gas drilling, and most importantly, to devise a plan to beef up inspection and enforcement efforts.

The 2013 Sunset staff report was even harder hitting. It recommended that commissioners be banned from taking money from parties involved in the agency's contested cases. It said that commissioners should just raise money during an

Table 14.5 Contributions by Check Size

Candidate (Party)	Checks <$1,000	%	Checks $1,000–$9,999	%	Checks ≥$10,000	%	All Itemized Contributions
Craddick (R)	$416,071	9%	$2,321,402	48%	$2,136,720	44%	$4,874,193
Sitton (R)	$99,003	3%	$1,169,477	32%	$2,420,188	66%	$3,688,668
Porter (R)	$209,320	8%	$1,504,731	59%	$844,500	33%	$2,558,551
Christian (R)	$87,397	8%	$450,990	41%	$572,500	52%	$1,110,887
Miller (L)	$25,807	20%	$20,200	16%	$80,000	63%	$126,007
Salinas (G)	$4,862	100%	$0	0%	$0	0%	$4,862
Yarbrough (D)	$0	NA	$0	NA	$0	NA	$0
Totals	**$842,460**	**7%**	**$5,466,800**	**44%**	**$6,053,908**	**49%**	**$12,363,168**

Note: Some percentages don't total 100% due to rounding.

18-month period surrounding an election (instead of throughout most of their six-year terms). That report also recommended that commissioners be forced to resign to run for another office and that the agency should develop rules to prevent informal, *ex parte* discussions of contested cases. The staff's more modest proposals this round may reflect an implicit recognition that the lawmakers charged with reforming the agency are themselves subject to considerable industry pressure. Indeed, some of the 10 lawmakers reviewing the latest Sunset staff report at a hearing in August 2016 took the Sunset staff to task for criticizing the agency. The "oil and gas industry is the heart and soul of the state of Texas," said Republican Rep. Dan Flynn. "And for us to go and attack an agency that's done a pretty good job, it just doesn't make sense to me."

In his classic 1981 study,[3] University of Texas professor David Prindle analyzed contributions to the six men who won 12 Railroad Commission elections from 1962 through 1978. Just looking at checks of $500 or more, Prindle found that the commissioners raised a *total* of $976,813 to win those 12 races (a now-quaint average of $81,400 per victory). The oil and gas industry supplied 69 percent of that total. Prindle concluded that the industry selected its regulators by ensuring that their candidates typically had 20 times more money than the combined totals of their opponents. Financial supremacy, he concluded, let industry candidates buy decisive name recognition in a low-profile, statewide race. Two major changes have occurred since Prindle published. First, the amounts of money involved have skyrocketed. Second, in Prindle's day the Democratic nominee always won, whereas in recent decades Republican nominees always prevail.[4] Texas can do much better than this ludicrous approach to regulating its energy industry.

NOTES

1. Another top donor is Jack Wood of Midland's Western National Bank, a major lender to the energy industry before and after Frost Bank bought it out.

2. Sitton and his consultants may have decided that having the Conservative Republicans of Texas promote Sitton would be more effective than Sitton promoting himself. Regardless of intent, the *effect* of these transactions was to make a wad of Sitton's petro contributions look like ideological contributions on his campaign finance reports.

3. "Petroleum Politics and the Texas Railroad Commission," David Prindle, University of Texas Press, Austin 1981.

4. Republican Barry Williamson beat resume-inflating Democratic Railroad Commissioner Lena Guerrero in 1992.

Data Appendix

Table 14.6 Contributions to Three Sitting Railroad Commissioners by Industry

Amount	Percent	Industry
*$6,999,303	*63%	*Energy/Nat'l Resources
$797,069	7%	Lawyers & Lobbyists
$712,781	6%	Other
$555,216	5%	Finance
$540,672	5%	Ideological/Single Issue
$347,367	3%	Real Estate
$258,175	2%	Construction
$221,335	2%	Miscellaneous Business
$206,239	2%	Unknown
$166,334	1%	Health
$133,827	1%	Agriculture
$90,850	1%	Transportation
$41,793	<1%	Communications
$37,850	<1%	Insurance
$12,600	<1%	Computers & Electronics
$11,121,412	**100%**	**Total**

*Includes electricity and solid waste interests not included in regulated-industry totals.

Table 14.7   Top Contributors to Commissioner Christi Craddick (July 2011 Through June 2016)

Amount	Contributor (Affiliation)	City	Industry
$625,937	Tom Craddick Campaign	Midland	Other
$205,390	Syed Javaid & Vicky Anwar (Midland Energy)	Midland	Energy/Nat'l Resources
$90,000	James L. Davis (West TX Gas/J. L. Davis Gas)	Midland	Energy/Nat'l Resources
$80,718	Mickey & Renee Long (Westex Well Services)	Midland	Energy/Nat'l Resources
$75,000	Trevor D. & Janice Rees-Jones (Chief Oil & Gas)	Dallas	Energy/Nat'l Resources
$67,380	Donald & Lynne Wood (Permian Enterprises)	Odessa	Energy/Nat'l Resources
$51,000	Blackridge Consulting	Austin	Lawyers & Lobbyists
$50,000	Terry & Pam Bailey (High Roller Wells)	Center	Energy/Nat'l Resources
$50,000	Kelcy & Amy Warren (Energy Transfer Partners)	Dallas	Energy/Nat'l Resources
$50,000	Jack Wood (Western National Bank)	Odessa	Finance
$45,420	Gary H. & Bev Martin (R. J. Mach./Falcon Bay Energy)	Midland	Energy/Nat'l Resources
$40,000	Rosalind & Arden Grover (Grover McKinney Oil)	Midland	Energy/Nat'l Resources
$40,000	S. Kirk Rogers (S. K. Rogers Oil)	Levelland	Energy/Nat'l Resources
$39,500	Good Government Fund	Fort Worth	Energy/Nat'l Resources
$37,000	Carlton "Carty" Beal (BTA Oil Producers)	Midland	Energy/Nat'l Resources
$36,000	Atmos Energy Corp.	Dallas	Energy/Nat'l Resources
$36,000	Parsley Coffin Renner LLP	Austin	Lawyers & Lobbyists
$35,000	Jeffery & Mindy Hildebrand (Hilcorp Energy)	Houston	Energy/Nat'l Resources
$35,000	Al G. Hill (A. G. Hill Partners)	Dallas	Energy/Nat'l Resources

Note: Above contributors gave $1,689,346, or 35 percent of what Christi Craddick raised.

Table 14.8   Top Contributors to Commissioner Ryan Sitton (Sept. 2013 Through June 2016)

Amount	Contributor (Affiliation)	City	Industry
$396,687	Conservative Republicans of TX	Houston	Ideological/Single Issue
$160,415	Mickey & Renee Long (Westex Well Services)	Midland	Energy/Nat'l Resources
$105,000	Trammell & Margaret Crow Holdings)	Dallas	Real Estate
$100,000	Chris Faulkner (Breitling Energy)	Dallas	Energy/Nat'l Resources
$80,115	Kelcy L. & Amy Warren (Energy Transfer Partners)	Dallas	Energy/Nat'l Resources
$75,000	Robert Beecherl (Piedra Resources/Verdad Oil)	Midland	Energy/Nat'l Resources
$75,000	Frosty & Rhonda Gilliam (Aghorn Energy)	Odessa	Energy/Nat'l Resources
$55,000	Syed Javaid & Vicky Anwar (Midland Energy)	Midland	Energy/Nat'l Resources
$53,648	Julia Jones Matthews (Dodge Jones Foundation)	Abilene	Energy/Nat'l Resources
$53,000	Dian Owen Graves Stai (Owen Healthcare)	Abilene	Health
$50,000	Cody & Tara Campbell (Double Eagle Dev.)	Fort Worth	Energy/Nat'l Resources

continued

Table 14.8 *continued*

Amount	Contributor (Affiliation)	City	Industry
$50,000	James L. Davis (West TX Gas/J. L. Davis Gas)	Midland	Energy/Nat'l Resources
$50,000	Trevor & Janice Rees-Jones (Chief Oil & Gas)	Dallas	Energy/Nat'l Resources
$40,000	James & Paula Henry (Henry Petroleum)	Midland	Energy/Nat'l Resources
$35,000	Lewis Burleson Properties	Midland	Energy/Nat'l Resources
$32,500	Tim & Terri Dunn (CrownQuest/Enerquest Oil)	Midland	Energy/Nat'l Resources
$32,500	Charles "Dick" Saulsbury (Saulsbury Industries)	Odessa	Energy/Nat'l Resources
$31,000	T. Boone Pickens (B. P. Capital)	Dallas	Finance

Note: Above contributors gave $1,474,865, or 40 percent of what Sitton raised.

Table 14.9   Top Contributors to Commissioner David Porter (Jan. 2010 Through June 2016)

Amount	Contributor (Affiliation)	City	Industry
$116,000	James L. Davis (West TX Gas/J. L. Davis Gas)	Midland	Energy/Nat'l Resources
$75,000	Grass Roots Institute of Texas	Arlington	Ideological/Single Issue
$60,000	Kelcy & Amy Warren (Energy Transfer Partners)	Dallas	Energy/Nat'l Resources
$57,500	Good Government Fund	Fort Worth	Energy/Nat'l Resources
$56,000	Parsley Coffin Renner	Austin	Lawyers & Lobbyists
$49,500	Courtney & Margaret Cowden (KC Operating)	Midland	Energy/Nat'l Resources
$44,437	James & Charlotte Finley (Finley Resources)	Fort Worth	Energy/Nat'l Resources
$42,445	Loyd W Powell (Cholla Petroleum)	Dallas	Energy/Nat'l Resources
$37,975	Linda Cowden (rancher)	Midland	Agriculture
$37,500	James & Paula Henry (Henry Petroleum)	Midland	Energy/Nat'l Resources
$35,000	Atmos Energy Corp.	Dallas	Energy/Nat'l Resources
$35,000	Trammell & Margaret Crow (Crow Holdings)	Dallas	Real Estate
$35,000	Harold C. Simmons (Contran Corp.)	Dallas	Finance
$30,000	Oscar Leo Quintanilla (Quintanilla Mgmt.)	San Antonio	Energy/Nat'l Resources
$27,500	Syed Javaid & Vicky Anwar (Midland Energy)	Midland	Energy/Nat'l Resources
$27,500	Tim & Terri Dunn (CrownQuest/Enerquest Oil)	Midland	Energy/Nat'l Resources
$25,000	Energy Transfer Partners	Houston	Energy/Nat'l Resources
$25,000	Jeffery & Mindy Hildebrand (Hilcorp Energy)	Houston	Energy/Nat'l Resources
$25,000	Anne & John Marion (Burnett Oil Co.)	Fort Worth	Energy/Nat'l Resources
$25,000	Patrick J. Moran (Moran Exploration)	Houston	Energy/Nat'l Resources
$25,000	Oilfield Water Logistics (OWL)	Dallas	Energy/Nat'l Resources

Note: Above contributors gave $891,357, or 35 percent of what Porter raised.

Table 14.10   Contributions to Four Railroad Commission Candidates by Industry

Amount	Percent	Industry
*$814,278	*66%	*Energy/Nat'l Resources
$99,156	8%	Ideological/Single Issue
$55,515	4%	Lawyers & Lobbyists
$55,001	4%	Unknown
$51,700	4%	Computers & Electronics
$39,450	3%	Agriculture
$30,771	2%	Communications
$24,032	2%	Health
$19,450	2%	Finance
$19,253	2%	Other
$17,000	1%	Construction
$6,750	1%	Miscellaneous Business
$3,700	<1%	Real Estate
$3,350	<1%	Insurance
$2,350	<1%	Transportation
$1,241,756	**100%**	**Total**

*Includes electricity and solid waste interests not included in regulated-industry totals.

Table 14.11   Top Contributors to Candidate Wayne Christian (Sept. 2013 Through Oct. 2016)

Amount	Contributor (Affiliation)	City	Industry
$155,000	Terry G. & Pam Bailey (High Roller Wells)	Center	Energy/Nat'l Resources
$51,145	T. Chris Cooper (Oilfield Water Logistics)	Dallas	Energy/Nat'l Resources
$50,646	Texas Oil & Gas Assn.	Austin	Energy/Nat'l Resources
$50,000	Dustin Bailey (CenTex Frac-Tanks)	Center	Energy/Nat'l Resources
$32,400	Texans for Lawsuit Reform	Austin	Ideological/Single Issue
$25,000	Stephen & Patricia Chazen (Occidental Petro.)	Pac. Pal. CA	Energy/Nat'l Resources
$20,000	James C. & Paula Henry (Henry Petroleum)	Midland	Energy/Nat'l Resources
$20,000	NGL Energy Operating	Tulsa, OK	Energy/Nat'l Resources
$15,000	AT&T, Inc.	Austin	Communications
$15,000	Chesapeake Energy Corp.	OK City	Energy/Nat'l Resources
$15,000	James L. Davis (West TX Gas/J. L. Davis Gas)	Midland	Energy/Nat'l Resources
$15,000	Laszlo & Adel Karalyos (GAIA Clearwater Corp)	Dallas	Energy/Nat'l Resources
$15,000	Marathon Oil Corp.	Houston	Energy/Nat'l Resources
$15,000	Anne W. & John L. Marion (Burnett Oil Co.)	Fort Worth	Energy/Nat'l Resources
$12,500	Exxon Mobil Corp.	Irving	Energy/Nat'l Resources
$12,500	Good Government Fund	Fort Worth	Energy/Nat'l Resources
$11,333	Young Conservatives of TX	Austin	Ideological/Single Issue
$10,300	Energy Transfer Partners	Houston	Energy/Nat'l Resources

Note: Above contributors gave $540,824, or 49 percent of what Christian raised.

Table 14.12   Top Contributors to Candidate Mark Miller (June 2014 Through Oct. 2016)

Amount	Contributor (Affiliation)	City	Industry
$42,000	Michael Chastain (retired software eng.)	Austin	Computers & Electronics
$20,000	Libertarian National Committee	Washington	Ideological/Single Issue
$20,000	Chris Rufer (Morning Star Co.)	Woodland CA	Agriculture
$6,700	Joel T. Trammell (Khorus)	Austin	Computers & Electronics
$2,832	Gil Robinson (retired doctor)	San Antonio	Health
$2,500	David M. Capshaw (AT&T)	Austin	Communications
$2,500	James M. Keller (photographer)	San Antonio	Communications
$1,000	Roxanne Elder (asset manager)	Austin	Finance
$1,000	David Hutzelman (Houston Media Source)	Houston	Communications
$1,000	Libertarian Party of Bexar County	San Antonio	Ideological/Single Issue
$1,000	Geoffrey Neale (Genama)	Bee Cave	Computers & Electronics
$1,000	Dixon Patrick (Dixon Process Automation)	Lago Vista	Misc. Business
$1,000	Paul Petersen (IT consultant)	Dallas	Computers & Electronics
$1,000	Kwaku Temeng (Aramco Services Co.)	Houston	Energy/Nat'l Resources

Note: Above contributors gave $103,532, or 82 percent of what Miller raised.

Table 14.13   Top Contributors to Candidate Martina Salinas (June 2014 Through Oct. 2016)

Amount	Contributor (Affiliation)	City	Industry
$2,332	Harris Co. Green Party	Houston	Ideological/Single Issue
$500	Wesson Gaige (retired)	Denton	Unknown
$500	Cristobal Rodriquez (Vaqueros night club)	Laredo	Misc. Business

Note: Above contributors gave $3,332, or 69 percent of what Salinas raised.

ARTICLE QUESTIONS

1) What are some of the connections between the industry and the agency the report's authors identify?
2) Are you persuaded by the report's description of cozy connections between the agency and the industry?
3) The report points to reforms recommended by the Sunset Commission. Do you believe that these reforms would resolve the conflict of interest issues?

Chapter 15

Criminal Justice in Texas

Criminal justice in Texas is carried out at the tense intersection of politics, personal freedom, and concerns about law and order. Crime and punishment issues are often filtered through the lens of state politics as candidates for office maneuver around a Texas public hostile to criminals but wary of punishing the innocent. The struggle to promote justice and punish criminals clashes with issues of fairness, racial equity in the application of laws, and enforceability. State officials face pressure to maintain stable order without eliminating protections that ensure equality and fairness.

Texans generally revere their law enforcement officers, believing them a critical frontline of defense against crime. The historical legacy of this view runs deep. The Texas Rangers, the state's oldest law enforcement agency, trace their roots back to Stephen F. Austin's call for a "group of rangers for the common defense" to defend the Texas frontier against attacks by Native Americans in 1823. Since then, the heritage of the Rangers has combined swift justice and punishment with outrages involving unnecessary use of force.

Texans have historically taken a tough stance on crime and criminals. Texas prides itself on its "tough on crime" attitude and "hang 'em high" approach to punishment. Nevertheless, pressure from both within and outside the system has led Texas to become a leader in reforming the criminal justice system. Michael Haugen, a policy analyst for Right on Crime at the Texas Public Policy Foundation, describes several ways that legislators have sought to remedy the problems associated with outmoded criminal justice policies. At the root of such troubles are legal issues associated with detaining individuals before trial and the financial burden to the state of doing so. Making the system more efficient and less expensive, Haugen finds, runs against the state's former "lock-'em-up" mentality but would improve the criminal justice system.

The legislature, seeking some control over the prison system, voted in 1842 to provide funds for the construction of a state penitentiary. Prisons were largely expected to become self-sufficient by growing crops or manufacturing items to generate revenue. Since then, the prison system has grown and shrunk while also adapting to new trends and responding to civil rights concerns. Most of the changes in the prison system that have occurred have been political, as elected and appointed officials shape the prison system in response to their political ideology.

Haugen argues that the state has saved billions of dollars by "thinking outside the cell." Texas has managed to reduce recidivism (criminal re-offending) and the number of prisons at the same time. Policies like graduated sanctions, curfews, extended probation, electronic monitoring, weekend jail, and diversion programs aim to divert people away from prisons while maintaining strict standards. Haugen argues that Texas's famed "tough on crime" philosophy should give way to one in which "necessity is the mother of all invention."

Texas's criminal justice system is not perfect. The system is complex, and on occasion, mistakes are made. Witnesses' memories of an event may be faulty, or police and prosecutors may become enamored with a certain story of the events, making charges without foundation stick and sending innocent individuals to prison. Texas Public Radio's Christopher Connelly explores the efforts of one former convict, who was sentenced to death but later exonerated, to help overturn convictions of wrongly incarcerated individuals. His personal experience led him to work to reform what he describes as Texas's "badly flawed" criminal justice system. Getting rid of the death penalty would remove one major problem, Connelly argues, but most Texans still approve of the practice, although the number of executions is lower than it has been in twenty years. Connelly suggests that there are many wrongfully convicted individuals in Texas prisons, but legislative changes to the legal system and improved DNA technology may provide more protections for the innocent.

State officials, often responding to public outcry, have often been punitive and harsh when dealing with criminals. But should such an attitude extend to Twitter? The *Texas Tribune*'s Madlin Mekelburg reports on a new rule from the Texas Department of Criminal Justice that limits Texas prisoners' use of social media, such as Facebook, Twitter, and Instagram, even if friends or family outside the prison run them. The department argues that this measure was adopted for security reasons, but opponents claim it limits free speech. In a world where social media serves as a critical connection between a person's community and environment, should prisoners be banned from accessing such outlets?

CHAPTER QUESTIONS

1) If Texas favors a "tough on crime" and "law and order" approach to criminal justice, why has it been the epicenter for many recent reforms?
2) What flaws or problems in the criminal justice system have prompted efforts to reform the system?
3) Are the solutions described by the authors sufficient in your view to remedy the problems in Texas's criminal justice system?

15.1) Right on Crime: Ten Years of Criminal Justice Reform

Texas Public Policy Foundation, 2017

MICHAEL HAUGEN

Texas's famed "tough on crime" sentencing policies came with high costs: punitive approaches for offenders and large expenses for taxpayers. Although jail populations ebb and flow monthly, they surged in the early 2000s, costing taxpayers more to house these individuals. Such ballooning costs were not tenable in a tight Texas budget, so legislators passed a "justice reinvestment" package to address this critical issue.

Michael Haugen, a policy analyst for the Texas Public Policy Foundation, argues that Texas has drawn acclaim for these efforts, which have led to the closing of prisons and a drop in crime. For Haugen, the prison issue is a fiscal issue, one that can be solved by more imaginative criminal justice policies. Many incarcerated individuals are low-level, nonviolent offenders, and many have mental illness or substance abuse problems. Several strategies to address these specialized jail populations have been attempted in recent years.

"Back-end" reforms to parole policies and community supervision programs have also had positive effects, with the expansion of drug courts, substance abuse programs, and diversion programs leading to the closure of four prisons and tens of millions of dollars saved. Here Haugen writes for a conservative policy foundation under the title "Right on Crime," but the solutions he describes were often supported by a bipartisan cast of legislators. Too, the outcomes that have been produced—lower recidivism, a reduction in crime rates, and less costly criminal justice programs—have been embraced by both parties.

If one were to search for an example to prove correct the old English proverb that "necessity is the mother of all invention," they could do no better than to look towards the pickle that Texas found itself in a decade ago with its burgeoning prison population.

Throughout much of the state's history, the question of what to do about criminal wrongdoing had a fairly straightforward answer: lock 'em up. Decades of "tough-on-crime" sentencing policies emphasized a punitive, carceral approach, especially as crime reached a fever-pitch throughout the 1970's and 80's. Coupled with a lack of faith on the part of judges and prosecutors in the effectiveness of potential alternatives to incarceration, Texas' prison population ballooned to well over 150,000 inmates by the early 2000's.

What to do with all of these offenders had a simple answer, as well: build more prisons. Certain realities have a habit of asserting themselves, however. And in the case of Texas' criminal justice system, the clock had finally run out on the efficacy of the just-build-more-prisons model—both in terms of simple economics and achieving good outcomes.

In 2007, the Texas Legislature faced an urgent situation. The Legislative Budget Board estimated that, in just five years' time, the state would need to build as many as 17,000 additional prison beds to keep pace with its growing rate of incarceration—at a cost of more than $2 billion. In a legislative session featuring an already tight budget, there was no longer any enthusiasm for continuing to construct costly new prisons—particularly when stubbornly high recidivism rates signaled the diminishing returns of simply warehousing offenders.

Then-House Speaker Tom Craddick's instructions to Jerry Madden—the then newly-appointed chairman of the House Corrections Committee and a current Right on Crime senior fellow—were simple: "Don't build new prisons, they cost too much."

Instead of signing off on a massive taxpayer bill, state leaders studied the drivers of prison growth and researched effective approaches to reducing recidivism. Legislators heard testimony from prosecutors and judges stating that low-risk, nonviolent offenders were often sent to prison for lack of effective alternatives. These criminal-justice professionals cited unwieldy probation caseloads along with lengthy waiting lists for drug courts or mental health treatment options, which make it difficult to supervise and treat offenders effectively.

After completing their lengthy survey, legislators came up with and adopted a stark alternative: an historic $241 million "justice reinvestment" package for treatment and diversion programs designed to stop prison expansion while protecting public safety. The front-end reform items included 800 new residential substance abuse treatment beds and 3,000 more outpatient substance abuse treatment slots — all to be used as initial options after sentencing and for those whose addiction problems undermine their compliance with community supervision.

Back-end reforms were no less substantial, and equally important. While examining drivers of prison growth, lawmakers discovered that the Board of Pardons and Paroles had been paroling offenders at a lower-than-possible clip because they lacked confidence that inmates were receiving necessary treatment in prison. The Board was also revoking a growing number of parolees because they had few other options. In fact, thousands of inmates approved for parole had to be wait-listed for either halfway houses or in-prison treatment programs. The result? Overflowing prisons.

So lawmakers filled the gap, adding 2,700 substance abuse treatment beds behind bars, 1,400 new intermediate sanction beds (a short-term program for those offenders who commit technical violations), and 300 halfway-house beds. They also capped parole caseloads at 75 to ensure closer supervision.

For a state system that had previously responded to capacity shortfalls by simply building new prisons, these reforms were a paradigm shift—and have exceeded expectations, both for public safety and cost control. Not only has the state averted the need to construct thousands of new prison beds and bolstered confidence in alternatives, but for the first time in its history, Texas is *closing* facilities: four adult units have been shuttered already, with an additional four slated for closure with the signature of the 2018–2019 budget into law.

Expanding treatment and community supervision capacity is great. Closing prisons is great. But achieving better public safety outcomes is the true measure of success, and Texas has been delivering.

In 2007, almost 16 percent of probationers failed and were revoked to prison. This figure fell to 14.7 percent by 2015. Thus, as more nonviolent offenders were diverted to community supervision instead of prison, probation success rates climbed. This likely stemmed from several factors, namely improved supervision—for instance, the use of graduated sanctions such as curfews to promote compliance—and court officials' assessment that many of these individuals could succeed given the right resources in the community.

The gains in parole are even more impressive: Even with 11,000 more people on parole today than in 2007, more than 17 percent fewer crimes are being alleged against parolees now than previously.

And crime rates? Nationwide, the index crime rate fell 20 percent between 2007 and 2014. In Texas, it fell 26 percent. Even more impressively, this occurred while its general population increased and its number of prisons decreased. Simply put, crime and incarceration can be addressed at the same time, and Texas (and other southern red states) have proven it.

Texas hasn't been idle since passing its initial reforms, either, with subsequent legislative sessions building on these earlier successes:

- In 2009, the Texas Department of Criminal Justice was authorized to restore "good time" credits that were previously revoked for minor infractions.
- In 2011, counties were allowed to enroll in performance incentive funding if they met certain requirements such as reducing

prison populations, reducing recidivism, increasing the number of probationers providing victims with restitution, and increasing probationers' employment rates.

- Also in 2011, judges were allowed to give "good time" credits for probationers if they perform certain tasks, such as earning a degree, paying the full amount of restitution, and completing treatment programs.
- In 2015 (and again in 2017, pending Gov. Abbott's signature), orders of nondisclosure were expanded to certain first-time, nonviolent offenders allowing them to seal their criminal records for employment, housing, and other purposes. Studies have consistently shown that proper housing and vocation are critical to successful reentry, and expanding nondisclosure laws will aid in this—while providing a free-market alternative to "ban the box" policies.

As reform efforts in Texas began to bear positive fruit in 2010, the decision was made to "take the show on the road," giving birth to Right on Crime. As the nation's premier conservative criminal justice reform initiative, Right on Crime seeks to leverage research and policy ideas—and mobilize strong conservative voices—to raise awareness of the growing support for effective reforms.

Thanks in part to Right on Crime's efforts since its inception, many other states have realized the utility of those reforms, especially in light of similar budgetary or capacity constraints that Texas experienced. In 2010, South Carolina passed a justice reinvestment package along the same vein of Texas' after lawmakers faced that ol' familiar pickle: change course, or face unacceptable prison population growth.

The results? Again, similar to Texas. The number of inmates has since fallen to under 21,000, and instead of building new prisons, the state has closed six of them—saving $33 million in operating costs.

In 2012, Georgia passed comprehensive adult corrections reforms in an attempt to avert expected population growth. Between 2011 and 2014, the state eliminated virtually all of its previous backlog of newly-sentenced offenders into prison and saved more than $25 million. Over the same period, its violent and property crime rate fell 8 percent, according to the Pew Charitable Trusts.

Alaska, Louisiana, and Maryland have all recently passed similar justice reinvestment packages, which are now informed by a decade's worth of data and experience that originated in large part here in Texas.

Those states that have passed justice reinvestment proposals have continued to see substantial reductions in crime rates and recidivism after their passage, while providing the sort of returns that the public demands of government: cost savings, increased sentencing flexibility for judges, an expansion of treatment beds for substance abuse, greater safety, and opportunities for wrongdoers to atone, get clean, and seize upon second chances.

These are the aims of the Center for Effective Justice and Right on Crime: To breathe some flexibility into a system that's been without it for a long time. We know we can save taxpayers money. We know what works to reduce recidivism. We know that finite prison space should be reserved for those "we're afraid of, not those we're mad at." We know that rehabilitation, not imprisonment, provides better outcomes for those who've fallen under the dark influence of drugs. And we know that, when possible, parents should be present in the lives of their children, rather than sit behind bars as unavailable wards of the state.

To accept the status quo is to accept a system that isn't working as well as it could. This should provide conservatives all the motivation they need to learn about criminal justice and seek to improve it—lest reality intrude to make decisions for us.

Necessity is the mother of all invention? Indeed, it can be. But *invention* has given way to *experience* in Texas and other states—who have led the nation toward a more free and prosperous future where crime rates remain low and the public enjoys a commitment to justice. Who will be next to learn from that experience?

ARTICLE QUESTIONS

1) What does the author argue the major problems confronting the criminal justice system in Texas were before reform efforts?
2) What programs does the author argue were successful in reducing jail and prison populations?
3) Texans tend to be seen as "tough on crime," but could saving money and promoting efforts to improve the justice system be enough to encourage Texans to embrace these changes?

15.2) What Do Exonerations Tell Us About the Death Penalty and the Criminal Justice System?

Texas Public Radio (KERA), January 26, 2017

CHRISTOPHER CONNELLY

Texas has long been associated with the death penalty. In the 1990s, when the state was cracking down on crime, Texas led the nation in executions. Thirty years later, fewer than 250 people (as of 2018) were on death row and the state put fewer people to death than at any other time in the last two decades. Growing worries about wrongful convictions and the improvement of technology that can help exonerate individuals wrongly accused of crimes has increased efforts to find justice for innocent people who have been incarcerated.

Radio station KERA's Christopher Connelly explores the story of one former convict who had been sentenced to death. Anthony Graves spent eighteen and a half years behind bars for a crime he didn't commit, and after he was released, he started a foundation to reexamine other questionable death sentences handed down by Texas juries. These efforts, along with those by other groups, have led to more than 300 exonerations since 1989. The state legislature has also investigated many of these issues in response to growing public concern. Will these high-profile mistakes lead the state to reform its use of the death penalty?

Texas is slated to execute Terry Edwards on Thursday evening. Barring an unexpected reprieve, Edwards will be the second man executed by the state this year. In Texas, 242 people sit on death row awaiting execution. Long the leading executioner in the U.S., the Lone Star State put to death fewer people last year than it has in two decades.

Death row is reserved for criminals who commit the most serious crimes, but Anthony Graves says not everyone who is sentenced to death is guilty. He should know. He spent almost two decades incarcerated after he was wrongfully convicted of murder. Most of those years were on death row, awaiting execution.

Graves was released from prison in 2010, after spending 18.5 years behind bars for a murder that he didn't commit.

"I always tell people don't forget the half, that was six more months," he said.

In 1992, Graves was wrongfully convicted as an accomplice to murder in the tiny town of Somerville, Texas. The murderer told police Graves helped him kill six people and burn down their house. The murderer later recanted, but the prosecutor proceeded to charge Graves, who was convicted and sentenced to death by the state of Texas. Graves said each day of his existence on death row was a grueling replay of the one before it.

"There was no life there," Graves said. "It was just waking up every day behind a 6-by-9 cage, no television, no nothing, just waiting to be executed."

Graves spent most of his time almost completely isolated. His only physical contact with other humans came when guards put on and took off his shackles to take him, alone, to the caged-off outdoor recreation area, or to the shower. One day, a decade or so into his sentence, Graves was shackled and taken to the prison warden's office. He told Graves that his execution was officially scheduled.

"It was just mind-boggling to me that this man was sitting across from me telling me that they're going to kill me for something I know absolutely nothing about. And how am I supposed to process this and then continue to carry on?" Graves recalls.

That execution was postponed, and Graves saw his execution scheduled and postponed again before his conviction was finally overturned. Four years later, Anthony Graves was exonerated and released. The prosecutor who put him in prison was later disbarred.

Now, Graves runs a foundation that re-examines questionable convictions and sentences, and sits on the board of the independent Houston crime lab that processes crime scene evidence. He's writing a book about his experience—he plans to call it "Infinite Hope"—and he has become an advocate for criminal justice reforms. These days, Anthony Graves says he has a good life. He lives in a large house on a tree-lined street in a nice neighborhood in Houston, with his dog named Papi.

"He is a Chihuahua mixed with a pit [bull]—don't ask me how that happened," Graves said, laughing. "I saw him on 'doggy oodles,' and I felt like I need to rescue him."

Graves' is far from an isolated case, says Innocence Project of Texas director Mike Ware, and his case exposes some of the problems that lead to wrongful convictions.

"What my experience has taught me is that there are many undetected wrongful convictions in Texas prisons," Ware said. "And I know that because I know when we look for them we find them."

More than 300 people have been exonerated in Texas since 1989. Together, they spent more than 1,700 years behind bars. Most exonerees weren't on death row, but 13 of them—including Anthony Graves—were.

Exonerations have skyrocketed in recent years. Part of that is science: more use of DNA evidence, and changes in accepted forensics science on arson, bite marks and other areas of expertise. Many prosecutors' offices have formed units that re-examine potential wrongful conviction cases. The Innocence Project and groups like it also look into questionable cases.

The exonerations have also spurred legislation.

"Exonerations tell us what the causes of wrongful convictions are. If we study them, they're like the black boxes on an airplane. They can tell us what goes wrong," said Nicole Casarez, the lawyer who helped free Anthony Graves. "And Texas has made some changes to address some of those issues," he said.

For instance, the Texas Legislature increased standards for eyewitness identification, which is often central in wrongful conviction cases. In 2013, Texas passed a law requiring prosecutors to turn over any evidence that raises doubt about a defendant's guilt. That year, it also passed a first-of-its-kind bill giving people convicted because of bad or outdated science the right to request a new trial.

More reforms are being proposed in Austin this session. But Casarez said there is a bigger, systemic disparity that the death penalty illuminates.

"There aren't any rich people on death row," Casarez said. "If you are poor, if you are unable to hire good counsel, you're much more likely to end up with the death penalty. And that's something I think we need to be concerned about."

"There's nothing wrong with questioning the process. If it's working well, it ought to withstand inspection," said Sen. John Whitmire, who leads the criminal justice committee in the Texas Senate.

The Houston senator said there are a number of ways the justice system still needs fixing, and he plans to propose more reforms this year.

Still, Whitmire said it's an incredibly complicated system and that people shouldn't look past the vast majority of death row inmates who have conclusively committed terrible crimes.

"I take it very seriously every time someone is executed," he said. "I reflect, I pause. Obviously, we have a responsibility to do it right. But personally, I support the death penalty."

Like Whitmire, 75 percent of Texans support the death penalty, according to a 2015 poll from the Texas Tribune and UT Austin. At the same time, 59 percent said they believe people are occasionally or often wrongfully convicted in death penalty cases.

Mike Ware from the Innocence Project said high-profile exonerations have made people question the infallibility of the criminal justice system.

"People understand that yes, innocent people are charged. And yes, completely innocent people are convicted. And in some circumstances, innocent people are sent to death row. And there have been some circumstances where people have been sent to death row and executed," he said.

While Ware and others point to credible evidence that the state has executed innocent people, there are significant legal, logistical and political barriers to definitively proving innocence after someone has been executed. Many point to the case of Todd Cameron Willingham as likely the clearest-cut example of how bad forensics could have resulted in the execution of an innocent man in Texas. The Death Penalty Information Center keeps a list of possibly innocent people in the US who have been executed.

Anthony Graves said for a lot of people, these are questions that they simply aren't confronted with. That's how it was for him, up until 1992.

"Before this happened to me, I didn't have an opinion about the death penalty," Graves said. "If someone got sentenced to death, well that was our law, so oh well, I didn't have an opinion one way or the other. And then the death penalty knocked on my door."

Still, while most people may not understand exactly how the criminal justice system fails people like him, Graves says there's also a willingness to remain ignorant of the scale of the problem.

"We still don't want to acknowledge that we have a badly flawed justice system, from top to bottom. And it starts with the way we think, and the way we see other people, those who don't look like us. We have to change that mentality before we can get real reform in our criminal justice system," he said.

Graves said reform efforts will always be too small, too weak, and too late until people are ready to grapple with the reality of capital punishment in Texas. In his estimation, the only way to make sure innocent people aren't executed is to get rid of the death penalty altogether.

ARTICLE QUESTIONS

1) What reforms have been put in place in Texas to ensure innocent individuals are not wrongly convicted?
2) Anthony Graves's lawyer argues that "there aren't any rich people on death row." What does she mean by that?
3) The author quotes Graves as saying that the system is "badly flawed," but a vast majority of Texans support the death penalty. Why do you believe this disagreement exists?

15.3) New Prison Rule Means Jailbirds Can't Tweet

Texas Tribune, April 14, 2016

MADLIN MEKELBURG

> In this *Texas Tribune* story, journalist Madlin Mekelburg reports on the Texas Department of Criminal Justice's decision to ban prisoners' use of social media accounts, such as Facebook, Twitter, and Instagram, even if friends or family outside of the prison run them. The department adopted the policy in part because convicted serial killer Elmer Wayne Henley was selling trinkets from prison through a Facebook page operated by someone outside the prison.
>
> Department officials claim the reason for the rule is to improve safety and security, but it has elicited free speech concerns from civil liberties groups. If prisoners and their friends and family on the outside are not allowed to use social media, these groups argue, this prohibition stifles free speech. Others question whether prisons can legally control what happens outside their walls. As the legal director for the Texas Civil Rights Project notes, "Prisons control the things inside the prisons. They don't traditionally get to pass prison policies that extend far beyond the bars."

Texas prison inmates shouldn't be allowed to have active social media accounts, even if friends or family on the outside actually run them, the Texas Department of Criminal Justice has decided.

Earlier this month, the department updated its criminal handbook to prohibit prisoners from having personal pages on Facebook, Twitter or Instagram run in their name by others. When pages violating the policy are discovered, the department plans to report the violations to the appropriate social network.

"What really prompted the rule was that social media companies now require some sort of specific rule in place that's going to prohibit offenders from maintaining their social media accounts," said department spokesman Jason Clark. "I can tell you increasingly it has become more difficult to ask those companies to take it down. They would come back to us and say, 'You don't have a specific policy that says they can't have it.'"

But the new rule is eliciting free-speech concerns from civil liberties groups and raising questions about how friends or family can advocate for inmates.

"I think that while TDCJ may have sincere goals in trying to implement this new policy, it raises very serious concerns about the stifling of free speech and frankly probably reaches far beyond, in terms of its impact," said Wayne Krause Yang, legal director for the Texas Civil Rights Project. "We don't know whether TDCJ is going to attempt to exercise, and has the power to enforce, this policy and against whom. If and when it does, it could present some very serious concerns."

A Facebook representative declined to comment on TDCJ's new prohibition but pointed to the company's policy for removing prisoner accounts when there is "a genuine risk of physical harm." The representative said this risk is demonstrated "by legal authority banning access to social media or by evidence that an inmate's access to our service poses a real-world security risk."

Facebook has a form on its website to submit requests for inmate accounts to be removed.

No specific inmate prompted the new policy, Clark said, but he pointed out that the department recently learned convicted Houston serial killer Elmer Wayne Henley was selling trinkets from prison through a Facebook account operated by another individual.

Clark said analysts with the Office of Inspector General may search for prohibited accounts, but the ban will primarily be enforced when officers within TDCJ catch wind of violations or when victims and their families report them. When an account violating the policy is discovered, Clark said the department will request the network remove it.

If the department finds evidence that an inmate "initiated someone to start and maintain the page," he said, they could be subject to disciplinary action for a "rule violation"—the lowest-level violation.

While the measure is aimed at accounts tied specifically to Texas inmates, Krause Yang said the prison system's reach exceeds its legal grasp.

"Typically, prisons control the things inside the prisons. They don't traditionally get to pass prison policies that extend far beyond the bars, and it seems like that's what they're trying to do here," he said. "Those types of policies have a name—they're called laws. They should be considered by the representatives of the people, too, because this policy doesn't just affect the people behind the bars."

State Rep. Joe Moody, vice chair of the House Criminal Jurisprudence Committee, said the legislature "deserves an opportunity to weigh in on things like this."

"It's not a small policy change," the El Paso Democrat said. "It's been a practice for a long time of inmates writing stuff to folks on the outside to post it on social media sites, and that's been a problem. That's definitely something that can be addressed legislatively."

While he acknowledged the policy could limit inmates' abilities to express themselves, Moody said it addresses just "one mechanism" inmates use to communicate with the outside world.

"There are other avenues that individuals who are incarcerated are able to raise awareness about their case," Moody said, pointing to websites and organizations that share things online on behalf of incarcerated individuals. "This is specifically saying you can't have a person running a social media site in the name of someone who is an inmate."

Gov. Greg Abbott's office declined a request for comment.

Uncertain about the policy's impact, Julie Strickland, a grant writer living in Florida who runs two social media sites for a death row inmate, said she has contacted an attorney for advice on handling her Facebook and Twitter accounts.

Strickland is trying to help free Rodney Reed, convicted of killing a woman during an aggravated sexual assault. Her sites are not run on Reed's behalf, but they include a community Facebook page titled, "Rodney Reed: Innocent on Texas Death Row" and a connected Twitter account.

Strickland said she thinks the policy is "complete bullshit."

"It sounds to me like the only reason they're implementing this is because their actions in the prison, which they like to keep very private, are just becoming way too public, and they don't like that," she said.

ARTICLE QUESTIONS

1) One opponent of the new rule who runs a Facebook page on behalf of a prisoner on death row calls the policy "complete bullshit." Do you agree?

2) What justification do prison officials give for limiting the social media use of incarcerated individuals? Do you agree with their logic?

3) Is the need for safety and control within prisons enough to justify a potential violation of inmates' free speech rights?

Chapter 16

Contemporary Public Policy Issues

Texas has historically been a state of small government and high self-reliance—and Texans by and large like it that way. Several policy issues that have recently been on the state's agenda highlight the Texas way of creating public policy. As with most public policy decisions, all of these choices have supporters and opponents.

Texas shares the longest contiguous border with another country of any state in the union. Consequently, immigration and border security have consistently ranked as Texans' top two concerns over the past several years. But tough talk on illegal immigration does not always translate to all sectors in Texas. *Texas Tribune* investigative reporter Jay Root argues that Texas business interests have partnered with immigration activists to limit the state's enforcement of laws prohibiting industries from hiring illegal workers. This alliance may seem unusual in the political arena, but, according to one lawmaker, big business support was important: "If we can get something done without putting a heavier hand on business, that's kind of the best way to handle it." Root wonders when the dogmatic political rhetoric surrounding illegal immigration will match up to the economic reality.

Immigration enforcement may be lax in the private sector, but legislators have recently been taking a hard look at local governments and their status as "sanctuary cities." In an editorial for *TribTalk*, Representative Paul Workman, a Republican legislator from Austin, examines the phenomenon of the sanctuary city, a local government (city or county) that refuses to cooperate with federal immigration law. Legislation passed and signed by Governor Abbott in 2017 banned local governments from establishing sanctuary cities and allowed law enforcement officers to ask detained individuals about their immigration status (a measure referred to as a "show me your papers" provision). According to Workman, the new law was necessary because the public safety of Texans is critical and local governments should not be allowed to pick and choose the laws they want to enforce.

School finance is another tough political issue the state faces. One veteran observer has remarked that school funding like no other issue "mixes lofty ideas with parochial politics."[1] The Texas Constitution requires the state to provide for "efficient and adequate" funding for its public schools. However, the funding system is complex. Schools are funded by a combination of state general revenue, local property taxes, and some federal taxes. Other funds come from one quarter of the state's motor fuel tax, one quarter of state taxes on the production of fossil fuels, and the state lottery. Finally, the state provides extra funds for students who need more support, such as students learning English, gifted and talented students, and students from low-income families.

Eventually, school finance conflicts got to be so bad that hundreds of school districts sued the state, claiming that the system underfunded schools, prevented Texas students from meeting academic standards, and created big disparities between wealthy and poor districts. The Texas Supreme Court found that the state's school finance system was "imperfect" and with "immense room for improvement" but did meet constitutional requirements. The Court urged the legislature to make transformational changes in response. So, how to fund public schools? Answers to the question underscore the complex situation facing Texas public schools.

One of the state's most revered experts on public school finance, former representative Jimmy Don Aycock, summarizes the state's difficulty in reforming the school finance system. Writing for the *Texas Tribune*, Aycock argues that the challenges of the funding system stem from its variability, depending largely on local property taxes instead of a more stable form of tax like an income tax. Similarly, efforts to comply with court rulings mandating that the state roughly equalize the funds spent per district creates legal controversy as rich school districts are asked to give funds to poor districts and poor districts struggle to educate a rapidly diversifying Texas. Alternatives to the current system all present difficult political choices, but Aycock invites us to think critically and responsibly about how to undertake the tough challenge of saving Texas's public schools.

NOTE

1. Paul Burka, "An F for Effort," *Texas Monthly*, June 2004, http://www.texasmonthly .com/politics/an-f-for-effort-2/.

CHAPTER QUESTIONS

1) Why are there differences in how the state enforces immigration laws depending on the sphere in which the violation occurs?
2) What are three criticisms identified by the authors of how the state is handling the problem of illegal immigration?
3) What problems in financing public schools have caused reform advocates to argue for overhauling the system?
4) The Texas Supreme Court held that the school finance system needed major reform but was not unconstitutional. What solutions for making the system stronger for Texas students have been identified?

16.1) In Texas, Lawmakers Don't Mess with Employers of Undocumented Workers

Texas Tribune, December 14, 2016

JAY ROOT

Despite hardline rhetoric against illegal immigration (which Lieutenant Governor Dan Patrick referred to as an "invasion"), investigative reporter Jay Root of the *Texas Tribune* finds that the same fervor has not been applied to the private workplace. Root describes the ability of private industry to avoid scrutiny regarding the hiring of illegal workers in the agriculture, construction, custodial services, and hospitality industries.

Why, in a state run by a political party so insistent that illegal immigration is a major issue, would Texas look the other way when it comes to clamping down on illegal employment? The reason, Root argues, is simple: powerful business interests rely on this source of labor, and there is bipartisan consensus that the current situation is good for the state's economic bottom line. Workers thus inhabit an underground labor market in which a "don't ask, don't tell" system allows employers to hire them without fear of punishment.

The state could address this issue by legalizing employment of individuals who are currently illegal or by more stringently regulating companies that hire undocumented workers. But legislative paralysis and the demand for illegal labor have made it difficult to build consensus and ultimately impossible, Root claims, to "secure the border."

Few Texas politicians have harnessed anger over illegal immigration like Republican Lt. Gov. Dan Patrick, who rose from talk radio host to powerful state leader largely on the strength of his incessant border security screeds.

Though he once embraced a foreign guest worker program himself, Patrick got elected lieutenant governor in 2014 in part by decrying what he called an "invasion" of disease-carrying immigrants and tying his GOP foes to policies that supposedly draw them here. He went on to become the top Texas cheerleader for immigration hardliner Donald Trump's presidential bid.

But there's one arena in the battles over illegal immigration that Patrick hasn't yet entered as lieutenant governor: the private workplace.

Despite promising during the 2014 race to crack down on Texas employers who hire undocumented workers, it was status quo last session in the state Senate that Patrick oversees. And illegal hiring practices in the Texas workplace, which the state has authority to police, have largely gone missing from his public outrage over the porous border and illegal immigration.

That's not political apostasy. It's the default posture in pro-business Texas—and one of the increasingly rare areas where Republicans and Democrats come together in common cause year after year.

Trump's ascendency to the White House may or may not change the hands-off approach in legislatures and Congress to the illegal hiring practices common in U.S. businesses. It certainly has the potential to shake things up in unprecedented ways—as Patrick and other Republicans gush. But if past performance and recent public pronouncements are any guide, Texas leaders will continue going easy on those who avail themselves of low-cost undocumented immigrant labor—particularly in agriculture, construction, janitorial services and the leisure and hospitality industry.

The reason is simple: Business interests rely on undocumented immigrant workers, while pro-immigrant activists fight to protect the labor rights of those facing abuse and exploitation. When the Chamber of Commerce and the American Civil Liberties Union are on the same side of an issue at the Capitol, they're hard to beat.

"We know what an important part immigrant labor plays in Texas, and to suddenly wipe out large sectors . . . would have a devastating impact on the Texas economy," said Bill Hammond, head of the influential Texas Association of Business, the state's top business advocacy group. "We need immigrant labor to do those tasks where not enough Americans will."

The left-right convergence—bringing businessmen and liberal immigration activists together—has been key in blocking legislation that would make life more difficult for undocumented immigrants in Texas, said Bill Beardall, executive director of the Equal Justice Center, a nonprofit law firm that advocates for immigrants and other low-wage workers in Austin.

"We begin each session of the Legislature highly concerned that some of these anti-immigrant bills are going to pass," Beardall said. "We've been extraordinarily successful in Texas in preventing that from happening."

Don't Ask, Don't Tell

While the deals get cut behind the scenes at the state Capitol, workers continue to live in the vast shadows of the underground labor market, where a "don't ask, don't tell" system allows employers to accept fake documents, fraudulently treat employees as "independent contractors" or simply pay them in cash under the table—all with little fear of punishment.

The workers are everywhere: at construction sites, behind the kitchen doors of popular restaurants, in the fields and—when the lights go out—emptying the trash and cleaning the toilets in office buildings and shopping centers.

An Austin janitor from southern Mexico, who preferred to use his nickname "Chunco," says he bought fake documents for about $100 to get a job cleaning Target stores. He told the *Texas Tribune* he and other undocumented workers were paid less than the minimum wage and got no overtime.

With the help of Beardall's Equal Justice Center, Chunco and other workers sued the retail giant for labor law violations. Target denied the allegations, blamed a contractor also named in the class action lawsuit and did not admit fault in a settlement brokered by the Equal Justice Center. The legal status of the workers was immaterial to the claims of wage law violations, so it's impossible to determine from the court records who in the chain of employment might have known that Chunco was in the country illegally.

He's now back at work on a custodial crew that cleans Target stores.

"In any company, store or wherever you go, you have to present a Social Security number and a permanent resident ID," Chunco said in his native Spanish. "What they want is to have something in which you identify yourself and that you do the work. They don't know or care how you got it."

Policymakers could potentially fix the problem by legalizing employment that is currently unauthorized, as backers of comprehensive immigration reform and proponents of guest worker programs through the ages have promoted.

Or they could get serious about regulating and heavily penalizing the companies and people who keep hiring undocumented workers—as conservative activists have urged Congress and legislatures to do with little enduring success.

Lawmakers have chosen the path of least resistance instead—political gridlock—allowing the problem to fester and prompting outrage in the electorate.

In the absence of a systematic fix, the high demand for illegal labor makes it virtually impossible to "secure" the southern border, said John Connolly, former executive associate director of Homeland Security Investigations in Washington, D.C.

"If you can come here and get a job and for 50 bucks, buy a Social Security card and some other type of documents and you get a job and you're getting paid, that's the pull. That's why you can come here," Connolly said. "If they're told, 'Look, don't come here anymore, they're enforcing the laws, you can't get jobs,' people aren't going to make that expense and make that long journey to come here to the United States."

A further border security complication: Many of the undocumented immigrant arrivals—nearly

6 out of 10, according to estimates by the Migration Policy Institute—aren't sneaking across a border at all but rather are overstaying legal visas. And many of the tens of thousands of Central Americans arriving at the U.S. border each month aren't running away from the U.S. Border Patrol when they cross. They look for the first uniformed agent they can find to turn themselves in and file a legal asylum claim.

Either way, the word is out: If you can get through all that manpower lined up on the U.S.-Mexico border, there is a job waiting for you hanging sheet rock, changing diapers, mowing lawns, whatever.

"The first thing you're going to do is send back messages to home," Connolly said. "To your hometown or wherever, and say, 'Hey, so and so is hiring and you make your way up here.'"

Business Usually Wins

While Texas has been under both Democratic and Republican rule, business interests have typically been able to douse a populist brush fire—like on immigration policy—even when the party in power is providing the fuel.

When former Republican Gov. Rick Perry was at the height of his power and sought to shore up his right flank ahead of a run for president in 2011, top business leaders joined with civil rights organizations to shoot down his effort to empower local police to crack down on undocumented immigrants in so-called "sanctuary cities." It was viewed as bad for business.

Those lined up against included one of Perry's largest state donors at the time, the late Houston billionaire homebuilder Bob Perry (no relation), perhaps best known for being the financier behind the infamous "swift boat" ads against 2004 Democratic nominee John Kerry; and Charles Butt, the billionaire chairman and CEO of H-E-B Grocery, a bipartisan political donor known for his support of public schools and opposition to private school voucher initiatives.

Their united opposition to the policing/immigration bill was recorded in an email, obtained by the *Texas Tribune* and other media outlets, sent June 23, 2011, by premier Austin lobbyist Buddy Jones. It was addressed to former state Rep. (and later Congressman) Pete Gallego, D-Alpine, then on the state House committee considering the bill in a special session whose agenda was announced and controlled by the Republican governor.

"They think it is very bad for Texas," Jones wrote to Gallego. "I wanted you to feel free to tell others that these two giants of Texas business are concerned that this is taking Texas in the wrong direction."

The bill died shortly thereafter.

Not much changed after Gov. Perry left town a couple of years ago. In the last session of the Texas Legislature, lawmakers adopted the moderate vision of Perry's successor, Gov. Greg Abbott, when it came to illegal hiring practices. It was the weakest possible iteration of a dozen bills proposing electronic employment verification (E-Verify) as a way of stopping undocumented immigrants from getting jobs here. Republican leaders didn't allow a public hearing on the tougher approaches, much less an up-or-down vote, legislative records show.

Instead, lawmakers voted to require E-Verify only for employees directly working for state government. Practically speaking, the law has had no measurable impact on government employment practices. The rule was already in effect under an executive order signed by Perry, the former governor. And the agency put in charge of implementing E-Verify rules for state government—the Texas Workforce Commission—says the Legislature never gave it the power to enforce the requirement, meaning compliance operates on the honor system. The agency has no records of anyone being turned down for state work because of the E-Verify rules, but they're not in charge of that, either, so assessing any impact from it appears to be impossible at this point.

The workforce commission is also supposed to police the kind of fraud that enables rampant hiring of undocumented immigrants by employers who dishonestly classify them as independent contractors instead of employees. But since the law took effect in 2014, the agency had penalized just 49 employers and issued only $138,000 in fines—$93,000 of them still uncollected as of late

October. The agency says state law keeps secret the names of the people or entities fined.

To put the paltry fines in perspective, an investigative report by McClatchy Newspapers (dubbed "Contract To Cheat") calculated that 38 percent of the 806,000 workers in the Texas construction industry alone (2011 data) were "misclassified" as contractors, the highest of the states the news outlet studied.

A huge number of them are undocumented.

Abbott declined to be interviewed for this story. So did the other major state leader who sets the legislative agenda, House Speaker Joe Straus, R-San Antonio. Straus's office released a written statement taking note of bills that might expand E-Verify; it said the speaker was "generally supportive of a guest worker program but also recognizes that such issues are within the purview of Congress and the federal government."

The governor wants Texas to "enhance E-Verify" but did not specify how he would do that in a written statement released by his press office.

"The governor believes the Trump Administration and Congress will deploy the necessary resources this upcoming year to secure our border once and for all," the statement said. "Until that happens, until the border is secure, any discussion of immigration reform is premature. Reforming the immigration system rests solely with the federal government."

Patrick took a single question from the *Tribune* about his views on policing the Texas workplace. He didn't directly answer what the state might do with its own considerable power to restore the rule of law in the Texas workplace but said with Trump in the White House, Washington had a "real shot" at both securing the border and fixing the nation's immigration woes.

"If we have real legal immigration reform and a president that America really believes has done his best to secure the border, then the question you asked me will be irrelevant in several years," Patrick said. His office declined to answer other questions about Patrick's border and immigration views.

For his part, Abbott explained his go-slow approach on E-Verify in a rare open-ended press conference in 2014, saying the government should set the example for the private sector "before the state goes about the process of imposing more mandates on private employers."

Fast forward to the approaching 2017 session of the Legislature, though, and most of the private workplace appears likely to remain a safe space for private employers who hire undocumented immigrants.

When it comes to mandatory E-Verify, Sen. Charles Schwertner, R-Georgetown, author of the 2015 bill, said extending it to all private employers is a non-starter for now in the Texas Legislature.

"We don't like a heavy hand on business," Schwertner said. "If we can get something done without putting a heavier hand on business, that's kind of the best way to handle it."

Schwertner is proposing instead to extend E-Verify to state government contractors. Most of them are covered already by former Gov. Perry's existing executive order, but Schwertner wants to make it permanent and enforceable. It's too early to say what the chances are for that limited measure.

Patrick's Earlier Battle

Though knowingly hiring people without proper work documents became a federal crime in 1986, states still have wide discretion to regulate business activity and punish certain companies or individuals that do it. Thanks to a Supreme Court ruling on Arizona's controversial immigration law, states gained the explicit power in 2011 to require private employers to use E-Verify, and at least nine states—Alabama, Arizona, Georgia, Louisiana, Mississippi, North Carolina, South Carolina, Tennessee and Utah—made it mandatory for most or all private sector employers, according to a tally by the National Conference of State Legislatures. How far state regulators go in enforcing the laws varies significantly.

Long before the ruling on the Arizona law, though, a small group of Texas lawmakers in 2009 got the chance to ponder using their own power to punish employers who illegally hire undocumented immigrants in violation of state labor and tax laws. The lead crusader of that ultimately doomed effort in the Senate: Dan Patrick.

Then a rank-and-file state senator, Patrick proposed legislation that would have suspended business licenses to employers who knowingly hire undocumented immigrants and pay them under the table in cash.

"For whatever reason—cheaper labor, a bigger workforce, less accountability or an unfair advantage to their competitors, some employers in Texas choose to operate outside those laws," Patrick said during a contentious public hearing on the bill. "Those employers might prefer to pay a fine when caught. In other words, do it now, ask forgiveness later. This is not the way a business operation in Texas should run."

Patrick said then that the state had clear power to take business licenses away from violators, and he noted the "green light" he got to pursue the crackdown in the form of an official state legal opinion. The author of that opinion: then-Attorney General Greg Abbott, now the governor.

"Federal immigration law allows for the state government to address the employment of illegal aliens in relation to licensing laws," Patrick told the Senate Committee on Transportation and Homeland Security. "I see this as a pro-business bill."

In that view he stood virtually alone, however, and Patrick seemed genuinely perplexed when a parade of business heavyweights unloaded a heap of criticism on his bill.

When the Texas Association of Business panned the measure, Patrick told Hammond, its influential CEO, that he thought he had the group's support in closed-door meetings. Hammond said if he gave that impression he "misspoke."

Patrick's exchange with chicken magnate Bo Pilgrim, founder of Pilgrim's Pride, was more illuminating and entertaining. Pilgrim is no stranger to the legislative process or the use of political influence in matters of business regulation.

In 1989 the folksy chicken processor grabbed national headlines for passing out $10,000 checks in the (then Democratic) Texas Senate in a bid—ultimately successful—to gain more protections for business owners who face lawsuits from injured workers.

In the 2009 hearing, Pilgrim confronted Patrick with a passage from the Bible, Leviticus 19:34, urging that the "aliens" among us be treated as though they were native-born.

"It don't state where it's a legal alien or not," Pilgrim scolded in his deep East Texas drawl.

Patrick tried to convince him that the bill could help companies like Pilgrim's because it would ensure unscrupulous competitors don't undercut the company by illegally hiring cheap, imported labor.

Pilgrim didn't budge. He urged Patrick to lay off state employers and instead focus his efforts on convincing a gridlocked U.S. Congress to pass sweeping immigration reform. In the meantime, he said undocumented workers will continue to flock across the border in search of work.

That's when Patrick reiterated his support for giving eventual legal status to foreign workers.

"I join you. We need to have a way to bring the workers here we need," Patrick answered. "But we in Texas cannot wait for the federal government to act."

As the hearing wound down, Patrick could see the writing on the wall. A virtual Who's Who of Texas business interests joined the Texas Association of Business and Pilgrim in opposing the bill, including representatives of the Texas Farm Bureau, the Texas Association of Builders, the Texas Nursery and Landscaping Association and the Texas Restaurant Association, to name a few.

The bill got closer than these efforts usually do: It went to a tie vote in committee, where it died on party lines—Republicans for it, Democrats against. A day later, on April 30, 2009, Patrick resurrected the measure and it was voted out of the committee, but moderate Lt. Gov. David Dewhurst never scheduled it for a vote on the Senate floor, records show.

"A New Slave Class"

Almost eight years have passed since Patrick attempted to rein in the worst business practices that, in his view, had turned undocumented immigrants into a "new slave class in this country."

Despite defeating Dewhurst in 2014 and taking the reins in the Texas Senate, though, state government hasn't moved any closer to punishing or shaming private employers along the lines Patrick advocated in 2009 and 2013.

Nor has the U.S. Congress delivered the comprehensive fix Patrick said he wanted just days after he was first elected to the Senate: "We should begin to put into place a guest worker program that identifies who is coming to our country so we can stop drugs and criminals at the border and at the same time bring the workers to Texas that our economy needs."

Patrick's press office did not respond to an email asking if Patrick still thinks a guest worker program is needed.

With the 2017 Texas legislative session just around the corner, Patrick and his fellow GOP leaders have another opportunity to solve the border and immigration woes they campaigned on. They have huge majorities in both houses of the Legislature.

While there are no signs yet they'll directly target the employers who continue to give jobs to undocumented immigrants, Republican leaders might again push up against powerful business interests in their drive to ban so-called "sanctuary cities." The devil, as usual, will be in the details.

If their final version defines sanctuary cities as those whose jails refuse to hand over "criminal aliens" wanted for possible deportation by Immigration and Customs Enforcement (ICE), they'll get little blowback from Texas business interests. All Texas sheriffs currently cooperate on such matters with ICE, and only one incoming one, Democratic Sheriff-elect Sally Hernandez of liberal Travis County, has made any serious noise about changing that.

But if they go back to the 2011 playbook that drew the ire of business titans like Bob Perry and Charles Butt—basically changing what immigration enforcement powers local police have—they should expect a fight.

"We don't believe that the state should be dictating to city councils and then police departments with regard to their attitudes and policy of dealing with immigrants," said Hammond of the Texas Association of Business. "It's not the purpose of the police department. That's the job of Immigration and Customs Enforcement."

ARTICLE QUESTIONS

1) Why does the author argue, "Texas leaders will continue going easy on those who avail themselves of low-cost undocumented immigrant labor"?

2) What groups have come together to block legislation that would increase enforcement of laws prohibiting businesses from hiring illegal workers?

3) What are three ways that illegal workers employed by Texas businesses in the underground labor market avoid being caught?

4) Do you believe that there is an equitable solution to the issues outlined that would be acceptable to all sides?

16.2) Outlawing Sanctuary Cities Protects Texans

TribTalk, December 8, 2016

PAUL WORKMAN

"Sanctuary cities" (cities that do not enforce federal immigration laws) are a controversial topic in the immigration debate in Texas, which is fueled by perceptions of cities going rogue and sensational murders by illegal immigrants. Legislation passed and signed by Governor Abbott in 2017 banned sanctuary cities, created civil and criminal penalties for police and elected officials who do not cooperate with Immigration and Customs Enforcement, and allowed law enforcement officers to ask detained individuals about their immigration status (a measure referred to as a "show me your papers" provision). Lawsuits were immediately filed suggesting the legislation would lead to racial profiling (despite a provision that banned it) and the usurpation of local control.

State representative Paul Workman, a Republican from the Austin area, argues in this *TribTalk* piece that sanctuary cities irresponsibly allow nonenforcement of federal laws, which is dangerous to Texans. Workman points to the murder of Kate Steinle, who was killed by an illegal immigrant in California, as a cautionary tale about the need to clamp down on illegal immigration. He also argues that the state must rein in municipalities and counties that refuse to carry out the law. He pushes aside criticism that the legislation would make local officers federal immigration agents and argues that it is the responsibility of Texas to protect its citizens.

The United States is a nation of laws—laws that apply equally to everyone, regardless of social, economic or political standing. This longstanding virtue is an important underpinning of the greatest nation the world has ever known. It is in this spirit that Texas has forged its path as a state of laws.

Unfortunately, this fundamental element of our justice system is being flouted by city and county officials across Texas who, by enacting sanctuary city policies, are not just turning a blind eye to the problem of illegal immigration but are encouraging it.

The overwhelming majority of Texas counties and municipalities are faithful in their execution of the law. However, when large cities such as Austin, Houston and Dallas ignore the laws on the books in order to facilitate their sanctuary city policies, their effects can be felt across the entire state.

Most Texans agree that the state must rein in these rogue policies, but how?

First, we must answer this simple question: What is a sanctuary city? From a criminal justice standpoint, a sanctuary city (or county) is a local government that refuses to cooperate with U.S. Immigration & Customs Enforcement.

For example, when an undocumented person is arrested, they are booked and their fingerprints are sent to ICE to process a criminal background check. If any red flags are raised by the results of the report, ICE may request local law enforcement to detain the individual for deportation, or may request that 24 hours' notice be given before the suspect is released. Most divisions of law enforcement honor ICE's requests to detain, but that is not the case in sanctuary cities, where local governments actually instruct law enforcement not to cooperate with ICE.

Many have falsely argued that a statewide ban on sanctuary cities would force local law enforcement officers to act as federal immigration officials. But the truth of the matter is local law enforcement is not being asked to determine anyone's immigration status, nor are they responsible for the prosecution or deportation of those here illegally.

Interestingly enough, local law enforcement routinely holds persons suspected of committing other federal crimes at the request of the U.S. government without complaint. We cannot allow local governments to pick and choose the laws they want to enforce.

The tragedy of Kate Steinle, who was murdered by an illegal immigrant with a criminal rap sheet in California last year, fueled national outrage over sanctuary cities, leading to the introduction of Kate's Law in Congress.

The first responsibility of any government is to protects its citizens, which is why I have filed legislation to outlaw sanctuary cities in Texas once in for all.

ARTICLE QUESTIONS

1) How does the author describe a "sanctuary city"?
2) What reasons does the author give for favoring legislation banning sanctuary cities? Are these reasons justified in your opinion?
3) What does the author argue is needed to require municipalities and counties to comply with federal immigration laws?

16.3) Why It's So Hard to Fund Public Education in Texas

TribTalk, October 11, 2016

JIMMY DON AYCOCK

> In the 1980s, Jimmy Don Aycock was frustrated by the vexing problem of school funding, so he ran for public office to get involved and help fix the situation. Thirty years later, as the "dean" of legislators and the most well-versed member of the Texas legislature on public education issues, Aycock, who had retired in 2016, was still unsatisfied with the state of public education.
>
> In this editorial, Aycock describes the problems facing public education funding and outlines some options for reform. Because school finance reform often requires politically unpopular higher taxes, politicians are reluctant to vote for it. Gaining the approval of educators, who are backed by powerful unions, is also difficult unless the spending increases are across the board. Equalizing spending (sometimes called "recapture") across a giant state with wildly different local revenues would require a statewide system for collecting taxes, which has been consistently rejected by the legislature and voters. Raising the fuel tax would be one way to generate needed funds, Aycock reports, but this option is also politically difficult for many legislators.
>
> Aycock pleads for serious consideration of all plans—with a school system as large and diverse as Texas, he argues, there are plenty of solutions, but no easy ones. Will political leaders have the courage to follow his advice?

As a parent, I was frustrated. Recent legislation was changing school funding. An array of tests was changing teaching. I felt the need to get involved and try to make the changes go as well as possible. I ran for and won a seat on the local school board.

The year was 1985.

Over 30 years later, I'm still frustrated. Since that time on the school board I've served on a college board and as a state representative. I've served on the Higher Ed Committee, chaired the Public Education Committee, chaired the Article III Appropriations Subcommittee (which deals with all education funding) and listened to thousands of hours of testimony and reports. While I certainly don't have all the answers, I think I know why education policy—especially the funding—is so hard.

First, the Texas Constitution simply states that schools should be "public," "free" and "efficient." It also states the Legislature is responsible for providing the system of education. Then it adds a requirement that the Legislature cannot use a statewide property tax to fund the system. And that's where it starts getting messy. Texas has no income tax and no state property tax, so our schools depend heavily on local property taxes. Unfortunately, there are vast differences in the "taxable wealth per student" from one area of the state to another. Also unfortunate is the fact that "taxable property wealth" has little or no correlation to the prosperity or poverty of the resident students.

Second is the Texas courts. Going back to the 1980s, a variety of cases have generated some interesting case law around school finance. In general, the courts require a substantial amount of "equalization," which means moving money from property-wealthy districts to property-poor districts—the so-called "Robin Hood" plan.

Third, as time goes by massive changes occur. Plans that seemed workable are altered by unexpected student growth, property value changes, demographic changes, technology changes, political shifts and other factors too numerous to mention.

Even if one could "fix school finance" today, the system would need to be fixed again very soon.

The Public Education Committee met for two days recently with the Appropriations Committee to discuss school finance. There are at least three immediate crises facing education funding in Texas. I would like to speak briefly to each.

- **Houston is facing "Recapture."** In short, property value increases have triggered the Robin Hood feature of the funding system requiring Houston ISD to send money to other districts. They can choose to write a check or they can choose to have commercial property reassigned to poorer districts. Either way is painful. Quite simply, the system doesn't function unless some form of redistribution occurs. Austin, Spring Branch and many others have faced this same issue. Houston cannot be treated differently. Dallas, if present trends continue, is probably only two to three years away from the same situation.
- **Many districts are about to lose Additional State Aid for Tax Reduction.** In 2006, districts were given state aid in exchange for property tax reduction. At the time, there were assurances the aid would be ongoing. In more recent years, the funding plan has been changed to expire in 2017. Some districts lose a little. Some would lose 40 percent or more of funding.
- **Fast-growing districts are caught between tax limits and continued growth.** About 75 or 80 of the state's 1,219 districts are absorbing most of the 80,000 new Texas students annually. A cap on bonded debt taxes—the interest and sinking, or I&S tax—prevents many of these districts from borrowing to build new schools while the growth just keeps coming.

These are just the three most pressing questions. There are plenty more, but unless we get a grip on these, the rest don't stand a chance. So what are the possibilities? A statewide property tax would solve the equity issues. It seems highly unlikely that such a constitutional amendment would pass.

Another possible solution is to reduce the number of taxing districts from over 1,000 to a much smaller number with less wealth variation. Last session I drafted House Bill 654, which took this approach. The concept would still redistribute taxable wealth but would do so within a group of districts with a common interest and common tax rate. The state funds would then be the same to every weighted student, thus avoiding distribution fights. While there are lots of kinks to work out in such a plan, I believe it may be the long-term solution since it doesn't require a constitutional amendment.

Any distribution plan must have funds to distribute. That amount will always be controversial. My personal opinion is that Texas needs to fund schools better than our current position, which is near the bottom of all U.S. states—by most measures, we get results near the national average with funding near the bottom. Remember that any added dollars will set off a fight about how to distribute them—a strong legislative disincentive.

Texas is a low-tax, low-service state, so any increase in taxes has political peril. A few years ago, I suggested an increase in the motor fuel tax. Under our Constitution, 25 percent of that tax goes directly into school funding, and the road fund gets 75 percent. These added funds, combined with savings from rising property values, would allow the state to raise the basic allotment to schools. As basic allotment increases, the problems of recapture and Additional State Aid for Tax Reduction are reduced sharply.

On a recent drive, I noticed gas price variation of more than 20 cents within 2 miles of my home. The fuel tax is transparent, consumption based, efficient to collect and dedicated in its use. That's exactly what conservatives demand from a tax. Yes, it's a tax increase. Yes, I got scolded when I presented it. But as our dependency on property taxes has risen, our complex funding mechanism continues to undergo multiple crises.

Various groups are coming forward with plans. All should be seriously considered. There are solutions, just no easy ones.

ARTICLE QUESTIONS

1) What problems does the author suggest are facing Texas's public schools?
2) The author mentions "recapture." What is recapture, and how does the author feel about the policy?
3) What solutions does the author claim would help alleviate the problems faced by Texas public schools?

Chapter 17

The Future of the Lone Star State

As it has at so many crossroads in its past, the Lone Star State is experiencing changes in demographics, education, energy, and politics that seem likely to transform the state in several fundamental ways.

The first selection in this chapter is from Texas-based journalist Richard Parker, who in his book *Lone Star Nation: How Texas Will Transform America* outlines two paths the state might take in the future to address economic inequality, unbalanced educational opportunity, and racial exclusion. First, he outlines a hypothetical "two-class" state in which opportunity is limited and cities are failing. Then, in a rosier alternative, he describes a thriving state that has chosen policies that harness diversity and maximize opportunity for all, especially younger and more racially diverse Texans. Which path will the state choose? Parker argues for the more encouraging model but finds that these goals often conflict with political realities.

Texans have always been "do it yourself" types, embracing the philosophy that a robust work ethic leads to success. This approach emphasizes personal achievement, individual freedoms, individual enterprise, and loyalty to self instead of others. Perhaps no other jobs better typify this Texan approach to work than farming and ranching,. Bryan Mealer, writing for London's *Guardian* newspaper, describes the hardscrabble daily life and complex challenges of modern ranchers. Natural disasters like wildfires, the siphoning off of employees to other professions, and trade fears have made the life of ranchers in Texas more difficult than ever.

The state's future will also undoubtedly be shaped by its largest, fastest-growing demographic group: Hispanics. This demographic transformation will impact many areas of Texas significantly, but, as Aliyya Swaby in the *Texas Tribune* argues, the changes to the state's public school system will be the most profound. The rocketing growth of Hispanics brings with it many challenges: greater dropout rates, lower English proficiency skills, urban segregation, and a lack of Hispanics in leadership positions. Fortunately, several solutions have been identified to these problems, including more interaction between parents and teachers, increased teacher language training, and more Hispanic teachers and administrators.

Pundits and politicians are vexed by the question of when Texas might turn blue, but if the Republicans have any safeguard against this trend, it is Congressman Will

Hurd of Texas's 23rd Congressional District. Once cruelly dubbed "Hurd the Nerd" in high school, he grew up tall and smart, became student body president at Texas A&M, joined the CIA to work in cybersecurity, and represents (as of 2018) the state's largest congressional district. In a spirited profile of the Republican rising star, *Politico*'s Tim Alberta digs into the congressman's humble past and charts his bright future. Democrats hope to take his seat and eventually turn the state more Democratic, but Hurd has a message for them: if they want it, he says, "come and get it."

CHAPTER QUESTIONS

1) What future challenges to Texas's status quo are identified by the authors in these excerpts?
2) What are the primary causes of the challenges identified?
3) Do you believe that the state is able to face these challenges?

17.1) Texas and America, 2050 (Chapter 14)

Lone Star Nation: How Texas Will Transform America, 2014

RICHARD PARKER

Texas-based journalist Richard Parker argues that Texas is at a crossroads: "There are no land-marks. But there are signs," he warns. One path the state could take is that of racial and eco-nomic exclusion; the other is that of expansion of opportunity and racial inclusion. In one hypothetical reality, Texans will miss the opportunity to get a quality education and become a permanent underclass. In the other, the state will expand opportunity and enhance representa-tive democracy. Parker's book *Lone Star Nation: How Texas Will Transform America* describes the impact of these two paths. He isn't shy about suggesting that the path of inclusion is, in his opinion, the correct course.

Unfortunately, he finds, many signs point to a future of economic decline and truncated edu-cational opportunities in Texas's largest cities, where more than 80 percent of Texans live. Still, the situation could be worse—and so he sketches a bleak dystopian future in which the state's institutions are failing its people and the economy is tanking. All except for certain privileged areas that enjoy prosperity are mired in misery. The prospect of this "two-class" system, Parker hopes, should be enough to shock policymakers into pursuing policies that help Texas maintain the promise of opportunity for its people.

Ultimately, Texas is at an important crossroads, a place on the high plains where two dusty tracks meet. There are no landmarks. But there are signs.

Down one path lies the choice of exclusiv-ity, essentially—and let's be blunt—to deny the totality of the American experience in the 21st century to people whose faces are not necessar-ily lily-white. These people, including many new arrivals and migrants to the cities and the sub-urbs, would be barred from good educations, col-lege, the middle class, and even the most basic act of citizenry, voting. Instead, these people would be consigned—unlike any previous majority in Texas and American history—to life in the under-class, while a tiny and aging majority controls the wealth and reserves all the political power solely for itself.

It is quite possible for Texans to go down this path. The current conservative Republican power structure is trying to fashion this very future through its actions, or lack of action, on education, which is the key to the middle class. In failing to confront the results of climate change vigorously, the same Republican power structure risks the demise of the economy in the coming years—forget the morality issue. And in jiggering the democracy, the same conservative Republican power structure is simply trying to limit it. Keeping nearly 1 million people from voting over the lack of an ID card, or denying big cities their own members of Congress is not democracy. It is oligarchy.

Down the other path lies the choice of inclu-sion, of expanding the teaching of the human mind, not narrowing it, of ensuring that the land-grant colleges educate all the young people—rural, urban, suburban, Anglo, Hispanic, African American, Asian American, women and men alike—who desire such an education. This is not a radical notion; it was hatched, along with the con-cept of land-grant universities in Texas in the 19th century as the very heritage of the landscape. The universities were apportioned land as assets of the people in order to create revenues, fees, and royal-ties to educate all Texans who came. And making sure that the land has water to sustain itself, and the people living on it, is hardly a flight of socialist fantasy. From Indian to cowboy to roughneck to suburbanite, doing so is merely the stewardship of a semi-arid land.

Down this path is the expansion of the right to vote, not to some new and unqualified class, but simply to all citizens who have never relinquished their right to vote by becoming felons. That's all. And down this path is the provision of duly-elected representation in government. These two rights are among the most simple, respected, and core tenets of a representative democracy.

On the face of it, the choice doesn't seem complicated. All of the signs leading down that first road, however, do list temptation and short-term gain as a destination. But those places are just waypoints of human avarice that will benefit those whose lot is favorable already. And when night falls in those places, instability and purgatory arise for them and everyone. The signs on the other road point to destinations that are more fruitful, though they are a little further away. These destinations will heal the afflicted and even harbor the comfortable when night falls. These destinations will prove more permanent for more people. All of them, after all, are migrants on the move across the plains of time.

The year is 2050.

All of the major cities of the Texas Triangle—Houston, Dallas-Fort Worth, Austin, and San Antonio—are dilapidated shells of their formerly booming selves. Unemployment is twice the national average. The city of San Antonio has declared bankruptcy. In each major city and even the smaller ones, like Corpus Christi and El Paso, specially appointed federal officials, known as masters, are making decisions on which schools to close.

In Austin, the state government flirted briefly with massive deficits but elected to keep taxes low and simply chose not to fund, beginning in 2015, the growth of enrollment in the state's sprawling public school system. Now there are too many students and not enough money. Of the state's 9 million students, two in three of these students are Hispanic. Half will never graduate from high school. Without taxpayer dollars approved by the legislature, the once-thriving public university system has continued to raise tuition and fees. Now, a public education in Texas costs at least $50,000 per year. But only 4.5 million public school

children here will finish high school anyway. And only one-tenth of them can afford college at any public university in the state. Those who can will simply leave; a new Texas diaspora is underway. Those who stay will struggle to find work.

Already the prospects for staying are quite clear: one in five people in San Antonio, 20 percent, are unemployed. The city government has sold off as many assets as it can: Public buildings, art museums and collections alike, even the old limestone football stadium that had hosted decades of Friday night games just off U.S. 281. The once world-renowned San Antonio Zoo was purchased by a private collector and though people can still occasionally hear the lions or bears roar at night, the zoo is closed to the public. Brackenridge Park, a vast urban park running through the center of the city, was sold years ago to developers. The municipal hospital system was auctioned off to a private company. Much of the health care industry which flourished in San Antonio in the late 20th century, focused on research, has become devoted to prolonging the lives of aging people with private insurance who can pay hefty fees for long-term care.

But the jobs in this sector are very low-paying service jobs, helping with menial tasks like cooking and cleaning for the wealthy, elderly remnants of the Anglo Baby Boom and Generation X. Bexar County, which surrounds metropolitan San Antonio, is not just the poorest county in the nation. It is the hungriest, too, with more people on food stamps than any other place in America, leading to its own set of health problems that range from malnourishment to obesity, diabetes, and heart and kidney failure. The average life span, for the first time in American history, is actually falling.

The people who do find work in San Antonio cannot afford the usual steps up the ladder of upward mobility. They cannot afford college for their children because they could not even afford to have bought a home in the first place. So, real estate values fall. With fewer property tax dollars there are fewer police and little work, the city is plagued with crime: From robberies to drug-trafficking to murder. San Antonio, in fact, has become the murder capital of the United States.

So, the tourists have largely stopped coming. The River Walk still is home to a dilapidated Hyatt and a Hard Rock, open only on weekends. But much of its length is abandoned and boarded up. Even the boats that once hauled tourists up and down the iconic little river are gone. The Alamo is closed to the public, behind a tall chain link fence topped by razor wire. There is talk of selling it and moving it, stone by stone, to Mexico City. On the north side of the city, Sea World and Six Flags have been torn down and sold, their once festive and packed playgrounds plowed under to make way for a scrap yard that is a sea of used electronics. Scrapped computers, mobile phones, and tablets arrive daily from all over North America for safe disposal of their hard metals which, improperly treated, would otherwise leach into the soil. That would have been a problem but rain is infrequent. The scrap yard is San Antonio's largest employer now and is so large that it can be seen by satellites in space. City leaders strangely boast that it is the largest such site anywhere in the world in the nearly futile quest to attract more industry.

Throughout Texas, a deep and distrustful two-class system has been firmly established. A handful of legislators in Austin are elected every two years. But not a single governor in over two centuries, now, of statehood has ever had a Hispanic surname. Restrictions on voting and successful court defenses of gerrymandering, enacted 35 years earlier, have generally worked to drive down Hispanic voting even as the Hispanic population swelled into an outright majority. Only two members of Congress from Texas have Hispanic surnames, one from Houston and one from San Antonio. No U.S. senator since Ted Cruz has even had a Hispanic surname. No woman has occupied a U.S. Senate seat from Texas since Republican Kay Bailey Hutchison retired in the first decade of the century. Nor has a woman ever sat in the governor's mansion in Austin in the 21st century—even though two did in the 20th. The leaders of most important corporations and all important financial institutions are Anglos who have lived in Texas for years or are freshly imported. Tiny and affluent Anglo enclaves are surrounded by razor wire, private security, and golf courses. In Dallas,

Highland Park has become the model for such communities throughout Texas.

At its heart is a wealthy, Anglo, and Christian university originally Methodist and now Baptist, with a much smaller enrollment. The university is ringed by fairly large homes, many of Georgian design and sturdy red brick. Leafy streets are patrolled by municipal police as well as Statewide, a hired security force largely made up of ex-military whose cars and weapons are easily mistaken for those of police. A complex barrier, modeled on the fence along the U.S.-Mexican border, has been erected around the entire city of Highland Park. Twenty feet tall, it is topped with the same kind of razor wire that is employed by the military as well as over 3,000 motion-activated sensors and 1,000 digital video cameras. Small drones with cameras, infrared, and listening devices fly the perimeter day and night and flit across town, recording everything.

There are precisely three checkpoints into and out of Highland Park. All the rest of the streets connecting to Dallas were closed off years ago, at first by hastily-imposed, concrete jersey barriers and later by the new fence. Police check the driver's licenses of all who enter, to verify either that addresses check out or that the driver is on a list of people invited by a resident or employer into the city. The peak times for traffic at the checkpoints are 8:00 a.m. and 6:00 p.m. because that is when landscape crews, house cleaners, and repairmen start their day in Highland Park—and later, when curfew is imposed. Violating it, or simply not having a state-issued ID card is grounds for immediate arrest. The jail is operated by a private contractor.

The urban cores of the big cities, however, are now where the super-rich live. During the boom times of the early 21st century, largely neglected downtowns were redeveloped with an eye toward older, affluent people downsizing from big homes as their children grew into adulthood. Many of these people remained in, say, downtown Austin even as the economy soured. Some were young couples; some were single. The couples were nearly uniformly childless. For the older ones, that period in life had come and gone. For the younger ones it was a simple matter of economics, particularly given the complications and costs of education. Nearly all are Anglo.

The 2nd Street corridor of downtown Austin is fairly emblematic. Steel and glass towers soar over what had been modest, old retail buildings and parking lots. A one-bedroom condominium can easily cost $1 million and rent is now the equivalent to the cost of living in Manhattan. Stylish retail shops, salons, gymnasiums, personal trainers, and expensive restaurants await on the streets below, patrolled heavily by the city's police force. The black-uniformed police in their black cars seem particularly zealous in their dedication to this zip code and its tax base—even if the Department of Justice has opened an investigation into the record number of shootings by the police of largely young, Hispanic males found in the area.

The city of Houston has had a Hispanic mayor, generally, for decades now. But the tax base has crumbled and the once thriving consumer economy—that built houses and bought the durable and non-durable goods that went inside them—has simply imploded. Services by the city and surrounding Harris County are on a shoestring. Roads and highways are still congested but they have long since buckled and filled with potholes so that drivers must now slowly navigate around them during the steaming commute. The waiting time for an ambulance or some kind of first responder in the event of an emergency is now longer in Houston than anywhere in the United States. And it has been that way for nearly 20 years. A popular bumper sticker reads: "If you're going to need an ambulance you'd better not need one in Houston."

So many people are now trying to leave Texas for parts elsewhere that it is impossible to rent a U-Haul trailer anywhere inside of the state's border. In each of the major cities a line stretches each day in front of the Mexican consulate. People—mostly Hispanic but African American and Anglo, too—are patiently seeking permission to immigrate to Mexico, where a middle class has now thrived for over 30 years. The American economy, after all, long ago slipped into second place as the Texas economy foundered. China is now the richest nation on earth.

The account above, of course, is a starkly dystopian scenario of the way that Texas could evolve if it goes down that first road, blazing a trail for the rest of the United States in its footsteps. Many of the examples, however, are quite real possibilities. Americans have witnessed in their own time the once unthinkable decay and collapse of Detroit, once one of the country's biggest and greatest cities, but now a shell of its former self and home to just a few hundred thousand residents. The drain of workers and students from Texas already happened in the 1980s when talent left the state in droves. The lack of municipal services, namely ambulances, was a reality in New Orleans during the same period when it was the murder capital of the United States. The examples of poverty and hunger are drawn from Hidalgo County in what is now metropolitan South Texas, not rural South Texas, in 2012. And the lynchpins that connect this fictional account of the future to the decisions of the present? Upward mobility. A college education. Prudent policy in a period of climate change. The right to vote. A functioning democracy. All of them mean the difference between continued and expanding prosperity or a descent into hopelessness, despair, and poverty.

The year is 2050.

The Texas economy now accounts for one in six dollars in the gross domestic product of the United States. One in 10 Americans calls Texas by a more familiar name: Home. And there are now 50 million Texans, vastly outstripping the projections. One, issued in 2009, forecast that 24 million Texans would live in the Lone Star state in 2025, a number surpassed more than a decade earlier.

More populous than California, Texas seats the largest delegation in the U.S. Congress in Washington. In just two years, another Texan will be president. She is the fourth Texan to occupy the White House, the second Hispanic, and the third woman, in fact. But by now, these are mere historical footnotes. Long a society divided by race, nationality, and ethnicity, Congress has decided that with the new census, the government will no longer track people's racial and ethnic identity. Intermarriage has made it ridiculously irrelevant anyway.

By now, Texas is the red hot super charger in the economic engine of the United States. Long feared that America would fall behind China in economic power, Texas has been the difference. The economy in Texas alone has eclipsed that of Germany, an inventive but aging society. The youthfulness of Texas, in fact, has provided a powerful edge over other economic rivals. Only Japan, China, and the United States itself boast a bigger economy than that of Texas. The successful rise of a Hispanic majority into the middle and upper classes in large numbers is replicated across America, which in 2050 becomes majority minority itself.

And while America remains the greatest global power in the world, with interests and relationships that span the earth and a military capable of securing them, it is also an increasingly Hispanic superpower. Indeed, after centuries of eyeing Europe, the Middle East, and then Asia, Washington has fixed its gaze more firmly on the Americas. From the wealth of Canada and the United States to the booming economies of Mexico, Venezuela, Brazil, Argentina, and Chile, the Americas have become the most educated, wealthy and powerful societies in the world. Europe never really recovered from the global financial meltdown of 2008. China's giant workforce has aged and is retiring. The nation that was once the workshop of the world became a comfortable consumer society, its economic growth slowed by debt, certainly, but cushioned by the comfort of its earlier success.

The world now belongs to the youngest, brightest, most energetic and unlikeliest of generations strung around the unlikeliest places in the world, the Philippines, Indonesia, Bangladesh, Nigeria, much of the Americas and—oddest of all—that relentless behemoth, the United States of America.

This account above is the other scenario.

Its facts and figures are drawn from the U.S. Census Bureau, a range of population projections, economic projections of major banks, the U.S. Federal Reserve in Dallas, and the work of interdisciplinary experts involved in a project called America 2050, which has tried to address everything from population growth to economic change to the infrastructure needs of the American economy in the 21st century.

The account above is best described as a projection, based upon a variety of current trends. But those trends cannot continue without investment in education to create a viable middle class forged out of the new Texas majority, as well as maintaining a representative democracy capable of making these choices—choices that address the economic effects of climate change, namely the availability of water.

Only these choices will lead to this future, this destination on that signpost out there on the crossroads. The opposite will lead to that other place: Perdition.

Back in the present, mid-2014 in Austin, the near future seems bright, on the one hand, and threatening on the other.

The economy continues to swell. Unemployment in Austin is well below 5 percent, and the city will likely add nearly 30,000 jobs, according to economist Angelos Angelous. On the other, another year of drought has come to visit or, rather, to stay. The politicians are crisscrossing the state, many with the usual agenda of God, guns, and gays but they're also calling once more for a crackdown on the border with Mexico, already one of the most militarized international boundaries on earth.

It is not clear that the Democratic Party offers Texas a brighter future, frankly. Based upon the performance of the Democratic Party nationally, that might be a dubious proposition. The Republicans may refuse to pass a comprehensive immigration reform bill. But the Democrats have a hard time thinking of Hispanics as anything but immigrants and that is an insufficient vision. Neither party seems to have grasped that Hispanic Texas wants what everyone else always wanted, a leg up into the middle class. According to Shaw, the University of Texas pollster, Hispanics have a strong interest in the economy—jobs and possibly entrepreneurship. "Any politician who doesn't address that," Shaw said, "is just another politician."

All that said, a return to genuinely competitive politics—in Texas and across America—would be a healthy development for the democracy, forget about one party or another. The emergence of a more competitive Democratic Party in Texas will likely not mean, however, the emergence of a terribly liberal strand of politics both in Texas and, as a result, nationally. Progressives hoping that somehow Texas will become a hotbed of left-wing politics are likely to be sorely surprised.

Instead, a successful brand of Democratic politics is likely to be more centrist than liberal in nature. Certainly, it would be free of the ideological straight-jacket of Republican politics—particularly on social issues—but Texas voters are likely to still want politicians dedicated to at the very least the platitudes of strong national security, a capitalist economy and, yes, the Second Amendment.

Already, the handful of successful Texas Democrats that exist readily pronounce themselves "pro-business Democrats." They seem to nearly stumble over their words trying to get that "pro-business" part out before that dirty, dreaded word, "Democrat." Nevertheless, the emergence of a competitive Democratic Party in Texas will not only push the state into the territory of purple, competitive politics—it will have the added effect of pushing American politics towards a place it sorely needs: The pragmatic center. The governor's mansion would no longer go to a candidate who can be elected with a minority of the electorate, further fractionalized by then peeling off the disproportionate number of conservative voters. It would instead go to the candidate who can forge coalitions of pragmatic conservatives and practical liberals into a strong center. The same would be true in presidential elections to a very powerful effect, given the state's 38 votes in the electoral college. And, on balance, this would be true of the House of Representatives and the Senate though House members have—and will always have—more license to buckle to petty special interests and powerful donors.

Politics aside, policy must confront the impacts of climate change head on, acknowledging that human activity is responsible for less rainfall and more evaporation in a hotter and drier Southwest. The plan for water resources approved in Austin is long on plans and very short on financing. It is also very heavy on 1950s and 1960s-era engineering solutions like more dams to hold back more freshwater in the rivers. But a hotter, drier climate will only evaporate more of that water. And the next generation of dams will only compound problems downstream, withholding water from farmers and ranchers and likely increasing the salinity of the Gulf of Mexico. The dam-building of the early 1960s may have already done that, damaging the ecosystem and nearly wiping out fish populations like those of the tarpon.

And nothing in Austin suggests that Texas will curtail its continued addiction to the problem of carbon emissions. Texas is the epicenter of the renaissance in American oil and gas. It also leads the nation in carbon emissions. No place, other than an increasingly arid Texas, has a greater responsibility—just for its own sake—in curbing the vicious cycle between the earth's heating and the pumping of carbon into an increasingly dry atmosphere.

At the University of Texas at Austin, Richard W. Fisher has come to talk about the economy. With his slicked-back salt and pepper hair and steel glasses, Fisher walks to the podium, looking like a taller and more youthful version of Donald Rumsfeld. The son of an Australian father and a South African mother, he is about as global a figure as any. A Californian raised in Mexico, product of Annapolis, Harvard, Oxford, and Stanford, a banker, diplomat and a Democrat, he was appointed to run the Dallas Federal Reserve by George W. Bush. Before the financial crisis of 2008, Fisher told other members of the Fed that he worried that a serious recession was in the offing and he opposed the cheap money policy of former Federal Reserve Chairman Ben Bernanke, who dumped billions of dollars into the big banks, but pumped comparatively little into the economy.

Fisher's talks are prone to colorful titles, nearly always illustrated by facts and figures showing how the Texas economy is performing better than the rest of America, reciting the state's status as the leading exporter, sending $280 billion in goods abroad even as it handles about half the nation's imports. He forecasts continued growth. He is bullish about Texas and down on his old home,

California. Increasingly, though, he wonders aloud about public policy choices including those about water and climate change that can damage a flowering economy. His urging is simple.

"If the fiscal and regulatory authorities that you elect and put into office to craft taxes, spending, and regulations do not focus their efforts on providing incentives for businesses to expand job-creating capital investment rather than bicker with each other for partisan purposes, our economy will continue to fall short and the middle-income worker will continue being victimized," he says. "In addition to being Longhorns and prosperous Texans, be bold Americans."

ARTICLE QUESTIONS

1) In what ways might a Texas on the "wrong path" fail to provide for Texans?
2) The author describes a "two-class" state in one of his hypothetical futures for Texas. What does he mean by this?
3) What would three impacts of Texas choosing the "wrong path" be?
4) Do you agree with the author about the "correct" path for Texas to take?

17.2) What Is the Future of the Texas Cowboy?

Guardian, June 19, 2017

BRYAN MEALER

Most non-Texans have the notion that Texas is full of cowboys, cowgirls, cattle, and tumbleweeds. Since a vast majority of Texans live in major cities, this iconic image isn't totally accurate, but farming and ranching have been major parts of the Texas economy and identity since the days when Texas was the western frontier. These lifestyles, and the economic arrangements that go along with them, are facing tough times, reports Bryan Mealer, writing for London's *Guardian* newspaper. Wildfires, the loss of potential employees who are drawn away from working the land, and trade fears have made the life of ranchers in Texas more complex than ever.

Mealer follows a few of these characters and their hardscrabble jobs and responsibilities to illustrate the difficulty and danger involved in such professions. The work is hard and the hours long, but Mealer describes a tight-knit bunch of individuals committed to their lives, even as they worry about the local implications of global trade. Despite such challenges, Mealer highlights the perseverance and determination of these ranchers, who illustrate the ways the state hangs on to its prideful frontier past and how that past is colliding with a more urban and technologically advanced future.

It's spring roundup time here on Texas's Spade ranch, when calves are branded and castrated and given their shots. In a time of big ranch conglomerates using drones and helicopters to move herds from above, the Spade cowboys pride themselves on being an old breed. They still gather their cattle by horseback, and they rope and drag their calves with tight, practiced loops. Their branding irons are still heated over a mesquite fire dug out of the red sand.

And when it comes to their horses, each man can ride like a bandit.

But the past year had been particularly harsh. In March, wildfires spread by heavy winds ravaged over a million acres across five states. Here in the Texas panhandle, it wiped out ranches and farms and overtook four people, along with thousands of cattle.

Before taking office, Donald Trump also raised anxieties by threatening to terminate NAFTA, which would jeopardize trade with two of America's biggest beef importers, Mexico and Canada. Trump had already rankled cattlemen by cancelling the Trans-Pacific Partnership, which the National Cattlemen's Beef Association, the industry's lobbyist, said is costing American ranchers around $400,000 a day in lost revenue in Japan (Hillary Clinton had promised to do the same). The only encouragement came in mid-May, when Trump announced a preliminary trade deal with China that could allow increased export of American beef, although the details are murky.

But on this first night of the roundup, as the sun sank low over the Canadian river breaks, the cowboys discussed a more pressing topic as they finished their chuck wagon supper.

"I tell you, it's hard finding a good hand these days," said Josh Ownbey, as he tucked into peach cobbler scooped from a Dutch oven.

Everyone agreed, especially here in Texas.

The oil and gas boom had lured away many a skilled cowboy and sent him threading drill pipe or pushing buttons on a frac truck. The money was fast and furious for small-town boys and vanished on Super Duty pickups, Easley trailers and diamond engagement rings. Many sold off their horse tack, convinced they'd never punch calves again. And when the boom busted two years ago, like booms always do, the men had returned to the ranches with borrowed kit and rusty mounts, heavily in debt and soft in the rear. Now they lived in town with their wives and demanded to go home after lunch.

Truth was, the demands of family and the modern world eventually weeded most men out of the life, since cowboy work was generally done on a freelance basis with little pay and no benefits.

Out of the eight cowhands assembled near the chuckwagon fire, only four have the pleasure of doing it full time. The Spade operate six divisions across the state, totaling nearly 300,000 acres, and the men live and work on its biggest ranch near Colorado City. The rest had found other jobs close to the trade and took day work to keep their skills sharp.

The person who'd hired them for the annual "spring works" is an old archetype, a cowboy they all admired. Jason Pelham is 6ft, 200lbs, and wears a standard bushy mustache. As foreman of the Panhandle Spade, his job is to oversee 22,000 acres of mostly rough terrain and care for the 600 cows who call it home.

At 52 years old, Pelham had been cowboying for most of his adult life. He's divorced with three grown daughters and lives alone in a small cabin on the ranch, removed from civilization by 30 miles of bone white caliche road. His only companions most days are his horses and a tank full of live rattlesnakes that live on his porch, which he catches along the roads and pastures to show visitors from the city. Come winter, when temperatures plunge below zero, he shelters calves in his living room under a framed portrait of John Wayne clutching his pistols.

As a cowboy, Pelham is widely known around these parts. Last February, he and his trusty roan Ninety (named for the brand along his hindquarters) had astonished the neighbors by chasing down and roping one of the wild Barbary sheep that live along the steep canyon walls—an accomplishment akin to lassoing a hummingbird. Pelham had taken video on his phone as proof.

He's also fearless in the rodeo arena, particularly at wild cow milking. For many years, he's served as the Spade team's "mugger," manhandling the thrashing, 1,400lb animals while a teammate squeezed milk into a beer bottle then legged it for the finish line. And Pelham was probably the only cowboy anyone could think of who'd been struck by lightning—while on horseback—and lived to tell about it. "I watched the fireball leave me and roll down the county road," he recalls.

The cowboys sleep in teepees around the cabin, while a few spread their canvas bedrolls along the porch, mindful of the rattlers. After a 5:30 a.m. breakfast, they gather outside in their spurs and shotgun chaps. Pelham sips a Henry's Hard Soda, his morning aperitif, and lays out the day's directive.

"We'll hit the creek bottoms and hill tops and push 'em against the Caprock," he tells them.

They drive to a high place near the north end of the pasture. Down below the valley yawned wild from recent rains, colored with Indian blanket, blackfoot daisy and green clusters of juniper and sage. The cowboys mount their horses and ride off in single file, becoming tiny specks against the country.

Pelham divides the men into two teams and points them south. Riding at a steady clip, one crew combs the chaparral and creek bottom, flushing mama cows and their calves, while the more experienced horsemen climb the ridge tops to scan for hideaways and strays. After about a mile, a dark mass emerges along the valley floor spewing a long cloud of dust, and riding behind it are the cowboys.

The bawling of the animals is so loud it echoes through the valley and the cowboys have to shout to be heard, screaming through their scarves that kept out the blowing dust. About 50 yards away, Pelham and the others pour diesel onto a pile of mesquite and set it ablaze, then nestle the Spade brands into the flames. They fill inoculation guns with Bovi-Shield Gold, a vaccine against respiratory disease, and another for blackleg.

Pelham motions for the branding to begin.

The first cowboy dips into the herd and throws his loop at the hind legs of a calf, then cinches it tight. He and his horse drag the calf through the soft buffalograss and deliver it to a pair of flankers, who hold it down while the others go to work.

In rapid succession, one man brands while another administers shots. Pelham uses his knife to remove a chunk from their ears—right side for bulls and left side for heifers—ensuring that months later, when a cowboy faced them head on, he could identify and sort them into pens. On the bull calves, he lobs off the scrotum to reveal the bright, egg-shaped testicles, which he pulls tightly between his bloody fingers and severs the cords. He then tosses the delicacies into a blue plastic bucket to distribute to friends.

"They remember eating them as kids and appreciate them," he says, sharpening his blade on a long leather string.

After two hours, all the calves are branded and are back with their mothers in the shade of the canyon wall. The cowboys check their phones and call their wives and sip bottles of beer. Pelham takes a fresh plug of Levi-Garrett chewing tobacco,

which he spikes with peppermint extract, and sorts through the pile of scrotums and ear tags to get a precise count on the morning's brand. He scribbles the number onto his palm, then leaves the heap of flesh in the dirt.

Time for lunch.

Back at camp, the cook serves a meal of chicken fried steak, mashed potatoes and fat buttermilk biscuits. The cowboys eat heartily in the sun and relive highlights from the morning's work.

One of the Spade hands, Marty Daniel, had displayed dazzling horsemanship, yet he lets the others brag on him while keeping his head toward his plate. After dessert, the cowboys step out of their boots and spurs, don their soft slippers and retire to their teepees to catch an afternoon nap.

Over the next two days, they brand another 500 calves and vaccinate 100 cows that thrash in the chute and spray them with excrement. Come fall, the steers will be sold to a feed yard in Dalhart or Colorado for $1,000 a head, if prices remain steady. From there, they'll likely end up as T-bones and briskets in stores and restaurants across America and Canada.

Other parts will be shipped around the globe: shoulder clods and tripe to Mexico, short ribs and chuck roll to South Korea, livers to Egypt, tongues to Japan. Last year, Canada and Mexico imported nearly $2bn in American beef, or about 28% of total export value.

The White House, after receiving an earful for its threat to terminate NAFTA, has since backpedaled in favor of perhaps renegotiating its terms. But even that makes Wesley Welch, the president and CEO of the Spade, nervous.

"If we're not able to trade normally with Mexico and Canada, it means we'd have to make up those sales domestically," Welch says as he helps work calves one morning. "That would drive down prices, which obviously would put a strain on ranchers."

When asked what he thought about Trump and NAFTA and how it might affect his livelihood, Pelham seems as dismissive as the cowboys seated around him. "What matters most down here is grass and water," Pelham says. "And that'll never change."

He thinks a little more about it, then declares what the 2% of Americans who grow and raise our food already know in their bones: "When it comes down to it, nobody really cares about us anyway."

Just that morning, the men had driven 200 head into a set of pens just yards from the Canadian river banks. The wildfires in March had stopped at the water's edge—the property line of the ranch—and spared the Spade's grass and cows. Everything on the other side had been ravaged, including 500 of the neighbor's cattle. Family ranch homes, stables and barns had gone up like kindling.

In the hours and days that followed, it wasn't Washington that had flocked in to help, but other farmers and ranchers from across the high plains, who donated bales of hay that continued to come in long convoys down the highway. They sent money, food and clothes, along with boxes of expensive handmade spurs and tack to replace those that had been burned.

Mother Nature and her fits of destruction had not changed in the centuries men had moved stock across the prairies. But neither had the people.

"We're the ones out here doing this every day," Pelham says. "All we've really got is each other."

Standing near the pens, he points across the river to where the fire-blackened ground was no longer visible. In its place now was a new carpet of green grass, just waiting for the next herd.

ARTICLE QUESTIONS

1) Why is trade so important to the lives of Texas ranchers?
2) Mealer quotes one of the ranch workers as saying, "When it comes down to it, nobody really cares about us anyway." What does the worker mean by that?
3) Why does the author argue that it is more difficult to find new "ranch hands" today than it was before?
4) What does the fate of the Texas cowboy (and cowgirl) say about the changing culture of Texas?

17.3) Texas School Districts Struggle to Recruit Bilingual Certified Teachers

Texas Tribune, February 21, 2017

ALIYYA SWABY

A tidal wave is coming, reports Aliyya Swaby in this *Texas Tribune* article about the skyrocketing growth of Hispanics in Texas public schools, which have seen the addition of more than 300,000 bilingual students in the past decade. This seismic change will alter the face of public education in Texas and bring myriad challenges: many Hispanics live below the poverty line, Texas teachers are not uniformly equipped to teach dual-language learners, the dropout rate is high for Hispanics, and schools are often segregated by race and income. School districts, the Texas Education Agency, policy experts, and community advocates have advanced several innovative solutions to these problems.

Unlike the changing demographic profile of Texas public school students, most Texas teachers remain white and female. Hispanic teachers make up only 26 percent of the teaching force, up from 20 percent a decade ago but still lower than the percentage of Hispanic students in public schools. Furthermore, there is a dearth of bilingual teachers to teach students whose first language is not English. Despite Texas's growing numbers of bilingual students, fewer than 6,000 full-time-employee equivalents are certified to teach them, according to Swaby's findings. The problem is particularly acute in larger districts like Houston, Dallas, and Corpus Christi.

Brenda Medina spends most of her time in the classroom translating lessons for her Corpus Christi ISD fourth-graders into English and Spanish because half her 20 students speak English and the other half need extra bilingual support.

A nine-year veteran, Medina is part of an overworked force of bilingual certified educators in the state—as more bilingual students file into Texas public school classrooms.

Kellye Loving, her principal at Oak Park Elementary, has worked hard to recruit teachers qualified to educate about 85 English-language learners at the school, including traveling to the Rio Grande Valley to interview candidates and persuade them to move to the Corpus Christi area. She has seven bilingual certified teachers, one in each grade, but some are stretched thin and have the maximum number of 22 students in one classroom.

"In the four years I've been here, I have lost three bilingual teachers because of retirement. That whole group of teachers is starting to retire, and there's no one to replace them," Loving said. This means teachers left in the classroom are bearing even more labor, and students are not receiving enough attention to meet their needs.

That makes it harder to get those English-language learners up to grade level in the same amount of time, Medina said. "The challenge is getting them to where they need to be," she said.

Oak Park Elementary is not alone in its need for more bilingual teachers. Texas schools have added more than 300,000 bilingual students in the past decade and have budgeted for 6,000 fewer full-time employee equivalents certified to teach them, according to the most recent data from the Texas Education Agency captured in the *Texas Tribune*'s Texas Public Schools Explorer.

"Full-time equivalent" or "FTE" measures the equivalent employees working full-time, with two half-time employees counted as one full-time employee.

The fluctuation in the numbers of bilingual FTEs in the past decade does not necessarily mark an exodus of bilingual certified teachers in Texas, according to Lauren Callahan, TEA spokeswoman.

Districts self-report the data on how much money they decide to allocate to each specialized program. Between 2005–06 and 2006–07, the count decreased by almost 3,000—which Callahan said can be attributed mostly to a decrease in the numbers Houston ISD reported between those years.

Houston reported 2,406.4 FTE bilingual teachers in 2005–06, and 203.2 the next academic year.

Dallas ISD accounted for another dip in the statewide count in the last decade, specifically between 2009–10 and 2010–11. The count for Dallas ISD went from 2,547.4 in 2009–10 to 323 in 2010–11. Representatives from Houston ISD and Dallas ISD did not immediately return requests for comment for this article.

Callahan stressed that these are not normal drop-offs and that she was not able to explain them. "We don't know why," she said. "I'm not going to know based on that number how many teachers we're talking about."

Since 2011, the number of bilingual FTEs in Texas has been consistently increasing. But bilingual and ESL teachers are still considered a shortage area in the state "because the certification process is so rigorous," Callahan said.

Teacher candidates know they will face tougher and pricier exams, as well as heavier workloads, as bilingual teachers, said Arcelia Hernandez, assistant professor of education at St. Edward's University. Bilingual teachers spend more time on their students than is reflected in their pay, even if they receive a targeted stipend, she said.

"There exists what I call a hidden labor of bilingual education. Even when bilingual teachers receive a stipend, the amount of work that is required from them far exceeds the financial compensation," she said. "They're always translating content, translating exams."

Teacher candidates often just get certified as English-only teachers, even if they take courses in the teacher preparation programs directed toward bilingual learning, Hernandez added.

Corpus Christi ISD educators said the bilingual certification exam has gotten significantly more difficult in the last several years, decreasing the pool of talent. Christian Gracia Cervantes, a first-grade bilingual teacher at Oak Park, passed the five-hour, computer-administered certification exam last summer. But she knows several people who failed it—often struggling with the listening section, which asks teachers to show an understanding of the language in social and professional contexts.

"There can be a lot of people talking at the same time, and they get nervous," Cervantes said. "They get frustrated while taking the test."

Corpus Christi ISD still needs about 13 bilingual certified teachers in elementary school classrooms to help support English-language learners in general education classrooms, said Yvonne Colmenero, the district's director of special programs.

Hernandez said she has met candidates who are "incredibly capable in the classroom" but unable to pass the bilingual certification exam, which she said does not take into account the range of linguistic connotations for words in the Spanish language. She suggested the state adopt an alternative

method of certifying bilingual teachers, allowing a panel to observe their teaching skills and decide whether they can do the job.

"There's a difference between passing the test and being a good teacher," she said.

Callahan said more than 4,000 educators yearly pass the bilingual or ESL certification exams. The passing rates on the test don't differ much from those on other subject tests, she said. Some teacher candidates come from programs that prepare them to succeed on the test more so than others.

Demographics of Teachers, Students

The 2015–16 numbers also show that the Texas teaching workforce is mostly white, female and in possession of bachelor's degrees, facts that have held steady over the past decade. The Texas public school student body has seen an increase in Hispanic students and a significant decrease in white students in the same time period.

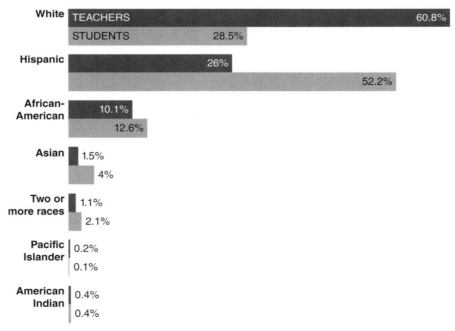

Figure 17.1 Demographics of Texas teachers doesn't mirror students   Here's a look at the racial breakdown of teachers and students in Texas public schools. While most teachers are white, most of the students are Hispanic.
Source: Texas Education Agency, Credit: Aditi Bhandari

While white teachers are more likely to head the classroom in Texas public schools, Hispanic students are more likely to be filling the chairs, according to the TEA data.

Just over 60 percent of teacher FTEs were white in 2015–16, compared with 69 percent in 2005. Hispanic teacher FTEs made up 26 percent of the teaching force, up from 20 percent a decade ago. Black teacher FTEs made up 10.1 percent, up one percentage point from 2005.

More than half of Texas public school students are Hispanic, and that percentage is increasing. About 46,000 more Hispanic students enrolled in Texas public schools in 2015–16 compared with the previous year, making up 52.2 percent of students in 2015–16. More than 2,000 fewer white students enrolled in Texas public schools in the same period, making up 28.5 percent of the student body in 2015–16. Black students remained at 12.6 percent.

Many Texas public school students are educated in districts where the vast majority of their classmates are of the same race. The data shows that 400 of 1,208 public schools in the state were more than 50 percent Hispanic last school year, 572 were more than 50 percent white, and 40 were more than 50 percent black. Just one, Universal Academy in Dallas County, is more than 50 percent Asian.

ARTICLE QUESTIONS

1) What are three challenges facing Texas public schools related to the growth of the Hispanic population?
2) Why are there too few bilingual teachers in Texas public schools?
3) The premise of the article is that students whose primary language is not English need teachers who can teach both languages. Do you agree with this, or do you think that students should be expected to learn in English only?
4) What solutions would help the state meet the challenges of a changing Texas public school student profile?

17.4) Will Hurd Is the Future of the GOP

Politico, May 5, 2017

TIM ALBERTA

It is fashionable among partisans and pundits to believe that Texas will become a Democratic-run state because of changing demographics. Republicans, however, aren't content to simply cede political ground they have dominated for more than thirty years. The future of the Republican Party, according to *Politico*'s Tim Alberta, may come in the form of Congressman Will Hurd, a tall, down-to-earth African American from San Antonio who was a former CIA agent and student body president at Texas A&M University. Hurd got involved in government because he was inspired to make a difference in an area in which he thought others lacked a proper viewpoint. "Their constituents were being represented by nincompoops" Alberta argues, paraphrasing Hurd's assessment of the issue.

Hurd has a tenuous hold on Texas's 23rd Congressional District, a seat he lost in 2010 but won in 2014 and 2016 by small margins. The district has been the subject of contention since federal courts found that it had been drawn to advantage a Republican over a Hispanic Democrat, but Alberta has another explanation for the Republicans' victory there: "Hurd is a phenom." Hurd is conservative, but Alberta quotes him as saying that voters should "forget about the labels" of politics and policy. Outside of Texas, he has even gained a slice of national fame by going on a "bipartisan road" with another member of Congress, El Paso's Democratic representative Robert "Beto" O'Rourke, to demonstrate that working together is not a bad thing in Washington, D.C.

Whether Hurd is able to hold onto his seat and make inroads for Republicans with a new generation of Texans is still unknown. Hurd himself has charted a course for his district and is working to mold himself as a statesman so he can continue to serve.

*If he can hold on to the toughest seat in Texas.

Drenched in yellow light and red fog, Robert Earl Keen scratches at his guitar and unloads the lyrics to his trademark anthem with several thousand boot-and-cowboy-hat-clad Texans howling along in delirium. This is the grand finale on a warm Saturday night at Floore's Country Store, among the holy sites in the "Texas Country" music scene, and I'm likely the only soul here who doesn't know the words. Luckily, it's not hard to catch on; at the end of each of the eight stanzas, Keen and his mob of devotees belt out the line that made him famous around these parts: *The road goes on forever, and the party never ends.*

The song isn't especially deep or meaningful—it's the story of two small-town social misfits who fall in love, arrange a meeting with Cuban drug dealers, steal their money, then kill the lawman who catches them, only to end with Sonny in the electric chair and Sherry driving a new Mercedes Benz—but the chorus provides an ideal thematic backdrop for a meeting of my own.

Drifting amid the sea of bodies in the poorly lit pavilion is Will Hurd, the congressman who represents Texas' behemoth 23rd District, which stretches from this suburb north of San Antonio, all the way to El Paso some eight hours west. Of the 36 congressional districts in Texas, 35 are safely controlled by Republicans or Democrats; Hurd's is the outlier. Not only is his district the biggest in the state—encompassing 58,000 square miles, covering all or parts of 29 counties, and including 820 miles of U.S.-Mexico border—it's easily the most competitive, with both parties pumping millions of dollars into the 23rd every election cycle. Hurd has agreed to let me drive with him across his district; over the next three days we will traverse infinite stretches of flat and long-forgotten highway, zigzagging between dusty outposts for discussions with constituents and local officials about issues as remote as the real estate they occupy. This is all part of the routine for Hurd, who, as a Republican in a 71 percent Hispanic district, must wage what is essentially a continuous, day-in-and-day-out campaign to keep his job. Serendipitously, before we depart on this odyssey, he wants to acquaint me with the stylings of Robert Earl Keen. *The road goes on forever, and the party never ends.*

Hurd is a 6'4" black guy at a country music concert; he's also a federal lawmaker who has become increasingly recognizable since winning his first term in 2014. Yet he mostly succeeds in not standing out. Keen salutes him from the stage halfway through his set, and a bunch of attendees—including two border patrol officers—stop him for a handshake. Otherwise, Hurd keeps a low profile, singing to himself and dancing with his girlfriend, Lynlie Wallace, who serves as chief of staff to state Rep. Lyle Larson and is currently running for a seat on the San Antonio City Council. Hurd, who is just shy of 40, grew up not far from here and today lives a few miles from this venue—close enough, he tells me after one of his staff members introduces us and hands me a Miller Lite from a red cooler, to hear these concerts from home. "Call me Will" is the first thing he says, which I dismiss as an aw-shucks tactic powerful people use to come across as everyday men. It's not until our trip ends that I realize nobody along the way—judges, construction workers, random constituents, his own staffers—has called the congressman anything except "Will."

The informality suits him: Hurd doesn't go out of his way to impress people, as he himself is not easily impressed. His foray into electoral politics was inspired by briefings he conducted with congressional members while working as an undercover CIA operative in the Middle East. More than once he encountered lawmakers who didn't grasp basic facts about the region like the distinction between

Sunni and Shia Muslims, and Hurd concluded that their constituents were being represented by nincompoops. ("It's OK for my brother not to know the difference between Sunni and Shia," Hurd likes to say, "because he sells cable for a living.") So he quit the agency after nearly a decade and came home, to Texas, launching a long-shot bid in 2010. He won the most votes in the district's Republican primary but lost the runoff. After retreating to the private sector—utilizing his intelligence and technological expertise to make some serious money as a cybersecurity adviser—he ran again in 2014, this time winning the GOP nomination and defeating incumbent Democratic Congressman Pete Gallego by roughly 2,400 votes. The outcome surprised strategists in both parties; Gallego, a Hispanic former lawyer, had represented much of the congressional district as a state lawmaker and was much better known in the area. Democrats felt certain they'd win a rematch in 2016 with presidential-year turnout—and that was *before* Trump won the GOP nomination. And yet somehow, despite Trump alienating Hispanics, despite Clinton winning the district by 4 percentage points, despite turnout nearly doubling between 2014 and 2016, Hurd won reelection, this time by just over 3,000 votes.

Democrats rationalize their defeat like this: The district is unfairly drawn to the GOP's advantage; Clinton failed to inspire low-propensity Hispanic voters; Gallego didn't raise sufficient money or hustle hard enough. There is, however, another explanation: Hurd is a phenom. Republicans and Democrats who have witnessed his ascent say he possesses a rare combination of competence as a policymaker, responsiveness as a representative and ferocity as a campaigner. Consider that during his first term—with Barack Obama, a Democrat, still occupying the White House—Hurd authored more bills that were signed into law than any other member of Congress. (Most aren't "sexy" bills of national interest, he says, but rather targeted toward his constituents, such as winning overtime pay for the Border Patrol.) Meanwhile, the freshman lawmaker found time to systematically explore every parcel of his district, assemble a staff that quickly became known as one of the most effective on Capitol Hill, and raise copious sums of

money to power a reelection bid that some in his party had privately written off.

"He's a survivor. He's always fought upstream," says James Aldrete, an Austin-based Democratic strategist who ran the Spanish-language media strategy for both Obama campaigns and Clinton 2016. "To be an African-American Republican in Texas is very rare. And to win, and then win again in a presidential year, which typically would swing the seat back into our corner, and to win with Trump at the top of the ticket, who's not being helpful to him, and he's able to distance himself from Trump while increasing his margin of victory . . ." Aldrete stops himself. He had pledged at the outset of our talk not to get carried away flattering Hurd on the record, and seemed disappointed in himself. "You've just got to give him credit," Aldrete quietly concludes.

Republicans have no such qualms in gushing about his potential. "I've been involved in Republican politics for over 30 years, and Democrats should be worried about Will Hurd," says Texas GOP Chairman Tom Mechler. "The sky is the limit. This guy is incredible." Of course, that's what any state party chairman worth his salt *should* say about a member of his congressional delegation. But the plaudits being showered on Hurd aren't perfunctory—and they're not just originating in Texas. When I told Kevin Seifert, the political consigliore to Speaker Paul Ryan who is responsible for raising tens of millions of dollars to protect the House Republican majority, that I was traveling to southern Texas for this story, he replied, "Will Hurd is my favorite member of Congress."

There's little for Republicans not to like: Hurd is a young, eloquent, dark-skinned, social media-savvy legislator who solves problems like a technocrat and speaks with an earned authority on national security. He is an intellectual asset to the party; the efficiency-obsessed Hurd, who wants to build a "cyber National Guard" of young computer whizzes to protect the nation's digital infrastructure, has been communicating with Trump's son-in-law, Jared Kushner, pitching projects for the White House's new Office of American Innovation. But Hurd is also unafraid of bucking the GOP and the president himself, especially in the interest of his district. He denounced Trump during the campaign, distancing himself in particular from the candidate's rhetoric about Mexican immigrants. He voted against Ryan's health care bill in early May, knowing the toll it would take on the many poor, isolated constituents he represents. And he has emerged as perhaps the most vocal opponent of Trump's plan to build a wall along the southern border, which he argues would hurt trade, send the wrong message and fail to keep out intruders.

Washington is talking about Hurd as a bonafide superstar who could represent the future of the Republican Party—but first, he must continue to survive in one of America's toughest congressional districts. Not only do Democrats have a price on his head; a federal court could redraw his district this summer to make it an even heavier demographic lift for Republicans. Hurd has already won twice under a map the court drew in 2013, and insists he's not worried—"Go ahead, redraw the maps," he says—but voting patterns there suggest he should be concerned.

"If you look at the history of this district, every single incumbent has gotten beat. There's not one member from this district that has ever retired because he or she wanted to," Gallego says, knowingly. "The same thing will happen to Will Hurd. It's just a question of when."

We're seated around an old wooden table in a small dining room in a simple, teal-colored house, one in a string of bungalows that line a working-class street in the northwest corner of San Antonio. This is the house Hurd grew up in. His parents purchased it when he was a newborn nearly 40 years ago, and it wasn't easy; Bob Hurd, who worked as a traveling salesman—and got used to being told, "We don't let n—— in here" as he approached pharmacy counters—remembers the redlining practices that made buying a home a nightmare for a black man and his white wife in south Texas circa 1975. They had invited me for Easter brunch before the congressman and I head west, and as we sit down to eat following some brief introductions, I lob a polite softball to jumpstart the conversation: "What's it like having your son in Congress?"

Hurd's mother, Mary Alice, does not hesitate. "It's his problem, not mine," she says. I almost spit out my orange juice at the unexpected hilarity of her response. But maybe she's not joking. Mary Alice is expressionless as she digs into her plate of scrambled eggs, sausage links, grits and biscuits with butter. Hurd's mother is a quiet woman with a shy smile, shoulder-length silver hair framing her round, bespectacled face. It's obvious that she is proud of her son—framed photos and newspaper clippings adorn his old room—but it's equally obvious that politics aren't exactly part of the family's DNA. The framed articles are from Texas A&M's student publication, *The Battalion*, marking his ascent to student body president and his time in office, yet there is no trace of his election and re-election to the U.S. House of Representatives.

"Your ass is crazy," Chuck Hurd recalls telling his brother when Will informed the family he was quitting the CIA to run for Congress after nine-and-a-half years as a covert operative. The Hurds were immensely proud of the dangerous and important work he was doing, and I got the distinct impression that they were less enamored of his political achievements. Chuck, the eldest of the three Hurd children—their middle sister, Liz, is away on vacation—is four inches shorter than his younger brother and probably 30 pounds heavier, built like a fullback and wearing a salt-and-pepper beard that makes him look the part of a blue-collar joe. (Clearly familiar with his brother's Sunni-Shia quip, Chuck tells me he doesn't merely *sell* cable, but is a sales manager who supervises other employees.)

If Chuck is straight out of central casting, so, too, is "William," as everyone here calls him. Tall and well-built with broad shoulders and enormous hands, the congressman has thinning black hair that is receding and meticulously combed back in small, slick waves. This feature, when combined with the rectangular glasses that tend to slip toward the tip of his nose and the slight under-bite he has owned since childhood, give him the distinguished appearance of an oil-painted parliamentarian, especially when glancing downward to read remarks or jot down thoughts in the mysterious red notebook he carries in his jacket everywhere he goes.

And yet Hurd doesn't always act the part. He cusses casually and laughs loudly, fitting in better with staff members than buttoned-down colleagues. He also talks with the slightest trace of a lisp from his childhood struggle with a speech impediment that had kids calling him "Hurd the Nerd," a nickname that still makes him shudder. ("Now I'm 6'4", 235 pounds, spent nine-and-a-half years in the CIA, and nobody messes with me," he tells a lunchroom full of wide-eyed third-graders in Fort Stockton.)

Hurd swears this career was never in the cards. His parents were conservative people in a conservative part of a conservative state, but there was no cheerleading for either party or dinner-table discussions of electoral developments. "I wouldn't say political talk was a staple of our house growing up," he tells me after brunch, laughing. Bob Hurd, who at 84 gets around slowly but cooks a mean breakfast, tells me with a mischievous smirk that he likes to tell people he's been a Republican "since Lincoln freed us," but it's clear there was no ideological indoctrination in the Hurd household. His youngest son identified with the GOP by cultural osmosis more than anything else, and found himself voting that way in college despite having no core set of political principles; his first presidential ballot, in 1996, was cast for Bob Dole over Bill Clinton—but only, Hurd says, because of Dole's military service.

It's hard to believe someone who ran for student body president did so without ideological conviction or future political aspiration. Hurd, however, insists he had neither. A computer-science major with a minor in international studies, he was set on attending Stanford only to fall in love with Texas A&M during a visit. The reason: its commitment to public service. Hurd didn't join the corps of cadets, and he wasn't politically active, but he threw himself into every other aspect of campus life. As a senior, he decided to mount an unlikely bid for student body president. He and some friends hoped for buzz by painting hundreds of ping-pong balls with his campaign logo—a black smile on a yellow face—and dumping them into the campus fountain. But the balls washed into one corner and went unnoticed. Hurd decided at

that point to try something different: meeting as many students as possible, one-on-one, especially those without a history of voting. It worked: He won the election with record-breaking voter turnout. "I learned there's no substitute for personal engagement," he tells me.

There were more lessons ahead, but they came at a steep price. Hurd had just fallen asleep around 3:00 in the morning in November 1999 when the phone rang. It was a friend—the older sister of his current chief of staff, Stoney Burke—telling him something had happened at "Bonfire," the Texas A&M tradition of building and burning a mountainous, wedding-cake-shaped structure of timber every year before the Aggies' annual grudge match against the University of Texas. The logs had collapsed, killing 12 students on the construction crew and shattering the community. Hurd found himself thrust into the spotlight, speaking at a memorial service that same day and representing the school in national media interviews ranging from CNN to NPR.

He seems uncomfortable talking about the experience, particularly when I ask how it might have shaped his approach to leadership and politics. But it's apparent that Hurd turned heads during that tragic period on campus. Bob Gates, the former CIA director and defense secretary, was serving as the interim dean of the university's George Bush School of Government and Public Service in 1999. He remembers being in awe of "Will's leadership skills, comforting people, bringing people together at a very difficult time for the university." When Gates learned that Hurd—who was taking former CIA operative Jim Olson's course, "Cold War Rhetoric and Intelligence"—was himself interested in joining the agency, they made a strong push on his behalf. Olson warned Hurd that he was unlikely to be recruited; he was young, had virtually no global experience and didn't even speak a second language. Yet Olson, who had taken his teaching job at the insistence of then-CIA Director George Tenet and former President George H. W. Bush, forcefully vouched for his pupil. "Because he was well-read, because of his interpersonal skills, his proven leadership," Olson remembers of the recommendation. "My job throughout my career was to evaluate and assess people. And Will just stood out."

Gates and Olson were thrilled at Hurd's recruitment, and through friends at the agency kept close tabs on their prized Aggie as he accepted dangerous assignments in Pakistan, Afghanistan, India and elsewhere. Hurd learned Urdu, grew several styles of beards, and with his ethnically ambiguous features managed to blend into—and find his way out of—lots of dangerous situations. The feedback was universally glowing: Hurd was headed for a corner office at the CIA, and quickly. "He was really regarded as a rising star," Gates tells me. "I had more than one conversation with people at the top"—he pauses—"They were very much aware of him." Olson, for his part, says Hurd "had the potential to lead the organization in a very senior position."

Gates and Olson, along with Hurd's CIA colleagues, were stunned and disappointed by his departure—especially when they learned it was for a congressional run. They weren't alone. "He could have done anything he wanted," Chuck Hurd tells me. "And he went from dealing with one set of terrorists and thieves to dealing with another set of terrorists and thieves." (The skill-set translates, as I learned when tracking Hurd off the House floor after his vote against the American Health Care Act. Seeing him on the phone but wanting a comment, I trailed him at a short distance as he weaved down a series of spiral staircases. He was five feet in front of me as we entered one final flight of stairs, yet when I emerged at the bottom—poof—he was gone.)

The shock of Hurd's career change didn't stop Chuck from being his brother's most active campaign volunteer. (Will still chides him for not knowing what a primary was.) And it didn't stop Gates from doing something he had never done. "Will is the only person I have ever formally endorsed—period," he tells me. When I ask about Hurd's potential, and the GOP's high expectations for him, Gates doesn't mask his own. "I have served eight presidents over a 50-year period," he says, chuckling. "And I think it's premature, but what I would say is he has the character and the integrity and the leadership skills for higher office."

Mary Alice Hurd is less vague. More surprising than her earlier response is what she tells me when I ask where she expects her son to be in 10 or 15 years. "President," she says.

"I'm sure you have stately feet, Sir."

One day later, Hurd can't decide whether to remove his shoes. The 23rd District looks like a deformed alligator whose wide-open jaws are chomping down on San Antonio from the west; we've traveled from its eyeball into its belly, the Monahans Sandhills State Park, where Hurd is shooting a video promoting the rolling dunes as a family vacation destination. Everything goes smoothly until Hurd reaches the scene where he'll slide down a dune on a green plastic saucer. Walking across sand in expensive dress shoes isn't a great option—just ask Richard Nixon—and neither is going barefoot. (Congressmen do have their dignity, after all.) But with a reporter watching—and Park Ranger Michael Smith promising no podiatric judgment—he can't turn back. Hurd takes off his socks and shoes, steps onto the hot khaki sand, mumbles about his "fat ass" keeping the vehicle stationary and trudges to the top. His muttering proves prescient: Try as he might, Hurd's sled won't budge. (The ranger shouts that it's the hot, sticky sand, then winks at me.) No matter. The shoot is a hit and Ranger Smith is ecstatic about the free publicity.

Of course, the park isn't all Hurd is promoting. As a sophomore lawmaker who prior to running for Congress had never stepped foot in most of this district, shoeless or otherwise, Hurd is playing catch-up. One smart technique is to constantly advertise his visits via social media. On Sunday evening, he posts from Lum's BBQ in Junction (population: 2,472), from a Davey Crockett statue he pulled off the highway to see in Ozona (population: 3,225) and then from a Dairy Queen just down the road. Hurd's preferred app is SnapChat; he controls the "HurdOnTheHill" account entirely from his personal phone. He posts roughly a third of his own Instagram photos, while his staff handles his accounts on Twitter and Facebook. This system allows Hurd and his team to churn out a prodigious amount of mutually beneficial posts; constituents are happy because their schools and towns and businesses get free exposure, and Hurd is happy because he is engaging constituents every day who he otherwise might never reach.

The 23rd District poses unique challenges as a political constituency; its raw size makes true representation almost impossible. For Hurd, the overwhelming Hispanic population would seem especially problematic—he doesn't speak Spanish, and doesn't plan to learn it—but he says the bigger obstacle was transcending the district's urban-rural divide. Having grown up in Bexar (pronounced "Bear") County, home of metropolitan San Antonio, Hurd learned quickly in his first campaign that West Texans resented anyone from "the big city" barging into their towns without proper humility. "I had to learn to leave my suit at the Bexar County line," he says.

This is still a work in progress. Hurd won in 2016 based on his dominance in Bexar County, where he topped Gallego by 14,000 votes. Democrats point out that Hurd lost the Hispanic vote district-wide, and rightly argue he would not have won without the Republican-heavy San Antonio suburbs. Hurd, though, won 18 of the other 28 counties that are part of the district, which suggests he hasn't simply catered to college-educated whites. He can't afford to: With Hispanics growing daily as a share of his voting-age constituency, and Trump proving historically unpopular early in his first term, Hurd must distance himself from the president and broaden his appeal in non-conservative precincts.

"There are a lot of second-generation people in this district, second-generation Hispanic immigrants who vote a straight Democratic ticket," says Ruben Falcon, a councilman in Fort Stockton who is also the city's former mayor and owner of Bienvenidos, Hurd's favorite restaurant in the district. Falcon says he voted for both Clinton and Hurd last November, and believes the sophomore congressman is chipping away the trend of straight-ticket voting that could threaten his career. "You can tell when it's just a bullshit handshake from a politician, and that's not him," Falcon says. "I think the thing that will save Will from the Trump haters is that he's out here so much, making all these connections in these communities."

In truth, Hurd has no choice. To survive here is to pursue every voter. That's why we started the day in Monahans (population: 7,617), then headed to Pecos (population: 9,213) before driving back to Fort Stockton (population: 8,482), where we stayed the night before and which, with its thousands of hotel rooms, is known as the premier rest-and-refuel stop for anyone traversing these parts of Texas. Representing such far-flung, isolated areas can be torture for a politician; it also can be strangely rewarding. Hurd lights up when he talks about Loving County, which, with 95 residents (at last unofficial count), stakes its claim as the least-populated county in America. It's a safely Republican area but Hurd was an unknown commodity when he first ventured there. "I've met all but 18 of them," he tells me. "And those 18 people don't want to be met." Hurd won 30 of the 40 votes cast there in 2014, and 54 of its 64 votes two years later.

"He is a hard worker. He is extremely conscientious," Ciro Rodriguez, the former Democratic congressman who represented the district from 2007 to 2011, says of Hurd. "I would disagree with him on his priorities and goals and objectives, but you have to admit, he's a hard worker and he moves around and he's responsive. He does all the right things from that perspective. Whoever runs against him has to match that."

Democrats are well aware. Fed up with Gallego after his back-to-back losses and alleged lethargy compared to Hurd, they are turning to fresh faces. San Antonio federal prosecutor Jay Hulings is viewed as a prize recruit among national Democrats, but the primary could get crowded, especially if a friendlier map emerges. Emily's List, the powerhouse pro-abortion-rights group that recruits female candidates, is said to be zeroing in on Judy Canales, a former Obama appointee who lives in Eagle Pass, as well as a mystery combat veteran from San Antonio.

Hard work is indeed necessary to win and protect a coin-flip district, but so too is the discipline—at least rhetorically—never to stray far from the middle of the electorate. Hurd, who is probably the least ideological politician I've ever met, had no trouble mastering this talent. At a roundtable with local officials in Monahans, Hurd emphasizes, as he does everywhere, that border security is a priority—but adds that building a wall is the "most expensive and least effective" way to achieve it. He strikes a disapproving tone on the Affordable Care Act, but tells them to "forget about the labels" of "repeal and replace" and says the only things he cares about are increasing access and decreasing costs. (It came as little surprise nearly three weeks later when he voted against Ryan's legislation; Hurd staffers told me that day the office got hundreds of phone calls and only one was in favor.) And when asked about recent foreign policy developments, Hurd says he supported Trump's missile strike in Syria—but speaks in cautionary tones about any American military intervention, especially on the Korean Peninsula, warning that North Korea has "the largest special forces in the world" and a leader who possesses "the capability and willingness to kill millions of people" across the border in South Korea.

Some of this, certainly, owes to Hurd's natural pragmatism and nuance. But he's also walking a tightrope at all times—and he knows it. The clearest (and funniest) example of this comes later Monday afternoon when, after a speech to a few dozen high school students in Pecos, Hurd asks for questions "on the CIA, Congress, robotics, anything." The first student to raise his hand is a Hispanic kid who came in wearing a 'Make America Great Again' hat. "What do you think about sanctuary cities?" he asks. Hurd grimaces. "You've got to enforce the law. It's that simple," he replies. Then, without so much as blinking, Hurd adds: "Let's talk about robotics."

Hurd's obsession with cultivating a centrist brand explains the now-famous "road trip" from San Antonio to Washington he took in March with Democratic Congressman Beto O'Rourke, who represents the neighboring district anchored in El Paso. It was fascinating not simply for the display of bipartisanship, but for the organically funny banter between two young politicians so eager to be perceived as moderates that they jumped in the car without necessarily expecting they would come to genuinely admire one another after 30 hours together with thousands of people watching via livestream. "Will's a great member of Congress," O'Rourke said to the camera at one point. "And if

I just allowed his party affiliation to determine whether or not we were going to work together, I wouldn't be spending any time with him."

Of course, this was a fuzzy sentiment wrapped in political calculation. The trip was O'Rourke's idea, and within weeks he had launched his Senate campaign against GOP incumbent Ted Cruz; naturally he used the adventure with Hurd to sow narratives of his centrist inclinations and contrast them against his polarizing right-wing opponent. Cruz allies were somewhat annoyed, but Hurd laughs at the suggestion that he might have unwittingly aided O'Rourke's effort to unseat his fellow Republican. "Look, a Democrat in Texas isn't going to win a statewide election—period," he says. "Did you tell Beto that?" I ask. Hurd grins. "He knows my opinion."

I didn't find one Republican complaining about Hurd helping O'Rourke. But a number of Democrats—who agree that Cruz can't be beaten—privately grumbled about O'Rourke boosting the bipartisan bonafides of someone they have a better chance of unseating in 2018, and who they fear could grow into a force in future statewide and perhaps even national elections. The road trip, skeptics in both parties say, was more about campaign strategy than congressional bipartisanship. We all know what Beto O'Rourke got out of it. What about Will Hurd?

Two unusual things strike me about the Texas congressman. The first is that he employs numerous staff members who aren't Republicans. His military and veteran caseworker, Jon, who lost a leg in Iraq (and has a wicked sense of humor about it) isn't shy about denouncing the party. His district staffer, Jenny, who drove with us from San Antonio, smiles and shakes her head no when I ask if she's a Republican. And his chief of staff, Stoney Burke, whom Hurd counts among his best friends and says will be "the only chief I'll ever have," used to work for Democrat Chet Edwards. When I ask Hurd about this, he looks surprised. Then he shrugs. "Your office is about getting things done for the district," he says. "So it's not a requirement."

The second is that Hurd has no rehearsed answer to one of the easiest questions for a politician.

After our thoroughly conviction-free discussion of how he came to identify as a Republican, I ask him which political figures were his inspirations and influences. This is a robotic answer for most everyone in his party: Ronald Reagan. And yet Hurd, despite growing up during the 1980s, struggles to produce a response. Finally, he settles on two figures: Teddy Roosevelt and George Washington. Solid choices, to be sure; they're half of Mt. Rushmore. But neither governed in the past century nor preached any sort of ideology that translates to today's political scene.

If anything, Hurd seems fundamentally distrustful of the GOP—especially its conservative most elements—when it comes to the treatment of women, minorities, gays, poor people and other groups. Its worst tendencies, he seems to believe, are embodied by Trump—which is maddening given they will share a ballot for the foreseeable future. "Do I have control over what he says? No," Hurd says. "Do I have to talk that way? No. And I'm not going to."

In some sense, Hurd's high-profile stand against the border wall isn't just about the wall itself. Yes, he passionately believes that a "virtual barrier"—cutting-edged fiber optic cables and high-definition cameras complimenting a few urban stretches of see-through fence, all monitored by a beefed up border-patrol monitoring the border—is a wiser use of money and a better way to protect the homeland. But he's not entirely unique in this regard; most Texas Republicans oppose Trump's sweeping proposal on the border. "Not even Ted Cruz, who is an idiot, and a Canadian, would agree to build that kind of wall in Texas," Rodriguez tells me.

Hurd's fight against the wall is sincere, but it doubles as a symbolic show of defiance against a president whose rhetoric offends his constituents and whose policies on immigration and NAFTA threaten their livelihoods in a region where the flow of people and goods underpins the economy. (To drive this point home, Hurd's staff arranges a trip across the border to Juárez on my final day in the district. We visit a technology incubator where American teenagers are working alongside their Mexican counterparts on computer chips and Hurd, both a science geek and a promoter of international commerce, can't hide his satisfaction.)

At one point, driving along a barren freeway with oil rigs toiling to our right, I ask Hurd how he can reconcile his approach with that of Trump, the leader of his party. "Well, he's *a member* of the party," Hurd says. "Just because somebody is in my party doesn't mean I can't be critical—I've been pretty clear about that. Yes, he's the titular head of the party. But he's just one person. And I completely disagree with people who say he's the standard-bearer. There's a lot of people that represent the Republican brand and conservatism."

But doesn't Trump speak for the party, I ask? "Shit, I don't know," Hurd says. "My thing is this: sphere of influence, sphere of control. What do I have control over? I have control over my actions and being an example to people. So that's what I spend time on. What does that mean for the broader party?" He takes another pause. "I look to good examples in the party, people like John Cornyn. That guy is really a great example of someone that people should grow up to be like."

It's an intriguing answer, because some people think Cornyn—the senior senator from Texas, the more moderate counterpart to Cruz, the No. 2 Republican in the Senate—is *exactly* who Hurd wants to grow up to be like. Whether Cornyn retires in 2020 or seeks another six-year term is the subject of intensifying speculation back home. If he leaves, Hurd could very well be his preferred successor. But this is where the tightrope routine could backfire: Texas is loaded with ambitious conservatives who are circling any open statewide office like vultures, and Hurd has cut such a moderate profile to survive in his own district that he might be rendered unacceptable to the right in a Republican primary.

"That definitely affects his ability to run statewide," says César Blanco, a Democratic state representative who formerly served as chief of staff to both Gallego and Rodriguez, and who is widely expected to run for O'Rourke's seat. Aldrete, the Obama and Clinton alum, says his party can only hope that conservatives crowd Hurd out of future races. "The fact that he's stymied because of them would be very helpful to Democrats."

Hurd is well aware of this potential predicament and laughs at the early handicapping of his future. "Cornyn's my boy. I've learned a lot from him," he says. "He's been incredibly helpful. And I think he's been underappreciated. . . . But I'm not plotting chess pieces. I evaluate opportunities as they arise."

He's clearly thinking ahead, though. At one point, Hurd engages me in a long conversation about demographics and my experience covering the presidential campaign in key primary states. To the extent he's making long-term chess moves, they are based on where the party—and his state—will be. And here's where Hurd hints at larger aspirations, arguing that the state's demographic transformation will produce a demand for more mainstream politicians. "Remember, everybody in Texas used to be Democrats," he says. "The tug-of-war will be over the center. My hypothesis is that 80 percent of Americans are around the center—40 percent left of center, 40 percent right of center—and they're all persuadable." A minute later, Hurd adds, "I just don't accept the premise that to win a primary you have to be the person furthest to the right."

He appears certain to test it sooner or later. Hurd is too young, too talented, too ambitious not to push the limits and enter the arena with bigger and better competition. But first, he has to hang onto the toughest seat in Texas, one of the toughest in America, where Democrats will continue to invest millions of dollars in hopes of taking it back and kneecapping his rapid ascent inside the Republican Party. Hurd, whose twin goals in Congress are to be a leader on national security and "the gold standard in constituent services," is growing more confident every single day, with every new social media post and every new voter he meets, that this district belongs to him.

"If you want it," Hurd says, "come and get it."

ARTICLE QUESTIONS
1) What event occurred at Texas A&M that made Hurd "stand out"?
2) What made Hurd want to run for office?
3) Why does Hurd identify with the Republican Party?
4) How does the author describe Hurd's attempts to win the 23rd Congressional District, a classic "swing district"?

1.1 – From Big, Hot, Cheap, and Right: What America Can Learn from the Strange Genius of Texas by Erica Grieder, copyright © 2013. Reprinted by permission of PublicAffairs, an imprint of Hachette Book Group, Inc.

1.2 – T. R. Fehrenbach (1996). "Chapter 5: The Society, in *The Seven Keys to Texas*." New York: AN [e-reads] Book.

1.3 – Lana Shadwick, "War on Christmas Comes to Texas School." Breitbart (online). December 9, 2016. http://www.breitbart.com/texas/2016/12/09/war-on-christmas-comes-to-texas-school/

2.1 – Brandon Formby, Chris Essig, and Annie Daniel. 2017. "Despite "Texas Miracle," Affordable Housing Difficult for Many Urban Dwellers." Texas Tribune, July 16.

2.2 – © 2014 Washington Monthly Publishing, LLC. Reprinted with permission of Washington Monthly.

2.3 – Brian Wellborn. 2017. Fiscal Notes: 2017 Legislative Wrap-Up. Office of the State Comptroller.

3.1 – Richard Parker (2014). "Chapter 2: Great Migrations, in Lone Star Nation: How Texas Will Transform America." New York" Pegasus Books.

3.2 – Steve White, et. al. Texas Demographic Center, "Texas Migration," http://demographics.texas.gov/Resources/publications/2017/2017_01_11_TexasMigration.pdf

3.3 – Rogelia Saenz (2016). "White Births, Migration Explain Why Texas Remains a Red State." San Antonio News Express, December 31, 2016. http://www.mysanantonio.com/opinion/commentary/article/White-births-migration-explain-why-Texas-remains-10827255.php

4.1 – Kiah Collier. 2016. "Texas Surpeme Court Rules School Funding System is Constitutional." Texas Tribune, May 13.

4.2 – John Colyandro and Russell Withers (2017). "Education Savings Accounts are Constitutional." TribTalk, Texas Tribune, January 24.

4.3 – Dean Galaro (2015). "Protests, Photography, and the First Amendment." TribTalk, November 12.

5.1 – Edgar Walters. 2016. "Texas Argues it Can Fix Foster Care Without Judge's Oversight." Texas Tribune, November 22.

5.2 – Jim Malewitz (2015). "George P. Bush Wades into Red River Fight with Feds." The Texas Tribune, December 1, 2016.

5.3 – Aaron Rippenkroeger. 2016. "Texans Will Not Abandon Refuges in Their Hour of Need." TribTalk, October 5.

6.1 – Mark Pulliam (2016). "Red State, Blue Cities." City Journal Magazine, Texas Rising Issue, https://www.city-journal.org/html/red-state-blue-cities-14731.html

6.2 – Matt Rinaldi (2015). "Liberty Trumps Local Control." TribTalk, March 12.

6.3 – Joel Nehlean (2016). "Who's Going to Pay for All of This" County Magazine, July 13. http://www.county.org/magazine/features/Pages/2016%20July/Who's-Going-to-Pay-for-All-of-This.aspx

7.1 – Jon Cassidy. 2016. "Broken By Design." City Journal Magazine. https://www.city-journal.org/html/broken-design-14736.html

7.2 – © ESPN. Reprinted courtesy of FiveThirtyEight.com.

7.3 – Ross Ramsey "Legislative Dance Partners Stepping on Each Others's Toes." The Texas Tribune, April 22, 2015

8.1 – From The Power of the Texas Governor: Connally to Bush by Brian McCall, Copyright © 2009. By permission of the University of Texas Press

8.2 – Greg Abbott. 2015. "Inaugural Address." https://gov.texas.gov/news/post/greg_abbott_delivers_2015_texas_inaugural_speech

8.3 – "Value in Diversity in Appointments." (2016). San Antonio Express News Editorial, April 25, 2016.

9.1 – Reprinted with permission from Texas Monthly

9.2 – Copyright 2016 POLITICO LLC

9.3 – Reprinted with permission from Texas Monthly

10.1 – The State of the Texas Judiciary (2017), Chief Justice Nathan L. Hecht. http://www.txcourts.gov/media/1437101/soj-2017.pdf

10.2 – Mark P. Jones (2017). "The Selection of Judges in Texas." Baker Institute of for Public Policy. http://www.bakerinstitute.org/media/files/files/b38e1ecc/POLI-pub-TexasJudges-011317.pdf

10.3 – Ross Ramsey (2015). "Should We Take Judges Out of the Fundraising Business?" Texas Tribune, May 15.

11.1 – Mark P. Jones, Renee Cross and Jim Granato. 2016. "The Texas Voter ID law and the 2016 Election: A Study of Harris County and Congressional District 23." https://ssl.uh.edu/class/hobby/voterid2016/voterid2016.pdf

11.2 – Alexa Ura. 2017. "Voting Rights Battle in Pasadena Could Have Texas-Wide Legal Ramifications." Texas Tribune, July 11.

11.3 – Bryan Jones (2017). "Why Can't Texans Register to Vote Online?" TribTalk, March 6. https://www.tribtalk.org/2017/03/06/why-cant-texans-register-to-vote-online/

11.4 – I'm still working on this one. Use standard citation format for now

12.1 – Sean P. Cunningham (2010). "Introduction" in Cowboy Conservatism: Texas and the Rise of the Modern Right. Lexington: University Press of Kentucky. 1-11

12.2 – From The New Republic, October 2014 © 2014 New Republic. All rights reserved. Used by permission and protected by the Copyright Laws of the United States. The printing, copying, redistribution, or retransmission of this Content without express written permission is prohibited.

12.3 – Max Krochmal (2016). "Texas Democrats Must Get Back to Their Progressive Roots." TribTalk, November 21.

12.4 – Brandon Formby, Christopher Connelly, and Alexa Ura (2017). "Can Texas Republicans Hold America's Reddest Large Urban County?" Texas Tribune, January 17.

13.1 – Eva DeLuna Castro (2017). "If Needed, Rainy Day Fund is There for Texas." TribTalk, Texas Tribune, January 5.

13.2 – Alex Samuels. 2017. "Why Can't We Create a Statewide Property Tax to Fund Public Education?" Texas Tribune, August 4.

13.3 – Texas Public Policy Foundation (2017). " A Review of the 85th Texas Legislature." https://www.texaspolicy.com/library/doclib/2017-85thLegislaturerecap-combined.pdf

13.4 – Ann Beeson (2017). "A Legislative Session Marked by Bruised Egos and Missed Opportunities." TribTalk, June 1, 2017.

14.1 – Ross Ramsey (2016). "The Long and Winding Road to the Texas Ethics Commission." Texas Tribune, July 22, 2016.

14.2 – © 2015 The Dallas Morning News, Inc

14.3 – Texans for Public Justice

15.1 – Christopher Connelly (2017). "What Do Exonerations Tell Us About the Death Penalty?" Texas Public Radio (KERA), January 26. http://tpr.org/post/what-do-exonerations-tell-us-about-death-penalty#stream/0

15.2 – Ten Years of Criminal Justice Reform in Texas. (2017, August 1). Retrieved from http://rightoncrime.com/2017/08/ten-years-of-criminal-justice-reform-in-texas/

15.3 – Madlin Mekelburg. 2016. "New Prison Rule Means Jailbirds Can't Tweet." April 14.

16.1 – Jay Root (2016). "In Texas, Lawmakers Don't Mess With Employers of Undocumented Workers." Texas Tribune, December 14.

16.2 – Paul Workman (2016). "Outlawing Sanctuary Cities Protects Texans." TribTalk, Texas Tribune, December 8.

16.3 – Jimmy Don Aycock (2016). "Why It's So Hard to Fund Public Education in Texas." TribTalk, Texas Tribune, October 11.

17.1 – Richard Parker (2014). "Chapter 14: Texas and America, 2050, in Lone Star Nation: How Texas Will Transform America." New York" Pegasus Books.

17.2 – Copyright Guardian News & Media Ltd 2017

17.3 – Copyright 2016 POLITICO LLC

Index

Figures and tables are indicated by "f" and "t" following page numbers.